MONEY, POWER, AND AI

In this ambitious collection, Zofia Bednarz and Monika Zalnieriute bring together leading experts to shed light on how artificial intelligence (AI) and automated decision-making (ADM) create new sources of profits and power for financial firms and governments. The chapter authors – who include public and private lawyers, social scientists, and public officials working on various aspects of AI and automation across jurisdictions – identify mechanisms, motivations, and actors behind technology used by Automated Banks and Automated States. They argue for new rules, frameworks, and approaches to prevent harms that result from the increasingly common deployment of AI and ADM tools. Responding to the opacity of financial firms and governments enabled by AI, *Money, Power, and AI* advances the debate on scrutiny of power and accountability of actors who use this technology. This title is available as Open Access on Cambridge Core.

Zofia Bednarz is a Lecturer at the University of Sydney Law School and researches the implications of new technologies for commercial and corporate law as an Associate Investigator in the ARC Centre of Excellence for Automated Decision-Making and Society.

Monika Zalnieriute is a senior lecturer (associate professor) at the University of New South Wales, Sydney and is a senior fellow at the Lithuanian Centre for Social Sciences. Her research on law and technology has been translated to German, Russian and Mandarin, and is widely drawn upon by scholars and organisations such as the Council of Europe, the World Bank, the European Parliament, and World Health Organization.

Money, Power, and AI

AUTOMATED BANKS AND AUTOMATED STATES

Edited by

ZOFIA BEDNARZ
University of Sydney

MONIKA ZALNIERIUTE
University of New South Wales

CAMBRIDGE
UNIVERSITY PRESS

CAMBRIDGE
UNIVERSITY PRESS

Shaftesbury Road, Cambridge CB2 8EA, United Kingdom

One Liberty Plaza, 20th Floor, New York, NY 10006, USA

477 Williamstown Road, Port Melbourne, VIC 3207, Australia

314–321, 3rd Floor, Plot 3, Splendor Forum, Jasola District Centre, New Delhi – 110025, India

103 Penang Road, #05-06/07, Visioncrest Commercial, Singapore 238467

Cambridge University Press is part of Cambridge University Press & Assessment, a department of the University of Cambridge.

We share the University's mission to contribute to society through the pursuit of education, learning and research at the highest international levels of excellence.

www.cambridge.org
Information on this title: www.cambridge.org/9781009334327

DOI: 10.1017/9781009334297

First published 2024

A catalogue record for this publication is available from the British Library.

Library of Congress Cataloging-in-Publication Data
NAMES: Bednarz, Zofia, editor. | Zalnieriute, Monika, editor.
TITLE: Money, power, and AI : automated banks and automated states / edited by Zofia Bednarz, University of Sydney; Monika Zalnieriute, University of New South Wales, Sydney.
OTHER TITLES: Money, power, and artificial intelligence
DESCRIPTION: Cambridge, United Kingdom ; New York, NY : Cambridge University Press, 2023. | Includes bibliographical references and index.
IDENTIFIERS: LCCN 2023027688 (print) | LCCN 2023027689 (ebook) | ISBN 9781009334327 (hardback) | ISBN 9781009334334 (paperback) | ISBN 9781009334297 (epub)
SUBJECTS: LCSH: Financial services industry–Law and legislation. | Internet banking–Law and legislation. | Financial services industry–Technological innovations. | Financial services industry–Data processing. | Electronic funds transfers–Law and legislation. | Financial institutions–Decision making–Computer programs. | Banks and banking–Automation. | Money–Law and legislation.
CLASSIFICATION: LCC K1081 .M66 2023 (print) | LCC K1081 (ebook) | DDC 346/.082170285467 8–dc23/eng/20230613
LC record available at https://lccn.loc.gov/2023027688
LC ebook record available at https://lccn.loc.gov/2023027689

ISBN 978-1-009-33432-7 Hardback

Contents

Contributors

Zofia Bednarz is the co-editor of this collection. She is a Lecturer at the University of Sydney Law School and an Associate Investigator at the Australian Research Council Centre of Excellence on Automated Decision-Making and Society. Zofia has an established track record in corporate law, financial services law, and the impact of new technologies on consumer protection regimes. She has published widely on these topics in leading journals and edited collections in both English and Spanish. She is the author of *Breach of Information Duties in the B2C E-Commerce: A Comparative Perspective* (Marcial Pons, 2019) and co-author of *International Encyclopaedia of Commercial and Economic Law – Spain* (Wolters Kluwer International, 1st ed. 2018, 2nd ed. 2022). She has also co-edited *Derecho de Sociedades: Los Derechos del Socio* (Company Law: Company Members' Rights) (Tirant lo Blanch, 2020).

José-Miguel Bello y Villarino is a Research Fellow at the Law School of the University of Sydney and the Institutions programme of the Australian Research Council Centre of Excellence for Automated Decision-Making and Society (ADM +S). He is a member of the Diplomatic Corps of Spain (on leave) and previously worked in different capacities for the European Union. In 2021 he was a Fulbright-Schuman scholar at the Harvard Law School. His current research focuses on regulatory approaches to ADM and AI, especially on how to deal with risks derived from the operation of AI systems from a comparative perspective.

Terry Carney AO is Emeritus Professor of Law at the University of Sydney Law School, where he served as Director of Research and Head of Department, and a visiting research professor at the University of Technology Sydney. The author of 11 books/monographs and over 250 academic papers, he is currently an associate investigator at the Australian Research Council Centre of Excellence for Automated Decision-Making and Society (ADM+S). He is an officer of the Order of Australia, a fellow of the Australian Academy of Law, former president

(2005–2007) of the International Academy of Law and Mental Health, and has chaired commonwealth bodies such as the National Advisory Council on Social Welfare and the Board of the Institute of Family Studies, along with various State enquiries into child welfare, adult guardianship, and health law.

Cary Coglianese is Edward B. Shils Professor of Law at the University of Pennsylvania Law School and the Director of Penn Program on Regulation. He specializes in the study of administrative law and regulatory processes, with an emphasis on technology and business–government relations in policy-making. The author of more than 200 articles, book chapters, and essays on administrative law and regulatory policy, Coglianese's recent book projects have included: *Achieving Regulatory Excellence; Does Regulation Kill Jobs?; Regulatory Breakdown: The Crisis of Confidence in U.S. Regulation; Import Safety: Regulatory Governance in the Global Economy*; and *Regulation and Regulatory Processes*. In addition to his work on the use of artificial intelligence by government agencies, he has written on climate change policy, public participation and transparency in federal rulemaking, voluntary environmental programs, and the role of waivers and exemptions in regulatory law. Prior to joining the Penn faculty, he spent a dozen years on the faculty at Harvard University's John F. Kennedy School of Government where he founded and chaired the school's Regulatory Policy Program and was an affiliated scholar at the Harvard Law School. A senior fellow of the Administrative Conference of the United States (ACUS), a federal agency that develops recommendations for improving the administrative aspects of government, Coglianese served for years as the chair of ACUS's Rulemaking Committee. He has also served as the chair and co-chair of several committees of the American Bar Association's section on administrative law as well as a member of the section's governing Council.

Tatiana Cutts is Associate Professor and researcher at the Centre for Artificial Intelligence and Digital Ethics at the University of Melbourne Law School. Her research spans private law and legal theory, often as these topics intersect with issues of technological innovation. Tatiana's recent monograph, Artificial Justice (OUP, 2023), makes the case for looking beyond equality when we assess the justice of predictive algorithms. She joined Melbourne Law School from the London School of Economics and Political Science in 2020, and received her D.Phil, BCL, and LLB from the University of Oxford. Tatiana has published in leading legal academic journals, including *Oxford Journal of Legal Studies, Law Quarterly Review*, and *Modern Law Review*.

Ainhoa Nadia Douhaibi is an adjunct researcher at the Open University of Catalonia (UOC) and intercultural policy consultant at the Barcelona City Council. She specialises in the analysis of racism, state surveillance, and Islamophobia. Her latest book published in 2019 *La radicalización del racismo*.

Islamofobia de estado y prevención antiterrorista (*The Radicalisation of Racism: State Islamophobia and Terrorism Prevention*) dissects the racist, capitalist, and colonial ideology underpinning Spain's counterterrorism policies.

Doron Goldbarsht, LLB, LLM (HUJI), PhD (UNSW), is the Director of the Financial Integrity Hub (FIH) and Senior Lecturer at Macquarie Law School, where he teaches banking and financial crime. He is an authority on anti-money laundering and counter-terrorist financing (AML/CTF) regulations, with expertise in the related fields of compliance and financial innovation. His recent books *Financial Crime and the Law: Identifying and Mitigating Risks* (Springer 2023, co-edited), *Financial Crime, Law and Governance: Navigating Challenges in Diverse Contexts* (Springer 2023, co-edited), *Financial Technology and the Law: Combating Financial Crime* (Springer, 2022, co-edited with Louis de Koker), and *Global Counter-Terrorist Financing and Soft Law: Multi-Layered Approaches* (Edward Elgar, 2020), as well as journal and chapter publications, focus on international AML/CTF standards and the mechanisms for their effective implementation and compliance at the national level.

Teresa Rodríguez de las Heras Ballell is Associate Professor of Commercial Law at the Universidad Carlos III de Madrid, Spain. Currently, she is an academic visitor at the University of Cambridge. In the academic year 2021–2022 she was Sir Roy Goode Scholar at the International Institute for the Unification of Private Law (UNIDROIT). Teresa is the delegate of Spain at the United Nations Commission on International Trade Law (UNCITRAL) on WG VI on secured transactions and WG IV on E-commerce (project on AI and automation in international trade and data transactions). She is an expert at UNCITRAL and UNIDROIT on digital economy projects and arbitrator at the Madrid Court of Arbitration and the Spanish Court of Arbitration. Teresa is a member of the European Commission Expert Groups: on Liability and New Technologies, the Observatory on Online Platform Economy, and on B2B Data Sharing and Cloud Computing. She is a member of the European Law Institute (ELI) Executive Committee and Council, the author of the ELI Guiding Principles on ADM in Europe, 2022, and co-reporter of the ELI Project on Algorithmic Contracts. She is a member of the International Academy of Commercial and Consumer Law, Artificial Intelligence Ethics Committee within the Spanish Bar Association, and of the Advisory Committee to Open Internet Governance Institute. Her past academic appointments include James J. Coleman Sr. Distinguished Visiting Professor of Law at Tulane Law School, Visiting Fellow at Harris Manchester College in Oxford University, Marie Curie Fellow at Centre of European Law and Politics of University of Bremen (Germany), and Chair of Excellence at Oxford University.

Aitor Jiménez is a sociologist, lawyer, and activist. He is a postdoctoral Research Fellow in the Australian Research Council Centre of Excellence for Automated

Decision-Making and Society at the University of Melbourne in the areas of Data Civics, Rights and Ownership for Automated Decision-Making. Previously, Aitor worked as a policy and legal analyst for progressive causes in Latin America and Europe, and as a human rights lawyer has defended cases of leftist activists and artists before the Spanish National Court. Aitor often writes for the media and collaborates with a range of civil society organisations interested in the development of forward-thinking alternatives for our digital futures. Aitor currently provides advice to progressive political parties in Spain on the regulation of fake news, public opinion, and the digital public sphere.

Ching-Fu Lin is Professor of Law at National Tsing Hua University (NTHU). Professor Lin received his LL.M. and S.J.D. from Harvard Law School with the honour of John Gallup Laylin Memorial Prize and Yong K. Kim Memorial Prize. He also holds a double degree in law (LL.B.) and chemical engineering (B.S.) from National Taiwan University. Professor Lin has served as visiting researcher/fellow at the Allens Hub for Technology, Law and Innovation at UNSW Sydney, Berkman Klein Center for Internet & Society at Harvard University, Graduate Institute of International and Development Studies in Geneva, Switzerland, and Petrie-Flom Center for Health Law Policy, Biotechnology, and Bioethics. His legal scholarship has appeared in many journals and edited volumes, including *European Journal of International Law, International & Comparative Law Quarterly, Harvard International Law Journal, Virginia Journal of International Law, University of Pennsylvania Journal of International Law, Melbourne Journal of International Law, Columbia Science and Technology Law Review,* and *Columbia Journal of Asian Law.*

Henrietta Lyons is a PhD candidate in Human Computer Interaction in the School of Computing and Information Systems at the University of Melbourne. She is working on a thesis titled 'Developing Human-Centred Explanations for Decisions Made by Artificial Intelligence'. Henrietta received her BCom and LLB from the University of Adelaide. She has co-authored a number of papers on fair and responsible AI, focusing on explainability and contestability of AI systems.

Paul Miller was appointed Ombudsman of New South Wales (NSW) on 1 May 2021, after holding a range of senior roles in the NSW public service, including General Counsel and Deputy Secretary (Legal and Cabinet) of the Department of Premier and Cabinet, and Deputy Secretary (Policy and Strategy) of the Department of Justice. In 2016, he was awarded the Australian Public Service Medal for outstanding public service through the provision of legal advice and freedom of information reforms.

Tim Miller is Professor of Artificial Intelligence in the School of Electrical Engineering and Computing Science at the University of Queensland. Tim's work lies at the intersection of artificial intelligence, interaction design, and cognitive science and psychology. His primary area of expertise is in artificial intelligence, with particular emphasis on human–AI interaction and collaboration; explainable Artificial Intelligence (XAI); decision-making in complex, multi-agent environments; and reasoning about action and knowledge. Tim has extensive experience developing novel and innovative solution with industry and defence collaborators.

Jeannie Marie Paterson is Professor of Law at Melbourne Law School and founding Co-director of the Centre for Artificial Intelligence and Digital Ethics at the University of Melbourne. Jeannie researches in the fields of consumer protection, banking, and consumer credit law, and the regulation of emerging digital technologies. Jeannie's particular research interests are in understanding digital vulnerability and regulatory interventions that recognise the information and power asymmetries in B2C relationships. She has published widely on these research topics in leading journals and edited collections.

Linda Przhedetsky is a doctoral candidate in law at the University of Technology, Sydney. Her research looks at how regulatory interventions can be used to protect consumers in contexts where automated decision-making tools are used to facilitate or limit access to essential services. Her PhD focuses on the use of tenant selection technologies in the private rental sector. Prior to pursuing academia, she worked across government, academia, civil society, and non-profit organisations. Linda is a research fellow at the Gradient Institute, a board member of the NSW Tenants' Union, and has previously served as an executive director of the Consumers' Federation of Australia. She is currently Associate Professor of Strategic AI at the Human Technology Institute, at the University of Technology Sydney.

Monika Zalnieriute is a senior lecturer (associate professor) the University of New South Wales. She is also a senior fellow at the Lithuanian Centre for Social Sciences. Her research on law and technology has been drawn upon by scholars and international organizations such as the *Council of Europe, World Bank, the European Parliament and World Health Organisation*. Monika's work has been published widely, including in *Modern Law Review, Harvard Journal of International Law, Cambridge Law Journal*, and *American Journal of International Law*, translated into Mandarin, Russian and German, and also appeared in international media outlets, such as *BBC* and *The Guardian*. She is the co-editor of *Cambridge Handbook of Facial Recognition in the Modern State* (CUP, 2024).

Foreword

Over the past decade, a movement for algorithmic accountability has highlighted the power of firms and government agencies determining persons' and entities' reputations, visibility in searches, financial standing, and even liberty. A promising line of work has compared the methods and power of governments and financial institutions. This new edited collection joins this established conversation, and advances it significantly.

Money, Power, and AI is an ambitious collection that sheds light on how artificial intelligence (AI) and automated decision-making (ADM), across diverse legal systems, bring new sources of profits and power to financial firms and governments. Several chapters offer approaches for holding powerful institutions accountable. The authors exemplify diverse perspectives, informed by their background as public or private lawyers, social scientists, and public officials, working on various aspects of AI and automation in different jurisdictions. In this way, they demonstrate an important point about algorithmic accountability: contributions from attorneys, social scientists, computer scientists, journalists, and many other professions are critical.

Eight years on from the publication of *The Black Box Society*,[1] many unnecessarily opaque governmental and corporate practices persist and proliferate, while few transparency gains have been achieved. Secrecy permeates the use of many critical AI and ADM tools by both public institutions and private corporations. The net effect is something like a one-way mirror, which shields powerful businesses and government agencies from scrutiny, while permitting these same advantaged entities to engage in ubiquitous surveillance of consumers, citizens, and communities. Moreover, from a law and political economy perspective, the intertwining of business and government frustrates accountability.

---

[1] Frank Pasquale, *The Black Box Society: The Secret Algorithms That Control Money and Information* (Cambridge: Harvard University Press, 2016).

The vast edifice of currency exchanges, derivatives, swaps, options, and countless other financial instruments rests on a foundation of law – or, to be more precise, rests on the relative power of one party to force another to obey the terms of contracts they have made. Though law to some extent shapes all markets, in finance it is fundamental. In fact, the 'products' traded are little more than legal recognitions of obligations to buy or sell, own or owe. This means that we deeply need books such as *Money, Power, and AI* which illuminate relationships among finance and government that are often obscured by legal and computational complexity.

The collection uniquely enriches our understanding of what it insightfully deems (in parallel) Automated Banks and Automated States, and proposes solutions to prevent, or at least mitigate, dangers that the use of AI and ADM poses in Automated Banks and Automated States. Reminiscent of Katharina Pistor's *The Code of Capital*,[2] several authors examine how legal systems, economies, and polities allow financial firms to use ADM to their advantage. Others focus on governments taking advantage of technology, noting misuse, overuse, and bias, as Ryan Calo and Danielle Citron have observed in their article 'The Automated Administrative State: A Crisis of Legitimacy'. Encouragingly, many of the same authors generally also acknowledge the opportunities that ADM can bring. The dose makes the poison, as Paracelsus advised, and sometimes better computing is needed to undo what worse computing has done.

By focusing on the use of AI for mitigation of financial crime and the role of the legal system in enabling and encouraging opaque AI, some authors raise deep questions for the legal profession. They rightly call for greater transparency and accountability in the use of automation in the financial industry, pointing to diverse harms and inefficiencies that occur even in seemingly low-risk contexts. The purported benefits of ADM in the financial industry may be outweighed by risks in some contexts, as the authors argue, and so careful and nuanced regulatory attention is needed.

However, this may not be easily achievable, giving the appeal of automated tools to government agencies, as discussed in Part II. A paradox may arise: just as the use of ADM in finance makes nuanced and personalised regulation all the more necessary, regulators may be encouraged to use 'regtech' (regulatory technology) and 'suptech' (supervisory technology) that is not up to the task. This is not to condemn regtech and suptech generally; in many cases, it may be capable of recognising problems far faster than human analysts. But several contributors to this volume paint a rather grim picture of state capacity across various jurisdictions, suggesting current personnel may not be poised to appropriately control the potential for abuse and misuse of powerful tools.

---

[2]   Katharina Pistor, *Code of Capital: How the Law Creates Wealth and Inequality* (Princeton: Princeton University Press, 2019).

The final part invites the readers to consider various possible safeguards preventing the harms raised in the previous parts. Mere procedural safeguards will not be enough to counter the unprecedented power of Automated Banks and Automated States. Substantive regulation, and a renewed commitment to human-centred empathy towards vulnerable citizens and consumers are also necessary to address harms arising in increasingly automated environments.

Money, power, and AI intersect, and experts have long called for suspect practices of industry and governments to be uncovered and addressed. This book answers the call admirably. The collection answers questions that are crucial for scholars, policymakers, and regulators to consider in the current socio-technical context. The book draws important parallels between financial industry 'private governance' and states' 'public governance', renewing aspects of the ADM research agenda. Similar automated tools have sparked forms of institutional isomorphism that sometimes improve efficiency, but also tend to have detrimental effects on citizens, consumers, and communities in terms of time demands, alienation, and new duties to interact with machines and understand their outputs. Replete with expert contributors addressing critical issues, this collection will shape scholarly and public understanding of Automated Banks and Automated States for years to come.

Frank Pasquale
Jeffrey D. Forchelli Professor of Law
Brooklyn Law School

Acknowledgements

We thank the authors for contributing to this book – your insights and determination make a change in this world, and it is great to have you as colleagues in the field. We are also grateful to Charis Chiu and Arundhati Suma Ajith for research assistance in editing the collection.

We are grateful to the Australian Research Council for funding received from the Centre of Excellence for Automated Decision-Making and Society (project number CE200100005) and a Discovery Early Career Research Award ('Artificial Intelligence Decision-Making, Privacy and Discrimination Laws', project number DE210101183). We would also like to thank the Santander Financial Institute, Fundación UCEIF (Spain) for the research prize awarded to Dr Zofia Bednarz.

Abbreviations

AAT	Administrative Appeals Tribunal
ADM	automated decision-making
ADMS	automated decision-making system
AI	artificial intelligence
AML	anti-money laundering
AUSTRAC	Australia's financial intelligence agency
CDD	customer due diligence
CJS	criminal justice system
COMPAS	Correctional Offender Management Profiling for Alternative Sanctions
DLT	distributed ledger technology
DMA	Digital Markets Act
DSA	Digital Services Act
DSP	Disability Support Pension
DTA	Digital Transformation Agency
EBA	European Banking Authority
ETF	exchange-traded fund
EVAAS	Educational Value-Added Assessment System
FATF	Financial Action Task Force
FOI	freedom of information
FTC	Federal Trade Commission
GDP	gross domestic product
GDPR	General Data Protection Regulation
GRR	General Recidivism Risk
JSCI	Job Seeker Classification Instrument
KYC	know your customer
MELD	Model for End-Stage Liver Disease
NATM	Non-Aligned Technologies Movement

NDIA	National Disability Insurance Authority
NDIS	National Disability Insurance Scheme
NFT	non-fungible token
NHS	National Healthcare System
NSW	New South Wales
OECD	Organisation for Economic Co-operation and Development
ORT	Opioid Risk Tool
PSI	pre-sentence investigation
SAMR	State Administration for Market Regulation
SCW	Supreme Court of Wisconsin
SPJ	structured professional judgement
VAM	value-added model
VRR	Violent Recidivism Risk
WTO	World Trade Organization

Introduction

AI at the Intersection of Money and Power

Monika Zalnieriute and Zofia Bednarz

Artificial intelligence (AI) and automated decision-making (ADM) tools promise money and unmatched power to banks and governments alike. As the saying goes, they will know everything about their citizens and customers and will also be able to predict their behaviour, preferences, and opinions. Global consulting firm McKinsey estimates that AI technologies will unlock $1 trillion in additional value for the global banking industry every year.[1] Governments around the world are getting on the AI bandwagon, expecting increased efficiency, reduced costs, and better insights into their populations.

AI, apart from being a fashionable term that many organisations and researchers like using, denotes a set of related techniques and tools, ranging from machine learning, natural language processing, and computer vision to speech recognition and robotics.[2] AI systems, incorporating these tools and techniques, on their own or combined, into hardware and software, have been described as 'systems that display intelligent behaviour by analysing their environment and taking actions – with some degree of autonomy – to achieve specific goals'.[3] In this book, we are mostly interested in AI tools, which are a subset of ADM. The ADM technology, including AI, is used to make decisions that affect individuals as citizens or consumers. The degree to which humans are involved in such decisions may vary, but the 'autonomy' of the AI tools should not be overestimated. Ultimately, they are only tools, or means to achieve certain goals, which are set by humans.

---

[1] McKinsey & Company, 'Building the AI Bank of the Future' (Global Banking Practice Report, May 2021) 5 <www.mckinsey.com/industries/financial-services/our-insights/building-the-ai-bank-of-the-future> accessed 29 April 2022.

[2] Michael Guihot and Lyria Bennett Moses, *Artificial Intelligence, Robots and the Law* (LexisNexis, 2020) 19.

[3] European Commission High-Level Expert Group on Artificial Intelligence, 'A Definition of AI: Main Capabilities and Disciplines' (8 April 2019) <https://ec.europa.eu/newsroom/dae/document.cfm?doc_id=56341> 1. Note, however, the Expert Group's disclaimer that its description and definition of AI 'is a very crude oversimplification of the state of the art'.

Many of the ADM and AI tools, which governments are eagerly applying today, have been developed and experimented with for decades in the private sector. Technology tools, along with the broader managerial culture, are often transferred from corporations to government departments. Governments also often fund the initial development of these tools, which are later commercialised by corporations. These interactions are often shielded from public eye with the help of legal rules and market practices, which prevent us from knowing how the latest technology is used by the industry and what new tools are being developed, let alone how to regulate their use. For example, China's Social Credit System has roots in automated credit scoring in the financial industry. Similarly, data-enabled fraud detection, used in the Australian 'Robo-debt' system, has long been a common practice in the banking industry. However, governments are not just the copycats in this relationship; they typically fund for the development of such ADM technologies, which are often shielded with trade secrecy laws.

This book explores the use of AI and ADM tools in the financial industry and public administration. Designing and applying AI and ADM tools in a close and mutually reinforcing relationship between the financial industry and governments – or what we call *Automated Banks* and *Automated States* – pose new threats to the accountability of public institutions and the regulation of financial industry alike. We understand *Automated Banks* as financial institutions investing in, and using, new technologies for increased efficiency and profits. Public administration, established to serve communities, closely follows the 'banks', adopting similar procedures, aims, and technology, resulting in *Automated States*. With an increasingly blurred line between public and private authority, this book aims at identifying new safeguards to ensure the rule of law, the protection of fundamental rights, and corporate and state accountability in the age of AI.

Financial industry, which has always been concerned with collecting data and analysing the information to be able to predict the future as accurately as possible, thus maximising their wealth (what we refer to as 'money'), has traditionally been regarded as private actors, as opposed to public governments. But the power that financial industry has over people in most societies can be compared to that of governments. Governments and financial industry have always been collaborating closely, engaging in a mutually reinforcing causal relationship, exchanging information and managerial culture, and participating in policy-making. That relationship is now evidenced in development and deployment of the AI and ADM technologies, which is at the core of this book.

The aim of this book is to encourage a dialogue between 'public' and 'private' legal scholars on accountability, better regulation, new safeguards, and scrutiny of AI applications in the financial industry and public administration. Drawing on socio-legal and critical studies, the book provides a platform for discussion of the use of AI and ADM tools by financial industry and government agencies and, importantly, their close interaction in this space. With its conceptual focus, not being tied to a specific jurisdiction, and diverse authors from Australia, Asia, the United States, and Europe, the book will appeal to wide audiences in research, policy and regulatory spheres, as well as general readers interested in knowing the new dynamics of power and wealth enabled by AI.

The book is organised into three main parts.

Titled *Automated Banks*, Part I examines how AI and ADM are used in the financial industry. The four chapters in Part I analyse the benefits, challenges, and opacity brought about by the use of AI and ADM tools, exploring how legal systems and market practices in financial industry often prevent effective control, scrutiny, and accountability of *Automated Banks*. In Chapter 1, Associate Professor Teresa Rodríguez de las Heras Ballell sets the scene for the discussion of AI in financial sector, discussing the trends in AI regulation using the example of the most recent developments in the European Union. The author argues that increasingly extensive automation of the financial industry flourishes under technology-neutral regulation. At the same time, the application of existing rules may not always lead to desired outcomes such as prevention of misconduct and resulting harms. Professor Jeannie Paterson, Professor Tim Miller, and Henrietta Lyons then analyse in Chapter 2 the notion of 'fintech innovation'. The authors demystify the kinds of capacities that are possible through the fintech technologies being offered to consumers, exploring the methods deployed by fintech solutions and interests behind them, in particular challenging a popular assumption that fintech innovation is of great benefit to marginalised communities with lower socio-economic backgrounds. Dr Doron Goldbarsht's analysis in Chapter 3 shows how legal rules aimed at preventing wrongdoing in the financial system and the use of AI tools by inter-governmental bodies fighting money laundering and terrorism financing vest the industry with unprecedented power. The author sheds light on the benefits and challenges of adopting AI to mitigate risks of financial crimes. Part I ends with Chapter 4 which analyses how the opacity surrounding the use of AI and ADM tools by financial entities is enabled, and even encouraged by the law. The co-editor of the book, Dr Zofia Bednarz, and Associate Professor Linda Przhedetsky unpack how financial entities often rely on rules and market practices protecting corporate secrecy, as well as those incentivising the use of AI and ADM tools, showing how the legal systems allow the technology to become a shield behind which corporations can hide their consumer scoring and rating practices. The authors then explore potential regulatory solutions that could break the opacity and ensure transparency, introducing direct accountability and scrutiny of ADM and AI tools, and reducing the control of financial corporations over people's data. Together, the chapters in Part I reveal the trends in the use of ADM and AI by the *Automated Banks*, how they are intertwined with the legal system, and lay the foundations for understanding their close interactions with the public sector, discussed in Part II.

Titled *Automated States*, Part II examines how AI and ADM tools are used in the public sector. In Chapter 5, Professor Terry Carney looks at the use of AI and ADM tools in welfare administration, and examines new challenges to the fundamental rights of the most vulnerable. Carney argues that existing safeguards for deployment of automated tools in public administration do not ensure decision-making values of transparency, quality, and responsiveness to the interests of citizens and communities. In Chapter 6, Paul Miller, an ombudsperson for community services in the Australian state of New South Wales, explores how the use of AI and ADM tools is shaping public administration, its impact on citizens, and how it affects scrutiny of public administration from a regulator's perspective. Dr José Miguel Bello y Villarino then focuses on legal challenges that incorporation of AI tools will bring in the *Automated State* in Chapter 7. The author discusses the distinct nature of AI technology through an exploration of the dual role of public administration: a state that executes policy and a state that designs policy. In the final chapter of this part, Chapter 8, Dr Aitor Jiménez and Ainhoa Douhaibi analyse the use of AI and ADM tools in welfare and surveillance through the lens of critical race studies. The authors use the example of Catalonia (Spain) to argue that AI and ADM technologies employed to control and monitor immigrant populations are rooted in colonial punitive governmental strategies. Together, the chapters in Part II explore the origins of the use of AI by public administration, the challenges it poses to fundamental rights of the vulnerable and marginalised, and the role of the administrative law in the *Automated State*. Part II lays the foundations for critical discussion and regulatory proposals for future regulation in Part III.

Titled *Synergies and Safeguards*, Part III asks how money, power, and AI tools are entwined and what new safeguards could ensure that *Automated Banks* and *Automated States* are accountable to their customers, citizens, and communities. This part is opened by Professor Cary Coglianese, with his Chapter 9 focusing on AI tools fulfilling administrative law's core values of expert decision-making and democratic accountability. Using the example of the US administrative law, the author points to a new challenge posed by a large-scale shift to the use of AI tools by government, ensuring that an *Automated State* is also an empathic one. Chapter 10 by Professor Ching-Fu Lin explores the blurred line between public and private authority in designing and applying AI tools. The author refers to important consequences resulting from ADM tools sorting individuals out, and citing the US case of *Houston Federation of Teachers v. Houston Independent School District* as a starting point, asks critical questions about the role of judicial review in scrutinising the use of ADM and AI tools. In Chapter 11, Associate Professor Tatiana Cutts critiques the broad consensus that human supervision holds the key to sound ADM and the resulting focus of academic and judicial spheres on ensuring that humans are equipped and willing to wield this ultimate decision-making power. The author argues that opaque ADM tools obscure the reasons for any given prediction, thus depriving the human decision-makers of appropriately weighing that prediction in their reasoning process and making a policy of using such opaque tools unjustified, however involved humans are along the way. In the concluding chapter of the book,

Chapter 12, co-editor Dr Monika Zalnieriute offers a counter-perspective in arguing that the traditional emphasis on procedural safeguards alone – or what she calls procedural fetishism – is insufficient to confront the unprecedented power of the *Automated States*. The author argues that only by shifting our perspective from procedural to substantive, can we search for new ways to regulate the future of *Automated States* and keep them accountable to their citizens and communities.

Collectively, the chapters in the book challenge the 'AI novelty' discourse, prevalent in both the financial industry and public administration. The authors look at the *Automated Banks* and *Automated States* – rather than the technology itself – to specifically emphasise the interests and actors behind the ADM and AI technology. The common theme of the contributions is the focus placed on practices or behaviours, of both government administration and private corporations, that technology enables or encourages, pointing to the recent socio-technological developments being a continuation of, rather than a radical departure from, earlier practices and technologies used. The innovation, so often cited by financial industry and governments, is neither really new nor that beneficial, especially from the point of view of the end-users subjected to it.

At the intersection of money, power, and technology, it becomes clear how the systematic use of ADM tools, which are neither reliable nor transparent, widens the gap in power asymmetry between the *Automated Banks* and *Automated States* on the one hand, and their customers, citizens, and communities on the other. Opacity and proneness to bias emerge as the most prominent characteristics of AI tools, impeding scrutiny of the practices of public administration and industry, and their accountability. The chapters in the book suggest that public and private collaboration becomes a black box barrier to enforcement where proprietary ADM systems are used.

The artificiality of divisions between private and public sectors, as well as public and private law disciplines, is at the heart of this book, which brings together different disciplines, different points of view, different arguments and jurisdictions. The book illustrates how money, power, and AI lead to blurred distinction between private and public sectors. And while the technology and the behaviour it enables are not new *per se*, the authors convincingly argue that new rules, frameworks, and approaches are necessary to prevent harms that increasingly common deployment of AI and ADM tools ultimately leads to.

PART I

Automated Banks

1

AI in the Financial Sector

Policy Challenges and Regulatory Needs

Teresa Rodríguez de las Heras Ballell

1.1 SETTING THE SCENE: AI IN THE FINANCIAL SECTOR

The progressive, but irrepressible, automation of activities, tasks, and decision-making processes through the systematic, pervasive application of AI techniques and systems is ushering in a new era in the digital transformation of the contemporary society and the modern economy.[1] The financial sector, traditionally receptive and permeable[2] to technological advances, is not oblivious to this process of intense and extensive incorporation of AI, for multiple purposes and under variegated forms.[3] The advantages and opportunities that AI solutions offer in terms of

---

[1] This marks the beginning of a second generation of digital transformation. The terminology 'first and second generation' to refer to the successive waves of emerging technologies is used and explained by the author in other previous publications. T Rodríguez de las Heras Ballell, *Challenges of Fintech to Financial Regulatory Strategies* (Madrid: Marcial Pons, 2019), in particular, pp. 61 et seq.

[2] Financial markets have been incorporating state-of-the-art digital communication channels and technological applications for more than two decades – International Finance Corporation (IFC), *Digital Financial Services: Challenges and Opportunities for Emerging Market Banks* (Report, 2017) footnote 42, p. 1. Regulation has been gradually accommodating these transformations: J Dermine, 'Digital Banking and Market Disruption: A Sense of déjà vu?' (2016) 20 *Financial Stability Review, Bank of France* 17.

[3] The study resulting from the survey conducted by the Institute of International Finance – *Machine Learning in Credit Risk*, May 2018 – revealed that traditional commercial banks are adopting technological solutions (artificial intelligence and machine learning and deep learning techniques) as a strategy to gain efficiency and compete effectively with new fintech entrants (Institute of International Finance, *Machine Learning in Credit Risk* (Report, May 2018). PwC's 2021 *Digital Banking Consumer Survey* (Survey 2021) confirms this same attitude of traditional banks to rethink their sales, marketing and customer interaction practices, models, and strategies (PwC, *Digital Banking Consumer Survey* (Report, 2021) <www.pwc.com/us/en/industries/banking-capital-markets/library/digital-banking-consumer-survey.html>. In this overhaul and modernisation strategy, the incorporation of digital technologies – in particular, the use of AI and machine learning models to deliver highly accurate personalised services – is a crucial piece.

efficiency, personalisation potential, risk management, and cost reduction have not gone unnoticed by the financial sector. On the contrary, the characteristics of AI systems seem to perfectly fit in with the features of financial services and to masterly address their most distinctive and challenging needs. Thus, the financial industry provides a receptive and conducive environment to the growing application of AI solutions.

Despite the spotlight on AI, the fact that AI solutions are usually applied, implemented, and incorporated in the financial activity in synergetic combination with other transformative and emerging technologies should not be disregarded. These are technologies such as big data, Internet of Things (IoT), cloud computing, distributed ledger technology (DLT), quantum computing, platform model, virtual reality, and augmented reality[4] that are synchronously present in the market, with similar levels of technical maturity,[5] commercial viability, and practical applicability. In fact, the multiplying effects triggered by such a combination of sophisticated technological ecosystems largely explain the perceived disruptive nature of AI and its actual impact.

With very diverse uses and applications, AI has penetrated financial markets across the board in an increasingly visible way.[6] Its alliance with analytical and predictive processing of big data by financial institutions[7] is perhaps the most telling dimension of a profound transformation of the industry, business strategies, risks, and operations.[8]

The perception of their usefulness[9] and, above all, of the timeliness and desirability of their increasingly pressing incorporation has been encouraged by markedly

---

[4] Capgemini, *World Fintech Report 2018* (Report, 2018) highlights the possibilities offered by emerging technologies for the delivery of customer-facing financial services – artificial intelligence, data analytics, robotics, DLT, biometrics, platforms, IoT, augmented reality, chatbots, and virtual assistants – pp. 20 et seq. Capgemini, *World Fintech Report 2021* (Report, 2021) confirms how the synergistic combination of these transformative technologies has opened up four routes for innovation in the financial sector: establishing ecosystems, integrating physical and digital processes, reorienting transactional flows, and reimagining *core* functions.

[5] World Economic Forum, *Forging New Pathways: The next evolution of innovation in Financial Services* (Report, 2020) 14 <www.weforum.org/reports/forging-new-pathways-the-next-evolution-of-innovation-in-financial-services>.

[6] According to the European Banking Authority (EBA), 64 per cent of European banks have already implemented AI-based solutions in services and processes, primarily with the aim of reducing costs, increasing productivity, and facilitating new ways of competing. EBA, *Risk assessment of the European Banking System* (Report, December 2020) 75.

[7] Joint Committee of the European Supervisory Authorities, *Final Report on Big Data* (Report JC/2018/04, 2018) <www.eba.europa.eu/sites/default/documents/files/documents/10180/2157971/77590961-de6f-4207-bb48-0797ce154ed9/Joint%20Committee%20Final%20Report%20on%20Big%20Data%20%28JC-2018–04%20%29.pdf?retry=1>.

[8] EBA, *Report on Big Data and Advanced Analytics* (Report EBA/REP/2020/01, 2020) <www.eba.europa.eu/sites/default/documents/files/document_library//Final%20Report%20on%20Big%20Data%20and%20Advanced%20Analytics.pdf> .

[9] European Securities and Markets Authority (ESMA), European Banking Authority (EBA), European Insurance and Occupational Pensions Authority (EIOPA), *Joint Committee*

different competitive conditions, precisely because of the impact of technology on market architecture and exceptional circumstances arising from the pandemic.[10] Indeed, this process of intense digital migration has altered the structure and conditions of competition in the market with the opening of new niches for the emergence of innovative fintech firms[11] and the sweeping entry of Big Tech in the financial services sector. The essential function of financial markets as mechanisms for the efficient allocation of savings to investment can take many different forms. Technological innovation has endowed the sector with new architectures[12] on a continuum that shifts from platform models[13] based on a centralised structure to decentralised or distributed models[14] – to varying degrees – that DLT[15] allows to articulate.[16]

Changes in market architecture and opportunities for the provision of new services and intermediation in the distribution of new financial assets and products have driven the emergence of new market players – crowdfunding platform operators, aggregators, comparators, robo-advisers, algorithm providers, social trading platform operators, and multilateral trading system operators – encouraged by low barriers to entry, promising business opportunities, cost reduction, and economies of scale.

Discussion Paper on automation in financial advice, (Discussion Paper JC 2015 080, 4 December 2015) <https://esas-joint-committee.europa.eu/Publications/Discussion%20Paper/20151204_JC_2015_080_discussion_paper_on_Automation_in_Financial_Advice.pdf>.
PwC, *Global Fintech Survey 2016, Beyond Automated Advice. How FinTech Is Shaping Asset & Wealth Management* (Report, 2016) 8, <www.pwc.com/gx/en/financial-services/pdf/fin-tech-asset-and-wealth-management.pdf>.

[10] Capgemini, *World Fintech Report 2021* (Report, 2021) <https://fintechworldreport.com/>: 'The consequences of the pandemic have made the traditional retail banking environment even more demanding'.

[11] According to the definition of the Financial Stability Board (FSB), *Financial Stability Implications from Fintech* (Report, June 2017) 7 <www.fsb.org/wpcontent/uploads/R270617.pdf>, fintech is defined as 'technology-enabled innovation in financial services that could result in new business models, applications, processes or products, with an associated material effect on the provision of financial services'.

[12] TF Dapp, 'Fintech Reloaded-Traditional Banks as Digital Ecosystems' (2015) *Deutsche Bank Research* 5.

[13] T Rodríguez de las Heras Ballell, 'The Legal Anatomy of Electronic Platforms: A Prior Study to Assess the Need of a Law of Platforms in the EU' (2017) 1 *The Italian Law Journal* 3, 149–76.

[14] IH-Y Chiu, 'Fintech and Disruptive Business Models in Financial Products, Intermediation and Markets – Policy Implications for Financial Regulators' (2016) 21 *Journal of Technology Law and Policy* 55.

[15] A Wright and P De Filippi, 'Decentralized Blockchain Technology and the Rise of Lex Cryptographia' (2015) <https://ssrn.com/abstract=2580664> .

[16] R Lewis et al, 'Blockchain and Financial Market Innovation' (2017) *Federal Reserve Bank of Chicago, Economic Perspectives* 7.

In this new landscape, complex relationships of cooperation[17] and competition[18] are established between entrants and incumbents.[19] The presence of new players in the market – offering complementary or instrumental services, creating new environments and channels of communication and intermediation, and adding value to traditional services and products – challenges the traditional scope of regulation and the classical limits of supervision.[20]

On the other hand, mobility restrictions, with closures, confinements, and limitations on travel aimed at containing the spread of the Covid-19 pandemic from the first quarter of 2020, although temporary, have turned the opportunity of digital banking into a survival necessity and even an obligation, in practice, for the proper provision of service and customer care. In a fully digital context for all customer interactions and operations, the use of AI for optimisation, personalisation, or recommendation is key. The processing of increasing amounts of data requires automated means. At this forced and exceptional juncture, many digitalisation initiatives have been prioritised to meet the needs of the changed circumstances. A bank that has completed its digital migration is in a very favourable and receptive position for AI solutions.

This trend, as a response to market demands, is met with increasing regulatory attention seeking to unleash the possibilities and contain the risks of AI. The European Union (EU) provides a perfect illustration. Efforts to define a harmonised regulatory framework for the market introduction, operation, and use of AI systems under certain prohibitions, requirements, and obligations crystallised in the proposed Regulation known as the AI Act.[21] From a sectoral perspective, the European

---

[17] According to the KPMG-Funcas report, *Comparison of Banking vs. Fintech Offerings* (Report, 2018) <https://assets.kpmg/content/dam/kpmg/es/pdf/2018/06/comparativa-oferta-%20banca-fintech.pdf> 48 per cent of domestic fintech firms are complementary to banks, 32 per cent are collaborative, and 20 per cent are competitors. It is estimated that 26 per cent of financial institutions have partnered with Big Tech or technology giants and a similar percentage plan to do so within the next twelve months – KPMG – Funcas, *La banca ante las BigTech* (Report, December 2019), presented in the framework of the Observatorio de la Digitalización Financiera (ODF).

[18] World Economic Forum, *Beyond Fintech: A Pragmatic Assessment of Disruptive Potential in Financial Services* (Report, 2017) <www.weforum.org/reports/beyond-Fintech-a-pragmatic-assessment-of-disruptive-potential-in-financial-services>.

[19] G Biglaiser, E Calvano, and J Crémer, 'Incumbency Advantage and Its Value' (2019) 28 *Journal of Economics & Management Strategy* 1, 41–48.

[20] Spanish Fintech and Insurtech Association (AEFI), *White Paper on Fintech Regulation in Spain* (White Paper, 2017) <https://asociacionfintech.es/wp-content/uploads/2018/06/AEFI_LibroBlanco_02_10_2017.pdf>. Basel Committee on Banking Supervision, *Sound Practices. Implications of Fintech Developments for Banks and Bank Supervisors* (Report, 2018).

[21] Proposal for a Regulation of the European Parliament and of the Council laying down harmonised rules in the field of artificial intelligence (Artificial Intelligence Act) and amending certain legislative acts of the Union, {SEC(2021) 167 final}. – {SWD(2021) 84 final}, {SWD (2021) 85 final}. – {SWD(2021) 85 final}, Brussels, 21.4.2021, COM(2021) 206 final, 2021/0106(COD). References to draft provisions will be made in this Paper to the drafting of the compromise text adopted on 3 November 2022 submitted to Coreper on 11 November 2022

Banking Authority (EBA) had already advocated the need to incorporate a set of fundamental principles to ensure the responsible use and implementation of safe and reliable AI in the banking sector.[22] Indeed, promoting safe, reliable, and high-quality AI in Europe has become one of the backbones of the EU's digital strategy as defined in the strategic package adopted on 19 February 2020. The White Paper on AI[23] and the European Commission Report on Safety and Liability Implications of AI, the *Internet of Things* and Robotics[24] define the coordinates for Europe's digital future.[25] The Ethics Guidelines for Trustworthy AI prepared by the independent High-Level Expert Group on AI in the European Union,[26] which takes the EBA as a reference, marked the first step towards the consolidation of a body of principles and rules for AI – explainability, traceability, avoidance of bias, fairness, data quality, security, and data protection. But the legal regime for the development, implementation, marketing, or use of AI systems requires incorporating other rules found in European legislation, in particular, the recently adopted Regulations on digital services and digital markets – Digital Services Act (DSA)[27] and Digital Markets Act (DMA),[28] or in some of the forthcoming instruments related to AI liability. Even so, it does not result in a coherent and comprehensive body of rules relating to the use of AI systems in the banking sector. It is necessary to compose a heterogeneous and plural set of rules that derive from sectoral regulations, result from the inference of general principles, apply standards from international harmonisation instruments, or project the rules on obligations, contracts, or liability through more or less successful schemes based on functional equivalence and technological neutrality.[29]

for a discussion scheduled on 18 November 2022 with the amendments subsequently adopted by the European Parliament on 14 June 2023.

[22] EBA, *Report on Big Data and Advanced Analytics* (Report EBA/REP/2020/01, 2020), 33–42.

[23] White Paper on *Artificial Intelligence – A European Approach to Excellence and Trust*, COM (2020) 65 final, Brussels, 19 February 2020.

[24] Report from the Commission to the European Parliament, the Council and the European Economic and Social Committee, *Report on the Security and Liability Implications of Artificial Intelligence, the Internet of Things and Robotics* (Report COM(2020) 64, 19 February 2020).

[25] Communication from the Commission to the European Parliament, the Council, the European Economic and Social Committee and the Committee of the Regions, *Shaping Europe's Digital Future*, COM(2020) 67 final, Brussels, 19 February 2020.

[26] 'Building Trust in Human-Centric AI', *European Commission* (Web Page) <https://ec.europa .eu/futurium/en/ai-alliance-consultation.1.html>.

[27] Regulation (EU) 2022/2065 of the European Parliament and of the Council of 19 October 2022 on a Single Market For Digital Services and amending Directive 2000/31/EC (Digital Services Act) (Text with EEA relevance), OJ L 277, 1–102.

[28] Regulation (EU) 2022/1925 of the European Parliament and of the Council of 14 September 2022 on contestable and fair markets in the digital sector and amending Directives (EU) 2019/ 1937 and (EU) 2020/1828 (Digital Markets Act) (Text with EEA relevance), OJ L 265, 1–66.

[29] Principles enshrined in international harmonisation instruments adopted by the United Nations: notably and essentially, 1996 Model Law on Electronic Commerce, 2001 Model Law on Electronic Signatures, 2005 Convention on the Use of Electronic Communications in International Trade, 2017 Model Law on Electronic Transmittable Documents <www .uncitral.un.org>.

The aim of this chapter is to follow this path, which starts with the observation of a growing and visible use of AI in the financial sector, moves into the regulatory and normative debate, and concludes with a reflection on the principles that should guide the design, development, and implementation of AI systems in decision-making (ADM) in the sector. To this end, the chapter is structured as follows. First, it explores the concept of an AI system, considering definitions proposed in the EU, especially in the AI Act, and the interaction of this term with other related terms such as ADM (Section 1.2.1). The various applications of AI in the financial sector in general and in the banking sector in particular are then explored (Section 1.2.2). This provides the conceptual basis for analysing the regulatory framework, including existing and emerging standards, applicable to AI systems, and concludes (Section 1.3) with a proposal of the main principles that should guide the design, implementation, and use of AI systems in the financial sector (Section 1.4).

1.2 CONCEPT AND TAXONOMY: AI SYSTEM AND ADM

The digital transformation is generating an intimate and intense intertwining of various technologies with socioeconomic reality. This implies not only recalibrating principles and rules, but also terminology and concepts. The legal response must be articulated with appropriate definitions and concepts with legal relevance that adequately grasp the distinctive features of technological solutions without falling into a mere technical description, which would make the law irremediably and forever obsolete in the face of technological progress. The law would rather opt for a functional categorisation, which understands the functions without prejudging the technological solution or the business model.

1.2.1 *AI Systems: Concept and Definition*

In the European legislation, whether in force or pending adoption, references to automation appear scattered and with disparate terminology. Both in the General Data Protection Regulation (GDPR),[30] or in the Digital Services Act references to automated individual decisions, algorithmic decisions, algorithmic content recommendation or moderation systems, algorithmic prioritisation, or the use of automatic or automated means for various purposes can be spotted. But there is no definition or explicit reference to 'AI' in the said texts. It is the future, and still evolving, AI Act that expressly defines 'AI systems', for the purposes of the regulation, in order to delimit its material scope of application.

---

[30] *Regulation (EU) 2016/679 of the European Parliament and of the Council of 27 April 2016 on the protection of natural persons with regard to the processing of personal data and on the free movement of such data, and repealing Directive 95/46/EC (General Data Protection Regulation)* [2016] OJ L 119/1.

The initial definition of AI system for the purposes of the proposed instrument in the European Commission's proposal was as follows: artificial intelligence system (AI system) means '*software that is developed using one or more of the techniques and approaches listed in Annex I and can, for a given set of human-defined objectives, generate outputs such as content, predictions, recommendations or decisions that influence the environments with which it interacts*' (Art. 3.1 AI Act).

With this definition, AI systems are defined on the basis of two components. First, the qualification as *learning systems* and thus separated from more traditional computational systems. That is, the fact that they employ or are developed using 'AI' techniques, which the AI Act would define in an Annex I, subject to further extension or modification, and which currently includes: machine learning strategies, including supervised, unsupervised, and reinforcement learning, employing a wide variety of methods, including deep learning; logic and knowledge-based strategies, especially knowledge representation, inductive (logic) programming, knowledge bases, inference and deduction engines, expert systems and (symbolic) reasoning; statistical strategies, Bayesian estimation, search and optimisation methods. Second, the influence on the environment with which they interact, generating outcomes such as predictions, recommendations, content, or actual decisions. Behind this definition lies the assumption that it is precisely the 'learning' capabilities of these systems that largely determine their disruptive effects[31] (opacity, vulnerability, complexity, data dependence, autonomy) and hence the need to reconsider the adequacy of traditional rules. This is, in fact, the reasoning that leads to rethink the rules of liability and thus assess their adequacy in the face of the distinctive features of AI as proposed in the report published on 21 November 2019, titled Report on Liability for Artificial Intelligence and other emerging technologies.[32] And it was issued by the Expert Group[33] on *New Technologies and Liability* advising the European Commission.[34]

---

[31] T Rodríguez de las Heras Ballell, 'Legal Challenges of Artificial Intelligence: Modelling the Disruptive Features of Emerging Technologies and Assessing Their Possible Legal Impact' (2019) 1 *Uniform Law Review* 1–13.

[32] European Commission, Report of the Expert Group in Its New Technologies Formation, *Report on Liability for Artificial Intelligence and Other Emerging Technologies* (Report, November 2019) <https://ec.europa.eu/transparency/regexpert/index.cfm?do=groupDetail .groupMeetingDoc&docid=36608>.

[33] European Commission, Expert Group on Liability and New Technologies, in Its Two Trainings, *New Technologies Formation and Product Liability Formation* <https://ec.europa .eu/transparency/regexpert/index.cfm?do=groupDetail.groupDetail&groupID=3592->.

[34] The author is a member of the Expert Group on Liability and New Technologies (New Technologies Formation), which assists the European Commission in developing principles and guidelines for the adaptation of European and national regulatory frameworks for liability in the face of the challenges of emerging digital technologies (Artificial Intelligence, Internet of Things, Big Data, Blockchain, and DLT). The Expert Group issued its *Report on Liability for Artificial Intelligence and Other Emerging Technologies* which was published on 21 November 2019. The views expressed by the author in this paper are personal and do not necessarily reflect either the opinion of the Expert Group or the position of the European Commission.

Along the same lines, the Commission adopted two related proposals in 2022: proposal for a directive on adapting non-contractual civil liability rules to artificial intelligence[35] and proposal for a directive of the European Parliament and of the Council on liability for defective products.[36]

However, the wording of this definition for AI systems in the Commission's proposal has been subject to significant reconsideration and might still evolve into its final wording. The compromise text submitted at the end of November 2021 by the Slovenian Presidency of the European Council (Council of the European Union, Presidency compromise text, 29 November 2021, 2021/0106(COD), here-after simply Joint Undertaking) proposed some changes to this definition.[37] The text, in its preamble, explains that the changes make an explicit reference to the fact that the AI system should be able to determine how to achieve a given set of pre-defined human objectives through learning, reasoning, or modelling, in order to distinguish them more clearly and unambiguously from more traditional software systems, which should not fall within the scope of the proposed Regulation. But also with this proposal, the definition of an AI system is stylised and structurally reflects the three basic building blocks: inputs, processes, and outputs.

Yet, a subsequent version version of the compromise text[38] of the AI Act offers another definition that refines the previous drafting and provides sufficiently clear criteria for distinguishing AI from simpler software systems. Thus, *AI system means a*

---

[35] *Proposal COM/2022/496 of 28 September 2022 for a Directive of the European Parliament and of the Council on adapting non-contractual civil liability rules to artificial intelligence (AI Liability Directive).*

[36] *Proposal COM/2022/495 of 28 September 2022 for a Directive of the European Parliament and of the Council on liability for defective products.*

[37] Artificial intelligence system (AI system) means a system that

    (i) receives machine and/or human-based data and inputs,

    (ii) infers how to achieve a given set of human-defined objectives using learning, reasoning, or modelling implemented with the techniques and approaches listed in Annex I, and

    (iii) generates outputs in the form of content (generative AI systems), predictions, recommendations, or decisions, which influence the environments it interacts with.

[38] The fourth compromise text is as follows:

On 5 July 2022, the Czech Presidency held a policy debate in WP TELECOM on the basis of a policy options paper, the outcomes of which were used to prepare the second compromise text. Based on the reactions of the delegations to this compromise, the Czech Presidency prepared the third compromise text, which was presented and dis-cussed in WP TELECOM on 22 and 29 September 2022. After these discussions, the delegations were asked to send in their written comments on the points they felt most strongly about. Based on those comments, as well as using the input obtained during bilateral contacts with the Member States, the Czech Presidency drafted the fourth compromise proposal, which was discussed in the WP TELECOM meeting on 25 October 2022. Based on these discussions, and taking into account final written remarks from the Member States, the Czech Presidency has now prepared the final version of the compromise text.

system that is designed to operate with a certain level of autonomy and that, based on machine and/or human-provided data and inputs, infers how to achieve a given set of human-defined objectives using machine learning and/or logic- and knowledge-based approaches, and produces system-generated outputs such as content (generative AI systems), predictions, recommendations, or decisions influencing the environments with which the AI system interacts. Some key elements of the initial definition are preserved or recovered in this recent version that finally narrows down the description of 'learning systems' to the definition to systems developed through machine learning approaches and logic- and knowledge-based approaches.

The definition is still evolving. In the latest compromise text[39] the new definition of AI system is 'a machine-based system that is designed to operate with varying levels of autonomy and that can, for explicit or implicit objectives, generate outputs such as predictions, recommendations, or decisions, that influence physical or virtual environments'.

Also, the European Parliament Resolution on liability for the operation of artificial intelligence systems[40] referred expressly to AI systems and formulated its own definition (Art. 3.a).[41] This Resolution contains a set of recommendations for a Regulation of the European Parliament and of the Council on civil liability for damage caused by the operation of AI systems. The proposal has not been adopted. Instead, the Commission proposed the abovementioned tandem of draft Directives, that follow a substantially different approach aimed to revise the Defective Product Liability rules so as to accommodate AI-driven products and to alleviate the burden of proof in fault-based liability scenarios on damages caused by AI systems.

The rest of the regulatory texts do not explicitly refer to AI, although they contain rules on algorithms, algorithmic systems of various types, automation or automatic decision-making. Thus, as mentioned above, the GDPR, the DSA, the DMA or, among others, the P2B Regulation[42] refer to algorithmic rating, algorithmic decision-making, algorithmic recommendation systems, algorithmic content moderation, algorithmic structures, automated profiling, or a variety of activities and actions performed by automated means. They include rules related to algorithms,

---

[39] Amendments adopted by the European Parliament on 14 June 2023 on the proposal for a regulation of the European Parliament and of the Council on laying down harmonised rules on artificial intelligence (Artificial Intelligence Act) and amending certain Union legislative acts (COM(2021)0206 – C9-0146/2021 – 2021/0106(COD)).

[40] Report with recommendations to the Commission on a civil liability regime for artificial intelligence (2020/2014(INL)), 5 October 2020 <www.europarl.europa.eu/doceo/document/A-9-2020-0178_ES.pdf>.

[41] (a) 'Artificial intelligence system' means any software-based or hardware-embedded system that exhibits behaviour simulating intelligence, inter alia, by collecting and processing data, analysing and interpreting its environment and taking action, with a degree of autonomy, to achieve specific objectives.

[42] *Regulation (EU) 2019/1150 of 20 June 2019 of the European Parliament and of the Council on promoting fairness and transparency for professional users of online intermediation services (Text with EEA relevance)* [2019] OJ L 186/57.

such as disclosure, risk assessment, accountability and transparency audits, on-site inspections, obtaining consent, etc. As the definition of AI systems proposed by the AI Act reveals, recommendations, decisions, predictions, or other digital content of any kind, as well as actions resulting from the system in or in relation to the environment, are natural and frequent *outputs* of AI systems. Consequently, regulatory provisions that in some way regulate algorithmic processes and decision-making by automated means in a variety of scenarios and for a variety of purposes are also relevant for the construction of the regulatory framework for AI in the European Union.

Provided that the AI system falls under the scope of application of the proposed AI Act, an AI system may be subject to the AI Act as well as to other rules depending on the specific purpose, the purpose for which it is intended or the specific action. As an illustration, if the system is intended to produce recommendations by a very large banking platform, the DSA (Art. 27) – applicable to any online platform – applies, or if the system is intended for profiling, the GDPR (Art. 22) would be relevant.

In conclusion, understanding the complementarity between the various legal texts that directly or indirectly address the use of AI systems for a variety of purposes and from a range of legal perspectives is fundamental to composing the current and future regulatory framework for AI, as discussed below.

1.2.2 *Current and Potential Uses of AI in the Financial Sector*

With varying degrees of intensity, AI systems are used transversally in the banking sector along the entire *front-line-mid-office-back-office* value chain. For customer service and interaction, AI systems offer extraordinary possibilities for personalisation, recommendation and profiling, account management, trading and financial advice (robo advisers), continuous service via chatbots and virtual assistants, and sophisticated Know Your Customer (KYC) solutions.[43] In the internal management of operations, AI solutions are applied in the automation of corporate, administrative and transactional processes, in the optimisation of various activities, or *compliance* management. For risk management, AI solutions are projected to improve fraud prevention mechanisms, early warning and cybersecurity systems, as well as being incorporated in predictive models for recruitment and promotion. Another interesting use[44] of advanced analysis models with *machine learning* is the calculation and determination of regulatory capital. Significant cost savings are estimated[45] if these models are used to calculate risk-weighted assets.

---

[43] See also discussion in Chapters 2–4 in this book.
[44] Although their effective use is still limited, there are very significant advantages that herald very promising expected implementation rates. EBA, *Report on Big Data and Advanced Analytics* (Report EBA/REP/2020/01, 2020) 20, figure 2.1.
[45] A Alonso and JM Carbó, 'Understanding the Performance of Machine Learning Models to Predict Credit Default: A Novel Approach for Supervisory Evaluation' (Working Paper No

Acknowledging this transversal and multipurpose use allows to anticipate some considerations of interest and relevance for legal analysis. It can be seen that automation has an impact on decision-making processes, actions, or operations of a diverse nature, which will be decisive in determining at least three elements.

First, the applicable regulatory regime – for example, whether it is used to automate compliance with reporting rules, to prevent fraud, to personalise customer offers, or to handle complaints via a chatbot. Second, the possible liability scenarios – for example, whether algorithmic biases and data obtained from social media for the credit scoring and creditworthiness assessment system could lead to systematic discriminatory actions. Third, the transactional context in which it is used – for example, in consumer relations with retail customers, in relations with the supervisor, or in internal relations with employees or partners.

The benefits deriving from the use of automation and AI and the expected gains from systematic and extensive application are numerous.[46] Algorithm-driven systems provide speed, simplicity, and efficiency in solving a multitude of problems. Automation drastically reduces transaction costs, enabling services that would otherwise be unprofitable, unaffordable, or unviable to be provided on reasonable and competitive terms. Cost reduction explains, for example, the burgeoning sector of robo-advisers[47] that have expanded the market beyond traditional financial advisers with appreciable benefits for consumers by diversifying supply, increasing competition, and improving financial inclusion.[48] Such expansion has facilitated financial advice to small investment and low-income investors on market terms.

ADM systems can therefore perform automated tasks and make mass decisions efficiently (high-frequency algorithmic trading, search engines, facial recognition, personal assistants, machine translation, predictive algorithms, and recommender systems). The use of automated means is critical for the large-scale provision of critical services in our society that would otherwise be impossible or highly inefficient (search, sorting, filtering, rating, and ranking).

However, the expansive and growing use of algorithms in our society can also be a source of new risks, can lead to unintended outcomes, have unintended consequences, or raise legal concerns and social challenges of many different kinds. ADM may be biased or discriminatory[49] as a result of prejudiced preconditions, based on stereotypes or aimed at exploiting user vulnerabilities, inadequate algorithm design,

---

2105, Banco de España March 2021) <www.bde.es/f/webbde/SES/Secciones/Publicaciones/PublicacionesSeriadas/DocumentosTrabajo/21/Files/dt2105e.pdf>.

[46] Deloitte, *Artificial Intelligence. Innovation Report* (Report, 2018).

[47] O Kaya, 'Robo-Advice: A True Innovation in Asset Management' (Research Paper, Deutsche Bank Research, *EU Monitor Global Financial Markets*, 10 August 2017) 9.

[48] T Bucher-Koenen, 'Financial Literacy, Cognitive Abilities, and Long-Term Decision Making: Five Essays on Individual Behavior' (2010) *Inauguraldissertation zur Erlangung des akademischen Grades eines Doktors der Wirtschaftswissenschaften der Universität Mannheim.*

[49] A Chander, 'The Racist Algorithm' (2017) 115 *Michigan Law Review* 1023.

or an insufficient or inaccurate training and learning data set.[50] The automation of ADM makes bias massive, amplified and distorted, and easily gain virality. In a densely connected society such as ours, virality acts as an amplifier of the harmful effects of any action. Negative impacts spread rapidly, the magnitude of the damage increases, and the reversibility of the effects becomes less likely and increasingly impractical. The incorporation of decision and learning techniques into increasingly sophisticated AI systems adds to the growing unpredictability of future response. This leads to greater unpredictability and unstoppable complexity that is not always consistent with traditional rules and formulas for attribution of legal effects and allocations of risk and liability (*infra* 3.1.2.2 and 3.1.2.3).

1.3 AN INITIAL REVIEW OF THE POLICY AND REGULATORY FRAMEWORK IN THE EUROPEAN UNION

The use of AI systems for decision-making and the automation of tasks and activities in the financial sector does not have a comprehensive and specific legal framework, either across the board or in its various sectoral applications.

The legal and regulatory framework needs to be assembled by the interlocking of legal provisions from various instruments and completed by the inference of certain principles from rules applicable to equivalent non-automated decisions. The application of the principle of functional equivalence (between automated and non-automated decisions with equivalent functions) guided by technological neutrality makes it possible to extract or extrapolate existing rules to the use of AI systems. However, as argued in the final part of this chapter, this effort to accommodate existing rules to the use of different technologies, under a non-discrimination approach on a medium basis, presents difficulties due to the distinctive characteristics of AI systems, thus compromising legal certainty and consistency. It is therefore suggested that a set of principles be formulated and a critical review of regulation be conducted to ensure that the European Union has a framework that provides certainty and encourages the responsible use of AI systems in the financial sector.

1.3.1 *The Expected Application of the Future AI Law to the Uses of AI in the Financial Sector*

The (future) AI Act is based on a risk-based classification of AI uses, applications, and practices, to which a specific legal regime is attached: prohibition, requirements for high-risk systems, transparency, and other obligations for certain low-risk systems. The classification of AI systems is not done on the basis of the employed technology but in conformity with the (intended, actual, reasonably expected) specific uses or applications. This means that there is no explicit sectoral selection, but certain

---

[50] S Barocas and A Selbst, 'Big Data's Disparate Impact' (2016) 104 *California Law Review* 671.

practices can be identified with preferred sectoral uses such as creditworthiness assessment, and automated credit rating determination.

1.3.1.1 Prohibited Practices under the AI Act and Their Relevance to Financial Activity

The prohibited practices under Article 5 of the AI Act does not at a first sight naturally embrace the expected uses of AI in the financial sector, but, to the extent that they are defined on the basis of certain effects, they cannot be fully ruled out and should be taken into consideration as red lines. Thus, for example, a personalised-marketing AI system that uses subliminal techniques to substantially alter behaviour in a way that may cause physical or psychological harm (Art. 5.a) or a loan offering and marketing system that exploits any of the vulnerabilities of a group of people based on age, physical or mental disability, or a specific social or economic situation (Art. 5.b).

As initially drafted, although slightly nuanced in subsequent versions (in the Joint Undertaking), the scenarios for the use of biometric identification systems or the assessment or classification of the trustworthiness of natural persons according to their social behaviour or personality are less likely to cover AI applications in the financial sector. The reason is because the prohibition is linked to their use by (or on behalf of) public authorities, or in publicly accessible spaces for law enforcement purposes (although there are still scenarios in which they could apply, such as precisely banks, mentioned in Recital 9 as 'publicly accessible spaces'). These requirements, questioned for being excessively restrictive, would leave outside the scope of prohibited use of the application in a private space – of an institution – of biometric recognition systems or even assessment systems (*social scoring*) that could be implemented to accompany a creditworthiness assessment or to profile the eligibility of applicants for banking products. Therefore, in the latest compromise text (14 June 2023), these restrictive criteria have been deleted. The prohibition is extended now to (Article 5.1.d) the use of 'real-time' remote biometric identification systems in publicly accessible spaces.

While the potential impact of the AI Act's on prohibitions of certain practices in the financial sector appears limited, the likelihood of these being systems classified as high risk is certainly much higher.

1.3.1.2 High-Risk Systems in the AI Act

Annex III of the AI Act provides a list of AI systems, related to eight areas (pursuant to the most recent version of the compromise text), defined by their use, purpose or aim, which will very easily reflect frequent applications of AI in the financial sector: systems for the remote biometric identification of natural persons (1.a Annex III), systems for recruitment or selection of natural persons or for making decisions on promotion or termination of employment relationships or assignment of tasks and monitoring and evaluation of performance (4.a and b Annex III), and, directly and obviously, systems for assessing the creditworthiness of natural persons or establishing their credit rating – with the exception of AI systems used for the purpose of detecting financial fraud – (5.b Annex III).

Confirming the application of the AI Act to certain uses of AI systems proposed by a financial institution will mean it being subject to certain more intensive requirements if it is qualified as high risk (Art. 8 AI Act). These are essentially audit, risk assessment and management, data governance (training, validation, and testing), technical documentation, event logging, cybersecurity, and transparency and reporting obligations to which financial institutions are by no means neither oblivious nor unfamiliar. They respond to a regulatory strategy of supervision and risk management that is well known in regulated sectors such as the financial sector. In fact, the need to avoid duplications, contradictions, or overlaps with sectoral regulations has been taken into account in the AI Act, in particular in relation to the financial sector already subject to risk management, assessment, and supervision obligations similar to those envisaged in the future Regulation – (see Recital 80, and Articles 17.3, 18.2, 20.2, 29.4, 61.4, 62.3). In this regard, the AI Act articulates some solutions to ensure consistency between the obligations of credit institutions under Directive 2013/36/EU[51] when they employ, operate, or place on the market IA systems in the exercise of their activity.

1.3.2 *Principles and Rules for the Use of AI Systems in Decision-Making*

However, the eventual application of the AI Act does not exhaust the regulatory framework of reference for the use of AI systems in the financial sector, nor, in fact, does it resolve a good number of questions that the implementation and subsequent operation of such systems in the course of their activity will generate. To this end, and for this reason, it is essential to explore other regulatory instruments and to discover legal avenues to answer a number of important questions. First, to what extent can automated systems be used with full functional equivalence for any activity, decision, or process without prior legal authorisation? Second, to what extent are decisions taken or assisted by AI systems attributed to the financial institution operating the system? Third, who bears the risks and liability for damage caused by the AI systems used?

---

[51] *Directive 2013/36/EU of the European Parliament and of the Council of 26 June 2013 relating to the taking up and pursuit of the business of credit institutions and the prudential supervision of credit institutions and investment firms, amending Directive 2002/87/EC and repealing Directives 2006/48/EC and 2006/49/EC Text with EEA relevance* [2013] OJ L 176/338.

1.3.2.1 On the Principle of Non-discrimination for the Use of AI in Decision-Making

Neither the AI Act nor, in principle, any other regulation expressly enables the use of AI systems to support decision-making or to automate specific tasks, processes, or activities.[52] Occasionally and incidentally, reference to automation is found in some texts, even simply in the recitals – Regulation (EU) 2020/1503/EU[53] to automatic investment in par. 20 – without further specification or development in the legal provisions. In other cases, this possibility is confirmed because reference is made to 'with or without human intervention' or 'by automatic means', as in the DSA – Art. 3 (s) on recommender systems, Art. 16(6) on means of notification and action, Art. 17 (3) on the statement of reasons. And in other cases, an express limitation to full automation of a decision-making process such as complaints handling on a platform – DSA, Art. 20(6) – is provided for.

Within this regulatory context, the question on the admissibility, validity, and enforceability of the use of AI systems must be approached on the basis of two backbone principles: the principle of functional equivalence and the principle of non-discrimination and technological neutrality. These principles lead to a positive and enabling initial response that allows the use of AI systems for decision-making or to assist in decision-making, to automate tasks, processes, and activities in a general way and without the need for prior express legislative recognition. There is no reason to deny this functional equivalence or to generally discriminate against the use of AI systems under analogous conditions. Subject-specific limits or sector-specific regulatory requirements might in practice restrict certain applications in the financial sector, but the basic rule is the feasibility of using AI in any activity and for any decision-making.

Naturally, the implementation of an IA system will require ensuring that the automated process is in compliance with the rules applicable to the same process, situation, or transaction if it were not automated. AI systems have to be designed, implemented, and operated in such a way that they comply with the rules that would apply to the legal nature of the decision or activity and, therefore, also to its regulatory treatment in the financial field. If the marketing of certain financial products is automated through a digital banking application, it should be ensured that the legal requirements for pre-contractual information are met. If an automated robo-adviser system is implemented, the requirements for financial advice must be met, if it is indeed categorised as such.

---

[52] See also arguments raised by Bednarz and Przhedetsky in Chapter 4 in this book as to the legal rules that incentivise the use of ADM and AI tools by financial entities.

[53] *Regulation (EU) 2020/1503 of the European Parliament and of the Council of 7 October 2020 on European providers of equity finance services to enterprises, and amending Regulation (EU) 2017/1129 and Directive (EU) 2019/1937 (Text with EEA relevance)* [2020] OJ L 347/1.

Despite the apparent simplicity of this principle of non-discriminatory recognition of AI, its effect is intense and powerful. It constitutes, in practice, a natural enabler for the multiple and intensive integration of AI in any area of financial activity, as a principle. As long as compliance with the rules and requirements applicable to the action or the equivalent non-automated process can be ensured, AI can be employed to make or assist in making any decision.

1.3.2.2 On the Attribution of Legal Effects

The particular complexity in the chain of design, development, implementation, and operation of AI systems with a set of actors involved, very often without prior agreement or coordination among them, raises a legal question of indisputable business relevance: to whom the legal effects, and thus the risks of a decision, or an action resulting from an automated process, are attributed.

Although this issue can be interpreted as a single attribution problem from a business perspective, from a legal point of view, it is useful to distinguish between two different, albeit related, issues.

First is the question to whom the decision – any decision with contractual relevance (offer, acceptance, modification, renegotiation, termination) – or the resulting action – commercial practice, compliance with supervision request – is to be attributed. That is, if a bank implements an application that incorporates a credit scoring system leading to the automated granting or refusal (without human intervention in each decision) of consumer credit applications, assessing credit-worthiness and the decision to accept or deny the credit request are attributable to the bank. Thus, if the credit is granted, the bank is the counterparty to the resulting credit contract; whereas, if it is unjustifiably denied, discriminating against certain groups, the bank would be the offender, violating, for example, the right not to be discriminated against. Similar reasoning would apply to the use of an AI system in an employee recruitment or promotion programme, or to a fraud detection and prevention system.

This attribution of legal effects is based on the formulation of the concept of 'operator'. This concept proposed by the Report on Liability for Artificial Intelligence and Other Emerging Technologies and subsequently taken over by the European Parliament Resolution of 2020[54] is based on two factors: control and benefit. Thus, the operator will be the centre of imputation of the legal effects insofar as it controls (or should be able to control) the risks of operating an AI system that it decides to integrate into its activity and, therefore, benefit from its operation.

---

[54] Report with recommendations to the Commission on a civil liability regime for artificial intelligence (2020/2014(INL)), 5 October 2020 <www.europarl.europa.eu/doceo/document/A-9-2020-0178_ES.pdf>.

This attribution of legal effects to the operator also has another important consequence. The operator cannot hide behind the automated or increasingly autonomous nature of the AI system used in order not to assume the consequences of the action or decision taken, nor can the bank consider attributing such effects to other actors involved in the life cycle of the AI system. Thus, for example, it cannot be attributed to the developer of the system, the distributor, or the provider of the data *per se* and vis-à-vis the bank customer. This is without prejudice to the possibility for the operator (the bank) to bring subsequent actions or remedies against these actors. However, the operator is who assumes the legal – legal or contractual – effects vis-à-vis the affected person concerned (customer).

Second, a question arises as to who should bear the risks and liability for damage caused by the operation of AI systems, as expounded below.

1.3.2.3 On Liability for Damage Caused by the Operation of AI Systems

The operation of an AI system can cause a wide range of damages. In certain sectors, substantial property damage and personal injury can be anticipated (autonomous vehicles, drones, home automation, care robots). Their applications in financial activities are linked to systemic risks, threats to economic stability and financial integrity, or cyclical responses and market shocks. But their malfunctioning can also simply cause massive data loss, disrupt access to services and products, generate misleading messages to customers about the status of their accounts, recommend unsuitable investments according to risk profile, or result in non-compliance with certain obligations vis-à-vis supervisory authorities. The use in rankings, recruitment services, content filtering, or virtual assistants for complaint handling opens the door to a far-reaching debate on their impact on fundamental rights and freedoms – freedom of expression, the right not to be discriminated against, the right to honour, and personality rights – but also on the competitive structure of the market or on the fairness of the commercial practices. Hence, the approach adopted by the proposed AI Act in Europe is based on the identification of certain AI practices, uses, or applications which, due to their particular risk or criticality, are prohibited, qualified as high risk and therefore subject to certain obligations and requirements, or subject to harmonised rules regulating their introduction on the market, their putting into service, and their use.[55]

---

[55] According to Article 1 of the proposal, the Regulation of the European Parliament and of the Council laying down harmonised rules in the field of artificial intelligence (Artificial Intelligence Act) states:

   (a) harmonised rules for the placing on the market, putting into service and use of artificial intelligence systems ("AI systems") in the Union;
   (b) prohibitions of certain artificial intelligence practices;
   (c) specific requirements for high-risk AI systems and obligations for operators of such systems;

However, in the face of such potentially negative effects, the fundamental question is whether, beyond the adoption of specific rules for AI systems aimed at controlling their use and mitigating their negative effects, traditional legal liability regimes are adequately equipped to manage the risks and effectively resolve the conflicts arising from such situations in complex technological environments.

In this respect, the European Union faces important legislative policy choices. First, to assess whether a thorough reform of the product liability regime[56] is necessary to accommodate AI systems.[57] The questions are manifold: are AI systems products?, is a decision of the AI system that causes damage necessarily the result of a defect?, and do the provisions of the Directive work adequately in the face of an AI system that has been updated since it was put on the market? Second, to consider whether it is appropriate to establish a harmonised liability regime specific to AI, as suggested in the abovementioned Parliament Resolution,[58] and if so, whether it should be an operator's liability and whether the distinction between strict liability for high-risk systems and fault-based liability for the rest is appropriate. The Proposal of the Commission in 2022[59] departs from the route initiated by the Parliament in 2020 as it proposes a Directive instead of a Regulation, and it puts forward a minimum and complementary harmonisation to national rules on (fault-based) (non-contractual) civil liability in a targeted manner with rules on specific aspects of fault-based liability rules at Union level.

1.4 CONCLUDING REMARKS: PRINCIPLES FOR THE RESPONSIBLE USE OF AI IN DECISION-MAKING

The principle of non-discrimination against the use of AI systems in any activity and for any decision-making enables intense and extensive automation in the banking (financial) sector through the implementation of AI solutions. Within this favourable and automation-friendly framework, compliance with the regulatory requirements demanded by the nature of the sectoral activity (*law-compliant AI systems*) must nevertheless be ensured and some specific limitations must be added which,

---

(d) harmonised transparency rules for certain AI systems;

(e) rules on market monitoring, and market surveillance governance; and enforcement

[56] *Council Directive 85/374/EEC of 25 July 1985 on the approximation of the laws, regulations and administrative provisions of the Member States concerning liability for defective products* [1985] OJ L 210/29.

[57] Proposal for a Directive on liability for defective products COM(2022) 495. BA Koch et al, 'Response of the European Law Institute to the Public Consultation on Civil Liability – Adapting Liability Rules to the Digital Age and Artificial Intelligence' (2022) 13 *Journal of European Tort Law* 1, 25–63 <https://doi.org/10.1515/jetl-2022-0002>.

[58] Proposal for a Directive on liability for defective products COM(2022) 495.

[59] Ibid.

by reason of their use or purpose (e.g. credit scoring, recruitment and promotion, biometric recognition), the future AI Act could prohibit or subject to certain obligations. To the extent that these AI systems are also employed to provide recommendations, personalise offers, produce rankings, or moderate content, additional rules (DSA, DMA, GDPR) could apply if they are used by financial institutions that have transformed their business model into an online platform.

Even so, there is neither a compact and coherent set of principles capable of guiding automation strategies nor a comprehensive body of rules that would provide full legal certainty for the implementation of AI systems in the banking sector. The highly distinctive characteristics of AI do not always make an application of existing rules under a technology-neutral and functional equivalence approach fully satis-factory, nor are the existing rules always feasible or workable in the AI context. Therefore, there are calls in the European Union for the complementation of the legal framework with other specific principles to crystallise a body of rules suitable for AI. The EBA also advocated for this strategy at sectoral level.

The formulation of ethical principles is certainly a starting point, but the integra-tion of AI systems in the course of an economic activity, throughout the transac-tional cycle and for business management requires a clear framework of duties and obligations. This is the endeavour that policymakers in the European Union and internationally must face now.[60] It is necessary to specify how AI systems should be designed, implemented, and commissioned to satisfy the principles of traceability, explainability, transparency, human oversight, auditability, non-discrimination, reasoned explanation of decisions, and access to a review mechanism for significant decisions. It will be key to understand how the provisions of the future AI Act interact with contract law and liability rules,[61] to what extent the classification of an AI system as high risk under the AI Act could imply the application of a strict liability regime (as previously proposed under the Parliament's resolution scheme, even if this approach has not been followed by the recent Commission's proposals for Directives), or what effects the failure to articulate a human-intervention mechanism under Art. 22 GDPR would have on the validity and effectiveness of an automated decision based on profiling, or what implications the failure of the

---

[60] The *European Law Institute*'s projects on *Smart Contract and Blockchain, Algorithmic Contracts* and *Innovation Paper on Guiding Principles for Automated Decision-Making in Europe* seek to contribute to this pre-legislative debate in the Union ('ELI Projects and Other Activities', *European Law Institute* (Web Page) <www.europeanlawinstitute.eu/pro jects-publications/>). At the international level, work has also started in the same direction, such as the new UNCITRAL/UNCITRAL work plan project on automation and the use of AI in international trade ('Working Group IV: Electronic Commerce', *United National Commission on International Trade Law* (Web Page) <https://uncitral.un.org/es/working_ groups/4/electronic_commerce>).

[61] C Codagnone, G Liva, and T Rodríguez de las Heras Ballell, *Identification and Assessment of Existing and Draft EU Legislation in the Digital Field* (Study, 2022) <www.europarl.europa .eu/thinktank/de/document/IPOL_STU(2022)703345>. Study requested by the AIDA special committee, European Parliament.

bank operator to comply with the requirements of the AI Act would have on the validity and the enforceability of the contract or on the eventual categorisation of certain bank practices as unfair commercial practices.It is essential for financial firms, referred to in this book as Automated Banks, to be provided with clear and coherent rules for the use and implementation of AI systems in decision-making. The law must be developed in combination with, and accompanied by, detailed (technical) standards, best practices, and protocols progressively and increasingly harmonised in the financial sector.

2

Demystifying Consumer-Facing Fintech

Accountability for Automated Advice Tools

Jeannie Paterson, Tim Miller, and Henrietta Lyons

2.1 INTRODUCTION: MONEY, POWER, AND AI

As the authors of this book recognise, money and power are intimately linked. For most consumers, access to banking services, credit, and a saving plan for retirement are necessary – although not sufficient – requirements for a stable, meaningful, and autonomous life. Conversely, financial hardship may have considerable impact on not only the financial but also the emotional well-being of consumers.[1] There are many causes of financial hardship, including high levels of personal debt, reliance on high-cost credit, lack of access to mainstream banking services, and unexpected circumstances such as unemployment or ill health.[2] Additionally, consumers are sometimes subject to fraudulent, deceptive, and dishonest practices, which can escalate their financial problems.[3] Moreover, many consumers find that they lack the time or skills to manage their day-to-day finances, select optimal credit products, or invest effectively for the future.[4]

So where does AI[5] – the third theme of this book – sit in this schema? The growing capacity of AI and related digital technologies has contributed to a burgeoning interest in the potential for financial technology ('fintech') to transform the

---

[1] See also Jodi Gardner, Mia Gray, and Katharina Moser (eds), *Debt and Austerity: Implications of the Financial Crisis* (Edward Elgar, 2020).

[2] See further Lucinda O'Brien et al, 'More to Lose: The Attributes of Involuntary Bankruptcy' (2019) 38 *Economic Papers* 15.

[3] Jeannie Paterson, 'Knowledge and Neglect in Asset-Based Lending: When Is It Unconscionable or Unjust to Lend to a Borrower Who Cannot Repay?' (2009) 20 *Journal of Banking and Finance Law and Practice* 18.

[4] See generally, Michael Trebilcock, Anthony Duggan, and Lorne Sossin (eds), *Middle Income Access to Justice* (University of Toronto Press, 2012).

[5] AI is a disputed category – we are using the term to cover automated decision-making processes informed by predictive analytics, machine learning techniques, and natural language processing.

way in which traditional banking and financial services are provided.[6] Governments across the globe have promoted the capacity of AI informed fintech to improve market competition and consumer welfare,[7] and have introduced initiatives to support the development of innovative fintech products within their jurisdictions.[8] Fintech products are increasingly being used by the financial services sector for internal processes, decision-making, and interactions with customers.[9]

Inside financial institutions, fintech products are assisting in fraud detection, cybersecurity, marketing, and onboarding new clients.[10] Fintech products are being developed to automate financial services firms' decisions about lending, credit-worthiness, and pricing credit and insurance.[11] In a consumer-facing role, fintech products are being used for communicating with customers, such as through chatbots (generative or otherwise),[12] and in providing access to financial products, for example, loan[13] or credit card online applications.[14] Fintech products are being developed to provide credit product comparisons for consumers looking for the best

[6]   See, for example, Ross P Buckley et al, 'Regulating Artificial Intelligence in Finance: Putting the Human in the Loop' (2021) 43(1) *Sydney Law Review* 43.
[7]   See, for example, the UK Financial Conduct Authority's innovation services, which aim to 'create room for the brightest and most innovative companies to enter the sector, support positive innovation to come to market in a controlled and sustainable way, support innovation that has genuine potential to improve the lives of consumers across all areas of financial services [and] support innovation delivered by a diverse range of participants, both in terms of the type of firm, and the people behind the developments': 'Our Innovation Services', *Financial Conduct Authority* (Web Page) <www.fca.org.uk/firms/innovation/our-innovation-services> accessed 11 July 2023. See also 'Competition in the Technology Marketplace', *Federal Trade Commission* (Web Page) <www.ftc.gov/advice-guidance/competition-guidance/indus try-guidance/competition-technology-marketplace> accessed 11 July 2023; Bank of England and Financial Conduct Authority, 'Machine Learning in UK Financial Services' (Web Page, October 2019) 3 <www.bankofengland.co.uk/report/2022/machine-learning-in-uk-financial-services> accessed 11 July 2023; Commonwealth Government, *Inquiry into Future Directions for the Consumer Data Right* (Final Report, October 2020) 19.
[8]   See, for example, 'Enhanced Regulatory Sandbox', *Australian Securities & Investments Commission (ASIC)* (Web Page, 1 September 2020) <https://asic.gov.au/for-business/innov ation-hub/enhanced-regulatory-sandbox> accessed 22 May 2022. Also, Philip Maume, 'Regulating Robo-Advisory' (2019) 55(1) *Texas International Law Journal* 49, 56.
[9]   OECD, *Personal Data Use in Financial Services and the Role of Financial Education: A Consumer Centric Analysis* (Report, 2020) 20 <www.oecd.org/daf/fin/financial-education/ Personal-Data-Use-in-Financial-Services-andthe-Role-of-Financial-Education.pdf> accessed 20 May 2022.
[10] Bank of England and Financial Conduct Authority, 'Machine Learning in UK Financial Services', 6.
[11] See, for example, *Zest* (Web Page) <www.zest.ai/> accessed 11 July 2023.
[12] OECD, *Personal Data Use in Financial Services*.
[13] See, for example, *Better* (Web Page, 2022) <https://better.com>; *Cashngo* (Web Page, 2022) <www.cashngo.com.au>; *Nano* (Web Page, 2022) <https://nano.com.au>; *Rocket Mortgage* (Web Page, 2022) <www.rocketmortgage.com>.
[14] See, for example, *Petal* (Web Page, 2022) <www.petalcard.com>.

deal.[15] However, the most common forms of consumer-facing fintech are, at the time of writing, financial advice tools[16] primarily for investing and budgeting.[17]

Consumer-facing fintech generally, and automated financial advice tools specifically, are often promoted as benefiting consumers by assisting them to make better decisions about credit, savings, and investment, and by providing these services in a manner that is more cost-effective, convenient, and consistent than could be provided by human advisers.[18] These features undoubtedly hold attractions for consumers. However, in our opinion, the allure of AI, and its financial market equivalent of fintech, should not be allowed to overshadow the limitations of, and the risks of harm inherent in, these technologies. As this book makes clear, whether used by governments or private sector firms, AI and automated decision-making tools raise risks of harm to privacy, efficacy, bias, and perpetrating existing power hierarchies. Albeit on a different scale, consumer-facing fintech, such as automated financial advice tools, carry many of the same kinds of risks, which equally demand regulatory attention and best practice for good governance. There has been little assessment of whether automated financial advice tools are effective in achieving improving the financial well-being of consumers. It is also unclear whether and to what extent such tools are equitable and inclusive, or conversely amplify existing bias or patterns of exclusion in financial services and credit markets.

Some of the potential risks of harm to consumers from automated financial advice tools will be addressed by existing law. However, we argue that there is a need to move past the commercial, and indeed political, promotion of 'AI' and 'fintech' to understand their specific fields of operation and demystify their scope. This is because the use of AI in this equation is not neutral or without friction. Automated advice tools raise discrete and unique challenges for regulatory oversight, namely opacity, personalisation, and scale. We therefore suggest, drawing on the key principles propounded in AI ethics frameworks, that the effective regulation of automated financial advice tools should require greater transparency about what is being offered to consumers. There should also be a regulatory commitment to ensuring the outputs of such tools are contestable and accountable, having regard to the challenges raised by the technology they utilise.

---

[15] See, for example, *LoanOptions.ai* (Web Page, 2022) <www.loanoptions.ai>.

[16] OECD, *Personal Data Use in Financial Services*, 20.

[17] 'What You Need to Know about How FinTech Apps Work', *Consumer Action* (Web Page, 16 February 2021) <www.consumer-action.org/english/articles/fintech_apps> accessed 20 May 2022.

[18] See, for example, Paul Smith and James Eyers, 'CBA in $134m Play to Be "AI Superpower"' (8 November 2021) *Australian Financial Review* <www.afr.com/technology/cba-aims-to-be-ai-superpower-with-us100m-tech-plunge-20211105-p596bx> accessed 20 May 2022. See also Daniel Belanche, Luis V Casaló, and Carlos Flavián, 'Artificial Intelligence in FinTech: Understanding Robo-Advisors Adoption among Customers' (2019) 119(7) *Industrial Management & Data Systems* 1411, 1411.

This chapter explores these issues, beginning with an overview of automated financial advice, focusing on what are currently the most widely available tools, namely 'robo' investment advice and budgeting apps. We discuss the risks of harm raised by these uses of AI and related technologies, arising from uncertainty about the quality of the service provided, untrammelled data collection, and the potential for bias, as well as the need for a positive policy focus on the impact of such tools on goals of equity and inclusion. We review the guidance provided by regulators, as well as the gaps and uncertainties in the existing regulatory regimes. We then consider the role of principles of transparency and contestability as preconditions to greater accountability from the firms deploying such tools, and more effective oversight by regulators.

2.2 ASPIRATION AND APPLICATION IN CONSUMER-FACING FINTECH

The term 'fintech' refers to the use of AI and related digital technologies to deliver financial products and services.[19] The AI used to deliver fintech products may include natural language processing in front-end interfaces to communicate effectively with clients and statistical machine learning models to make predictions that inform financial decision-making. 'Consumer-facing' fintech refers to the use of fintech to provide services to consumers, as opposed to use by professional investors, business lenders, or for back-room banking processes. As already noted, perhaps the most prominent form of fintech service offered to consumers, as opposed to informing the internal processes of financial institutions, is automated financial advice, primarily about investing and budgeting.

The aims of most fintech products are to allow services to be delivered at scale, reducing human handling of information, and, in the case of consumer-facing fintech, benefiting consumers. Automated financial advice tools typically purport to offer a low-cost option for financial advice derived from insights from consumer data and statistical analysis and provided through an accessible interface using state-of-the-art processing to identify and respond to consumers' financial aims. The commonly stated aspiration of governments and regulators in supporting the development of these and other fintech products is to promote innovation and to provide low-cost, reliable, and effective financial services to consumers.[20] Some fintech

---

[19] Dirk A Zetsche et al, 'From Fintech to Techfin: The Regulatory Challenges of Data-Driven Finance' (2018) 14(2) *NYU Journal of Law & Business* 393, 400; Bonnie G Buchanan, *Artificial Intelligence in Finance* (Report, The Alan Turing Institute, 2019) 1 <www.turing.ac.uk/sites/default/files/2019-04/artificial_intelligence_in_finance_-_turing_report_0.pdf> accessed 11 July 2023.

[20] The Australian Government, The Treasury, *Consumer Data Right Overview* (Report, September 2019) 2 <https://treasury.gov.au/sites/default/files/2019-09/190904_cdr_booklet .pdf> accessed 11 July 2023; OECD, *Personal Data Use in Financial Services*, 15.

providers express aspirations to be more inclusive and empower ordinary people to participate in the financial and banking sectors.[21]

There are undoubted attractions in such aspirations.[22] The majority of consumers do not seek financial planning advice,[23] probably because it is perceived as being too expensive.[24] Yet many consumers find financial matters difficult or confusing. This is due to a combination of factors, including low financial literacy, limits on time, and the impact of behavioural biases on decision-making. In principle, automation should allow financial services providers to lower the cost and improve the consistency of advice,[25] as well as providing the convenience of an on-demand service.[26] Additionally, by using consumers' own data, automated financial advice tools have the potential to be uniquely tailored to those consumers' individual

---

[21] See, for example, 'Built to Make Investing Easier', *Betterment* (Web Page) <www.betterment .com/investing> accessed 20 May 2022: 'Automated technology is how we make investing easier, better, and more accessible'. See also 'About Us', *Robinhood* (Web Page) <https:// robinhood.com/us/en/about-us> accessed 11 July 2023: 'We're on a mission to democratize finance for all'.

[22] Australian Securities & Investments Commission (ASIC), *Providing Digital Financial Product Advice to Retail Clients* (Regulatory Guide 255, August 2016) para 255.3 <https://download .asic.gov.au/media/vbnlotqw/rg255-published-30-august-2016-20220328.pdf> accessed 11 July 2023: 'digital advice has the potential to be a convenient and low-cost option for retail clients who may not otherwise seek advice'.

[23] Ibid para 255.3, noting that only around 20 per cent of adult Australians seek personal financial advice. See also The Australian Government, The Treasury, *Financial System Inquiry: Interim Report* (Report, July 2014) paras 3.69–3.70 <https://treasury.gov.au/sites/default/files/2019-03/ p2014-fsi-interim-report.pdf> accessed 15 May 2022. See also Deloitte Access Economics, *ASX Australian Investor Study* (Report, 2017) <www2.deloitte.com/content/dam/Deloitte/au/ Documents/Economics/deloitte-au-economics-asx-australian-investor-study-190517.pdf> accessed 20 May 2022; Australian Securities & Investments Commission, *Regulating Complex Products* (Report 384, January 2014) 16–18 <https://download.asic.gov.au/media/lneb1sbb/ rep384-published-31-january-2014-03122021.pdf> accessed 11 July 2023.

[24] Consumers more commonly seek advice from mortgage brokers when seeking to buy a home, which is paid by commissions from banks. Doubts have been raised about the extent to which conflicts of interest undermine the value of the service to consumers and indeed the extent of the benefit provided which is often of unreliable quality. See Australian Securities & Investments Commission, *Review of Mortgage Broker Remuneration* (Report 516, March 2017) 17 <https://download.asic.gov.au/media/4213629/rep516-published-16-3-2017-1.pdf> accessed 11 July 2023; Productivity Commission, *Competition in the Australian Financial System* (Inquiry Report No 89, 2018) 301 <www.pc.gov.au/inquiries/completed/financial-system/report> accessed 11 July 2023. See also generally Jeannie Marie Paterson and Elise Bant, 'Mortgage Broking, Regulatory Failure and Statutory Design' (2020) 31(1) *Journal of Banking and Finance Law and Practice* 7. Also, generally Maume, 'Regulating Robo-Advisory', 50: noting the FCA estimates that in the United Kingdom there are sixteen million people in this financial advice gap.

[25] Bob Ferguson, 'Robo Advice: An FCA Perspective' (Annual Conference on Robo Advice and Investing: From Niche to Mainstream, London, 2 October 2017) <www.fca.org.uk/news/ speeches/robo-advice-fca-perspective> accessed 20 May 2020; Maume, 'Regulating Robo-Advisory', 69.

[26] Tom Baker and Benedict Dellaert, 'Regulating Robo Advice across the Financial Services Industry' (2018) 103 *Iowa Law Review* 713, 714.

circumstances.[27] Indeed, this is one of the premises behind Australia's consumer data right, which aims to give consumers control over their data to promote innovation and competition in the banking sector.[28]

Currently, the two main kinds of automated financial advice tools are robo-advisers and budgeting apps.[29] Though these tools will no doubt evolve, they provide a simpler, less personalised service than might be envisaged by the 'AI' label commonly attached to them.

2.2.1 *Robo-Advisers*

Robo-advisers[30] provide 'automated financial product advice using algorithms and technology and without the direct involvement of a human adviser'.[31] In principle, robo-advice might cover automated advice about any topic relevant to financial management, such as budgeting, borrowing, investing, superannuation, retirement planning, and insurance. Currently, most robo-advisers provide automated investment advice and portfolio management.[32]

Typically, robo-advice services begin with consumers answering a questionnaire about their goals, expectations, and aptitude for risk. An investment profile for consumers is derived from this information, based on their goals and capacity to bear risk. An algorithm matches consumers' profiles with an investment portfolio available through the advisory firm to produce an investment recommendation.[33] Should a consumer choose to follow the advice and invest in that portfolio, many robo-advisers will also manage the portfolio on an ongoing basis, keeping it within the parameters recommended for the consumer. Consumers generally pay a fee for the service provided by the robo-adviser, often a percentage of the amount invested, with minimum investment amounts required to access the service.

---

[27] '10 Things Consumers Need to Know about FinTech', *Consumers International* (Web Page) <www.consumersinternational.org/news-resources/blog/posts/10-things-consumers-need-to-know-about-fintech> accessed 20 May 2022.

[28] Australian Government, The Treasury, *Consumer Data Right Overview*, 2; Edward Corcoran, *Open Banking Regulation around the World* (Report, BBVA, 11 May 2020) <www.bbva.com/en/open-banking-regulation-around-the-world> accessed 20 May 2022.

[29] See also Jeannie Marie Paterson, 'Making Robo Advisers Careful' (2023) *Law and Financial Markets Review* 18.

[30] See, for example, *Betterment* (Web Page) <www.betterment.com> accessed 11 July 2023; *Robinhood* (Web Page) <https://robinhood.com/us/en/about-us> accessed 11 July 2023; *Wealthfront* (Web Page) <www.wealthfront.com/> accessed 11 July 2023.

[31] ASIC, *Providing Digital Financial Product Advice to Retail Clients*, para 255.1.

[32] Financial Conduct Authority, *Automated Investment Services: Our Expectations* (Report, 21 May 2018) <www.fca.org.uk/publications/multi-firm-reviews/automated-investment-services-our-expectations> accessed 11 July 2023.

[33] Belanche et al, 'Artificial Intelligence in FinTech', 1413; Dominik Jung et al, 'Robo-Advisory: Digitalization and Automation of Financial Advisory' (2018) 60(1) *Business & Information Systems Engineering* 81, 81.

Robo-advice is sometimes described as 'trading with AI'.[34] This language might be thought to suggest specialised insights into the stock market uniquely tailored to consumers' needs and arrived at through sophisticated machine learning models. The practice is more straightforward. At the time of writing, robo-advisers do not rely on state-of-the-art AI technology, such as using neural networks to process data points and make predictions about stock market moves, or link individual profiles to unique investment strategies. As Baker and Dellaert explain, the matching process will be based on 'a model of how to optimise the fit between the attributes of the financial products available to the consumer and the attributes of the consumers who are using the robo-advisor'.[35] The robo-adviser will typically build the consumer profile based on the entry questionnaire and match this with an investment strategy established using financial modelling techniques and based on the investment packages already offered by firm. The process will usually have been automated through some form of expert system – a hand coded application of binary rule identified by humans. Ongoing management of the consumer's portfolio will be done on a similar basis, often using exchange-traded funds (ETFs) that 'require no or less active portfolio management'.[36]

Unlike human financial advisers, robo-advice tools typically do not provide budgeting or financial management advice to consumers.[37] Their recommendations are limited to the kinds of investment that will match consumers' investment profiles. Robo investment advisers do not provide advice on matters of tax, superannuation, asset management, or savings, and they do not yet have the capacity to provide this more nuanced advice.[38] Sometimes robo-advice tools are used in conjunction with human financial advisers who will provide a broader suite of advice. Automated budgeting tools are also increasingly available on the market.

2.2.2 *Budgeting Tools*

Budgeting tools allow consumers to keep track of their spending by categorising expenses and providing dashboard-style visualisations of spending and saving.[39] Some banks offer budgeting tools to clients, and there are many independent service

---

[34] See, for example, *Jaaims* (Web Page) <www.jaaimsapp.com> accessed 11 July 2023.

[35] Baker and Dellaert, 'Regulating Robo Advice across the Financial Services Industry', 734.

[36] Jung et al, 'Robo-Advisory: Digitalization and Automation of Financial Advisory', 82.

[37] Maume, 'Regulating Robo-Advisory', 53. But see, providing both investment and budgeting advice, *Douugh* (Web Page) <https://douugh.com/> accessed 11 July 2023.

[38] Sophia Duffy and Steve Parrish, 'You Say Fiduciary, I Say Binary: A Review and Recommendation of Robo-Advisors and the Fiduciary and Best Interest Standards' (2021) 17 *Hastings Business Law Journal* 3, 5.

[39] See, for example, *Goodbudget* (Web Page) <https://goodbudget.com/> accessed 11 July 2023; *Mint* (Web Page) <https://mint.intuit.com/> accessed 11 July 2023; *MoneyBrilliant* (Web Page) <https://moneybrilliant.com.au/> accessed 11 July 2023; *Empower* (Web Page) <www.personalcapital.com/> accessed 11 July 2023; *Spendee* (Web Page) <www.spendee.com/> accessed 11 July 2023; *Toshl* (Web Page) <https://toshl.com/> accessed 11 July 2023;

providers. Some neo-banks have, additionally, consolidated their brand around their in-built budgeting tools.[40]

As with robo-advisers, automated budgeting tools collect information about consumers through an online questionnaire. Budgeting tools also typically require consumers to provide access to their bank accounts, in order to scrape transaction data from that account,[41] or alternatively rely on data-sharing arrangements.[42] Based on this information, the services provided by budgeting tools include categorising and keeping track of spending; providing recommendations about budgeting; and monitoring savings.[43] In some cases, the tools will transfer funds matching consumers' savings goals to a specific account, provide bill reminders, make bill payments, monitor information about credit scores, suggest potential savings through various cost-cutting measures or identifying alternative service providers.[44] Additionally, automated budgeting tools may provide articles and opinion pieces about financial matters, such as crypto, non-fungible tokens (NFTs), or budgeting.[45] Some budgeting tools have a credit card option,[46] and at least one is linked to a 'buy now-pay later' provider.[47]

Automated budgeting tools often describe their service as relying on AI.[48] Again, however, they do not, as might have been expected from this terminology, typically provide a personalised plan for saving derived from insights from multiple data points relating to consumers. They may use some form of natural language processing to identify spending items. Primarily, somewhat like robo-advisers, they rely on predetermined, human-coded rules for categorising spending and presenting

Rocketmoney (Web Page) <www.rocketmoney.com/> accessed 11 July 2023; *Wemoney* (Web Page) <www.wemoney.com.au> accessed 11 July 2023.

[40] See, for example, *UpBank* (Web Page) <https://up.com.au/> accessed 11 July 2023; *Revolut* (Web Page) <www.revolut.com/en-AU/> accessed 11 July 2023; *Pluto Money* (Web Page) <https://plutomoney.app/> accessed 11 July 2023.

[41] See Han-Wei Liu, 'Two Decades of Laws and Practice around Screen Scraping in the Common Law World and Its Open Banking Watershed Moment' (2020) 30(2) *Washington International Law Journal* 28.

[42] See e.g. Frollo using Australia's open banking regime: <www.instagram.com/p/CHzG3winmBo/>.

[43] See *Choice* (Web Page) <www.choice.com.au/money/financial-planning-and-investing/creating-a-budget/buying-guides/budgeting-software> accessed 11 July 2023; *Select* <www.cnbc.com/select/best-budgeting-apps/> accessed 11 July 2023.

[44] Joris Lochy, 'Budgeting Apps – A Red Ocean Looking for a Market' (Blog Post, 8 March 2020) <https://bankloch.blogspot.com/2020/03/budgeting-apps-red-ocean-looking-for.html> accessed 20 May 2020.

[45] See e.g. *Spendee* (Web Page) <www.spendee.com/> accessed 11 July 2023.

[46] See e.g. *Mint* (Web Page) <https://mint.intuit.com/> accessed 11 July 2023; *Rocketmoney* (Web Page) <www.rocketmoney.com/> accessed 11 July 2023.

[47] E.g., Zippay provides a budgeting function (Web Page) <https://zip.co/au> accessed 11 July 2023.

[48] See e.g. 'We Combine Best-in-Breed AI Driven Categorization and Analytics with a Deep Set of Features That Are Proven to Work', *Budget Bakers* (Web Page) <https://budgetbakers.com/> accessed 11 July 2023.

savings. Most budgeting tools are free, although some charge for a premium service. This means that the tools are funded in other, more indirect ways, including through selling targeted advertisements on the app, fees for referrals, commissions for third-party products sold on the app, the sale of data (usually aggregated), and in some cases a percentage of the savings where a lower cost service or provider is identified for consumers.[49]

2.3 REGULATION AND RISK IN CONSUMER-FACING FINTECH

This brief survey of available automated financial advice tools aimed at consumers suggests that they are operating with a fairly narrowly defined scope and using relatively straightforward digital processes. The tools may evolve into the future to make greater use of such state-of-the-art AI, such as using generative AI for providing general advice to consumers. However, even in their current form, the tools pose risks of harm to consumers that are more than fanciful, and similar to those raised by AI generally. The risks arising from AI are becoming increasingly well recognised, including poor efficacy, eroding privacy, data profiling, and bias and discrimination.[50] These risks are also inherent in consumer-facing fintech and automated financial advice tools. Moreover, we suggest they are only partially addressed by existing law. While financial services law commonly imposes robust obligations on those providing financial advice, those obligations may not squarely address the issues arising from the automated character of the advice, particularly issues of bias. Additionally, some automated advice tools, such as budgeting apps, may fall outside of these regimes. It is therefore worth considering these issues in more detail.

2.3.1 *Quality of Performance*

One of the notable features of automated financial advice is that consumers are unlikely to be able to scrutinise the quality of the service provided. Consumers will typically turn to automated advice tools because they lack skills in the relevant area, be it investing or budgeting. This lack of expertise makes it difficult for them to assess the quality of the advice they receive.[51] There is not a lot of information for consumers in selecting between different tools, as compared to standard consumer goods. While some rankings of automated financial advice tools have emerged, these often focus on ease of use – the interface, syncing with bank data, fees

---

[49] Joris Lochy, 'Budgeting Apps – A Red Ocean Looking for a Market'.
[50] See Zofia Bednarz, 'There and Back Again: How Target Market Determination Obligations for Financial Products May Incentivise Consumer Data Profiling' [2022] *International Review of Law, Computers & Technology* <www.tandfonline.com/doi/10.1080/13600869.2022.2060469> accessed 20 May 2022.
[51] Baker and Dellaert, 'Regulating Robo Advice across the Financial Services Industry', 723.

charged – rather than the quality of the advice provided,[52] and some ranking reviews include sponsored content.[53] Accordingly, at least at this point in time, automated financial advice tools may be very much a credence good – for which assertions of quality are all that is available to consumers. Unless the advice provided by the tools is patently bad, it may not be apparent that the poor quality of the automated process is to blame, as opposed to other external factors. Indeed, without a point of comparison, which is effectively excluded by the personalised nature of the service, it may be difficult for consumers to identify poor quality advice at all.

There is currently little academic research on the extent to which consumers are well-served by automated financial advice tools, particularly when weighted against possible costs in terms of data-sharing.[54] There have been a number of concerns raised in the literature about how well the tools may function. Although robo-advisers may operate in a manner that is more objective and consistent than human financial advisers,[55] this does not mean they operate free from the influence of commissions, which may be coded into their advisory process. It is unclear to what extent the recommendations provided by automated financial advice tools are personalised to consumers, as opposed to being generic or based on broad target groupings. Additionally, concerns have been raised about the relatively small number of investment options actually held by robo-investment advisers.[56] While automated budgeting tools may assist consumers by providing an accessible, straightforward, and visual way of monitoring spending,[57] this does not necessarily translate

---

[52] See, e.g., Tamika Seeto, '6 Budgeting and Savings Apps Worth Checking Out in 2022', *Canstar* (Blog Post, 15 March 2022) <www.canstar.com.au/budgeting/budgeting-apps/> accessed 20 May 2022; *Choice* (Web Page) <www.choice.com.au/money/financial-planning-and-investing/creating-a-budget/articles/how-we-test-budgeting-apps> accessed 20 May 2022.

[53] See also Christy Rakoczy, 'Best Budgeting Software: Fight the Right Software for Any Budgeting Goal', *Investopedia* (Web Page) <www.investopedia.com/personal-finance/best-budgeting-software/> accessed 22 May 2022: 'We recommend the best products through an independent review process, and advertisers do not influence our picks. We may receive compensation if you visit partners we recommend. Read our advertiser disclosure for more info'.

[54] Jung et al, 'Robo-Advisory: Digitalization and Automation of Financial Advisory', 84.

[55] Lukas Brenner and Tobias Meyll, 'Robo-Advisors: A Substitute for Human Financial Advice?' (2020) 25 *Journal of Behavioral and Experimental Finance* 100275.

[56] Duffy and Parish, 'You Say Fiduciary, I Say Binary', 23.

[57] Yaron Levi and Shlomo Benartzi, 'Mind the App: Mobile Access to Financial Information and Consumer Behavior' (17 March 2020) 9: 'The interpretation of our results is that the mobile apps have a causal impact on the attention and spending behavior among consumers that decided to adopt it.' <http://dx.doi.org/10.2139/ssrn.3557689> accessed 22 May 2022.

into long-term savings[58] or improved financial literacy.[59] It is further possible that one of the main functions of at least some budgeting apps is to obtain consumers' attention in order to market other financial services, such as credit cards, as well as the opportunity for the providers to profit from the use or sale of consumer data for marketing and data analytics.[60]

In consumer transactions – particularly those that are complex, hard for consumers to monitor, or which carry the risk of high impact harms – reliance is usually placed on regulators to take 'ex ante' measures for ensuring that the products supplied to consumers are acceptably safe and reliable. Financial services regulators in jurisdictions such as Australia, the United Kingdom, the European Union, and the United States of America have responded to the rise of robo-advisers by affirming that the existing regulatory regime applies to this form of advice.[61] Financial services providers are typically subject to an array of statutory conduct obligations, which overlap, albeit imperfectly, with their fiduciary duties arising under general law.[62] These statutory duties require firms to manage conflicts of interest,[63] act in their clients' best interests,[64] ensure the suitability of the advice provided,[65] and take

---

[58] Evan Kuh, 'Budgeting Apps Have Major Faws When It Comes to Helping Users Actually Save', *CNBC* (Halftime Report, 13 June 2019) <www.cnbc.com/2019/06/13/budgeting-apps-don't-help-users-save-money.html>; Rhiana Whitson, 'Would You Use a Budgeting App? There Are Some Big pros and cons to Consider', *ABC Online* (News Report, 4 August 2021) <www.abc.net.au/news/2021-08-04/how-do-you-keep-track-of-your-budget-we-look-at-your-options/100342676>.

[59] Stefan Angel, 'Smart Tools? A Randomized Controlled Trial on the Impact of Three Different Media Tools on Personal Finance' (2018) 74 *Journal of Behavioral and Experimental Economics* 104–11: adolescent users of a smartphone budgeting app check their current account balance more than a control group. However, the app did not have a significant effect on subjective or objective financial knowledge indicators.

[60] See discussion of the data use below.

[61] ASIC, *Providing Digital Financial Product Advice to Retail Clients*; United States Securities and Exchange Commission, *Commission Interpretation Regarding Standard of Conduct for Investment Advisers* (Release No IA-5248, 2019) 12–18.

[62] See generally Simone Degeling and Jessica Hudson, 'Financial Robots as Instruments of Fiduciary Loyalty' (2018) 40 *Sydney Law Review* 63.

[63] See e.g., *Corporations Act 2001* (Cth) s 912A(1)(aa), requiring financial services licensees to have 'adequate arrangements' for 'managing' conflicts of interest.

[64] *Corporations Act 2001* (Cth) s 961B(1); Securities and Exchange Commission, 'Commission Interpretation Regarding Standard of Conduct for Investment Advisers'; Securities and Exchange Commission, *Regulation Best Interest: The Broker Dealer Standard of Conduct* (Release No 34-86031, 5 June 2019). Also, Duffy and Parish, 'You Say Fiduciary, I Say Binary'; Han-Wei Liu et al, 'In Whose Best Interests? Regulating Financial Advisers, the Royal Commission and the Dilemma of Reform' (2020) 42 *Sydney Law Review* 37.

[65] 'COBS 9.2 Assessing suitability', *Financial Conduct Authority (United Kingdom) Handbook* (Web Page) <www.handbook.fca.org.uk/handbook/COBS/9/2.html>; *European Parliament and Council Directive 2014/65/EU of 15 May 2014 Markets in Financial Instruments Directive II* [2014] OJ L 173/349, art 25(2). Also, *Corporations Act 2001* (Cth) pt 7.8A (design and distribution obligations).

reasonable care in proving the advice.[66] These obligations should, in principle, assist in addressing concerns about the quality of the service provided by robo-advisers.[67] Nonetheless, some uncertainties remain, including, for example, whether the category-based approach deployed by robo-advisers fits with statutory requirements for personalised advice that is suitable for the individual consumer.[68]

Regulators have additionally stated they expect firms providing robo-advice to have a 'human in the loop', in the sense of a person with 'an understanding of the technology and algorithms used to provide digital advice' and who are 'able to review the digital advice generated by algorithms'.[69] Recommendations for a human overseeing the automated advice leave open the question of what that human should be monitoring – is it merely compliance with existing law applying to the giving of advice, or should there be other considerations taken into account, arising from the automated character of the advice?

In terms of the issue of automation, regulators have focused on the informational aspects of the process. They have emphasised that firms providing automated advice should give consideration to the way in which the information on which the advice is based is collected from consumers so as to ensure it is accurate and relevant, especially because there is no human intermediary to pick up possible discrepancies or errors. Regulators have also advised firms to take care in the way the advice is framed and explained, given the potential for misunderstanding and error in an automated process.[70] Issues of information gathering and reporting are important but they are only part of the challenge presented by automation for consumer protection law and policy. Moreover, they tend to represent a very individualised response to the risks of harm to consumers relying on automated financial advice, focusing on what consumers need to provide and understand, as opposed to the substance of the process through which advice is provided.

Notably, there is typically no specific law or regulatory guidance that applies to automated budgeting tools, which do not involve financial services. These tools will be subject to general consumer protection regimes, which typically prohibit

---

[66] *Australian Securities and Investments Commission Act 2001* (Cth) s 12ED; *Investment Advisers Act Release No. 3060* (28 July 2010) (United States).

[67] See Paterson, 'Making Robo-Advisers Careful'; ASIC, *Providing Digital Financial Product Advice to Retail Clients*, para 255.55.

[68] Melanie L Fein, 'Regulation of Robo-Advisers in the United States' in Peter Scholz (ed), *Robo-Advisory* (Palgrave Macmillan, 2021), 112.

[69] ASIC, *Providing Digital Financial Product Advice to Retail Clients*, paras 255.60, 255.73; Division of Investment Management, *Robo Advisers* (IM Guidance Update No 2017-02, February 2017) 8 <www.sec.gov/investment/im-guidance-2017–02.pdf> accessed 20 May 2022.

[70] Financial Conduct Authority, 'Automated Investment Services – Our Expectations'; European Securities Markets Authority, *Guidelines on Certain Aspects of the MiFID II Suitability Requirements* (Guidelines, 28 May 2018); Division of Investment Management, *Robo Advisers* (IM Guidance Update No 2017-02, February 2017) 3–6 <www.sec.gov/investment/im-guidance-2017-02.pdf> accessed 22 May 2020.

misleading conduct, and mandate reasonable care and skill in the provision of services.[71] Uncertainties about the application of existing law to automated advice give rise to the question of whether other kinds of regulatory mechanisms are required to complement sector-specific or general consumer protection law in order to address the risks of harms that are specific to the use of AI and related digital technologies. In answering this question, we suggest that, at minimum, the risks around data collection and bias need to be considered.

2.3.2 *The Data/Service Trade-Off*

Automated financial advice tools operate on the core premise that consumers necessarily hand over data to obtain the service. A firm may be using consumer data for the dual purposes of providing advice and making a return for itself, such as through promoting other products for a commission on sales, up-selling add-on products for a fee, or on-selling the data for profit.[72] This behaviour is particularly apparent in the case of budgeting apps, which are typically free. As already noted, these services earn income through in-app advertising, fees, and commissions for referrals and potentially through selling aggregated consumer data, as well as targeted advertising. Notably, the privacy terms of automated budgeting tools commonly allow the collection of a wide range of consumer data and the use of that data for a number of purposes, including improving the service and related company group services, marketing, and, in aggregated form, sharing with third parties.[73]

Data protection and privacy law impose obligations on the collection and processing of data.[74] However, the key requirements of notice and consent typically found under these regimes may easily be met in automated advice contexts because the exchange is at the heart of the transaction. Consumers provide their data in order to obtain the advice they need. While consumers may be unaware of how much information they are handing over, there is some evidence that consumers,

---

[71] Jeannie Paterson and Yvette Maker, 'AI in the Home: Artificial Intelligence and Consumer Protection' in Ernest Lim and Phillip Morgan (eds), *The Cambridge Handbook of Private Law and Artificial Intelligence* (Cambridge: Cambridge University Press, forthcoming, 2024).

[72] On this trade-off, see also Matthew Adam Bruckner, 'The Promise and Perils of Algorithmic Lenders' Use of Big Data' (2018) 93 *Chicago-Kent Law Review* 3. Also, Zetsche et al, 'From Fintech to Techfin', 427.

[73] See, especially 'Inuit Privacy Policy', *Mint* (Web Page) <www.intuit.com/privacy/statement/> accessed 11 July 2023; 'Privacy Policy', *Frollo* (Web Page) <https://frollo.com.au/privacy-policy/> accessed 11 July 2023; 'Privacy Policy', *Pocketguard* (Web Page) <https://pocketguard.com/privacy/> accessed 11 July 2023.

[74] See, eg, *Regulation (EU) 2016/679 on the protection of natural persons with regard to the processing of personal data and on the free movement of such data, and repealing Directive 95/46/EC (General Data Protection Regulation)* [2016] OJ L119/1; *Data Protection Act 2018* (UK); *Privacy Act 1988* (Cth); *California Consumer Privacy Act*, 1.81.5 Cal Civ Code § 1798.100–1798.199.100 (2018).

particularly younger consumers, are prepared to trade data for cheaper, more efficient financial services.[75] However, to the extent consumers are ill or under-informed about the quality of the service being provided by automated advice tools, the data-for-service bargain may look thinner than they might have at first thought.[76] Under the fintech service model, consumers provide personal data to obtain a personalised and cost-effective service but have few objective measures as to the quality of what is actually being provided.

2.3.3 Bias and Exclusion

In discussing legal and regulatory responses to the growing influence of AI and related technologies, much attention has rightly been given to their role in amplify-ing surveillance, bias and discrimination.[77] The technologies may use personal data to profile consumers, which in turn allows firms to differentiate between different consumers and groups with a high degree of precision, leading to risks of harmful manifestations of targeted advertising, or differential pricing.[78] Bias and error are particular concerns in firms' use of AI technologies for decision-making, including in decisions about lending,[79] credit,[80] or insurance.[81] Automated lending decisions and credit scoring might be more objective than human-made decisions and might benefit cohorts that have previously been disadvantaged by human prejudice.[82] But there is no guarantee this is the case, and indeed the outcomes may be worse for these groups. Differential treatment of already disadvantaged groups – such as minoritiy or low-income cohorts – may already be embedded in the practices and processes of the institution. To the extent this data is used in credit-scoring models or

[75] OECD, *Personal Data Use in Financial Services*, 20.
[76] Ibid; Bednarz, 'There and Back Again'.
[77] Centre for Data Ethics and Innovation, *Review into Bias in Algorithmic Decision-Making* (Report, November 2020) 21.
[78] Ryan Calo, 'Digital Market Manipulation' (2014) 82 *George Washington Law Review* 995; Bednarz, 'There and Back Again'.
[79] See generally Ari Ezra Waldman, 'Power, Process, and Automated Decision-Making' (2019) 88 (2) *Fordham Law Review* 613; Australian Human Rights Commission, *Human Rights and Technology* (Final Report, 2021).
[80] Emmanuel Martinez and Lauren Kirchner, 'The Secret Bias Hidden in Mortgage-Approval Algorithms' (25 August 2021) *The Markup* <https://themarkup.org/denied/2021/08/25/the-secret-bias-hidden-in-mortgage-approval-algorithms> accessed 22 May 2022.
[81] See, e.g., Ramnath Balasubramanian, Ari Libarikian, and Doug McElhaney, McKinsey & Co, *Insurance 2030: The Impact of AI on the Future of Insurance* (Report, 12 March 2021) <www.mckinsey.com/industries/financial-services/our-insights/insurance2030-the-impact-of-ai-on-the-future-of-insurance> accessed 22 May 2022; Zofia Bednarz and Kayleen Manwaring, 'Keeping the (Good) Faith: Implications of Emerging Technologies for Consumer Insurance Contracts' (2021) 43 *Sydney Law Review* 455, 470–75.
[82] Jennifer Miller, 'A Bid to End Loan Bias' (20 September 2020) *The New York Times* <https://link.gale.com/apps/doc/A635945144/AONE?u=unimelb&sid=bookmark-AONE&xid=164a6017> accessed 22 May 2022.

to inform automated decisions, historical unequal treatment may be amplified[83] or distorted.[84] Unequal treatment may, moreover, be difficult to identify or address where it is based, not directly on protected attributes, but on proxies for those attributes found in the training data.[85]

Bias may also be embedded in automated advice tools used by consumers. For example, a robo-advice tool might exhibit bias by treating a person who takes time off work for childrearing as going through a period of precarious employment or being unable to hold down steady employment. An automated budgeting tool might exhibit bias by characterising products for menstruation as discretionary spending, instead of essentials. There are complex technical and policy decisions to be made in identifying and responding to the risks of unacceptable bias in automated financial advice tools.[86] Consumer protection and financial services law have not traditionally have not been central to this process, which is primarily the domain of human rights law. However, decisions based on historical prejudice may be unconscionable or unfair, contrary to consumer protection law. Certainly, in the United States, the Federal Trade Commission has indicated that discriminatory algorithms would fall foul of its jurisdiction to respond to unfair business practices.[87]

A related issue concerns financial exclusion. Fintech innovators and government initiatives to encourage innovation often refer to an aspiration of promoting inclusion and overcoming exclusion.[88] There are few findings on the extent to which this aspiration is achievable. There are plausible reasons why automated advice tools may fail to assist, or assist adequately, consumers already excluded from mainstream financial or banking services, or consumers who have had less engagement with the mainstream banking system, such as where they are 'not accessing or using financial services in a mainstream market in a way that is appropriate to their needs'.[89] Financially excluded consumers might not be offered meaningfully relevant advice tools because there is no relevant or useful data about them or because they are

---

[83] Andeas Fuster et al, 'Predictably Unequal? The Effects of Machine Learning on Credit Markets' (2022) 77(1) *Journal of Finance* 1.

[84] Will Douglas Heaven, 'Bias Isn't the Only Problem with Credit Scores – and No, AI Can't Help' MIT *Technology Review* (Blog Post, 17 June 2021) <www.technologyreview.com/2021/06/17/1026519/racial-bias-noisy-data-credit-scores-mortgage-loans-fairness-machine-learning/> accessed 20 May 2020; Laura Blattner and Scott Nelson, 'How Costly Is Noise? Data and Disparities in Consumer Credit' (2021) arXiv 2105.07554 <https://arxiv.org/abs/2105.07554> accessed 20 May 2022.

[85] See also Zetsche et al, 'From Fintech to Techfin', 424.

[86] See, e.g., Sian Townson, 'AI Can Make Bank Loans More Fair' *Harvard Business Review* (Article, 6 November 2020) <https://hbr.org/2020/11/ai-can-make-bank-loans-more-fair>.

[87] Elisa Jillson, 'Aiming for Truth, Fairness, and Equity in Your Company's Use of AI' *Federal Trade Commission Business Blog* (Blog Post, 19 April 2021) <www.ftc.gov/business-guidance/blog/2021/04/aiming-truth-fairness-equity-your-companys-use-ai> accessed 22 May 2022.

[88] Commonwealth Government, *Inquiry into Future Directions for the Consumer Data Right*, 66, 172. See also Zetsche et al, 'From Fintech to Techfin', 418–22.

[89] Emma Leong and Jodi Gardner, 'Open Banking in the UK and Singapore: Open Possibilities for Enhancing Financial Inclusion' (2021) 5 *Journal of Business Law* 424, 426.

unlikely to be sufficiently profitable for financial services providers to develop products suited to them. These consumers may also find that the models on which the advisory tools are based are inaccurate when applied to their circumstances.

For example, investment tools may be of little value to consumers struggling to make ends meet and with no savings to invest. The models used by automated budgeting tools may have a poor fit with consumers living on very low incomes and for whom cutting back on discretionary spending is not an option available. In these circumstances, the tools will do little to improve equity, leaving unrepresented groups without advice, or relevantly personalised advice. Moreover, there may be a real risk of harm. Inept recommendations may subject consumers to harms of financial over-commitment or lull inexperienced consumers into a false sense of financial security. At a more systematic level, the availability of automated advice tools for improving financial well-being may feed into longstanding liberal rhetoric about the value of individual responsibility, as opposed to government initiatives for improving overall financial well-being.

It is possible to envisage services that would be useful to financially excluded consumers or consumers experiencing financial harshi, such as for example, advice on affordable loans and other services.[90] Emma Leong and Jodi Gardner point to proposed uses of Open Banking in the United Kingdom to provide tools that assist with better managing fluctuating incomes.[91] The United Kingdom Financial Conduct Authority notes there are some apps on the market providing legal aid and welfare support advice.[92] These kinds of initiatives are likely to require a deliberate policy decision to initiate rather than arising 'naturally' in the market.[93] This is because there would seem to be little commercial incentive for firms to invest in tools specifically tailored to low-income or otherwise marginalised consumers from whom there is little likelihood of ongoing lucrative return to the firm, without government support.

2.4 NEW REGULATORY RESPONSES TO THE RISKS OF AUTOMATED FINANCIAL ADVICE

Automated financial advice tools illustrate the continuing uncertainties in regulating consumer-facing fintech and AI informed consumer products. We have seen

---

[90] See, e.g., *Tully* (Web Page) <https://tullyapp.com>; *Touco* (Web Page) <https://usetouco.com>.

[91] Leong and Gardner, 'Open Banking in the UK and Singapore', 429.

[92] Financial Conduct Authority, *Call for Input: Open Finance* (Publication, 2019) 8 [2.11], discussed in Commonwealth Government, *Inquiry into Future Directions for the Consumer Data Right*, 66.

[93] Commonwealth Government, *Inquiry into Future Directions for the Consumer Data Right*, 171.

that regulators will need to adapt existing regimes to the new ways in which services are being provided to consumers, which requires attention not only to the risks in providing advice but in the automation of advice. We further suggest that regulators need to be cognisant of the ways in which the AI and digital technologies informing the tools raise unique challenges for regulation. Opacity is a key concern in any regulatory response to making AI systems more accountable.[94] Automated financial advice tools may not currently rely on sophisticated AI, in the sense of deep learning or neural networks. Nonetheless, they are for commercial (if not technical) reasons highly opaque as to the technology being utilised and how recommendations are reached. Their very purpose is to provide advice without significant human intervention and at scale, which may amplify harms of bias or error in the system.[95] The tools typically purport to provide output on factors personal to the consumer, which may make it difficult to determine whether an adverse outcome is unfortunate, a systematic error or failure of a legal duty.[96]

One response to navigating the challenges of regulating consumer-facing fintech is provided by the principles of ethical AI.[97] Principles of AI ethics are sometimes criticised as too general to be useful.[98] The principles operate as a form of soft law – they are not legally binding and must necessarily be supplemented by legal rules.[99] However, principles of AI ethics may be effective when operationalised to apply to specific contexts and when used in conjunction with other forms of regulation. The principles provide the preconditions for responsible use of AI and automated decision tools by firms. They also provide an indication of what regulators should demand from firms deploying such technology to reduce the risk of harm to consumers.[100] While there are various formulations of the principles of ethical

[94] See Jenna Burrell, 'How the Machine "Thinks": Understanding Opacity in Machine Learning Algorithms' (2016) 3(1) *Big Data & Society* 1; Jennifer Cobbe, Michelle Seng Ah Lee, and Jatinder Singh, 'Reviewable Automated Decision-Making: A Framework for Accountable Algorithmic Systems' (ACM Conference on Fairness, Accountability, and Transparency, 1–10 March 2021) <https://ssrn.com/abstract=3772964> accessed 22 May 2022.

[95] William Magnuson, 'Artificial Financial Intelligence' (2020) 10 *Harvard Business Law Review* 337, 340.

[96] Bednarz, 'There and Back Again'; Martinez and Kirchner, 'The Secret Bias Hidden in Mortgage-Approval Algorithms'.

[97] See Anna Jobin, Marcello Ienca, and Effy Vayena, 'The Global Landscape of AI Ethics Guidelines' (2019) 1 *Nature Machine Intelligence* 389, 389: 'Our results reveal a global convergence emerging around five ethical principles (transparency, justice and fairness, non-maleficence, responsibility and privacy)'.

[98] Australian Human Rights Commission, *Human Rights and Technology*, 54; Brent Mittelstadt, 'Principles Alone Cannot Guarantee Ethical AI' (2019) 1 *Nature Machine Intelligence* 501.

[99] Lorne Sossin and Charles W Smith, 'Hard Choices and Soft Law: Ethical Codes, Policy Guidelines and the Role of the Courts in Regulating Government' (2003) 40 *Alberta Law Review* 867.

[100] Jake Goldenfein, 'Algorithmic Transparency and Decision-Making Accountability: Thoughts for Buying Machine Learning Algorithms' in Cliff Bertram, Asher Gibson, and Adriana Nugent (eds), *Closer to the Machine: Technical, Social, and Legal Aspects of AI* (Office of the Victorian Information Commissioner, 2019) 43: '[T]he time and place for instilling public

AI,[101] key features typically include requirements for AI to be transparent and explainable,[102] along with mechanisms for ensuring accountability[103] and – at least in the Australian government's principles[104] – contesting adverse outcomes.[105]

2.4.1 *Transparency and Explanations*

Principles of ethical AI typically require the use of such technologies to be transparent.[106] A starting place for transparency is to inform consumers when AI is being used in an interaction with them. Applied to automated financial advice tools, transparency must mean more than informing consumers that AI is being used to provide advice. Consumers choosing to turn to a robo-adviser or budgeting app will usually be aware of the automated character of the advice. Consumers also require transparency in the kind of technology being used to provide that advice: i.e. is it based in machine learning or a hand coded expert system. Additionally, a principle of transparency would require firms to inform consumers clearly about the scope of the service that is being provided, including the limitations of the technology in terms of personalised or expert advice.[107] If the advice provided is generalised to

---

values like accountability and transparency is in the design and development of technological systems, rather than after-the-fact regulation and review'.

[101] See Jobin et al, 'The Global Landscape of AI Ethics Guidelines', 389: 'Our results reveal a global convergence emerging around five ethical principles (transparency, justice and fairness, non-maleficence, responsibility and privacy)'.

[102] Australian Government Department of Industry, Science, Energy and Resources, *Australia's Artificial Intelligence Ethics Framework* (Report, 2019) <www.industry.gov.au/data-and-publi cations/building-australias-artificial-intelligence-capability/ai-ethics-framework> accessed 22 May 2022; Australian Council of Learned Academics, *The Effective and Ethical Development of Artificial Intelligence: An Opportunity to Improve Our Wellbeing* (Report, July 2019) 132; Australian Human Rights Commission, *Human Rights and Technology*, 49; European Commission, *Artificial Intelligence: A European Approach to Excellence and Trust* (White Paper, 2020) 20; Select Committee on Artificial Intelligence, *AI in the UK: Ready, Willing and Able?* (Report, HL 2017–2019) 38.

[103] Jobin et al, 'The Global Landscape of AI Ethics Guidelines'; Institute of Electrical and Electronics Engineers, *Ethically Aligned Design: A Vision for Prioritizing Human Well-Being with Autonomous and Intelligent Systems* (Report, 2019) 21; Australian Council of Learned Academics, *The Effective and Ethical Development of Artificial Intelligence*, 105; Australian Human Rights Commission, *Human Rights and Technology*, 50.

[104] Henrietta Lyons, Eduardo Velloso, and Tim Miller, 'Conceptualising Contestability: Perspectives on Contesting Algorithmic Decisions' (2021) 5 *Proceedings of the ACM on Human-Computer Interaction* <https://arxiv.org/abs/2103.01774> accessed 22 May 2022.

[105] See Australian Government Department of Industry, Science, Energy and Resources, *Australia's Artificial Intelligence Ethics Framework*; European Commission, High-Level Expert Group on Artificial Intelligence, *Ethics Guidelines for Trustworthy AI* (Guidelines, 8 April 2019) <https://digital-strategy.ec.europa.eu/en/library/ethics-guidelines-trustworthy-ai> accessed 20 May 2022.

[106] See Australian Government Department of Industry, Science, Energy and Resources, *Australia's Artificial Intelligence Ethics Framework*.

[107] Financial Conduct Authority, *Automated Investment Services: Our Expectations*; ASIC, *Providing Digital Financial Product Advice to Retail Clients*, para 255.98.

broadly defined categories of consumers, then this should be made clear, to counter consumers' expectations of a unique and personal experience.

To the extent that consumers overestimate the capacities of fintech, transparency in way the advice is produced is important to ground expectations and allow scrutiny of the veracity of claims made about it. For regulators, transparency is key to overseeing the performance of the tools. Transparency is key to allowing bias or distortions in the scope of advice to be identified, scrutinised and, in some instances, rectified. Regulation can support the imperative for firms to take these ethical demands seriously, including by treating them as necessary elements of statutory obligations of suitability or best interests, and essential to ensuring that claims about the operation of the product are not misleading. For example, the process of automation, and its claims to objectivity and consistency, may make consumers overconfident about the advice and more likely to act on it.[108] This might suggest an obligation on firms to be scrupulously clear on the limits of what is able to provided by automated advice tools, and of the insights that can be derived from the technology being utilised.[109]

Transparency in ethical AI is closely associated with initiatives in AI 'explanations' or 'explainability'.[110] Explanations in this sense do not lie in the details of the code. Rather, explainable AI considers the kind and degree of information that should be provided in assisting the various stakeholders in the decision or recommendation process to understand why decisions were taken or the factors that were significant in reaching a recommendation.[111] Explainable AI aims to provide greater transparency into the basis for automated decisions, predictions, and recommendations.[112] There are different ways in which explanations may be provided, and indeed the field of study in computer science is still developing.[113] Possibilities include the use of counterfactuals, feature disclosure scores, weightings of influential factors, or a

---

[108] See also Brenner and Meyll, 'Robo-Advisors: A Substitute for Human Financial Advice?' (substitution effect of robo-advisers is especially driven by investors concerned about investment fraud from human advisers).

[109] See Jeannie Paterson, 'Misleading AI' (2023) 34 (Symposium) *Loyola University Chicago School of Law Consumer Law Review* 558.

[110] See Select Committee on Artificial Intelligence, 'AI in the UK', 40; Australian Human Rights Commission, *Human Rights and Technology*, 75.

[111] On explanations, see Tim Miller, 'Explanation in Artificial Intelligence: Insights from the Social Sciences' (2019) 267(1) *Artificial Intelligence* 1; Sandra Wachter, Brent Mittelstadt, and Chris Russell, 'Counterfactual Explanations without Opening the Black Box: Automated Decisions and the GDPR' (2018) 31 *Harvard Journal of Law & Technology* 841; Jonathan Dodge et al, 'Explaining Models: An Empirical Study of How Explanations Impact Fairness Judgment' (International Conference on Intelligent User Interfaces, Marina del Ray, 17–20 March 2019).

[112] Tim Miller, 'Explainable Artificial Intelligence: What Were You Thinking?' in N Wouters, G Blashki, and H Sykes (eds), *Artificial Intelligence: For Better or Worse* (Future Leaders, 2019) 19, 21; Wachter et al, 'Counterfactual Explanations without Opening the Black Box', 844.

[113] Umang Bhatt et al, 'Explainable Machine Learning in Deployment' (Conference on Fairness, Accountability, and Transparency, Barcelona, January 2020) 648.

preference for simpler models where high levels of accuracy are not as imperative.[114] Overall, however, a requirement for explanations would assist in scrutinising the basis of the recommendations produced through automated financial advice tools.

For lawyers, suggesting that a core element in the regulation of automated financial advice tools should focus on requirements related to transparency/explanations may seem a surprising aspiration.[115] Disclosure as a consumer protection strategy has increasingly fallen out of favour, particularly in the regulation of financial services and credit. The insights into decision-making from behavioural psychology have shown that mere information disclosure does not lead to better decisions by consumers. Consumers are subject to bounded rationality which means they rely on rules of thumb, heuristics, and behavioural bias rather than information.[116] In this light, it may be thought that any demand for greater transparency in automated financial advice tools may be of marginal utility. However, in a consumer protection context, consumers' interests are substantially protected by regulators, and therefore transparency and explanations are relevant to both consumers seeking to protect their interests, and regulators charged with overseeing the market. Explanations should be provided in a form that is meaningful to the recipient.[117] This means that the detail and technicality of the information provided may need to differ between consumers and regulators.[118] In other words, the requirements should be scaled according to who is receiving the explanation.

2.4.2 Accountability

Principles of AI ethics typically require mechanisms for ensuring firms are accountable for the operation of the technologies.[119] To have impact, accountability will require more than allocating responsibility for supervising the AI to a person. There is little worth in having a 'human in the loop' in circumstances where the design of the AI or automated tool means it is difficult for that person genuinely to oversee,

---

[114] See Miller, 'Explanation in Artificial Intelligence: Insights from the Social Sciences'; Wachter et al, 'Counterfactual Explanations without Opening the Black Box'.

[115] See also Karen Yeung and Adrian Weller, 'How Is "Transparency" Understood by Legal Scholars and the Machine Learning Community' in Mireille Hildebrandt et al (eds), *Being Profiled: Cogitas Ergo Sum* (Amsterdam University Press, 2018); John Zerilli et al, 'Transparency in Algorithmic and Human Decision-Making: Is There a Double Standard?' (2019) 32 *Philosophy and Technology* 661.

[116] See generally Robert A Hillman and Jeffrey J Rachlinski, 'Standard-Form Contracting in the Electronic Age' (2002) 77 *New York University Law Review* 429; Russell Korobkin, 'Bounded Rationality, Standard Form Contracts, and Unconscionability' (2003) 70 *University of Chicago Law Review* 1203.

[117] Wachter et al, 'Counterfactual Explanations without Opening the Black Box', 843. See also Miller, 'Explanation in Artificial Intelligence: Insights from the Social Sciences'.

[118] See Wachter et al, 'Counterfactual Explanations without Opening the Black Box', 843.

[119] Lyons et al, 'Conceptualising Contestability'.

interrogate or control the tool.[120] Accountability for automated financial advice tools should therefore require a firm to implement systematic processes for reviewing the operations and performance of the tools.[121] A commitment to accountability may therefore require firms to have processes for scrutinising the data on which the AI is trained, its ongoing use, and its outputs.[122] A model for the kind of robust approach required might be found in the audits increasingly recommended for AI used in public sector decision-making.[123] Such processes should aim to ensure the veracity of the tools and are a critical element in addressing and redressing concerns about bias, equity, and inclusion.[124]

2.4.3 *Contestability*

There is little utility in requiring transparency and accountability in AI systems if there is no mechanism available to those affected by an AI or automated decision for acting to challenge an outcome that is erroneous, discriminatory, or otherwise flawed. Some formulations of AI ethical principles respond to this issue by requiring processes for contesting adverse outcomes.[125] While accountability processes should aim to be proactive in preventing these kinds of problems, contestability is a mechanism for individuals, advocates, or regulators to respond to harms that do occur.

Lyons et al. make the point that little is currently known about 'what contestability in relation to algorithmic decisions entails, and whether the same processes used to contest human decisions ... are suitable for algorithmic decision-making'.[126] Contestability for automated decisions may not be able simply to follow existing mechanisms for dealing with individual complaints or concerns. The models informing AI may be complex and opaque, thus creating challenges for review by subject domain experts who may nonetheless be unfamiliar with the technology.

---

[120] Madeleine Clare Elish, Moral Crumple Zones: Cautionary Tales in Human-Robot Interaction (pre-print) (1 March 2019). Engaging Science, Technology, and Society (pre-print) <http://dx.doi.org/10.2139/ssrn.2757236>.

[121] See also Cobbe et al, 'Reviewable Automated Decision-Making: A Framework for Accountable Algorithmic Systems' (discussing the principle of reviewability as a core element of accountability for automated decision-making systems).

[122] Baker and Dellaert, 'Regulating Robo Advice across the Financial Services Industry', 724. Cf Proposal for a Regulation (EU) 2021/1016 Laying Down Harmonised Rules on Artificial Intelligence (Artificial Intelligence Act) and Amending Certain Union Legislative Acts [2021] (EU AI Draft Regulations).

[123] Compare Cobbe et al, 'Reviewable Automated Decision-Making: A Framework for Accountable Algorithmic Systems'.

[124] Brent Mittelstad, 'Auditing for Transparency in Content Personalization Systems' (2016) 10 *International Journal of Communication* 4991.

[125] See, e.g., Australian Government Department of Industry, Science, Energy and Resources, *Australia's Artificial Intelligence Ethics Framework*.

[126] Lyons et al, 'Conceptualising Contestability', 1–2.

Additionally, scale creates a challenge. This is because one of the benefits of automated decision-making is that it can operate on a scale that is not possible for human decision-makers or advisers, and yet this makes processes for individual review potentially unmanageable.

The inquiry into what contestability requires may be different in the context of automated financial advice tools, as opposed to public sector use of automated decision-making. Consumers using automated advice tools will not be challenging a decision made about their rights to access public resources or benefits. Rather they will be challenging the advice given to them, the consistency of this advice with any representations about the tool, or compliance with any applicable regulatory regimes. Nonetheless, complexity and scale remain significant challenges. It is possible that the field of consumer protection law may have insights given its focus on both legal rights and structural mechanisms for protecting consumers' interests in circumstances where there are considerable imbalances in power, resources, and information, which in some ways mirrors concerns around AI contestability. For example, in this context of automated financial advice tools, contestability for poor outcomes may come through the oversight provided by ombudsmen and regulators, rather than traditional litigation. These inquiries have the capacity to look at systemic errors, thus bringing expertise and capacity to review processes through which advice or recommendations are provided, rather than necessarily reopening every decision.

2.5 CONCLUSION

The triad of money, power, and AI collide in fintech innovation, which sees public and private sector support for using AI, along with blockchain and big data, in the delivery of financial services. Currently, the most prominent forms of fintech available to consumers are automated advice tools for investing and budgeting. These tools offer advantages of low cost, convenient and consistent advice on matters consumers often find difficult. Without discounting these attractions, we have argued that the oft-stated aspiration of automated advice financial tools in democratising personal finance should not distract attention from their potential to provide only a marginally useful service, while extracting consumer data and perpetuating the exclusion of some consumer cohorts from adequate access to credit, advice and banking. From this perspective, consumer-facing fintech provides a exemplary example of the need for careful regulatory attention being provided to the use of AI and related technologies even in seemingly low-risk contexts. Fintech tools that hold out to consumers a promise of expertise and assistance should genuinely be fit for the purpose. Consumers are unlikely to be able to monitor this quality themselves. As such, robust standards of transparency, accountability, and contestability that facilitate good governance and allow adequate regulatory oversight are crucial, even for these modest applications of AI.

3

Leveraging AI to Mitigate Money Laundering Risks in the Banking System

Doron Goldbarsht[*]

3.1 INTRODUCTION

Money laundering involves the transfer of illegally obtained money through legitimate channels so that its original source cannot be traced.[1] The United Nations estimates that the amount of money laundered each year represents 2–5 per cent of global gross domestic product (GDP); however, due to the surreptitious nature of money laundering, the total could be much higher.[2] Money launderers conceal the source, possession, or use of funds through a range of methods of varying sophistication, often involving multiple individuals or institutions across several jurisdictions to exploit gaps in the financial economy.[3]

As major facilitators in the global movement of money, banks carry a high level of responsibility for protecting the integrity of the financial system by preventing and obstructing illicit transactions. Many of the financial products and services they offer are specifically associated with money laundering risks. To ensure regulatory compliance in the fight against financial crime, banks must develop artificial intelligence (AI) about emerging money-laundering processes and create systems that effectively target suspicious behaviour.[4]

'Smart' regulation in the financial industry requires the development and deployment of new strategies and methodologies. Technology can assist regulators, supervisors, and regulated entities by alleviating the existing challenges of anti-money laundering (AML) initiatives. In particular, the use of AI can speed up risk

[*] The author wishes to thank Isabelle Nicolas for her excellent research assistance.
[1] *Black's Law Dictionary* (2009), 1097.
[2] 'Money Laundering', *United Nations Office on Drugs and Crime* (Web Page) <www.unodc .org/unodc/en/money-laundering/overview.html>.
[3] Ana Isabel Canhoto, 'Leveraging Machine Learning in the Global Fight against Money Laundering and Terrorism Financing: An Affordances Perspective' (2021) 131 *Journal of Business Research* 441 at 449.
[4] Ibid, 449.

identification and enhance the monitoring of suspicious activity by acquiring, processing, and analysing data rapidly, efficiently, and cost-effectively. It thus has the potential to facilitate improved compliance with domestic AML legal regimes. While the full implications of emerging technologies remain largely unknown, banks would be well advised to evaluate the capabilities, risks, and limitations of AI – as well as the associated ethical considerations.

This chapter will evaluate compliance with the Financial Action Task Force (FATF) global standards for AML,[5] noting that banks continue to be sanctioned for non-compliance with AML standards. The chapter will then discuss the concept of AI, which can be leveraged by banks to identify, assess, monitor, and manage money laundering risks.[6] Next, the chapter will examine the deficiencies in the traditional rule-based systems and the FATF's move to a more risk-oriented approach, which allows banks to concentrate their resources where the risks are particularly high.[7] Following this, the chapter will consider the potential for AI to enhance the efficiency and effectiveness of AML systems used by banks, as well as the challenges posed by its introduction. Finally, the chapter will offer some concluding thoughts.

3.2 ENFORCEMENT AND DETECTION: THE COST OF NON-COMPLIANCE

The FATF sets global standards for AML, with more than 200 jurisdictions committed to implementing its recommendations.[8] It monitors and assesses how well countries fulfil their commitment through legal, regulatory, and operational measures to combat money laundering (as well as terrorist financing and other related threats).[9] Pursuant to the FATF recommendations, banks must employ customer due diligence (CDD) measures.[10] CDD involves the identification and verification of customer identity through the use of other sources and data. Banks should conduct CDD for both new and existing business relationships.[11] They have a duty to monitor transactions and, where there are reasonable grounds to suspect criminal activity, report them to the relevant financial intelligence agency.[12] Banks must conduct their operations in ways that withstand the scrutiny of customers,

---

[5] FATF, *The FATF Recommendations* (Report, 2012) 7 <www.fatf-gafi.org/media/fatf/documents/recommendations/pdfs/FATF%20Recommendations%202012.pdf>.
[6] FATF, *Opportunities and Challenges of New Technologies for AML/CTF* (Report, 2021) 5 <www.fatf-gafi.org/media/fatf/documents/reports/Opportunities-Challenges-of-New-Technologies-for-AML-CFT.pdf>.
[7] Ibid, 31.
[8] Doron Goldbarsht, 'Who's the Legislator Anyway? How the FATF's Global Norms Reshape Australian Counter Terrorist Financing Laws' (2017) 45 *Federal Law Review* 127. See also 'About', FATF (Web Page) <www.fatf-gafi.org/about/whoweare/#d.en.11232>.
[9] FATF, *The FATF Recommendations*.
[10] Ibid, Recommendation 10.
[11] Ibid, Recommendations 10, 11.
[12] Ibid, Recommendation 20.

shareholders, governments, and regulators. There are considerable consequences for falling short of AML standards.

In a 2021 report, AUSTRAC, Australia's financial intelligence agency, assessed the nature and extent of the money laundering risk faced by Australia's major banks as 'high'. The report highlighted the consequences for customers, the Australian financial system, and the community at large.[13] It drew attention to impacts on the banking sector – including financial losses, increased compliance costs, lower share prices, and increased risk of legal action from non-compliance – as well as reputational impacts on Australia's international economic security.[14]

In this climate of heightened regulatory oversight, banks continue to be sanctioned for failing to maintain sufficient AML controls. In 2009, Credit Suisse Group was fined US$536 million for illegally removing material information, such as customer names and bank names, so that wire transfers would pass undetected through the filters at US banks. The violations were conducted on behalf of Credit Suisse customers in Iran, Sudan, and other sanctioned countries, allowing them to move hundreds of millions of dollars through the US financial system.[15] Also in 2009, Lloyds Banking Group was fined US$350 million after it deliberately falsified customer information in payment records, 'repairing' transfers so that they would not be detected by US banks.[16] In 2012, US authorities fined HSBC US$1.9 billion in a money laundering settlement.[17] That same year, the ING Bank group was fined US$619 million for allowing money launderers to illegally move billions of dollars through the US banking system.[18] The Commonwealth Bank of Australia was fined A$700 million in 2017 after it failed to comply with AML monitoring requirements and failed to report suspicious matters worth tens of millions of dollars.[19] Even after becoming aware of suspected money laundering, the bank

---

[13] AUSTRAC, *Australia's Major Banks: Money Laundering and Terrorism Financing Risk Assessment* (Report, 2021) <www.austrac.gov.au/sites/default/files/2021–09/Major%20Banks%20ML_TF_Risk%20Assessment%202021.pdf>.

[14] Ibid.

[15] Department of Justice, Office of Public Affairs, 'Credit Suisse Agrees to Forfeit $536 Million in Connection with Violations of the International Emergency Economic Powers Act and New York State Law' (Media Release, 16 December 2009) <www.justice.gov/opa/pr/credit-suisse-agrees-forfeit-536-million-connection-violations-international-emergency>.

[16] Andrew Clark, 'Lloyds Forfeits $350 m for Disguising Origin of Funds from Iran and Sudan' (10 January 2009) *The Guardian* <www.theguardian.com/business/2009/jan/10/lloyds-forfeits-350m-to-us>.

[17] Associated Press, 'HSBC to Pay $1.9b to Settle Money-Laundering Case' (11 December 2012) *CBC News* <www.cbc.ca/news/business/hsbc-to-pay-1-9b-to-settle-money-laundering-case-1.1226871>.

[18] Toby Sterling and Bart H Meijer, 'Dutch Bank ING Fined $900 Million for Failing to Spot Money Laundering' (4 September 2018) *Reuters* <www.reuters.com/article/us-ing-groep-settlement-money-laundering-idUSKCN1LK0PE>.

[19] AUSTRAC, 'AUSTRAC and CBA Agree $700 m Penalty' (Media Release, 4 June 2018) <www.austrac.gov.au/austrac-and-cba-agree-700m-penalty>.

failed to meet its CDD obligations while continuing to conduct business with suspicious customers.[20] In 2019, fifty-eight AML-related fines were issued world-wide, totalling US$8.14 billion – more than double the amount for the previous year.[21] Westpac Bank recently agreed to pay A$1.3 billion fine – an Australian record – for violating the Anti-Money Laundering and Counter-Terrorism Financing Act 2006. Westpac had failed to properly report almost 20 million international fund transfers, amounting to over A$11 billion, to AUSTRAC, thereby exposing Australia's financial system to criminal misuse.[22] In 2020, Citigroup agreed to pay US$400 million fine after engaging in what US regulators called 'unsafe and unsound banking practices', including with regard to money laundering.[23] The bank had previously agreed to a US$97.4 million settlement after 'failing to safe-guard its systems from being infiltrated by drug money and other illicit funds'.[24] The severity of these fines reflects the fact that non-compliance with AML measures in the banking industry is unacceptable to regulators.[25] More recently, AUSTRAC accepted an enforceable undertaking from National Australia Bank to improve the bank's systems, controls, and record keeping so that they are compliant with AML laws.[26]

The pressure on banks comes not only from increased regulatory requirements, but also from a marketplace that is increasingly concerned with financial integrity and reputational risks.[27] A bank's failure to maintain adequate systems may have consequences for its share price and its customer base. Citigroup, for example, was

---

[20] Ibid.

[21] Brian Monroe, 'More than $8 Billion in AML Fines Handed Out in 2019, with USA and UK Leading the Charge: Analysis' (2021) ACFCS <www.acfcs.org/fincrime-briefing-aml-fines-in-2019-breach-8-billion-treasury-official-pleads-guilty-to-leaking-2020-crypto-compliance-out look-and-more/>.

[22] AUSTRAC, 'AUSTRAC and Westpac Agree to Proposed $1.3bn Penalty' (Media Release, 24 September 2020) <www.austrac.gov.au/news-and-media/media-release/austrac-and-westpac-agree-penalty>.

[23] Emily Flitter, 'Citigroup Is Fined $400 Million over "Longstanding" Internal Problems' (7 October 2020) *New York Times* <www.nytimes.com/2020/10/07/business/citigroup-fine-risk-management.html>.

[24] Michael Corkery and Ben Protess, 'Citigroup Agrees to $97.4 Million Settlement in Money Laundering Inquiry' (22 May 2017) *New York Times* <www.nytimes.com/2017/05/22/business/dealbook/citigroup-settlement-banamex-usa-inquiry.html>.

[25] Richard Grint, Chris O'Driscoll, and Sean Paton, *New Technologies and Anti-money Laundering Compliance: Financial Conduct Authority* (Report, 31 March 2017) <www.fca .org.uk/publication/research/new-technologies-in-aml-final-report.pdf>.

[26] AUSTRAC, 'AUSTRAC Accepted Enforceable Undertaking from National Australia Bank' (Media Release, 2 May 2022) <www.austrac.gov.au/news-and-media/media-release/enforce able-undertaking-national-australia-bank>.

[27] Barry R Johnston and Ian Carrington, 'Protecting the Financial System from Abuse: Challenges to Banks in Implementing AML/CFT Standards' (2006) 9 *Journal of Money Laundering* 49.

fined in 2004 for failing to detect and investigate suspicious transactions. The bank admitted to regulators that it had 'failed to establish a culture that ensured ongoing compliance with laws and regulations'. Within one week of the announcement by regulators, the value of Citigroup shares had declined by 2.75 per cent.[28]

It is, therefore, in the best interests of the banks themselves to manage risks effectively and to ensure full compliance with the domestic legislation that implements the FATF recommendations, including by retaining senior compliance staff.[29] Despite the high costs involved, banks have largely expressed a strong commitment to improving their risk management systems to protect their own integrity and that of the financial system – as well as to avoid heavy penalties, such as those detailed above.[30] Yet, while banks continue to invest in their capabilities in this area, they also continue to attract fines. This suggests that the current systems are inadequate for combating financial crime.

The current systems rely on models that are largely speculative and rapidly outdated.[31] Fraud patterns change constantly to keep up with technological advancements, making it difficult to distinguish between money laundering and legitimate transactions.[32] But while emerging technologies can be exploited for criminal activity, they also have the potential to thwart it.[33] AI has proven effective in improving operational efficiency and predictive accuracy in a range of fields, while also reducing operational costs.[34] Already, some banks have begun using AI to automate data in order to detect suspicious transactions. Indeed, AI could revolutionise the banking industry, including by improving the banking experience in multiple ways.[35]

---

[28] Ibid, 52.

[29] Raghad Al-Shabandar et al, 'The Application of Artificial Intelligence in Financial Compliance Management', in *Proceedings of the 2019 International Conference on Artificial Intelligence and Advanced Manufacturing* (New York: Association for Computing Machinery, 2019).

[30] KPMG, *Global Anti-money Laundering Survey: How Banks Are Facing Up to the Challenge* (2004), cited in Johnston and Carrington, 'Protecting the Financial System', 58.

[31] Howard Kunreuther, 'Risk Analysis and Risk Management in an Uncertain World' (2002) 22 *Risk Analysis* 655, cited in Canhoto, 'Leveraging Machine Learning', 443.

[32] Zhiyuan Chen et al, 'Machine Learning Techniques for Anti-money Laundering (AML) Solutions in Suspicious Transaction Detection: A Review' (2018) 57 *Knowledge and Information Systems* 245.

[33] Grint et al, *New Technologies and Anti-money Laundering Compliance: Financial Conduct Authority*.

[34] Institute of International Finance, *Machine Learning in Anti-money Laundering: Summary Report* (Report, 2018) <www.iif.com/portals/0/Files/private/32370132_iif_machine_learning_in_aml_-_public_summary_report.pdf>.

[35] Praveen Kumar Donepudi, 'Machine Learning and Artificial Intelligence in Banking' (2017) 5 *Engineering International* 84.

3.3 LEVERAGING AI FOR AML

AI simulates human thought processes through a set of theories and computerised algorithms that execute activities that would normally require human intellect.[36] It is, in short, the ability of a computer to mimic the capabilities of the human mind. The technology uses predictive analytics through pattern recognition with differing degrees of autonomy. Machine learning is one of the most effective forms of AI for AML purposes.[37] It can use computational techniques to gain insights from data, recognise patterns, and create algorithms to execute tasks – all without explicit programming.[38] Standard programming, in contrast, operates by specific rules that are developed to make inferences and produce outcomes based on input data.[39] Machine learning initiatives allow AML systems to conduct risk assessments with varying levels of independence from human intervention.[40] Deep learning, for example, is a form of machine learning that builds an artificial neural network by conducting repeated tasks, allowing it to improve the outcome continuously and solve complex problems by adapting to environmental changes.[41] Although there are many machine learning techniques, AI has four main capabilities for AML purposes: anomaly detection, suspicious behaviour monitoring, cognitive capabilities, and automatic robotic processing.[42] The effectiveness of these capabilities depends largely on processing power, the variability of data, and the quality of data, thus requiring some degree of human expertise.

The processes involved in AI can be broadly grouped into supervised and unsupervised techniques. Supervised techniques use algorithms to learn from a training set of data, allowing new data to be classified into different categories. Unsupervised techniques, which often operate without training data, use algorithms to separate data into clusters that hold unique characteristics. Researchers maintain that algorithmic processes have the potential to detect money laundering by classifying financial transactions at a larger scale than is currently possible – and with greater accuracy and improved cost-efficiency.[43]

---

[36] Ana Fernandez, 'Artificial Intelligence in Financial Services', *Economic Bulletin*, June 2019, 1.

[37] FATF, *Opportunities and Challenges of New Technologies for AML/CTF*, 22.

[38] Pariwat Ongsulee, 'Artificial Intelligence, Machine Learning and Deep Learning' (15th International Conference on ICT and Knowledge Engineering, 2017).

[39] Steven S Skiena, *The Algorithm Design Manual* (London: Springer, 2008), cited in Canhoto, 'Leveraging Machine Learning', 443.

[40] Isabel Ana Canhoto and Fintan Clear, 'Artificial Intelligence and Machine Learning as Business Tools: A Framework for Diagnosing Value Destruction Potential' (2020) 63 *Business Horizons* 183, cited in Canhoto, 'Leveraging Machine Learning', 444.

[41] FATF, *Opportunities and Challenges of New Technologies for AML/CTF*, 22.

[42] Alessa, *Webinar – An Executive Guide on How to Use Machine Learning and AI for AML Compliance* (Video, 2019) <www.youtube.com/watch?v=k46_UY4DGXU>.

[43] While this chapter is primarily concerned with the adoption of AI by banks for AML purposes, AI is also increasingly relied on by AML regulators. Occurring in parallel with increased regulatory demands, the evolution of AI in regulatory technology promised to improve

3.4 THE SHIFT TO A RISK-BASED APPROACH

One of the most significant obstacles for banks seeking to meet their compliance obligations is the difficulty of appropriately detecting, analysing, and mitigating money laundering risks – particularly during CDD and when monitoring transactions.[44] Currently, transaction monitoring and filtering technology is primarily rule-based, meaning that it is relatively simplistic and predominantly focused on automated and predetermined risk factors.[45] The system operates as a 'decision tree', in which identified outliers generate alerts that require investigation by other parties. Thus, when a suspicious activity is flagged, a compliance officer must investigate the alert and, if appropriate, generate a suspicious matter report.[46]

In order to minimise the costs and time required to investigate suspicious transactions, it is essential to detect them accurately at the first instance.[47] In rule-based systems, the task is made all the more difficult by the high false positive rate of the alerts, which is believed to be above 98 per cent.[48] If risk assessment in low-risk situations is overly strict, unmanageable numbers of false positive identifications can cause significant operational costs.[49] Conversely, if risk assessments are too lax, illicit transactions can slip through unnoticed.[50] These static reporting processes make it difficult to analyse increasingly large volumes of data, making them impractical on the scale required by banks. It has thus become necessary for banks to choose between the efficiency and the effectiveness of their AML processes.

Moreover, the rule-based systems rely on human-defined criteria and thresholds that are easy for money launderers to understand and circumvent. The changing

---

compliance monitoring, as well as reduce costs, which undoubtedly motivated its uptake. See Hannah Harris, 'Artificial Intelligence and Policing of Financial Crime: A Legal Analysis of the State of the Field' in Doron Goldbarsht and Louis de Koker (eds), *Financial Technology and the Law* (Cham: Springer, 2022); Lyria Bennett Moses and Janet Chan, 'Algorithmic Prediction in Policing: Assumptions, Evaluation, and Accountability' (2018) 28 *Policing and Society* 806; Douglas W Arner, Janos Barberis, and Ross Buckley, 'FinTech, RegTech, and the Reconceptualization of Financial Regulation' (2017) 37 *Northwestern Journal of International Law and Business* 390.

44 FATF, *Opportunities and Challenges of New Technologies for AML/CTF*, 11.

45 Institut Polytechnique de Paris, 'More AI, and Less Box-Ticking, Says FATF in AML/CTF Report' (Media Release, 13 July 2021) <www.telecom-paris.fr/more-ai-less-box-ticking-fatf-aml-cft>.

46 Dattatray Vishnu Kute et al, 'Deep Learning and Explainable Artificial Intelligence Techniques Applied for Detecting Money Laundering – A Critical Review' (IEEA Access, 2021) 82301.

47 Ibid, 82301.

48 McKinsey & Company, *Transforming Approaches to AML and Financial Crime* (Report, 2019) 14 <www.mckinsey.com/~/media/McKinsey/Business%20Functions/Risk/Our%20Insights/Transforming%20approaches%20to%20AML%20and%20financial%20crime/Transforming-approaches-to-AML-and-financial%20crime-vF.pdf>.

49 Jingguang Han et al, 'Artificial Intelligence for Anti-money Laundering: A Review and Extension' (2020) 2 *Digital Finance* 213.

50 Ibid, 219.

patterns of fraud make it difficult for rule-based systems and policies to maintain their effectiveness, thus allowing money laundering transactions to be misidentified as genuine.[51] AML systems are designed to detect unusual transaction patterns, rather than actual criminal behaviour. Rule-based systems thus have the potential to implicate good customers, initiate criminal investigations against them, and thereby damage customer relationships – all without disrupting actual money laundering activities. This is because the systems were designed for a relatively slow-moving fraud environment in which patterns would eventually emerge and be identified and then incorporated into fraud detection systems. Today, criminal organisations are themselves leveraging evolving technologies to intrude into organisational systems and proceed undetected.[52] For example, AI allows criminals to use online banking and other electronic payment methods to move illicit funds across borders through the production of bots and false identities that circumnavigate AML systems.[53]

According to the FATF, implementing a risk-based approach is the 'cornerstone of an effective AML/CFT system and is essential to properly managing risks'.[54] Yet many jurisdictions continue to use antiquated rule-based systems, leading to defensive compliance. To keep pace with modern crime and the increasing volume and velocity of data, banks need a faster and more agile approach to the detection of money laundering. They should reconsider their AML strategies and evolve from traditional rule-based systems to more sophisticated risk-based AI solutions. By leveraging AI, banks can take a proactive and preventive approach to fighting financial crime.[55]

3.5 ADVANTAGES AND CHALLENGES

3.5.1 _Advantages_

New technologies are key to improving the management of regulatory risks. Banks have begun exploring the use of AI to assist analysts in what has traditionally been a manually intensive task to improve the performance of AML processes.[56] In 2018, US government agencies issued a joint statement encouraging banks to use innovative methods, including AI, to further efforts to protect the integrity of the financial

[51] FATF, _Opportunities and Challenges of New Technologies for AML/CTF_, 12.
[52] Alessa, _Webinar_.
[53] Richard Paxton, 'Is AI Changing the Face of Financial Crimes and Money Laundering?' (26 August 2021) _Medium_ <https://medium.com/@alacergroup/is-ai-changing-the-face-of-financial-crimes-money-laundering-912ceod168bd>.
[54] FATF, _Opportunities and Challenges of New Technologies for AML/CTF_, 13.
[55] Ibid, 13.
[56] Ilze Calitz, 'AI: The Double-Edged Sword in AML/CTF Compliance' (27 January 2021) _ACAMS Today_ <www.acamstoday.org/ai-the-double-edged-sword-in-aml-ctf-compliance/>.

system against illicit financial activity.[57] The United Kingdom Financial Conduct Authority has supported a series of public workshops aimed at encouraging banks to experiment with novel technologies to improve the detection of financial crimes.[58] AUSTRAC has invested in data analysis and advanced analytics to assist in the investigation of suspicious activity.[59] Indeed, developments in AI offer an opportunity to fundamentally transform the operations of banks, equipping them to combat modern threats to the integrity of the financial system.[60] And, where AI reaches the same conclusions as traditional analytical models, this can confirm the accuracy of such assessments, ultimately increasing the safeguards available to supervisors.[61] Although machine learning remains relatively underutilised in the area of AML, it offers the potential to greatly enhance the efficiency and effectiveness of existing systems.[62]

3.5.1.1 Improved Efficiency

Incorporating AI in AML procedures can reduce the occurrence of false positives and increase the identification of true positives. In Singapore, the United Overseas Bank has already piloted machine learning to enhance its AML surveillance by implementing an AML 'suite' that includes know-your-customer (KYC), transaction monitoring, name screening, and payment screening processes.[63] The suite provides an additional layer of scrutiny that leverages machine learning models over traditional rule-based monitoring systems, resulting in real benefits. In relation to transaction monitoring, the recognition of unknown suspicious patterns saw an increase of 5 per cent in true positives and a decrease of 40 per cent in false positives. There was a more than 50 per cent reduction in false positive findings in relation to name screening.[64]

---

[57] Board of Governors of the Federal Reserve System, Federal Deposit Insurance Corporation, Financial Crimes Enforcement Network, National Credit Union Administration, and Office of the Comptroller of the Currency, *Joint Statement on Innovative Efforts to Combat Money Laundering and Terrorist Financing* (3 December 2018).

[58] AUSTRAC, *Annual Report 2020–21* (Report, 2021) 21.

[59] Ibid.

[60] Bob Contri and Rob Galaski, 'How AI Is Transforming the Financial Ecosystem' (2018), cited in Deloitte and United Overseas Bank, *The Case for Artificial Intelligence in Combating Money Laundering and Terrorist Financing: A Deep Dive into the Application of Machine Learning Technology* (Report, 2018) 4.

[61] FATF, *Opportunities and Challenges of New Technologies for AML/CTF*, 14.

[62] Mark Luber, cited in Markets Insider, 'Machine Learning and Artificial Intelligence Algorithm Paves New Ways for Anti-money Laundering Compliance in LexisNexis Risk Solutions' Award-Winning Solution' (Media Release, 14 November 2018) <https://markets.businessinsider.com/news/stocks/machine-learning-and-artificial-intelligence-algorithm-paves-new-ways-for-anti-money-laundering-compliance-in-lexisnexis-risk-solutions-award-winning-solution-1027728213>.

[63] Deloitte and United Overseas Bank, *The Case*, 25.

[64] Ibid, 29.

AI has the capability to analyse vast volumes of data, drawing on an increased number of variables. This means that the quality of the analysis is enhanced and the results obtained are more precise.[65] At the same time, utilising AI in AML can increase productivity by reducing staff work time by 30 per cent.[66] By combining transactional data with other information, such as customer profile data, it is possible to investigate AML risks within days. In contrast, traditional methods that review isolated accounts often require months of analysis. Additionally, banks can use AI to facilitate the live monitoring of AML standards, which can also improve governance, auditability, and accountability.[67] Overall, the use of machine learning has resulted in a 40 per cent increase in operational efficiency, reinforcing the notion that investment in AI initiatives may have positive implications for the reliability of AML processes.[68]

3.5.1.2 Reduced Compliance Costs

By leveraging AI, banks have an opportunity to reduce costs and prioritise human resources in complex areas of AML.[69] It has been estimated that incorporating AI in AML compliance procedures could save the global banking industry more than US$1 trillion by 2030[70] and reduce its costs by 22 per cent over the next twelve years.[71] The opportunities for cost reduction and improved productivity and risk management offer convincing incentives for banks to engage AI and machine learning to achieve greater profitability.[72] With increased profits, banks could further improve the accuracy of AML systems and, in the process, advance the goals of AML.[73]

3.5.1.3 Increased Inclusiveness

Digital tools have the potential to increase financial inclusion, promoting more equitable access to the formal financial sector.[74] Customers with less reliable forms of identification – including First Nations peoples and refugees – can access banking services through solutions such as behavioural analytics, which reduces

---

[65] Fernandez, 'Artificial Intelligence', 2.
[66] Deloitte and United Overseas Bank, *The Case*, 29.
[67] FATF, *Opportunities and Challenges of New Technologies for AML/CTF*, 20.
[68] Deloitte and United Overseas Bank, *The Case*, 29.
[69] Financial Stability Board, *Artificial Intelligence and Machine Learning in Financial Services: Market Developments and Financial Stability Implications* (Report, 1 November 2017) 23.
[70] 'Strengthening AML Protection through AI' (July 2018) *Financier Worldwide Magazine* <www.financierworldwide.com/strengthening-aml-protection-through-ai#.YV6BGioRrw4>.
[71] Ibid.
[72] Financial Stability Board, *Artificial Intelligence and Machine Learning in Financial Services*, 9.
[73] Ibid, 25.
[74] Ratna Sahay et al, 'Financial Inclusion: Can It Meet Multiple Macroeconomic Goals?' (IMF Staff Discussion Note SDN/15/17, September 2015).

the burden of verification to one instance of customer onboarding. Utilising AI makes banks less reliant on traditional CDD, offering enhanced monitoring capabilities that can be used to manage verification data.[75]

3.5.2 *Challenges*

Despite the growing recognition of the potential for AI to improve the accuracy, speed, and cost-effectiveness of AML processes, banks remain slow to adopt these technologies due to the regulatory and operational challenges involved.[76] Significant hurdles to wider adoption persist and these may continue to stifle innovations in AML compliance.

3.5.2.1 Interpretation

The difficulty of interpreting and explaining the outcomes derived from AI technologies is among the main barriers to securing increased support for these tools.[77] The Basel Committee on Banking Supervision has stated that, in order to replicate models, organisations should be able to demonstrate developmental evidence of theoretical construction, behavioural characteristics, and key assumptions; the types and use of input data; specified mathematical calculations; and code-writing language and protocols.[78] Yet artificial neural networks may comprise hundreds of millions of connections, each contributing in some small way to the outcomes produced.[79] Indeed, as technological models become increasingly complex, the inner workings of the algorithms become more obscure and difficult to decode, creating 'black boxes' in decision-making.[80]

In the European Union, the increased volume of data processing led to the adoption of the General Data Protection Regulation (GDPR) in 2016.[81] The

---

[75] FATF, *Opportunities and Challenges of New Technologies for AML/CTF*, 17.
[76] Grint et al, *New Technologies and Anti-money Laundering Compliance: Financial Conduct Authority*.
[77] FATF, *Opportunities and Challenges of New Technologies for AML/CTF*, 36.
[78] Financial Stability Board, *Artificial Intelligence and Machine Learning in Financial Services*, 28.
[79] Erik Brynjolfsson and Andrew McAfee, 'Artificial Intelligence, for Real', *Harvard Business Review: The Big Idea* (July 2017) 10 <https://starlab-alliance.com/wp-content/uploads/2017/09/AI-Article.pdf>.
[80] Financial Stability Board, *Artificial Intelligence and Machine Learning in Financial Services*, 26.
[81] *Regulation (EU) 2016/679 of the European Parliament and of the Council of 27 April 2016 on the protection of natural persons with regard to the processing of personal data and on the free movement of such data, and repealing Directive 95/46/EC (General Data Protection Regulation)* [2016] OJ L 119/1. See Christa Savia, 'Processing Financial Crime Data under the GDPR in Light of the 5th Anti-money Laundering Directive', Thesis, Örebro Universitet (2019) <www.diva-portal.org/smash/get/diva2:1353108/FULLTEXT01.pdf>.

GDPR aims to ensure that the data of individuals is protected – particularly in relation to AML procedures, which often collect highly personal data.[82] With respect to AI and machine learning, Recital 71 specifies that there is a right to obtain an explanation of the decision reached after algorithmic assessment. Because regulated entities remain responsible for the technical details of AI solutions, fears persist concerning accountability and interpretability where technologies cannot offer robust transparency.[83] While the GDPR expects that internal compliance teams will understand and defend the algorithms utilised by digital tools, compliance officers working in banks require expertise and resources to do so. It may take a long period of time for even the most technologically literate of supervisors to adjust to new regulatory practices.[84] Efforts to improve the interpretation of AI and machine learning are vital if banks are to enhance risk management and earn the trust of supervisors, regulators, and the public.

3.5.2.2 Data Quality

The data utilised to train and manage AI systems must be of high quality.[85] Machine learning models are not self-operating; they require human intervention to ensure their optimal functioning.[86] In other words, machines cannot think for themselves. Rather, they merely execute and learn from their encoded programming.[87] Since machine learning is only as good as its input, it is crucial that the models used are based on relevant and diverse data.[88] Where money-laundering transactions have not previously been identified by the system, it may be difficult for machine learning to detect future instances.[89] Moreover, false positives would be learned into the system if the training data included them.[90] Therefore, it is essential that data quality is monitored on an ongoing basis to ensure thorough data analysis and regular data cleansing. This serves to highlight the vital importance of vigilant human collabor-

[82] Savia, 'Processing Financial Crime Data'.
[83] Penny Crosman, 'Can AI's "Black Box" Problem Be Solved?' (1 January 2019) *American Banker* 2.
[84] FATF, *Opportunities and Challenges of New Technologies for AML/CTF*, 36.
[85] Ibid, 41.
[86] Alessa, *Webinar*.
[87] Lyria Bennett Moses, 'Not a Single Singularity' in Simon Deakin and Christopher Markou (eds), *Is Law Computable? Critical Perspectives on Law and Artificial Intelligence* (Oxford: Hart, 2020) 207.
[88] Mireille Hildebrandt, 'Code-Driven Law: Freezing Future and Scaling the Past' in Simon Deakin and Christopher Markou (eds), *Is Law Computable? Critical Perspectives on Law and Artificial Intelligence* (Oxford: Hart, 2020) 67.
[89] Ibid, 67.
[90] McKinsey & Company, *Transforming Approaches to AML and Financial Crime*.

ation in the technological implementation of AI to ensure that models are well maintained and remain effective.[91]

3.5.2.3 Collaboration

The inexplicable nature of AI, especially machine learning processes, has sparked concerns that are exacerbated by the lack of data harmonisation between actors and users.[92] Currently, customer privacy rules and information security considerations prevent banks from warning each other about potentially suspicious activity involving their customers. While some customers rely on a single financial services provider for all their banking requirements, criminals often avoid detection by moving illicit proceeds through numerous financial intermediaries.[93] The FATF has reported that intricate schemes involving complex transaction patterns are difficult and sometimes impossible to detect without information from counterparty banks or other banks providing services to the same customer.[94] Nevertheless, the FATF's rules to prevent 'tipping off' support the objective of protecting the confidentiality of criminal investigations.[95]

While data standardisation and integrated reporting strategies simplify regulatory reporting processes, they also raise various legal, practical, and competition issues.[96] It is likely that the capacity of banks to model will continue to be limited by the financial transactions that they themselves process.[97] Moreover, where information is unavailable across multiple entities, some technological tools may not be cost-effective.[98] On the other hand, stronger collaboration may introduce the risk of data being exploited on a large scale.[99] There is as yet no 'model template' in relation to private sector information sharing that complies with AML and data protection and privacy requirements. However, information sharing initiatives are being explored and should be considered in targeted AI policy developments.

---

[91] Ibid.
[92] FATF, *Opportunities and Challenges of New Technologies for AML/CTF*, 38.
[93] FATF, *Partnering in the Fight against Financial Crime: Data Protection, Technology and Private Sector Information Sharing* (Report, July 2022) 12 <www.fatf-gafi.org/media/fatf/documents/Partnering-int-the-fight-against-financial-crime.pdf>.
[94] Ibid.
[95] FATF, *The FATF Recommendations*, Recommendation 21.
[96] Juan Carlos Crisanto et al, *From Data Reporting to Data Sharing: How Far Can Suptech and Other Innovations Challenge the Status Quo of Regulatory Reporting?* (Financial Stability Institute Insights No 29, 16 December 2020) 2.
[97] FATF, *Stock Take on Data Pooling, Collaborative Analytics and Data Protection* (Report, July 2021), 11 <www.fatf-gafi.org/media/fatf/documents/Stocktake-Datapooling-Collaborative-Analytics.pdf>.
[98] FATF, *Opportunities and Challenges of New Technologies for AML/CTF*, 41.
[99] Financial Stability Board, *Artificial Intelligence and Machine Learning in Financial Services*, 31.

3.5.2.4 Privacy

Due to the interconnectedness of banks and third party service providers, cyber risks are heightened when tools such as AI and machine learning are used and stored in cloud platforms. Concentrating digital solutions might exacerbate these risks.[100] These regulatory challenges reinforce the desire to maintain human-based supervisory processes so that digital tools are not replacements but rather aids in the enhancement of regulatory systems.[101] Article 22 of the GDPR provides that subjects of data analysis have the right not to be subject to a decision with legal or significant consequences 'based solely on automated processing'.[102] The FATF also maintains that the adoption of AI technology in AML procedures requires human collaboration, due to particular concerns that technology is incapable of identifying emerging issues such as regional inequalities.[103]

3.5.2.5 Bias

Although algorithmic decision-making may appear to offer an objective alternative to human subjectivity, many AI algorithms replicate the conscious and unconscious biases of their programmers.[104] This may lead to unfairly targeting the financial activities of certain individuals or entities, or it may produce risk profiles that deny certain persons access to financial services. For example, AI and machine learning are increasingly being used in relation to KYC models.[105] Recommendation 10 of the FATF standards requires banks to monitor both new and existing customers to ensure that their transactions are legitimate.[106] Without the incorporation of AI, existing KYC processes are typically costly and labour-intensive.[107] Utilising AI can help evaluate the legitimacy of customer documentation and calculate the risks for banks where applications may seem to be fake.[108] The data input team should ensure that it does not unintentionally encode systemic bias into the models by using attributes such as employment status or net worth.[109] Transactional

---

[100] Crisanto et al, *From Data Reporting*, 5.
[101] FATF, *Opportunities and Challenges of New Technologies for AML/CTF*, 39.
[102] *General Data Protection Regulations*, art. 22.
[103] FATF, *Opportunities and Challenges of New Technologies for AML/CTF*, 39.
[104] Ibid, 41.
[105] KYC is an element of CDD that aims to prevent people from opening accounts anonymously or under a false name. See FATF, *Opportunities and Challenges of New Technologies for AML/CTF*, 43.
[106] FATF, *The FATF Recommendations*, Recommendation 10.
[107] Financial Stability Board, *Artificial Intelligence and Machine Learning in Financial Services*, 20.
[108] Ibid, 20.
[109] Finextra, 'Responsible Artificial Intelligence for Anti-money Laundering: How to Address Bias' (Blog, 1 September 2021) <www.finextra.com/blogposting/20830/responsible-artificial-intelligence-for-anti-money-laundering-how-to-address-bias>.

monitoring is less vulnerable to such biases, as it does not involve personal data such as gender, race, and religion. Nonetheless, AI and machine learning algorithms could implicitly correlate those indicators based on characteristics such as geographical location.[110] If not implemented responsibly, AI has the potential to exacerbate the financial exclusion of certain populations for cultural, political, or other reasons.[111] The use of these digital tools may thus lead to unintended discrimination.[112] Such concerns are heightened by the fact that the correlations are neither explicit nor transparent.[113] Therefore, regulators must remain mindful of the need to limit bias, ensure fairness, and maintain controls. The evolving field of discrimination-aware data mining may assist the decision-making processes that flow through information technology to ensure that they are not affected on unjust or illegitimate grounds.[114] It does this by recognising statistical imbalances in data sets and leveraging background information about discrimination-indexed features to identify 'bad' patterns that can then be either flagged or filtered out entirely.[115]

3.5.2.6 Big Data

The term 'big data' refers to large, complex, and ever-changing data sets and the technological techniques that are relevant to their analysis.[116] Policymakers and technical organisations have expressed significant concerns over the potential misuse of data.[117] There are also apprehensions that the lack of clarity around how data is handled may lead to potential violations of privacy.[118] In addition, there are uncertainties surrounding the ownership of data, as well as its cross-border flow.[119] Nonetheless, the primary focus should remain on the *use* of big data, rather

---

[110] Financial Stability Board, *Artificial Intelligence and Machine Learning in Financial Services*, 27.

[111] World Bank, *Principles on Identification for Sustainable Development: Toward the Digital Age* (Report, 2021) <https://documents1.worldbank.org/curated/en/213581486378184357/pdf/Principles-on-Identification-for-Sustainable-Development-Toward-the-Digital-Age.pdf>.

[112] Financial Stability Board, *Artificial Intelligence and Machine Learning in Financial Services*, 27.

[113] Lyria Bennett Moses and Janet Chan, 'Using Big Data for Legal/Law Enforcement Decisions: Testing the New Tools' (2014) 37 *UNSW Law Journal* 672.

[114] Bettina Berendt and Sören Preibusch, 'Better Decision Support through Exploratory Discrimination-Aware Data Mining: Foundations and Empirical Evidence' (2014) 22 *Artificial Intelligence and Law* 180.

[115] Ibid, 180.

[116] Janet Chan and Lyria Bennett Moses, 'Making Sense of Big Data for Security' (2016) 57 *British Journal of Criminology* 299.

[117] Ibid, 314.

[118] FATF, *Opportunities and Challenges of New Technologies for AML/CTF*, 43.

[119] Financial Stability Board, *Artificial Intelligence and Machine Learning in Financial Services*, 37.

than its collection and storage, as issues pertaining to use have the potential to cause the most egregious harm.[120]

3.5.2.7 Liability

The issues discussed above raise questions of liability regarding who will carry the burden of any systemic faults that result in the loss or corruption of data and related breaches of human rights.[121] While artificial agents are not human, they are not without responsibility.[122] Because it is impossible to punish machines, questions of liability are left to be determined between system operators and system providers.[123] This situation can be likened to a traffic accident in which an employee injures a pedestrian while driving the company truck. While the employer and the employee may both be liable for the injuries, the truck is not.[124] These issues enliven questions of causation. Will the use of AI and machine learning be considered a *novus actus interveniens* that breaks the chain of causation and prevents liability from being attributed to other actors?[125] The answer to this question will largely depend on the characteristics of artificial agents and whether they will be considered as mere tools or as agents in themselves, subject to liability for certain data breaches or losses. Despite the impact of automation processes on decision-making, doubts remain as to whether AI uses 'mental processes of deliberation'.[126] Due to the collaborative nature of AI technology and human actors, it is generally assumed that AI is merely an instrument and that accountability will be transferred to banks and developers.[127] Therefore, where supervisors can be considered legal agents for the operation of artificial technology, they may incur liability on the basis of that agency relationship.[128] Alternatively, where system developers are negligent as far as security vulnerabilities are concerned, they may be liable for the harm caused by unauthorised users or cyber criminals who exploit these deficiencies.[129] Thus, supervisors and

---

[120] US President's Council of Advisors on Science and Technology, cited in Moses and Chan, 'Using Big Data', 647.

[121] Fernandez, 'Artificial Intelligence', 6.

[122] Samir Chopra and Laurence F White, 'Tort Liability for Artificial Agents' in Samir Chopra and Laurence F White (eds), *A Legal Theory for Autonomous Artificial Agents* (Ann Arbor: University of Michigan Press, 2011) 120.

[123] Ibid, 154.

[124] Leon E Wein, 'The Responsibility of Intelligent Artifacts: Toward an Automation Jurisprudence' (1992) 6 *Harvard Journal of Law and Technology* 110, cited in Chopra and White, 'Tort Liability', 121.

[125] Chopra and White, 'Tort Liability', 122.

[126] *Pintarich v Federal Commissioner of Taxation* (2018) 262 FCR 41; [2018] FCAFC 79. This case is relevant to the applicability of judicial review to decisions made by machines.

[127] Financial Stability Board, *Artificial Intelligence and Machine Learning in Financial Services*, 26.

[128] Chopra and White, 'Tort Liability', 130.

[129] Ibid, 126.

developers have a duty of care to ensure that they take reasonable steps to prevent harm or damage.[130] It is possible that, as a result of its continued advancement, machine learning may eventually be granted legal personhood. Rights and obligations would therefore belong to the technology itself, excusing operators and developers from liability.[131] However, this viewpoint remains highly contested on the basis that AI does not possess 'free will', since it is programmed by humans and has little volition of its own.[132] Banks must not underestimate the importance of these concerns. They should ensure that AI and machine learning are carefully implemented with well-designed governance in place so that risks and liabilities are not unintentionally heightened by the use of new technologies.[133] Strong checks and balances are required at all stages of the development process.[134]

3.5.2.8 Costs

Banks must consider the costs of maintaining, repairing, and adapting new AI systems.[135] While AI models have the potential to improve the cost-efficiency of AML compliance, it may be difficult for banks – especially smaller institutions – to budget for high-level AI solutions.[136] Moreover, there are associated indirect costs that require firms to invest in additional funding – for example, updating existing database systems to make them compatible with new AI solutions and hiring staff with appropriate technical expertise.[137]

3.5.3 *Consideration*

AI and machine learning have the potential to provide banks with effective tools to improve risk management and compliance with regard to AML. However, if these new technologies are not introduced with care and diligence, they could adversely

---

[130] Ibid, 125.

[131] Samir Chopra and Laurence F White, 'Personhood for Artificial Agents' in Samir Chopra and Laurence F White (eds), *A Legal Theory for Autonomous Artificial Agents* (Ann Arbor: University of Michigan Press, 2011). In Australia, AI has already been granted recognition as an inventor in patent applications, suggesting that there is a cultural shift occurring that challenges assumptions in relation to the influence and abilities of AI. See Alexandra Jones, 'Artificial Intelligence Can Now Be Recognised as an Inventor after Historic Australian Court Decision' (1 August 2021) *ABC News* <www.abc.net.au/news/2021-08-01/historic-decision-allows-ai-to-be-recognised-as-an-inventor/100339264>.

[132] Chopra and White, 'Personhood', 173.

[133] Financial Stability Board, *Artificial Intelligence and Machine Learning in Financial Services*, 26.

[134] Basel Committee on Banking Supervision, *Revisions to the Principles for Sound Management of Operational Risk* (Report, 2021) 16.

[135] FATF, *Opportunities and Challenges of New Technologies for AML/CTF*, 40.

[136] Canhoto, 'Leveraging Machine Learning', 448.

[137] Merendino et al (2018), cited in Canhoto, 'Leveraging Machine Learning', 448.

affect AML systems by introducing greater burdens and risks. Some of the challenges presented by AI are similar to those posed by other technology-based solutions aimed at identifying and preventing money laundering. Machine learning, however, offers a relatively new and unique method of classifying information based on a feedback loop that enables the technology to 'learn' through determinations of probability.[138] Banks can thus analyse and classify information through learned anomaly detection algorithms, a technique that is more effective than traditionally programmed rule-based systems.[139] At the same time, the utilisation of AI can exacerbate the complexity and severity of the challenges inherent in AML compliance, particularly in relation to interpretation and explanation.[140] As discussed above, machine learning algorithms usually do not provide a rationale or reasoning for the outcomes they produce, making it difficult for compliance experts to validate the results and deliver clear reports to regulators.[141] This is particularly concerning for banks, where trust, transparency, and verifiability are of great importance to ensure satisfaction and regulatory confidence.[142] Nonetheless, in the current regulatory climate, it seems almost inevitable that banks will continue to leverage AI for AML compliance.

3.6 CONCLUSION

The traditional framework for AML compliance is largely premised on old banking models that do not adequately keep pace with the modern evolution of financial crime. Traditional rule-based monitoring systems are clearly inadequate to detect the increasingly sophisticated methods and technologically advanced strategies employed by criminals. Banks are burdened with false positives while most money laundering transactions remain unidentified, posing a significant threat to the integrity of banks and the financial system itself. Banks that do not meet their compliance obligations expose themselves to significant pecuniary losses and reputational damage.[143]

The FATF has highlighted the potential of innovative technologies such as AI and machine learning to make AML measures faster, cheaper, and more effective than current monitoring processes. While rule-based algorithms remain relevant, harnessing AI and machine learning holds great promise for increasing the accuracy

---

[138] FATF, *Opportunities and Challenges of New Technologies for AML/CTF*, 22.

[139] Deloitte and United Overseas Bank, 'The Case', 25; Fernandez, 'Artificial Intelligence', 2; FATF, *Opportunities and Challenges of New Technologies for AML/CTF*, 20.

[140] Kute et al, 'Deep Learning', 82313.

[141] Ouren Kuiper et al, 'Exploring Explainable AI in the Financial Sector: Perspectives of Banks and Supervisory Authorities' in Luis A Leiva et al (eds), *Artificial Intelligence and Machine Learning* (Cham: Springer, 2022) 105.

[142] Ibid, 105.

[143] Grint et al, *New Technologies and Anti-money Laundering Compliance: Financial Conduct Authority*.

of risk identification and heightening its efficiency due to the large analytical capacity of these processes. While these initiatives may be costly and risky to implement, they offer an excellent return on investment for banks that seek to strengthen their internal AML regime. The implementation of AI is increasingly recognised as the next phase in the fight against financial crime.

Due to the various regulatory and operational challenges that are likely to arise, banks should approach the adoption and implementation of AI with cautious optimism. They should ensure that sophisticated AI and machine learning models can be adequately understood and explained. To achieve optimal outcomes, these technologies should operate in conjunction with human analysis, particularly in areas of high risk. However, banks should be aware that the emphasis on collaboration between analysts, investigators, and compliance officers with regard to AI technology may introduce its own legal and ethical complications relating to privacy, liability, and various unintended consequences, such as customer discrimination.

In the increasingly complex environment of financial crime and AML regulation, banks should thoroughly consider the advantages and challenges presented by AI and machine learning as they move towards the transformation of risk assessment by leveraging AI to mitigate money laundering risks.

4

AI Opacity in the Financial Industry and How to Break It

Zofia Bednarz and Linda Przhedetsky[*]

4.1 INTRODUCTION

Automated Banks – the financial entities using ADM and AI – feed off the culture of secrecy that is pervasive and entrenched in automated processes across sectors from 'Big Tech' to finance to government agencies, allowing them to avoid scrutiny, accountability, and liability.[1] As Pasquale points out, 'finance industries profit by keeping us in the dark'.[2]

An integral part of the financial industry's business model is the use of risk scoring to profile consumers of financial services, for example in the form of credit scoring, which is a notoriously opaque process.[3] The use of non-transparent, almost 'invisible' surveillance processes and the harvesting of people's data is not new: financial firms have always been concerned with collecting, aggregating, and combining data for the purposes of predicting the value of their customers through risk scoring.[4] Automation[5] introduces a new level of opacity in the financial industry, for example through the creation of AI models for which explanations are not provided – either deliberately, or due to technical explainability challenges.[6]

[*] The authors would like to thank Arundhati Suma Ajith for excellent research assistance.
[1] Frank Pasquale, *The Black Box Society* (Cambridge: Harvard University Press, 2015) 187.
[2] Ibid.
[3] Janine S Hiller and Lindsay Sain Jones, 'Who's Keeping Score?: Oversight of Changing Consumer Credit Infrastructure' (2022) 59(1) *American Business Law Journal* 61, 104.
[4] Pernille Hohnen, Michael Ulfstjerne, and Mathias Sosnowski Krabbe, 'Assessing Creditworthiness in the Age of Big Data: A Comparative Study of Credit Score Systems in Denmark and the US' (2021) 5(1) *Journal of Extreme Anthropology* 29, 34–35.
[5] Solon Barocas and Andrew D Selbst, 'Big Data's Disparate Impact' (2016) 104(3) *California Law Review* 671, 673–77.
[6] Alejandro Barredo Arrieta et al, 'Explainable Artificial Intelligence (XAI): Concepts, Taxonomies, Opportunities and Challenges toward Responsible AI' (2020) 58 *Information Fusion* 82, 99–101.

In this chapter we argue that the rise of AI and ADM tools contributes to opacity within the financial services sector, including through the intentional use of the legal system as a 'shield' to prevent scrutiny and blur accountability for harms suffered by consumers of financial services. A wealth of literature critiques the status quo, showing that consumers are disadvantaged by information asymmetries,[7] complicated consent agreements,[8] information overload,[9] and other tactics that leave consumers clueless if, when, and how they have been subject to automated systems. If consumers seek to access a product or service, it is often a requirement that they be analysed and assessed using an automated tool, for example, one that determines a credit score.[10] The potential harms are interlinked and range from financial exclusion to digital manipulation to targeting of vulnerable consumers and privacy invasions.[11] In our analysis we are mostly concerned with discrimination as an example of such harm,[12] as it provides a useful illustration of problems enabled by opacity, such as significant difficulty in determining if unfair discrimination has occurred at all, understanding the reasons for the decision affecting the person or group, and accessing redress.

The rules we examine will differ among jurisdictions, and our aim is not to provide a comprehensive comparative analysis of all laws that provide potential protections against scrutiny and increase the opacity of ADM-related processes of Automated Banks. We are interested in exploring certain overarching tendencies, using examples from various legal systems, and showing how financial firms may take advantage of the complex legal and regulatory frameworks applicable to their operations in relation to the use of AI and ADM tools.

As the use of AI and ADM continues to grow in financial services markets, consumers are faced with the additional challenge of knowing about, and considering how their ever-expanding digital footprint may be used by financial institutions. The more data exists about a person, the better their credit score (of course within certain limits, such as paying off debts on time).[13] The exact same mechanism may

---

7   Peter Cartwright, 'Understanding and Protecting Vulnerable Financial Consumers' (2014) 38 (2) *Journal of Consumer Policy* 119, 121–23.
8   Frederik Borgesius, 'Consent to Behavioural Targeting in European Law: What Are the Policy Implications of Insights from Behavioural Economics?' (Conference Paper for Privacy Law Scholars Conference, Berkeley, CA, 6–7 June 2013).
9   Petra Persson, 'Attention Manipulation and Information Overload' (2018) 2(1) *Behavioural Public Policy* 78.
10 Andrew Grant and Luke Deer, 'Consumer Marketplace Lending in Australia: Credit Scores and Loan Funding Success' (2020) 45(4) *Australian Journal of Management* 607.
11 Zofia Bednarz and Kayleen Manwaring, 'Risky Business: Legal Implications of Emerging Technologies Affecting Consumers of Financial Services' in Dariusz Szostek and Mariusz Zalucki (eds), *Internet and New Technologies Law: Perspectives and Challenges* (Baden: Nomos, 2021) 59–74.
12 Aaron Klein, Brookings Institution, *Reducing Bias in AI-Based Financial Services* (Report, 10 July 2020) <www.brookings.edu/research/reducing-bias-in-ai-based-financial-services/>.
13 Hohnen et al, 'Assessing Creditworthiness', 36.

underpin 'open banking' schemes: consumers who do not have sufficient data – often vulnerable people, such as domestic violence victims, new immigrants, or Indigenous people – cannot share their data with financial entities, may be excluded from accessing some products or offered higher prices, even if their actual risk is low.[14]

In Australia, consumers have claimed that they have been denied loans due to their use of takeaway food services and digital media subscriptions.[15] Credit rating agencies such as Experian explicitly state that they access data sources that reflect consumers' use of new financial products, including 'Buy Now Pay Later' schemes.[16] As more advanced data collection, analysis, and manipulation technologies continue to be developed, there is potential for new categories of data to emerge. Already, companies can draw surprising inferences from big data. For example, studies have shown that seemingly trivial Facebook data can, with reasonable accuracy, predict a range of attributes that have not been disclosed by users: in one study, liking the 'Hello Kitty' page correlated strongly with a user having '[d]emocratic political views and to be of African-American origin, predominantly Christian, and slightly below average age'.[17]

Unless deliberate efforts are made, both in the selection of data sets and the design and auditing of AMD tools, inferences and proxy data will continue to produce correlations that may result in discriminatory treatment.[18]

This chapter proceeds as follows. We begin Section 4.2 with discussion of rules that allow corporate secrecy around AI models and their data sources to exist, focusing on three examples of such rules. We discuss the opacity of credit scoring processes and the limited explanations that consumers can expect in relation to a financial decision made about them (Section 4.2.1), trade secrecy laws (Section 4.2.2), and data protection rules which do not protect de-identified or anonymised information (Section 4.2.3). In Section 4.3 we analyse frameworks that incentivise the use of ADM tools by the financial industry, thus providing another 'protective

[14] Zofia Bednarz, Chris Dolman, and Kimberlee Weatherall, 'Insurance Underwriting in an Open Data Era – Opportunities, Challenges and Uncertainties' (Actuaries Institute 2022 Summit, 2–4 May 2022) 10–12 <https://actuaries.logicaldoc.cloud/download-ticket?ticketId= 09c77750-aa90-4ba9-835e-280ae347487b>.

[15] Su-Lin Tan, 'Uber Eats, Afterpay and Netflix Accounts Could Hurt Your Home Loan Application' (5 December 2018) *Australian Financial Review* <www.afr.com/property/uber-eats-afterpay-and-netflix-accounts-could-hurt-your-home-loan-application-20181128-h18ghz>.

[16] 'Credit Bureau', *Experian Australia* (Web Page) <www.experian.com.au/business/solutions/credit-services/credit-bureau>. 'Secured from critical sectors of the Australian credit industry as well as from niche areas such as Specialty Finance data, short-term loans (including Buy Now Pay Later) and consumer leasing, enabling a more complete view of your customers'.

[17] Michal Kosinski, David Stillwell, and Thore Graepel, 'Private Traits and Attributes Are Predictable from Digital Records of Human Behavior' (2013) 110 *Proceedings of the National Academy of Sciences of the United States of America* 5805.

[18] Anya ER Prince and Daniel Schwarcz, 'Proxy Discrimination in the Age of Artificial Intelligence and Big Data' (2020) 105(3) *Iowa Law Review* 1257, 1273–76.

layer' for Automated Banks, again discussing two examples: financial product governance regimes (Section 4.3.1) and 'open banking' rules (Section 4.3.2). The focus of Section 4.4 is on potential solutions. We argue it is not possible for corporate secrecy and consumer rights to coexist, and provide an overview of potential regulatory interventions, focusing on preventing Automated Banks from using harmful AI systems (Section 4.4.1), aiding consumers understand when ADM is used (Section 4.4.2), and facilitating regulator monitoring and enforcement (Section 4.4.3). The chapter concludes with Section 4.5.

4.2 RULES THAT ALLOW CORPORATE SECRECY TO EXIST

4.2.1 *Opacity of Credit Scoring and the (Lack of) Explanation of Financial Decisions*

Despite their widespread use in the financial industry, credit scores are difficult for consumers to understand or interpret. A person's credit risk has traditionally been calculated based on 'three C's': collateral, capacity, and character.[19] Due to the rise of AI and ADM tools in the financial industry, the 'three C's' are increasingly being supplemented and replaced by diverse categories of data.[20] An interesting example can be found through FICO scores, which are arguably the first large-scale process in which automated computer models replaced human decision-making.[21] FICO, one of the best-known credit scoring companies,[22] explains that their scores are calculated according to five categories: 'payment history (35%), amounts owed (30%), length of credit history (15%), new credit (10%), and credit mix (10%)'.[23] These percentage scores are determined by the company to give consumers an understanding of how different pieces of information are weighted in the calculation of a score, and the ratios identified within FICO scores will not necessarily reflect the weightings used by other scoring companies. Further, while FICO provides a degree of transparency, the ways in which a category such as 'payment history' is calculated remains opaque: consumers are not privy to what is considered a 'good' or a 'bad' behaviour, as represented by data points in their transaction records.[24]

Globally, many credit scoring systems (both public and private) produce three-digit numbers within a specified range to determine a consumer's creditworthiness. For example, privately operated Equifax and Trans Union Empirica score

[19] Eric Rosenblatt, *Credit Data and Scoring: The First Triumph of Big Data and Big Algorithms* (Cambridge: Elsevier Academic Press, 2020) 1.
[20] Hiller and Jones, 'Who's Keeping Score?', 68–77.
[21] Rosenblatt, *Credit Data and Scoring*, 7.
[22] Hohnen et al, 'Assessing Creditworthiness', 36.
[23] 'What's in My FICO® Scores?', *MyFico* (Web Page) <www.myfico.com/credit-education/whats-in-your-credit-score>.
[24] Consumer Financial Protection Bureau, 'The Impact of Differences between Consumer- and Creditor-Purchased Credit Scores' (SSRN Scholarly Paper No 3790609, 19 July 2011) 19.

consumers in Canada between 300 and 900,[25] whereas credit bureaus in Brazil score consumers between 1 and 1,000.[26] In an Australian context, scores range between 0 and 1,000, or 1,200, depending on the credit reporting agency.[27] By contrast, other jurisdictions use letter-based ratings, such as Singapore's HH to AA scale which corresponds with a score range of 1,000–2,000,[28] or blacklists, such as Sweden's payment default records.[29]

Credit scoring, it turns out, is surprisingly accurate in predicting financial break-downs or future loan delinquency,[30] but the way different data points are combined by models is not something even the model designer can understand using just intuition.[31] Automated scoring processes become even more complex as credit scoring companies increasingly rely on alternative data sources to assess consumers' creditworthiness, including 'predictions about a consumer's friends, neighbors, and people with similar interests, income levels, and backgrounds'.[32] And a person's credit score is just one of the elements lenders, Automated Banks, feed into their models to determine a consumer's risk score. It has been reported that college grades, and the time of day an individual applies for a loan have been used to determine a person's access to credit.[33] These types of data constitute 'extrinsic data' sources, which consumers are unknowingly sharing.[34]

The use of alternative data sources is purported as a way of expanding consumers' access to credit in instances where there is a lack of quality data (such as previous loan repayment history) to support the underwriting of consumers' loan.[35] Applicants are often faced with a 'Catch-22 dilemma: to qualify for a loan, one

---

[25] 'What Is a Good Credit Score?', *Equifax Canada* (Web Page) <www.consumer.equifax.ca/personal/education/credit-score/what-is-a-good-credit-score>; 'FICO Score 10, Most Predictive Credit Score in Canadian Market', *FICO Blog* (Web Page) <www.fico.com/blogs/fico-score-10-most-predictive-credit-score-canadian-market>.

[26] Frederic de Mariz, 'Using Data for Financial Inclusion: The Case of Credit Bureaus in Brazil' (SSRN Paper, *Journal of International Affairs*, 28 April 2020).

[27] 'Credit Scores and Credit Reports', *Moneysmart* (Web Page) <https://moneysmart.gov.au/managing-debt/credit-scores-and-credit-reports>.

[28] 'Credit Score', *Credit Bureau* (Web Page) <www.creditbureau.com.sg/credit-score.html>.

[29] 'Payment Default Records', *Swedish Authority for Privacy Protection* (Web Page) <www.imy.se/en/individuals/credit-information/payment-default-records/>.

[30] Or even car accidents one will have in the future, Rosenblatt, *Credit Data and Scoring*, 6.

[31] Ibid, 7.

[32] Mikella Hurley and Julius Adebayo, 'Credit Scoring in the Era of Big Data' (2016) 18 *Yale Journal of Law and Technology* 148, 151.

[33] Hiller and Jones, 'Who's Keeping Score?', 68–77.

[34] Zofia Bednarz and Kayleen Manwaring, 'Hidden Depths: The Effects of Extrinsic Data Collection on Consumer Insurance Contracts' (2022) 45(July) *Computer Law and Security Review: The International Journal of Technology Law and Practice* 105667.

[35] 'Examining the use of alternative data in underwriting and credit scoring to expand access to credit' (Hearing before the Task Force on Financial Technology of the Committee on Financial Services, U.S. House of Representatives, One Hundred Sixteenth Congress, First Session July 25, 2019) <www.congress.gov/116/chrg/CHRG-116hhrg40160/CHRG-116hhrg40160.pdf>.

must have a credit history, but to have a credit history one must have had loans'.[36] This shows how ADM tools offer more than just new means to analyse greater than ever quantities of data: they also offer a convenient excuse for Automated Banks to effectively use more data.

Of course, increasing reliance on automated risk scoring is not the origin of unlawful discrimination in financial contexts. However, it is certainly not eliminating discriminatory practices either: greater availability of more granular data, even when facially neutral, leads to reinforcing of existing inequalities.[37] Automated Banks have been also shown to use alternative data to target more vulnerable consumers, who they were not able to reach or identify when only using traditional data on existing customers.[38] The quality change that AI tools promise to bring is to 'make the data talk': all data is credit data, if we have the right automated tools to analyse them.[39]

Collection, aggregation, and use of such high volumes of data, including 'extrinsic data', also make it more difficult, if not impossible, for consumers to challenge financial decisions affecting them. While laws relating to consumer lending (or consumer financial products in general) in most jurisdictions provide that some form of explanation of a financial decision needs to be made available to consumers,[40] these rules will rarely be useful in the context of ADM and AI tools used in processes such as risk scoring.

This is because AI tools operate on big data. Too many features of a person are potentially taken into account for any feedback to be meaningful. The fact that risk

---

[36] Hohnen et al, 'Assessing Creditworthiness', 38.

[37] Hiller and Jones, 'Who's Keeping Score?', 87–96; Bartlett et al, 'Consumer-Lending Discrimination in the FinTech Era' (2022) 143(1) *Journal of Financial Economics* 30.

[38] Hiller and Jones, 'Who's Keeping Score?', 92–93.

[39] Quentin Hardy, 'Just the Facts: Yes, All of Them' (25 March 2012) *The New York Times* <https://archive.nytimes.com/query.nytimes.com/gst/fullpage-9A0CE7DD153CF936A15750C0A9649D8B63.html>.

[40] See for example: US: Equal Credit Opportunity Act (ECOA) s 701, which requires a creditor to notify a credit applicant when it has taken adverse action against the applicant; Fair Credit Reporting Act (FCRA) s 615(a), which requires a person to provide a notice when the person takes an adverse action against a consumer based in whole or in part on information in a consumer report; Australia: Privacy Act 1988 (Cth) s 21P, stating that if a credit provider refuses an application for consumer credit made in Australia, the credit provider must give the individual written notice that the refusal is based wholly or partly on credit eligibility information about one or more of the persons who applied; Privacy (Credit Reporting) Code 2014 (Version 2.3) para 16.3 requiring a credit provider who obtains credit reporting information about an individual from a credit reporting bureau and within 90 days of obtaining that information, refuses a consumer credit application, to provide a written notice of refusal, informing the individual of a number of matters, including their right to access credit reporting information held about them, that the refusal may have been based on the credit reporting information, and the process for correcting the information; UK: lenders are not required to provide reasons for loan refusal, even when asked by a consumer, but s 157 Consumer Credit Act 1974 requires them to indicate which credit reporting agency (if any) they used in assessing the application.

scores and lending decisions are personalised make it even more complicated for consumers to compare their offer with anyone else's. This can be illustrated by the case of Apple credit card,[41] which has shown the complexity of investigation necessary for people to be able to access potential redress: when applying for personalised financial products, consumers cannot immediately know what features are being taken into account by financial firms assessing their risk, and subsequent investigation by regulators or courts may be required.[42] The lack of a right to meaningful explanation of credit scores and lending decisions based on the scores makes consumers facing Automated Banks and the automated credit scoring system quite literally powerless.[43]

4.2.2 *Trade Secrets and ADM Tools in Credit Scoring*

The opacity of credit scoring, or risk scoring more generally, and other automated assessment of clients that Automated Banks engage in, is enabled by ADM tools which 'are highly valuable, closely guarded intellectual property'.[44] Complementing the limited duty to provide explanation of financial decisions to consumers, trade secrets laws allow for even more effective shielding of the ADM tools from scrutiny, including regulators' and researchers' scrutiny.

While trade secrets rules differ between jurisdictions, the origin and general principles that underpin these rules are common across all the legal systems: trade secrets evolved as a mechanism to protect diverse pieces of commercial information, such as formulas, devices, or patterns from competitors.[45] These rules fill the gap where classic intellectual property law, such as copyright and patent law, fails – and it notably fails in relation to AI systems, since algorithms are specifically excluded from its protection.[46] Recent legal developments, for example the European Union

---

[41] Neil Vidgor, 'Apple Card Investigated after Gender Discrimination Complaints' (10 November 2019) *The New York Times* <www.nytimes.com/2019/11/10/business/Apple-creditcard-investigation.html>.

[42] See e.g. Corrado Rizzi, 'Class Action Alleges Wells Fargo Mortgage Lending Practices Discriminate against Black Borrowers' (21 February 2022) *ClassAction.org* <www.classaction .org/news/class-action-alleges-wells-fargo-mortgage-lending-practices-discriminate-against-black-borrowers> or Kelly Mehorter, 'State Farm Discriminates against Black Homeowners When Processing Insurance Claims, Class Action Alleges' (20 December 2022) *ClassAction. org* <www.classaction.org/news/state-farm-discriminates-against-black-homeowners-when-pro cessing-insurance-claims-class-action-alleges>; Hiller and Jones, 'Who's Keeping Score?', 83–84.

[43] Hiller and Jones, 'Who's Keeping Score?', 65.

[44] Consumer Financial Protection Bureau, 'The Impact of Differences between Consumer- and Creditor-Purchased Credit Scores' (SSRN Scholarly Paper No 3790609, 19 July 2011) 5.

[45] Brenda Reddix-Smalls, 'Credit Scoring and Trade Secrecy' (2012) 12 *UC Davis Business Law Journal* 87, 115.

[46] Katarina Foss-Solbrekk, 'Three Routes to Protecting AI Systems and Their Algorithms under IP Law: The Good, the Bad and the Ugly' (2021) 16(3) *Journal of Intellectual Property Law & Practice* 247, 248.

Trade Secrets Directive,[47] or the US Supreme Court case of *Alice Corp. v CLS Bank*,[48] mean that to protect their proprietary technologies, companies are now turning to trade secrets.[49] In practice, this greatly reduces the transparency of the ADM tools used: if these cannot be protected through patent rights, they need to be kept secret.[50]

The application of trade secrets rules leads to a situation in which financial entities, for example lenders or insurers, who apply third party automated tools to assess creditworthiness of their prospective clients might not be able to access the models and data they use. Using third party tools is a common practice, and the proprietary nature of the tools and data used to develop and train the models will mean financial entities using these tools may be forced to rely on the supplier's specifications in relation to their fairness as they may not be able to access the code themselves.[51]

Secrecy of ADM tools of course has implications for end users, who will be prevented from challenging credit models, and is also a barrier for enforcement and research.[52] Trade secret protections apply not only to risk scoring models, but often extend also to data sets and inferences generated from information provided by individuals.[53] Commercial entities openly admit they 'invest significant amounts of time, money and resources' to draw inferences about individuals 'using [. . .] proprietary data analysis tools', a process 'only made possible because of the [companies'] technical capabilities and value add'.[54] This, they argue, makes the data sets containing inferred information a company's intellectual property.[55]

The application of trade secrets rules to credit scoring in a way that affects the transparency of the financial system is not exactly new: '[t]he trade secrecy surrounding credit scoring risk models, and the misuse of the models coupled with the lack of governmental control concerning their use, contributed to a financial industry wide recession (2007–2008)'.[56]

---

[47] *Directive (EU) 2016/943 of the European Parliament and of the Council of 8 June 2016 on the protection of undisclosed know-how and business information (trade secrets) against their unlawful acquisition, use and disclosure* [2016] OJ L 157/1.

[48] 573 U.S. 208 (2014).

[49] Foss-Solbrekk, 'Three Routes to Protecting AI Systems and Their Algorithms under IP Law', 248; Meghan J Ryan, 'Secret Algorithms, IP Rights and the Public Interest' (2020) 21(1) *Nevada Law Journal* 61, 62–63.

[50] Ryan, 'Secret Algorithms', 62–63.

[51] Hiller and Jones, 'Who's Keeping Score?', 83.

[52] Reddix-Smalls, 'Credit Scoring and Trade Secrecy', 117; see also Bartlett et al, 'Consumer-Lending Discrimination in the FinTech Era'.

[53] Gintarė Surblytė-Namavičienė, *Competition and Regulation in the Data Economy: Does Artificial Intelligence Demand a New Balance?* (Cheltenham: Edward Elgar, 2020).

[54] Facebook, 'Submission to the Australian Privacy Act Review Issues Paper' (6 December 2020) 25 <www.ag.gov.au/sites/default/files/2021–02/facebook.PDF>.

[55] Ibid.

[56] Reddix-Smalls, 'Credit Scoring and Trade Secrecy', 89.

In addition to trade secrets laws, a *sui generis* protection of source code of algorithms is being introduced in international trade law through free trade agreements,[57] which limit governments from mandating access to the source code. The members of the World Trade Organization (WTO) are currently negotiating a new E-commerce trade agreement, which may potentially include a prohibition on government-mandated access to software source code.[58] WTO members, including Canada, the EU, Japan, South Korea, Singapore, Ukraine, and the United States support such a prohibition,[59] which in practice will mean a limited ability for states to adopt laws that would require independent audits of AI and ADM systems.[60] It is argued that adoption of the WTO trade agreement could thwart the adoption of the EU's AI Act,[61] demonstrating how free trade agreements can impose another layer of rules enhancing the opacity of AI and ADM tools.

4.2.3 *'Depersonalising' Information to Avoid Data and Privacy Protection Laws: Anonymisation, De-identification, and Inferences*

Automated Banks' opacity is enabled by the express exclusion of 'anonymised' or 'de-identified' data from the scope of data and privacy protection laws such as the GDPR.[62] In its Recital 26, the GDPR defines anonymised information as not relating to 'an identified or identifiable natural person' or as 'data rendered anonymous in such a manner that the data subject is not or no longer identifiable'. This allows firms to engage in various data practices, which purport to use anonymised data.[63] They argue they do not collect or process 'personal information', thus avoiding the application of the rules, and regulatory enforcement.[64] Also, consumers to whom privacy policies are addressed believe that practices focusing on information that does not directly identify them have no impact on their privacy.[65] This

---

[57] Kristina Irion, 'Algorithms Off-Limits?' (FAccT'22, 21–24 June 2022, Seoul) 1561 <https://dl .acm.org/doi/pdf/10.1145/3531146.3533212>.

[58] Ibid.

[59] Ibid.

[60] Ibid, 1562.

[61] Proposal for a Regulation of the European Parliament and of the Council Laying Down Harmonised Rules on Artificial Intelligence (AI Act) and Amending Certain Union Legislative Acts [2021] OJ COM 206.

[62] *Regulation (EU) 2016/679 of the European Parliament and of the Council of 27 April 2016 on the protection of natural persons with regard to the processing of personal data and on the free movement of such data, and repealing Directive 95/46/EC (GDPR)* [2016] OJ L 119/1, Recital (26); *Australian Privacy Act 1988* (Cth) s 6.

[63] Katharine Kemp, 'A Rose by Any Other Unique Identifier: Regulating Consumer Data Tracking and Anonymisation Claims' (August 2022) *Competition Policy International TechReg Chronicle* 22.

[64] Ibid.

[65] Ibid, 23.

in turn may mean privacy policies are misrepresenting data practices to consumers, which could potentially invalidate their consent.[66]

There is an inherent inconsistency between privacy and data protection rules and the uses and benefits that ADM tools using big data analytics promise. Principles of purpose limitation and data minimisation[67] require entities to delimit, quite strictly and in advance, how the data collected are going to be used, and prevent them from collecting and processing more data than necessary for that specific purpose. However, this is not how big data analytics, which fuels ADM and AI models, works.[68] Big data means that 'all data is credit data', incentivising the Automated Banks to collect as much data as possible, for any possible future purpose, potentially not known yet.[69] The exclusion of anonymised or de-identified data from the scope of the protection frameworks opens doors for firms to take advantage of enhanced analytics powered by new technologies. The contentious question is at which point information becomes, or ceases to be, personal information. If firms purchase, collect, and aggregate streams of data, producing inferences allowing them to describe someone in great detail, including their age, preferences, dislikes, size of clothes they wear and health issues they suffer from, their household size and income level,[70] but do not link this profile to the person's name, email, physical address, or IP address – would it be personal information? Such a profile, it could be argued, represents a theoretical, 'model' person or consumer, built for commercial purposes through aggregation of demographic and other information available.[71]

De-identified data may still allow a financial firm to achieve more detailed segmentation and profiling of their clients. There are risks of harms in terms of 'loss of privacy, equality, fairness and due process' even when anonymised data is used.[72] Consumers are left unprotected against profiling harms due to such 'narrow interpretation of the right to privacy as the right to anonymity'.[73]

---

[66] Ibid, 27–29.

[67] See e.g. Art. 5 GDPR.

[68] Tal Zarsky, 'Incompatible: The GDPR in the Age of Big Data' (2017) 4(2) *Seton Hall Law Review* 995, 1004–18.

[69] Ibid, 1010.

[70] Wolfe Christl and Sarah Spiekermann, *Networks of Control: A Report on Corporate Surveillance, Digital Tracking, Big Data & Privacy* (Vienna: Facultas, 2016); Forbrukerrådet (Norwegian Consumer Council), *Out of Control: How Consumers Are Exploited by the Online Advertising Industry* (Report, 14 January 2020) 19–22.

[71] Ibid.

[72] Mireille Hildebrandt, 'Profiling and the Identity of the European Citizen' in Mireille Hildebrandt and Serge Gutwirth (eds), *Profiling the European Citizen: Cross-Disciplinary Perspectives* (New York: Springer, 2008) 305–9; Sandra Wachter, 'Data Protection in the Age of Big Data' (2019) 2 *Nature Electronics* 6, 7.

[73] N Chami et al, 'Data Subjects in the Femtech Matrix: A Feminist Political Economy Analysis of the Global Menstruapps Market' (Issue Paper 6, Feminist Digital Justice, December 2021) 4.

There is also discussion as to the status of inferences under data and privacy protection laws. Credit scoring processes are often based on inferences, where a model predicts someone's features (and ultimately their riskiness or value as a client) on the basis of other characteristics that they share with others deemed risky by the model.[74] AI models may thus penalise individuals for 'shopping at low-end stores', membership in particular communities or families, and affiliations with certain political, religious, and other groups.[75] While AI-powered predictions about people's characteristics are often claimed to be more accurate than those made by humans,[76] they may also be inaccurate.[77] The question is if such inferences are considered personal information protected by privacy and data laws.

Entities using consumers' data, such as technology companies, are resisting against expressly including inferred information in the scope of data and privacy protections. For example, Facebook openly admitted that '[t]o protect the investment made in generating inferred information and to protect the inferred information from inappropriate interference, inferred information should not be subject to all of the same aspects of the [Australian Privacy Act] as personal information'.[78] The 'inappropriate interference' they mention refers to extending data correction and erasure rights to inferred information.

Second, there is an inherent clash between the operation of privacy and data protection rules and the inference processes AI tools are capable of carrying out. Any information, including sensitive information, may be effectively used by an ADM system, even though it only materialises as an internal encoding of the model and is not recorded in a human understandable way. The lack of explicit inclusion of inferred information, and its use, within the privacy and data protection frameworks provides another layer of opacity shielding financial firms (as well as other entities) from scrutiny of their ADM tools.

When information is 'depersonalised' in some way: de-identified on purpose through the elimination of strictly personal identifiers,[79] through use of anonymous 'demographic' data, through 'pseudonymisation' practices, or because it is inferred from data held (either personal or already de-identified), the result is the same – privacy and data protection rules do not apply. The firms take advantage of that exclusion, sometimes balancing on the thin line between legal and illegal data processing, making their data practices non-transparent to avoid scrutiny by consumers and regulators.

---

[74] Hurley and Adebayo, 'Credit Scoring in the Era of Big Data', 183.
[75] Ibid.
[76] Wu Youyou, Michal Kosinski, and David Stillwell, 'Computer-Based Personality Judgments Are More Accurate than Those Made by Humans' (Research Paper, *Proceedings of the National Academy of Sciences* 112(4): 201418680, 12 January 2015).
[77] Hurley and Adebayo, 'Credit Scoring in the Era of Big Data', 183.
[78] Facebook, 'Submission to the Australian Privacy Act Review Issues Paper', 25–26.
[79] CM O'Keefe et al, *The De-Identification Decision-Making Framework* (CSIRO Reports EP173122 and EP175702, 18 September 2017), ix.

As a US judge in a recent ruling put it: '[i]t is well established that there is an undeniable link between race and poverty, and any policy that discriminates based on credit worthiness correspondingly results in a disparate impact on communities of color'.[80] The data used in large-scale AI and ADM models is often de-identified or anonymised, but it inherently mirrors historical inequalities and biases, thus allowing the Automated Banks to claim impartiality and avoid responsibility for the unfairness of data used.

The reason why privacy and data protection rules lack clear consideration of certain data practices and processes enabled by AI may be due to these tools and processes being relatively new and poorly understood phenomena.[81] This status quo is however very convenient for the companies, who will often raise the argument that 'innovation' will suffer if more stringent regulation is introduced.[82]

4.3 RULES THAT INCENTIVISE THE USE OF ADM TOOLS BY FINANCIAL ENTITIES

In addition to offering direct pathways allowing Automated Banks to evade scrutiny of their AI and ADM models, legal systems and markets in the developed world have also evolved to incentivise the use of automated technology by financial entities. In fact, the use of ADM and AI tools is encouraged, or sometimes even mandated,[83] by legal and regulatory frameworks. After all, the fact that they are *told to* either use the technology, or to achieve outcomes that can effectively only be reached with the application of the tools in question, provides a basis for a very convenient excuse. Though this is mainly an unintended effect of the rules, it should not be ignored.

In this section, we discuss two examples of rules that increase the secrecy of AI or ADM tools used in the context of risk scoring: financial products governance rules and 'open banking' regimes.

---

[80] Office of the Insurance Commissioner Washington State, *Final Order on Court's Credit Scoring Decision; Kreidler Will Not Appeal* (Media Release, 29 August 2022) <www.insurance.wa.gov/news/final-order-courts-credit-scoring-decision-kreidler-will-not-appeal>.

[81] For example, Prof Sandra Wachter has pointed out the GDPR is based on an outdated concept of a 'nosey neighbour': Sanda Wachter, 'AI's Legal and Ethical Implications' *Twimlai* (Podcast, 23 September 2021) <https://twimlai.com/podcast/twimlai/ais-legal-ethical-implications-sandra-wachter/>.

[82] Microsoft Australia, 'Microsoft Submission to Review of the Privacy Act 1988' (December 2020) 2–3 <www.ag.gov.au/sites/default/files/2021–02/microsoft-australia.PDF>; Facebook, 'Submission to the Australian Privacy Act Review Issues Paper', 25.

[83] See Zofia Bednarz, 'There and Back Again: How Target Market Determination Obligations for Financial Products May Incentivise Consumer Data Profiling' (2022) 36(2) *International Review of Law, Computers & Technology* 138.

4.3.1 *Financial Products Governance Rules*

Financial firms have always been concerned with collecting and using data about their consumers, to differentiate between more and less valuable customers. For example, insurance firms, even before AI profiling tools were invented (or at least before they were applied at a greater scale) were known to engage in practices referred to as 'cherry-picking' and 'lemon-dropping', setting up firms' offices at higher floors in buildings with no lifts, so that it would be harder for disabled (potential) clients to reach them.[84] There is a risk that the widespread data profiling and use of AI tools may exacerbate issues relating to consumers' access to financial products and services. AI tools may introduce new or replicate historical biases present in data,[85] doing so more efficiently, in a way that is more difficult to discover, and at a greater scale than was possible previously.[86]

An additional disadvantage resulting from opaque risk scoring systems is that consumers may miss out on the opportunity to improve their score (for example, through the provision of counterfactual explanations, or the use of techniques including 'nearby possible worlds').[87] In instances where potential customers who would have no trouble paying back loans are given low risk scores, two key issues arise: first, the bank misses out on valuable customers, and second, there is a risk that these customers' rejections, if used as input data to train the selection algorithm, will reinforce existing biases.[88]

Guaranteeing suitability of financial services is a notoriously complicated task for policymakers and regulators. With disclosure duties alone proving largely unsuccessful in addressing the issue of consumers being offered financial products that are unfit for purpose, policymakers in a number of jurisdictions, such as the EU and its Member States, the United Kingdom, Hong Kong, Australia, and Singapore, have started turning to product governance regimes.[89] An important component of these

---

[84] Marshall Allen, 'Health Insurers Are Vacuuming Up Details about You: And It Could Raise Your Rates' (17 July 2018) *NPR* <www.npr.org/sections/health-shots/2018/07/17/629441555/healthinsurers-are-vacuuming-up-details-about-you-and-it-could-raise-your-rates>.

[85] Australian Human Rights Commission, *Using Artificial Intelligence to Make Decisions: Addressing the Problem of Algorithmic Bias* (Technical Paper, November 2022) 34–44.

[86] E Martinez and L Kirchner, 'Denied: The Secret Bias Hidden in Mortgage-Approval Algorithms' (25 August 2021) *The Markup*.

[87] Sandra Wachter, Brent Mittelstadt, and Chris Russell, 'Counterfactual Explanations without Opening the Black Box: Automated Decisions and the GDPR' (2018) 31(2) *Harvard Journal of Law & Technology* 841, 848.

[88] European Union Agency for Fundamental Rights, *Bias in Algorithms: Artificial Intelligence and Discrimination* (Report, 2022) 8–9 <https://fra.europa.eu/sites/default/files/fra_uploads/fra-2022-bias-in-algorithms_en.pdf>.

[89] Hannah Cassidy et al, 'Product Intervention Powers and Design and Distribution Obligations: A Cross-Border Financial Services Perspective' (Guide, Herbert Smith Freehills, 11 June 2019) <www.herbertsmithfreehills.com/latest-thinking/product-intervention-powers-and-design-and-distribution-obligations-in-fs>.

financial product governance regimes is an obligation placed on financial firms, which issue and distribute financial products, to ensure their products are fitness-for-purpose and to adopt a consumer-centric approach in design and distribution of the products. In particular, a number of jurisdictions require financial firms to delimit the target market for their financial products directed at retail customers, and ensure the distribution of the products within this target market. Such target market is a group of consumers of a certain financial product who are defined by some general characteristics.[90]

Guides issued by regulators, such as the European Securities and Markets Authority[91] and the Australian Securities and Investment Commission,[92] indicate which consumers' characteristics are to be taken into account by financial firms. The consumers for whom the product is intended are to be identified according to their 'likely objectives, financial situation, and needs',[93] or five 'categories': the type of client, their knowledge and experience, financial situation, risk tolerance, and objective and needs.[94] For issuers or manufacturers of financial products these considerations are mostly theoretical: as they might not have direct contact with clients, they need to prepare a *potential* target market, aiming at *theoretical* consumers and their *likely* needs and characteristics.[95] Both issuers and distributors need to take reasonable steps to ensure that products are distributed within the target market, which then translates to the identification of real consumers with specific needs and characteristics that should be compatible with the potential target markets identified. Distributors have to hold sufficient information about their end clients to be able to assess if they can be included in the target market,[96] including:

– indicators about the likely circumstances of the consumer or a class of consumers (e.g. concession card status, income, employment status);

– reasonable inferences about the likely circumstances of the consumer or a class of consumers (e.g. for insurance, information inferred from the postcode of the consumer's residential address); or

---

[90] Martin Hobza and Aneta Vondrackova, 'Target Market under MiFID II: the Distributor's Perspective' (2019) 14 *Capital Markets Law Journal* 518, 529.

[91] European Securities and Markets Authority (ESMA), 'Guidelines on MiFID II Product Governance Requirements' (ESMA35-43-620, 5 February 2018).

[92] Australian Securities and Investment Commission (ASIC), 'Regulatory Guide 274: Product Design and Distribution Obligations' (December 2020).

[93] ASIC, 'Regulatory Guide 274', para 274.6.

[94] ESMA, 'Guidelines on MiFID II Product Governance Requirements', 34–35.

[95] ESMA, 'Final Report: Guidelines on MiFID II Product Governance Requirements' (ESMA35-43-620, 2 June 2017) 34, para 17.

[96] 'The MiFID II Review – Product Governance: How to Assess Target Market' *Ashurst* (Financial Regulation Briefing, 3 October 2016) <www.ashurst.com/en/news-and-insights/legal-updates/mifid-12-mifid-ii-product-governance-how-to-assess-target-market/#:~:text=Regular%20review%20by%20the%20manufacturer,how%20to%20get%20that%20information>.

– data that the distributor may already hold about the consumer or similar consumers, or results derived from analyses of that data (e.g. analysis undertaken by the distributor of common characteristics of consumers who have purchased a product).[97]

Financial products governance frameworks invite financial firms to collect data on consumers' vulnerabilities. For example in Australia, financial firms need to consider vulnerabilities consumers may have, such as those resulting from 'personal or social characteristics that can affect a person's ability to manage financial interactions',[98] as well as those brought about by 'specific life events or temporary difficulties',[99] in addition to vulnerabilities stemming from the product design or market actions.

The rationale of product governance rules is to protect financial consumers, including vulnerable consumers,[100] yet the same vulnerable consumers may be disproportionately affected by data profiling, thus inhibiting their access to financial products. Financial law is actively asking firms to collect even more data about their current, prospective, and past customers, as well as the general public. It provides more than a convenient excuse to carry out digital profiling and collect data for even more precise risk scoring – it actually *mandates* this.

4.3.2 *How 'Open Banking' Increases Opacity*

Use of AI and ADM tools, together with ever-increasing data collection feeding the data hungry models,[101] is promoted as beneficial to consumers and markets, and endorsed by companies and governments. Data collection is thus held out as a necessary component of fostering AI innovation. Companies boast how AI insights allow them to offer personalised services, 'tailored' to individual consumer's needs. McKinsey consulting firm hails 'harnessing the power of external data' noting how

---

[97] ASIC, 'Regulatory Guide 274', para. 277.180.
[98] ASIC's RG para. 274.47 provides examples of such personal and social characteristics: 'speaking a language other than English, having different cultural assumptions or attitudes about money, or experiencing cognitive or behavioural impairments due to intellectual disability, mental illness, chronic health problems or age'.
[99] ASIC, 'Regulatory Guide 274' para. 274.47: 'an accident or sudden illness, family violence, job loss, having a baby, or the death of a family member'.
[100] For example, Indigenous Australians, whose lack of financial literacy historically made them an easy target for mis-selling of inadequate products: Commonwealth of Australia, *Royal Commission into Misconduct in the Banking, Superannuation and Financial Services Industry* (Interim Report Vol. 2, 2018) 452–57.
[101] Machine Learning in particular has been described as 'very data hungry' in the World Economic Forum and Deloitte; WEF and Deloitte, *The New Physics of Financial Services: Understanding How Artificial Intelligence Is Transforming the Financial Ecosystem* (Report, August 2018) <www.weforum.org/reports/the-new-physics-of-financial-services-how-artificial-intelligence-is-transforming-the-financial-ecosystem/>.

'few organizations take full advantage of data generated outside their walls. A well-structured plan for using external data can provide a competitive edge'.[102]

Policymakers use the same rhetoric of promoting 'innovation' and encourage data collection through schemes such as open banking.[103] The aim of open banking is to give consumers the ability to direct companies that hold financial data about themselves to make it available to financial (or other) companies of the consumer's choice. Thus, it makes it possible for organisations to get access to consumers' information they could never get from a consumer directly, such as for example their transaction data for the past ten years.

Jurisdictions such as the EU, United Kingdom, Australia, and Hong Kong have recently adopted regulation promoting open banking, or 'open finance' more generally.[104] The frameworks are praised by the industry as 'encourag[ing] the development of innovative products and services that help consumers better engage with their finances, make empowered decisions and access tailored products and services'.[105]

While open banking is making it possible for financial firms to develop new products for consumers, the jury is still out as to the scheme's universally positive implications for consumers and markets.[106] One thing that is clear, however, is that because of its very nature, open banking contributes to information and power asymmetry between consumers and Automated Banks.

Traditionally, in order to receive a financial product, such as a loan or an insurance product, consumers would have to actively provide relevant data, answering questions or prompts, in relation to their income, spending, age, history of loan repayments, and so on. Open banking – or open finance more broadly – means that consumers can access financial products without answering any questions. But these questions provided a level of transparency to consumers: they knew what they were being asked, and were likely to understand why they were being asked such questions. But when an individual shares their 'bulk' data, such as their banking transaction history, through the open banking scheme, do they really know what a financial firm is looking for and how it is being used? At the same time, in such a setting, consumers are deprived of control over which data to share (for

---

[102] Mohammed Aaser and Doug McElhaney, 'Harnessing the Power of External Data' (Article, 3 February 2021) *McKinsey Digital*.

[103] Nydia Remolina, 'Open Banking: Regulatory Challenges for a New Forum of Financial Intermediation in a Data-Driven World' (SMU Centre for AI & Data Governance Research Paper No 2019/05, 28 October 2019).

[104] EMEA Center for Regulatory Strategy, 'Open Banking around the World' *Deloitte* (Blog Post) <www.deloitte.com/global/en/Industries/financial-services/perspectives/open-banking-around-the-world.html>.

[105] UK Finance, 'Exploring Open Finance' (Report, 2022) <www.ukfinance.org.uk/system/files/2022–05/Exploring%20open%20finance_0.pdf>.

[106] Joshua Macey and Dan Awrey, 'The Promise and Perils of Open Finance' *Harvard Law School Forum on Corporate Governance* (Forum Post, 4 April 2022) <https://corpgov.law.harvard.edu/2022/04/04/the-promise-and-perils-of-open-finance/>.

example, they cannot just hide transaction data on payments they made to merchants such as liquor stores or pharmacies). The transparency for financial firms when data is shared is therefore significantly higher than in 'traditional' settings – but for consumers the process becomes more opaque.[107]

4.4 CAN CORPORATE SECRECY COEXIST WITH CONSUMER RIGHTS? POSSIBLE REGULATORY SOLUTIONS

ADM tools contribute to maintaining corporate secrecy of Automated Banks, and as we argue in this chapter, legal systems perpetuate, encourage, and feed the opacity further. The opacity then increases the risk of consumer harm, such as discrimination, which is more difficult to observe, and more challenging to prove.

In this section we provide a brief outline of potential interventions that may protect against AI-facilitated harms, particularly if applied synchronously. This discussion does not aim to be exhaustive, but rather aims to show something can be done to combat the opacity and resulting harms.

Interventions described in academic and grey literature can be divided into three broad categories: (1) regulations that prevent businesses from using harmful AI systems in financial markets, (2) regulations that aid consumers to understand when ADM systems are used in financial markets, and (3) regulations that facilitate regulator monitoring and enforcement against AI-driven harms in financial markets. Approaches to design (including Transparency by Design[108]) are not included in this list, and while they may contribute to improved consumer outcomes, they are beyond the scope of this chapter.

The somewhat provocative title of this section asks if corporate secrecy is the real source of the AI-related harms in the described context. The interventions outlined below focus on preventing harms, but can the harms really be prevented if the opacity of corporate practices and processes is not addressed first? Corporate secrecy is the major challenge to accountability and scrutiny, and consumer rights, including right to non-discrimination, cannot be guaranteed in an environment as opaque as it currently is. We submit that the regulatory interventions urgently needed are the ones that prevent secrecy first and foremost. AI and ADM tools will continue to evolve, and technology as such is not a good regulatory target[109] – the focus must be on harm prevention. Harms can only be prevented if the practices of financial firms, such as credit scoring discussed in this chapter, are transparent and easily monitored both by regulators and consumers.

[107] Bednarz et al, 'Insurance Underwriting in an Open Data Era'.
[108] Heike Felzmann et al, 'Towards Transparency by Design for Artificial Intelligence' (2020) 26 (6) *Science and Engineering Ethics* 3333, 3343–53.
[109] Lyria Bennett Moses, *How to Think about Law, Regulation and Technology: Problems with 'Technology' as a Regulatory Target* (SSRN Scholarly Paper No ID 2464750, Social Science Research Network, 2013) 18–19.

4.4.1 *Preventing Automated Banks from Designing Harmful AI Systems*

International and national bodies in multiple jurisdictions have recently adopted, or are currently debating, various measures with an overarching aim of protecting consumers from harm. For example, the US Federal Trade Commission has provided guidance to businesses using AI, explaining that discriminatory outcomes resulting from the use of AI would contravene federal law.[110] The most comprehensive approach to limiting the use of particular AI tools can be found in the EU's proposed *Artificial Intelligence Act*. Its Recital 37 specifically recommends that 'AI systems used to evaluate the credit score or creditworthiness of natural persons should be classified as high-risk AI systems'. This proposal is a step towards overcoming some opaque practices, through the provision of 'clear and adequate information to the user' along with other protections that enable authorities to scrutinise elements of ADM tools in high-risk contexts.[111] Early criticisms of the proposed Act note that while a regulatory approach informed by the context in which ADM is used has some merit, it does not cover potentially harmful practices such as emotion recognition and remote biometric identification,[112] which could be used across a range of contexts, generating data sets that may later be used in other markets such as financial services.

An alternative approach to regulating AI systems before they are used in markets is to limit the sources of information that can be used by ADM tools, or restrict the ways in which information can be processed. In addition to privacy protections, some jurisdictions have placed limitations on the kinds of information that can be used to calculate a credit score. For example, in Denmark, the financial services sector can use consumers' social media data for marketing purposes but is explicitly prohibited from using this information to determine creditworthiness.[113] Similarly, the EU is considering a Directive preventing the use of personal social media and health data (including cancer data) in the determination of creditworthiness.[114] Such prohibitions are, however, a rather tricky solution: it may be difficult for the regulation to keep up with a growing list of data that should be excluded from

---

[110] Elisa Jilson, 'Aiming for Truth, Fairness and Equity in Your Company's Use of AI' *US Federal Trade Commission* (Business Blog Post, 19 April 2021) <www.ftc.gov/business-guidance/blog/2021/04/aiming-truth-fairness-equity-your-companys-use-ai>.

[111] European Commission, 'Regulatory Framework Proposal on Artificial Intelligence' *European Commission* (Web Page) <https://digital-strategy.ec.europa.eu/en/policies/regulatory-framework-ai#:~:text=encourages%20dangerous%20behaviour.-,High%20risk,life%20(e.g.%20scoring%20of%20exams>.

[112] Daniel Leufer, 'EU Parliament's Draft of AI Act: Predictive Policing Is Banned, but Work Remains to Protect People's Rights' (4 May 2022) *Access Now* <www.accessnow.org/ai-act-predictive-policing/>.

[113] Hohnen et al, 'Assessing Creditworthiness'.

[114] Proposal for a Directive of the European Parliament and of the Council on consumer credits [2021] OJ COM 347 (47).

analysis.[115] One way of overcoming this challenge would be to avoid focusing on restricted data sources, and instead create a list of acceptable data sources, which is a solution applied for example in some types of health insurance.[116]

Imposing limits on how long scores can be kept and/or relied on by Automated Banks is another important consideration. In Australia, credit providers are bound by limits that stipulate the length of time that different pieces of information are held on a consumer's file: credit providers may only keep financial hardship information for twelve months from the date the monthly payment was made under a financial hardship arrangement, whereas court judgements may be kept on record for five years after the date of the decision.[117] In Denmark, where the credit reporting system operates as a 'blacklist' of people deemed more likely to default, a negative record (for instance, an unpaid debt) is deleted after five years, regardless of whether or not the debt has been paid.[118] A challenge with these approaches is that the amount of time particular categories of data may be kept may not account for proxy data, purchased data sets, and/or proprietary scoring and profiling systems that group consumers according to complex predictions that are impossible to decode.

4.4.2 *Aiding Consumers Understand When ADM Systems Are Used in Financial Services*

Despite the development of many principles-based regulatory initiatives by governments, corporates, and think tanks,[119] few jurisdictions have legislated protections that require consumers to be notified if and when they have been assessed by an automated system.[120] In instances where consumers are notified, they may be unable to receive an understandable explanation of the decision-making process, or to seek redress through timely and accessible avenues.

Consumers face a number of challenges in navigating financial markets, such as understanding credit card repayment requirements[121] and failing to accurately

---

[115] For examples of such potentially harmful data sources see: Pasquale, *The Black Box Society*, 21, 31; Hurley and Adebayo, 'Credit Scoring in the Era of Big Data', 151–52, 158; Hiller and Jones, 'Who's Keeping Score?'.

[116] E.g., health insurers in the United States under the US Public Health Service Act, 42 USC § 300gg(a)(1)(A) may only base their underwriting decisions on four factors: individual or family coverage; location; age; and smoking history.

[117] 'Your Credit Report', *Financial Rights Legal Centre* (Web Page, 6 February 2017) <https://financialrights.org.au/>.

[118] Hohnen et al, 'Assessing Creditworthiness', 40.

[119] Anna Jobin, Marcello Ienca, and Effy Vayena, 'The Global Landscape of AI Ethics Guidelines' (2019) 1(9) *Nature Machine Intelligence* 389, 2–5.

[120] See e.g. Art. 22 GDPR.

[121] Jack B Soll, Ralph L Keeney, and Richard P Larrick, 'Consumer Misunderstanding of Credit Card Use, Payments, and Debt: Causes and Solutions' (2013) 32(1) *Journal of Public Policy & Marketing* 66, 77–80.

assess their credit.[122] For individuals, it is crucial to understand how they are being scored, as this will make it possible for them to be able to identify inaccuracies,[123] and question decisions made about them. Credit scoring is notoriously opaque and difficult to understand, so consumers are likely to benefit from requirements for agencies to simplify and harmonise how scores are presented.[124]An example of a single scoring system can be found in Sri Lanka, where credit ratings, or 'CRIB Scores' are provided by the Central Information Bureau of Sri Lanka, a public-private partnership between the nation's Central Bank and a number of financial institutions that hold equity in the Bureau. The Bureau issues CRIB Score reports to consumers in a consistent manner, utilising an algorithm to produce a three-digit number ranging from 250 to 900.[125] In Sri Lanka's case, consumers are provided with a singular rating from a central agency, and although this rating is subject to change over time, there is no possibility of consumers receiving two different credit scores from separate providers.

Providing consumers with the opportunity to access their credit scores is another (and in many ways complementary) regulatory intervention. A number of jurisdictions provide consumers with the option to check their credit report and/or credit score online. For example, consumers in Canada[126] and Australia[127] are able to access free copies of their credit reports by requesting this information directly from major credit bureaus. In Australia, consumers are able to receive a free copy of their credit report once every three months.[128]

However, such approaches have important limitations. Credit ratings are just one of many automated processes within the financial services industry. Automated Banks, with access to enough data, can create their own tools going outside the well-

---

[122] Marsha Courchane, Adam Gailey, and Peter Zorn, 'Consumer Credit Literacy: What Price Perception?' (2008) 60(1) *Journal of Economics and Business* 125, 127–38.

[123] Beth Freeborn and Julie Miller, *Report to Congress under Section 219 of the Fair and Accurate Credit Transactions Act of 2003* (Report, January 2015) i <www.ftc.gov/system/files/docu ments/reports/section-319-fair-accurate-credit-transactions-act-2003-sixth-interim-final-report-federal-trade/150121factareport.pdf>. In one study of 1001 US consumers, 26 per cent found inaccuracies in their credit reports.

[124] Heather Cotching and Chiara Varazzani, *Richer Veins for Behavioural Insight: An Exploration of the Opportunities to Apply Behavioural Insights in Public Policy* (Behavioural Economics Team of the Australian Government, Commonwealth of Australia, Department of the Prime Minister and Cabinet, 2019) 1, 14. Studies have shown simplifying and standardising information in consumer markets aids comprehension and assists consumers in making choices that result in better outcomes.

[125] Credit Information Bureau of Sri Lanka, 'CRIB Score Report Reference Guide' (Guide) <www.crib.lk/images/pdfs/crib-score-reference-guide.pdf>.

[126] 'Getting Your Credit Report and Credit Score' *Government of Canada* (Web Page) <www .canada.ca/en/financial-consumer-agency/services/credit-reports-score/order-credit-report .html>.

[127] 'Access Your Credit Report' *Office of the Australian Information Commissioner* (Web Page) <www.oaic.gov.au/privacy/credit-reporting/access-your-credit-report>.

[128] Ibid.

established credit rating systems. Also, it is consumers who are forced to carry the burden of correcting inaccurate information which is used to make consequential decisions about them, while often being required to pay for the opportunity to do so.[129]

In addition, explainability challenges are faced in every sector that uses AI, and there is considerable investigation ahead to determine the most effective ways of explaining automated decisions in financial markets. It has been suggested that a good explanation is provided when the receiver 'can no longer keep asking why'.[130] The recent EU Digital Services Act[131] emphasises such approach by noting that recipients of online advertisements should have access to 'meaningful explanations of the logic used' for 'determining that specific advertisement is to be displayed to them'.[132]

Consumer experience of an AI system will depend on a number of parameters, including format of explanations (visual, rule-based, or highlighted key features), their complexity and specificity, application context, and variations suiting users' cognitive styles (for example, providing some users with more complex information, and others with less).[133] The development of consumer-facing explainable AI tools is an emerging area of research and practice.[134]

A requirement of providing meaningful feedback to consumers, for example, through counterfactual demonstrations,[135] would make it possible for individuals to understand what factors they might need to change to receive a different decision. It would also be an incentive for Automated Banks to be more transparent.

4.4.3 *Facilitating Regulator Monitoring and Enforcement of ADM Harms in Financial Services*

The third category of potential measures relies on empowering regulators, thus shifting the burden away from consumers. For example, regulators need to be able

---

[129] Some consumers discovered that their reports 'featured inconsistent or misleading claims descriptions and statuses, included personal information unrelated to insurance at all, and no explanation of the terms used to assist in comprehensibility'. See Roger Clarke and Nigel Waters, *Privacy Practices in the General Insurance Industry* (Financial Rights Legal Centre Report, April 2022) vii <https://financialrights.org.au/wp-content/uploads/2022/04/2204_PrivacyGIReport_FINAL.pdf>.

[130] Leilani Gilpin et al, 'Explaining Explanations: An Overview of Interpretability of Machine Learning' (2019) v3 *arXiv*, 2 <https://arxiv.org/abs/1806.00069>.

[131] Regulation (EU) 2022/2065 of the European Parliament and of the Council of 19 October 2022 on a Single Market for Digital Services and amending Directive 2000/31/EC (Digital Services Act) [2022] OJ L 277/1, para 27.10.2022.

[132] Ibid, para 52.

[133] Yanou Ramon et al, 'Understanding Consumer Preferences for Explanations Generated by XAI Algorithms' (2021) *arXiv*, 9–14 <http://arxiv.org/abs/2107.02624>.

[134] Jessica Morley et al, 'From What to How: An Initial Review of Publicly Available AI Ethics Tools, Methods and Research to Translate Principles into Practices' (2020) 26(4) *Science and Engineering Ethics* 2141.

[135] Rory Mc Grath et al, 'Interpretable Credit Application Predictions with Counterfactual Explanations' (2018) v2 *arXiv*, 4–7 <https://arxiv.org/abs/1811.05245>.

to 'look under the hood' of any ADM tools, including these of proprietary character.[136] This could be in a form of using explainable AI tools, access to raw code, or
ability to use dummy data to test the model. A certification scheme, such as quality
standards, is another option, the problem however is the risk of 'set and forget
approach'. Another approach to providing regulators insight into industry practices
is the establishment of regulatory sandboxes, which nevertheless have limitations.[137]

Financial institutions could also be required to prove a causal link between the
data that they use to generate consumer scores, and likely risk. Such approach would
likely reduce the use of certain categories of data, where correlations between data
points would not be supported by a valid causal relationship. For example, Android
phone users are reportedly safer drivers than iPhone users,[138] but such rule would
prevent insurers from taking this into account when offering a quote on car
insurance (while we do not suggest they are currently doing so, in many legal
systems they could). In practice, some regulators are looking at this solution. For
example, while not going as far as requiring direct causal link, the New York State
financial regulator requires a 'valid explanation or rationale' for underwriting of life
insurance, where external data or external predictive models are used.[139] However,
such approach could result in encouraging financial services providers to collect
more data, just to be able to prove the causal link,[140] which may again further
disadvantage consumers and introduce more, not less, opacity.

4.5 CONCLUSIONS

Far from being unique to credit scoring, the secrecy of ADM tools is a problem
affecting multiple sectors and industries.[141] Human decisions are also unexplainable
and opaque, and ADM tools are often made out to be a potential, fairer and more
transparent, alternative. But the problem is secrecy increases, not decreases,
with automation.[142]

There are many reasons for this, including purely technological barriers to
explainability. But also, it is obviously cheaper and easier not to design and use

---

[136] Ada Lovelace Institute, *Technical Methods for the Regulatory Inspection of Algorithmic Systems in Social Media Platforms* (December 2021) <www.adalovelaceinstitute.org/wp-content/uploads/2021/12/ADA_Technical-methods-regulatory-inspection_report.pdf>.

[137] Sophie Farthing et al, *Human Rights and Technology* (Australian Human Rights Commission, 1 March 2021) 1, 95–97.

[138] Henry Hoenig, 'Sorry iPhone Fans, Android Users Are Safer Drivers' *Jerry* (Blog Post, 20 April 2023) <https://getjerry.com/studies/sorry-iphone-fans-android-users-are-safer-drivers>.

[139] New York State Department of Financial Services Circular Letter No 1 (2019), 18 January 2019, 'RE: Use of External Consumer Data and Information Sources in Underwriting for Life Insurance'.

[140] Gert Meyers and Ine Van Hoyweghen, '"Happy Failures": Experimentation with Behaviour-Based Personalisation in Car Insurance' (2020) 7(1) *Big Data and Society* 1, 4.

[141] See for example Chapters 8, 10 and 11 in this book.

[142] Pasquale, *The Black Box Society*.

transparent systems. As we argue in this chapter, opacity is a choice made by organisations, often on purpose, as it allows them to evade scrutiny and hide their practices from the public and regulators. Opacity of ADM and AI tools used is a logical consequence of the secrecy of corporate practices.

Despite many harms caused by opacity, the legal systems and market practice have evolved to enable or even promote that secrecy surrounding AI and ADM tools, as we have discussed using examples of rules applying to Automated Banks. However, the opacity and harms could be prevented with some of the potential solutions which we have discussed in this chapter. The question is whether there is sufficient motivation to achieve positive social impact with automated tools, without just focusing on optimisation and profits.

PART II

Automated States

5

The Automated Welfare State

Challenges for Socioeconomic Rights of the Marginalised

Terry Carney[*]

More recently, administrative agencies have introduced 'new public analytics' approaches, using data-driven technologies and risk models to reshape how commonplace administrative decisions are produced.[1]

5.1 INTRODUCTION

Artificial intelligence (AI) is a broad church. Automated decision-making (ADM), a subset of AI, is the form of technology most commonly encountered in public administration of the social services, a generic term which includes income support (social security) and funding or provision of services such as disability support funding under Australia's National Disability Insurance Scheme (NDIS). New public analytics is a label that nicely captures how ADM is deployed as the contemporary form of public administration.[2]

ADM has long been an integral aid to the work of hard-pressed human administrators exercising their delegated social security powers in Centrelink (the specialist service delivery arm of the federal government department called Services Australia). Early digitisation of social security benefits administration not only resulted in considerable efficiency gains but provided the guide-rails that protected against the more egregious errors or decline in decision-making quality as staffing was drastically reduced in scale and shed higher levels skills and experience.

---

[*] The author is indebted to research assistance provided by Arundhati Ajith.

[1] Jennifer Raso, 'Unity in the Eye of the Beholder? Reasons for Decision in Theory and Practice in the Ontario Works Program' (2020) 70 (Winter) *University of Toronto Law Journal* 1, 2.

[2] Karen Yeung, 'Algorithmic Regulation: A Critical Interrogation' (2018) 12(4) *Regulation & Governance* 505; Lina Dencik and Anne Kaun, 'Introduction: Datification and the Welfare State' (2020) 1(1) *Global Perspectives* 12912; Raso, 'Unity in the Eye of the Beholder?'; Lena Ulbricht and Karen Yeung, 'Algorithmic Regulation: A Maturing Concept for Investigating Regulation of and through Algorithms' (2022) 16 *Regulation & Governance* 3.

Automation as such has not been the issue; the issue is a more recent one of a breakneck rush into a 'digital first future'[3] and the abysmal failure of governance, design, ethics, and legal rectitude associated with the $1.8 billion robodebt catastrophe.[4] As Murphy J observed in his reasons approving the class action settlement, this was a 'shameful chapter in the administration of the Commonwealth social security system and a massive failure of public administration [which] should have been obvious to the senior public servants charged with overseeing the Robodebt system and to the responsible Minister at different points'; a verdict echoed by the Royal Commissioner in her July 2023 Report.[5]

ADM is only a technology. Like all new technologies, there are extremes of dystopian and utopian evaluative tropes, though a mature assessment often involves a more ambiguous middle ground.[6] Like the history of other new technological challenges to law, the answers may call for innovative new approaches, rather than extension of existing remedies. Robodebt was ultimately brought to heel by judicial review and class actions, but the much vaunted 'new administrative law' machinery of the 1970s[7] was seriously exposed. Merits review failed because government 'gamed it'[8] while the other accountability mechanisms proved toothless.[9] So radical new thinking is called for.[10] AI for its part ranges in form from computational aids (or automation) to neural network 'machine learning' systems. Even agreed taxonomies of AI are still in development, including recently by the first Organisation for Economic Co-operation and Development (OECD), with its four-fold schema of context; data and input; AI model; and task and output.[11]

The focus of this chapter on social security and social services is apt, because Services Australia (as the former Department of Human Services is now called) was envisaged by the Digital Transformation Agency ('DTA' formerly 'Office') as 'the first

[3] Terry Carney, 'Artificial Intelligence in Welfare: Striking the Vulnerability Balance?' (2020) 46 (2) *Monash University Law Review* 23.
[4] Tapani Rinta-Kahila et al, 'Algorithmic Decision-Making and System Destructiveness: A Case of Automatic Debt Recovery' (2021) 31(3) *European Journal of Information Systems* 313; Peter Whiteford, 'Debt by Design: The Anatomy of a Social Policy Fiasco – Or Was It Something Worse?' (2021) 80(2) *Australian Journal of Public Administration* 340.
[5] *Prygodicz v Commonwealth of Australia (No 2)* [2021] FCA 634, para [5]: Royal Commission into the Robodebt Scheme, Report (Canberra: July 2023).
[6] Penny Croft and Honni van Rijswijk, *Technology: New Trajectories in Law* (Abingdon, Oxford: Routledge, 2021) 4–16.
[7] Brian Jinks, 'The "New Administrative Law": Some Assumptions and Questions' (1982) 41(3) *Australian Journal of Public Administration* 209.
[8] Joel Townsend, 'Better Decisions?: Robodebt and Failings of Merits Review' in Janina Boughey and Katie Miller (eds), *The Automated State* (Sydney: Federation Press, 2021) 52–69.
[9] Terry Carney, 'Robo-debt Illegality: The Seven Veils of Failed Guarantees of the Rule of Law?' (2019) 44(1) *Alternative Law Journal* 4.
[10] Maria O'Sullivan, 'Automated Decision-Making and Human Rights: The Right to an Effective Remedy' in Janina Boughey and Katie Miller (eds), *The Automated State* (Sydney: Federation Press, 2021) 70–88.
[11] *Framework for the Classification of AI Systems – Public Consultation on Preliminary Findings* (OECD AI Policy Observatory, 2021).

department to roll out intelligent technologies and provide new platforms to citizenry, in accordance with the then DTA's roadmap for later adoption by other agencies'.[12] The focus of this chapter is on the associated risk of digital transformation in the social services, of three main forms. First, the risk due to the heightened vulnerabilities of clients of social services.[13] Second, the risk from inadequate design, consultation, and monitoring of ADM initiatives in the social services.[14] And finally, the heightened risk associated with particular ADM technologies.

The next section of the chapter (Section 5.2) reviews selected ADM/AI examples in social services in Australia and elsewhere. To draw out differences in levels of risk of various initiatives it takes as a loose organising principle Henman's[15] observation that the risks and pitfalls of AI increase along a progression – lowest where it involves recognising 'patterns', higher where individuals are 'sorted' into categories, and highest where AI is used to make 'predictions'. Section 5.3 discusses the harm inflicted on vulnerable clients of social services when ADM and AI risks are inadequately appreciated, and some options for better regulation and accountability. It questions both the capacity of traditional judicial and administrative machinery in holding AI to account, and the relevance and durability of those 'values' in the face of the transformational *power* of this technology to subordinate and *remake* law and social policy to instead reflect AI values and processes.

Restoration of trust in government is advanced in a short conclusion (Section 5.4) as being foundational to risk management in the social services. Trust is at the heart of the argument made for greater caution, more extensive co-design, and enhanced regulatory oversight of ADM in the social services.

5.2 ISSUES POSED BY AUTOMATION AND ADM

Three issues in particular stand out for social services in Australia. First, the comprehensibility or otherwise of the system for citizens engaging with it. Second, the compatibility or otherwise of ADM in case management. Finally, the risks and benefits of 'predictive' ADM in the social services.

5.2.1 *Comprehensibility Issues*

5.2.1.1 Early Centrelink Adoption of Digitisation and Decision Aids

Prior to robodebt, Centrelink clients concerns mainly centred on intelligibility of digitised social security records and communications, and the ability to understand

---

[12] Alexandra James and Andrew Whelan, '"Ethical" Artificial Intelligence in the Welfare State: Discourse and Discrepancy in Australian Social Services' (2022) 42(1) *Critical Social Policy* 22 at 29.

[13] Virginia Eubanks, *Automating Inequality: How High-Tech Tools Profile, Police, and Punish the Poor* (New York: St Martins Press, 2017).

[14] Joe Tomlinson, *Justice in the Digital State: Assessing the Next Revolution in Administrative Justice* (Bristol: Policy Press, 2019).

[15] Paul Henman, 'Improving Public Services Using Artificial Intelligence: Possibilities, Pitfalls, Governance' (2020) 42(4) *Asia Pacific Journal of Public Administration* 209, 210.

automation of rate calculations or scoring of eligibility tools. The ADEX and MultiCal systems for debt calculations generate difficult-to-comprehend and acronym-laden print-outs of the arithmetic. This is because the measures were designed for convenience of internal inputting of data rather than ease of consumer comprehension.

The combination of deeply unintelligible consumer documentation and time-poor administrators often leaves too little time to detect less obvious keying or other errors. Internal review officer reconsiderations instead often focus on very basic sources of error such as couple status.[16] While external merits tribunal members do have the skills and expertise to penetrate the fog[17] this only rectifies a very small proportion of such errors (only 0.05% in the case of robodebts), and only for those with the social capital or resources to pursue their concern.

Lack of transparency of communications with run-of-the-mill social security clients remains problematic for want of investment in provision of the 'public facing' front-end interfaces (or correspondence templates) to convert an almost 100 per cent digital environment into understandable information for the public. Instead, new investment was initially in pilots to classify and file supporting documents for claims processing.[18] Only in recent years were expressions of interest sought for general customer experience upgrades of the MyGov portal,[19] reinforced by allocation of $200 million in the 2021–2022 budget for enhancements to provide a 'simpler and more tailored experience for Australians based on their preferences and inter-actions', but also including virtual assistants or chatbots.[20]

Comprehensibility of debt calculations and other routine high incidence transac-tions to ordinary citizens surely should be the first reform priority. Transparency to citizens certainly hinges on it. Availability of accurate information to recipients of ADM-based welfare is fundamental to individual due process. This was demon-strated by the contrast between Australia's failure to explain adequately the basis of yearly income variations under its unlawful 'robodebt' calculations, compared to the way case officers in the Swedish student welfare program provided explanations and

---

[16] Daniel Turner, 'Voices from the Field' (Paper presented at the *Automated Decision Making (ADM) in Social Security and Employment Services: Mapping What Is Happening and What We Know in Social Security and Employment Services* (Brisbane, Centre of Excellence for Automated Decision Making and Society (ADM + S), 5 May 2021).

[17] Terry Carney, 'Automation in Social Security: Implications for Merits Review?' (2020) 55(3) *Australian Journal of Social Issues* 260.

[18] This is a machine learning optical character reading system developed by Capgemini: Aaron Tan, 'Services Australia Taps AI in Document Processing' (16 October 2020) *ComputerWeeklyCom* <www.computerweekly.com/news/252490630/Services-Australia-taps-AI-in-document-processing>.

[19] Sasha Karen, 'Services Australia Seeks Customer Experience Solutions for myGov Platform Upgrade' (9 February 2021) ARN <www.arnnet.com.au/article/686126/services-australia-seeks-customer-experience-solutions-mygov-platform-upgrade/>.

[20] Asha Barbaschow, 'All the Tech within the 2021 Australian Budget' (11 May 2021) ZDNet <www.zdnet.com/article/all-the-tech-within-the-2021-australian-budget/>.

an immediate opportunity to rectify inaccurate information.[21] Even review bodies such as the Administrative Appeals Tribunal (AAT) would benefit from comprehensibility of the basis of decisions. It would benefit from time freed up to concentrate on substantive issues, due to no longer having to pick their way through the morass of computer print-outs and multiple acronyms simply to create an accessible narrative of issues in dispute.[22]

5.2.2 *ADM Case Management Constraints*

5.2.2.1 The (Aborted) NDIS Chatbot

The NDIS is seen as a pathbreaker for digitisation in disability services.[23] But the National Disability Insurance Authority (NDIA) was obliged to abort roll-out of its sophisticated chatbot, called Nadia.

Nadia was designed to assume responsibility for aspects of client interaction and case management. The chatbot was built as a machine learning cognitive computing interface, involving 'data mining and pattern recognition to interact with humans by means of natural language processing'.[24] It was to have an ability to read and adjust to emotions being conveyed, including by lightening the interaction such as by referencing information about a person's favourite sporting team. However, it did not proceed beyond piloting. As a machine learning system it needed ongoing access to a large training set of actual NDIS clients to develop and refine its accuracy. Rolling it out was correctly assessed as carrying too great 'a potential risk, as one incorrect decision may disrupt a person's ability to live a normal life'.[25]

This risk of error is a serious one, not only for the person affected by it, but also to the confidence of people in public administration. Given the sophistication required of 'human' chatbots, it presently must be doubted whether a sufficient standard of performance and avoidance of risk can be attained for vulnerable social security or disability clients. As Park and Humphrey[26] suggest, that ability to give human-like cues to end users means that the chatbot 'need[s] to be versatile and

---

[21] Monika Zalnieriute, Lyria Bennett Moses, and George Williams, 'The Rule of Law and Automation of Government Decision-Making' (2019) 82(3) *Modern Law Review* 425.

[22] Carney, 'Automation in Social Security'. Marginalised citizens may however benefit from human-centred (a 'legal design approach') to AI technologies to broaden access to justice at a relatively low cost: Lisa Toohey et al, 'Meeting the Access to Civil Justice Challenge: Digital Inclusion, Algorithmic Justice, and Human-Centred Design' (2019) 19 *Macquarie Law Journal* 133.

[23] Gerard Goggin et al, 'Disability, Technology Innovation and Social Development in China and Australia' (2019) 12(1) *Journal of Asian Public Policy* 34.

[24] Sora Park and Justine Humphry, 'Exclusion by Design: Intersections of Social, Digital and Data Exclusion' (2019) 22(7) *Information, Communication & Society* 934, 944.

[25] Ibid, 946.

[26] Ibid.

adaptable to various conditions, including language, personality, communication style and limits to physical and mental capacities'. This inability of ADM to bridge the 'empathy gap' is why it is so strongly argued that such administrative tasks should remain in the hands of human administrators.[27] Even smartphone digital reporting proved highly problematic for vulnerable income security clients such as young single parents under (now abolished) ParentsNext.[28] So, it was surely hoping too much to expect better outcomes in the much more challenging NDIS case management environment.

Such issues are not confined to Australia or to case management software of course. Ontario's 'audit trail' welfare management software, deployed to curb a perceived problem of over-generosity, was found to have 'decentred' or displaced caseworkers from their previous role as authoritative legal decision-makers.[29] The caseworkers responded by engaging in complicated work-arounds to regain much of their former professional discretion. As Raso concluded, '[s]oftware that requires individuals to fit into pre-set menu options may never be sophisticated enough to deliver complex social benefits to a population as diverse as [Ontario's welfare] recipients'.[30]

A US federal requirement to automate verification of Medicaid remuneration of disability caregivers provides yet another example. The state of Arkansas adopted an inflexibly designed and user-unfriendly service app (with optional geo-location monitoring). This proved especially problematic for clients who were receiving 'self-directed' care. Care workers were unable to step outside the property boundaries on an errand or to accompany the person without triggering a 'breach' of the service being provided. Unlike Virginia, Arkansas had neglected to take advantage of the ability to exempt self-care, or remove problematic optional elements.[31]

5.2.2.2 NDIA's Aborted ADM Assessment and Planning Reforms

In 2021 public attention was drawn to an NDIA proposal to replace caseworker evaluations by objective rating 'scores' when assessing eligibility for the NDIS, and

---

[27] See Chapter 9 in this book: Cary Coglianese, 'Law and Empathy in the Automated State'.

[28] Carney, 'Automation in Social Security'; Simone Casey, 'Towards Digital Dole Parole: A Review of Digital Self-service Initiatives in Australian Employment Services' (2022) 57(1) *Australian Journal of Social Issues* 111. A third of all participants in the program experienced loss or delay of income penalties, with Indigenous and other vulnerable groups overrepresented: Jacqueline Maley, '"Unable to Meet Basic Needs": ParentsNext Program Suspended a Third of Parents' Payments' (11 August 2021) *Sydney Morning Herald* <www.smh.com.au/politics/federal/unable-to-meet-basic-needs-parentsnext-program-suspended-a-third-of-parents-payments-20210811-p58hvl.html>.

[29] Jennifer Raso, 'Displacement as Regulation: New Regulatory Technologies and Front-Line Decision-Making in Ontario Works' (2017) 32(1) *Canadian Journal of Law and Society* 75, 83.

[30] Ibid, 93.

[31] Virginia Eubanks and Alexandra Mateescu, '"We Do Not Deserve This": New App Places US Caregivers under Digital Surveillance' (28 July 2021) *Guardian Australia* <www.theguardian.com/us-news/2021/jul/28/digital-surveillance-caregivers-artificial-intelligence>.

to also serve as a basis for providing indicative packages of funding support. This was shelved on 9 July 2021,[32] at least in that form.[33] The measure was designed to address inequities around access and size of packages. The stated policy objective was to improve equity of access between different disability groups and between those with and those without access to a good portfolio of recent medical reports, as well as reduce staffing overheads and processing time.[34] Subjective assessments of applicant-provided medical reports were to have been replaced by objective 'scores' from a suite of functional incapacity 'tools'. Rating scores were designed not only to improve consistency of NDIS access decisions, but also generate one of 400 personas/presumptive budgets.[35]

The rating tool and eligibility leg of this reform was not true ADM. That aspect mirrored the historical reform trajectory for Disability Support Pension (DSP) and Carer Allowance/Payments (CA/CP). Originally eligibility for DSP (then called Invalid Pension, IP) was based on showing that an applicant experienced an actual or real life 85 per cent 'incapacity for work'.[36] In the 1990s this was transformed from an enquiry about the real human applicant to becoming an abstraction – assessing the theoretical ability or not of people with that class of functional impairment to be able to perform any job anywhere in the country – and requiring minimum scores under impairment tables rating functional impairment (leaving extremely *narrow* fields/issues for subjective classification of severity). These and associated changes significantly reduced the numbers found eligible for these payments.[37] Similar

---

[32] The reforms were opposed by the NDIS Advisory Council and abandoned at a meeting of Federal and State Ministers: Luke Henriques-Gomes, 'NDIS Independent Assessments Should Not Proceed in Current Form, Coalition's Own Advisory Council Says' (8 July 2021) *Guardian Australia* <www.theguardian.com/australia-news/2021/jul/08/ndis-independent-assessments-should-not-proceed-in-current-form-coalitions-own-advisory-council-says>; Muriel Cummins, 'Fears Changes to NDIS Will Leave Disabled without Necessary Supports' (7 July 2021) *Sydney Morning Herald* <www.smh.com.au/national/fears-changes-to-ndis-will-leave-disabled-without-necessary-supports-20210706-p58756.html> .

[33] The NDIA outlined significant changes to the model immediately prior to it being halted: Joint Standing C'tte on NDIS, *Independent Assessments* (Joint Standing Committee on the National Disability Insurance Scheme, 2021) 24–27 <https://parlinfo.aph.gov.au/parlInfo/download/committees/reportjnt/024622/toc_pdf/IndependentAssessments.pdf;fileType=application%2Fpdf>.

[34] Helen Dickinson et al, 'Avoiding Simple Solutions to Complex Problems: Independent Assessments Are Not the Way to a Fairer NDIS' (Melbourne: Children and Young People with Disability Australia, 2021) <https://apo.org.au/sites/default/files/resource-files/2021–05/apo-nid312281.pdf>.

[35] Ibid; Marie Johnson, '"Citizen-Centric" Demolished by NDIS Algorithms', *InnovationAus* (Blog Post, 24 May 2021) <'Citizen-centric' demolished by NDIS algorithms (innovationaus.com)>; Joint Standing C'tte on NDIS, *Independent Assessments*.

[36] The original IP test was a subjective one of whether the real applicant with their actual abilities and background could obtain a real job in the locally accessible labour market (if their disability rendered them an 'odd job lot' they qualified).

[37] Terry Carney, *Social Security Law and Policy* (Sydney: Federation Press, 2006) ch 8; Terry Carney, 'Vulnerability: False Hope for Vulnerable Social Security Clients?' (2018) 41(3) *University of New South Wales Law Journal* 783.

changes were made for CA and CP payments. The proposed NDIS assessment tools, distilled from a suite of existing measures and administered by independent assessors (as for DSP), followed the disability payment reform pathway. The risks here were twofold. First that the tool would not adequately reflect the legislative test; second, that the scoring basis would not be transparent or meaningful to clients of the NDIS and their family and advisers.[38]

The reform did however have a genuine ADM component in its proposed case planning function. The assessment tool was intended not only to determine eligibility for NDIS access but also to then generate one of 400 different 'template' indicative funding packages. This leg of the proposed reform was criticised as robo-planning which would result in lower rates of eligibility, smaller and less appropriate packages of support, and loss of individualisation (including loss of personal knowledge reflected in medical reports no longer to be part of the assessment) along with a substantial reduction of human engagement with case planners.[39]

This was a true deployment of ADM in social services, highlighting Henman's middle range risks around ADM categorisation of citizens, as well as risks from devaluing professional casework skills, as further elaborated in the next section.

5.2.3 *Predictive ADM*

Risks associated with ADM are arguably most evident when it is predictive in character.[40] This is illustrated by the role predictive tools play in determining the level and adequacy of employment services for the unemployed in Australia,[41] and the way compliance with the allocated program of assistance to gain work is tied to retention of eligibility for or the rate of unemployment payments.[42] The accuracy or otherwise of the prediction is key to both experiences.

5.2.3.1 Predictive ADM Tools in Employment Services and Social Security

Predictive ADM tools to identify those at greatest risk of long-term unemployment operate by allocating people to homogenous bands according to predictors

[38] Joint Standing C'tte on NDIS, *Independent Assessments*, ch 5, 9–13.
[39] Asher Barbaschow, 'Human Rights Commission Asks NDIS to Remember Robo-debt in Automation Push' ZDNet (Blog Post, 22 June 2021) <www.zdnet.com/article/human-rights-commission-asks-ndis-to-remember-robo-debt-in-automation-push/>.
[40] Henman, 'Improving Public Services Using Artificial Intelligence', 210.
[41] Mark Considine, Phuc Nguyen, and Siobhan O'Sullivan, 'New Public Management and the Rule of Economic Incentives: Australian Welfare-to-Work from Job Market Signalling Perspective' (2018) 20(8) *Public Management Review* 1186.
[42] Simone Casey, 'Job Seeker' Experiences of Punitive Activation in Job Services Australia' (2022) 57(4) *Australian Journal of Social Issues* 847–60 <https://doi.org/10.1002/ajs1004.1144>; Simone Casey and David O'Halloran, 'It's Time for a Cross-Disciplinary Conversation about the Effectiveness of Job Seeker Sanctions' *Austaxpolicy* (Blog Post, 18 March 2021) <www.austaxpolicy.com/its-time-for-a-cross-disciplinary-conversation-about-the-effectiveness-of-job-seeker-sanctions/>.

unemployment duration (statistical profiling). These statistical profiling predictions are much more accurate than random allocation, but still misclassify some individuals. They also fail to identify or account for *causal* reasons for membership of risk bands.[43] Human assessments are also liable to misclassify, but professional caseworkers lay claim to richer understandings of causal pathways, which may or may not be borne out in practice.

Predictive tools are constructed in two main ways. As an early pioneer, Australia's Job Seeker Classification Instrument (JSCI) was developed and subsequently adjusted using logistic regression.[44] Other international designs are constructed using machine learning which interrogates very large data sets to achieve higher accuracy of prediction, as in the Flemish tool.[45] As with all ADM predictive tools, reflection and reinforcement of bias is an issue: '[b]y definition, high accuracy models trained on historical data to satisfy a bias preserving metric will often replicate the bias present in their training data'.[46]

While there is a large literature on the merits or otherwise of possible solutions for unacceptable bias and discrimination in AI, statistical profiling poses its own quite nuanced ethical challenges. Membership of a racial minority is associated with longer durations of unemployment for instance. But the contribution of racial minority to allocation to a statistical profile band can be either bitter or sweet. Sweet if placement in that band opens a door to *voluntarily* obtaining access to employment services and training designed to counteract that disadvantage (positive discrimination). Bitter if band placement leads to involuntary imposition of requirements to participate in potentially punitive victim blaming programs such as work for the dole. This risk dilemma is real. Thus, a study of the Flemish instrument found that jobseekers not born in the country were 2.6 times more likely to wrongly be classified as at high risk of long-term unemployment.[47]

Nor is the issue confined to the more obvious variables. It arises even with superficially more benign correlations, such as the *disadvantage* actually suffered from having a long duration of employment for a single employer prior to becoming unemployed. Its inclusion in the predictive algorithm is more acceptable if this results in accessing programs to help counter the disadvantage, such as projecting

43 Bert van Landeghem, Sam Desiere, and Ludo Struyven, 'Statistical Profiling of Unemployed Jobseekers' (2021) 483(February) *IZA World of Labor* 5–6 <https://doi.org/10.15185/izawol.15483>.

44 Sam Desiere, Kristine Langenbucher, and Ludo Struyven, 'Statistical Profiling in Public Employment Services: An International Comparison' (OECD Social, Employment and Migration Working Papers, Paris, OECD Technical Workshop, 2019) 10, 14, 22–23.

45 van Landeghem et al, 'Statistical Profiling of Unemployed Jobseekers'.

46 Sandra Wachter, Brent Mittelstadt, and Chris Russell, 'Bias Preservation in Machine Learning: The Legality of Fairness Metrics under EU Non-Discrimination Law' (2021) 123(3) *West Virginia Law Review* 735, 775.

47 Sam Desiere and Ludo Struyven, 'Using Artificial Intelligence to Classify Jobseekers: The Accuracy-Equity Trade-Off (2020) 50(2) *Journal of Social Policy* 367.

the human capital benefits of past loyalty to the previous employer compared to likely future sunk costs associated with other applicants with more varied employment histories. But its inclusion is ethically more problematic if it only exposes the person to greater likelihood of incurring income support or other sanctions. Other examples of predictive legal analytics also show that the normative aspect of the law is often supplanted by causal inference drawn from a data set, which may or may not reflect the relevant legal norms.[48]

To a considerable degree, the contribution of statistical profiling hinges on the *way* it is used. The lack of engagement with causal factors and the arbitrariness or bias of some variables constituting the algorithm is magnified where caseworkers are left with little scope for overriding the initial band allocation. This is the case with Australia's JSCI, a risk compounded by lack of transparency of the algorithm's methodology.[49] These risks are lessened in employment services systems which leave caseworkers in ultimate control, drawing on assistance from a profiling tool. That is the way the tools are used in Germany, Switzerland, Greece, and Slovenia.[50]

This analysis of the risks associated with predictive tools in employment services is consistent with findings from other areas of law. For example decisions grounded in pre-established facts, such as aspects of aggravating and mitigating criminal sentencing considerations may be more amenable to computation, overcoming perceived deficiencies of instinctive synthesis sentencing law.[51] Distinguishing between administrative decisions as either rule-based or discretionary may prove also useful, because ADM applied to discretionary decisions may result in a failure to lawfully exercise discretion.[52] Discretionary tasks high in complexity and uncertainty arguably fare better under human supervision and responsibility, such as by a caseworker.[53]

For its part, Australia mitigates the risk of JSCI predictive errors in two ways. First, an employment services assessment may be conducted by a contracted health or allied health professional in certain circumstances. This is possible where it is shown

---

[48] Emre Bayamlıoğlu and Ronald Leenes, 'The "Rule of Law" Implications of Data-Driven Decision-Making: A Techno-regulatory Perspective' (2018) 10(2) *Law, Innovation and Technology* 295.

[49] Jobactive Australia, 'Assessments Guideline – Job Seeker Classification Instrument (JSCI) and Employment Services Assessment (ESAt)' (Canberra: 3 June 2020) <www.dese.gov.au/down load/6082/assessments-guideline-job-seeker-classification-instrument-jsci-and-employment-ser vices-assessment/22465/document/pdf>.

[50] Desiere et al, 'Statistical Profiling in Public Employment Services', 9–10.

[51] Nigel Stobbs, Dan Hunter, and Mirko Bagaric, 'Can Sentencing Be Enhanced by the Use of Artificial Intelligence?' (2017) 41(5) *Criminal Law Journal* 261.

[52] Justice Melissa Perry, 'AI and Automated Decision-Making: Are You Just Another Number?' (Paper presented at the *Kerr's Vision Splendid for Administrative Law: Still Fit for Purpose? – Online Symposium on the 50th Anniversary of the Kerr Report*, UNSW, 21 October 2021) <www.fedcourt.gov.au/digital-law-library/judges-speeches/justice-perry/perry-j-20211021>.

[53] Justin B Bullock, 'Artificial Intelligence, Discretion, and Bureaucracy' (2019) 49(7) *The American Review of Public Administration* 751.

that there are special barriers to employment, a significant change of circumstances or other indications of barriers to employment participation.[54] The weakness of this is that it occurs only in exceptional circumstances, rather than as part of routine caseworker fine tuning of the overly crude and harsh streaming recommendations resulting from application of the JSCI. So it is essentially confined to operating as a vulnerability *modifier*.

Second, a new payment system has been introduced to break the overly rigid nexus between the JSCI determined stream and the level of remuneration paid to employment providers for a person in that stream. The old rigid payment regime was exposed as perverse both by academic research[55] and the government's own McPhee Report.[56] Rather than encourage investment in assisting people with more complex needs it perversely encouraged parking or neglect of such cases in order to concentrate on obtaining greater rewards from assisting those needing little if any help to return to work. The New Enhanced Services model decouples service levels and rates of payment to providers for achieved outcomes, 'which provides some additional flexibility, so a participant with a High JSCI but no non-vocational barriers can be serviced in Tier 1 but still attract the higher outcome payments'.[57]

The obvious question is why Australia's employment services structure and JSCI instrument survived with so little refinement to its fundamentals for nearly two decades after risks were first raised.[58] Davidson argues convincingly that path-dependence and cheapness were two main reasons why it took until the McPhee Report to effect systemic change.[59] It is suggested here that another part of the answer lies in a lack of appetite for and difficulty of realising processes of co-design with welfare clients and stakeholders. Certainly, recent experience with co-design in

[54] DSS, *Guide to Social Security Law* (Version 1.291, 7 February 2022) para 1.1.E.104 <http://guides.dss.gov.au/guide-social-security-law> .

[55] Considine et al, 'New Public Management and the Rule of Economic Incentives'.

[56] Employment Services Expert Advisory Panel, *I Want to Work* (Canberra: Department of Jobs and Small Business, 2018) <https://docs.jobs.gov.au/system/files/doc/other/final_-_i_want_to_work.pdf>.

[57] Australia, 'New Employment Services Enhanced Services Payment Model Frequently Asked Questions 13 January 2021' (Web Page, 2023) <www.google.com/url?sa=t&rct=j&q=&esrc=s&source=web&cd=&ved=2ahUKEwjw8K_rxp_vAhVh7nMBHSc8A4YQFjACegQIDBAD&url=https%3A%2F%2Fwww.dese.gov.au%2Fdownload%2F10457%2Fnew-employment-services-enhanced-services-payment-model-frequently-asked-questions%2F19947%2Fnew-employment-services-enhanced-services-payment-model-frequently-asked-questions%2Fpdf&usg=AOvVaw0UUO6DiA_ymmo5HEeqjLqR>.

[58] Mark Considine, *Enterprising States: The Public Management of Welfare-to-Work* (Cambridge: Cambridge University Press, 2001); Terry Carney and Gaby Ramia, *From Rights to Management: Contract, New Public Management and Employment Services* (The Hague: Kluwer Law International, 2002).

[59] Peter Davidson, 'Is This the End of the Job Network Model? The Evolution and Future of Performance-Based Contracting of Employment Services in Australia' (2022) 57(3) *Australian Journal of Social Issues* 476.

Denmark demonstrates that it is possible to construct a more sophisticated and balanced system which avoids the worst of the adverse effects of statistical profiling and welfare conditionality.[60] The case for co-production with users is not new to Australian public administration.[61] Co-design is particularly favoured where risks of discrimination and exclusion are present.[62]

In theory co-design of employment services should also be possible in Australia, but the history of top-down and very harsh 'work-first' welfare-to-work policies[63] suggests that its realisation is unlikely.

5.3 RESPONDING TO THE 'POWER' OF AI

[I]n our current digital society, there are three phenomena that simultaneously connect and disconnect citizens from government and impede millions of individuals from exercising their rights on equal terms: bureaucracy, technology, and power asymmetries.[64]

ADM and AI technology in the social services carries a potential both to harm participants as well as to radically transform services by compressing the range of social policy options considered in program design much in the same way these technologies can change the bases of legal accountability (Section 5.3.2).

The power of poorly conceived ADM and AI to inflict unacceptable harm on vulnerable citizens reliant on social services is well established. The challenge here lies in finding ways of mitigating that risk, as discussed below.

5.3.1 *The Vulnerability Challenge in Social Services*

Common to assessing all of these examples of automation and artificial intelligence in welfare is the impact on vulnerable clients. That vulnerability cannot be over-stated. As Murphy J wrote in approving the robodebt class action settlement in *Prygodicz*:

---

[60] Flemming Larsen and Dorte Caswell, 'Co-Creation in an Era of Welfare Conditionality – Lessons from Denmark' (2022) 51(1) *Journal of Social Policy* 58.

[61] Bill Ryan, 'Co-production: Option or Obligation?' (2012) 71(3) *Australian Journal of Public Administration* 314.

[62] Joel Tito, BGC Foundation Centre for Public Impact, *Destination Unknown: Exploring the Impact of Artificial Intelligence on Government* (Report, 2017) <www.centreforpublicimpact .org/assets/documents/Destination-Unknown-AI-and-government.pdf>; Elisa Bertolini, 'Is Technology Really Inclusive? Some Suggestions from States Run Algorithmic Programmes' (2020) 20(2) *Global Jurist* 1–76 <https://doi.org/10.1515/gj-2019-0065>; Perry, 'AI and Automated Decision-Making'.

[63] Simone Casey, 'Social Security Rights and the Targeted Compliance Framework' (2019) February, *Social Security Rights Review* <www.nssrn.org.au/social-security-rights-review/ social-security-rights-and-the-targeted-compliance-framework/>; Casey, 'Job Seeker' Experiences'.

[64] Sofia Ranchordas and Louisa Scarcella, 'Automated Government for Vulnerable Citizens: Intermediating Rights' (2022) 30(2) *William & Mary Bill of Rights Journal* 373, 375.

It is fundamental that before the state asserts that its citizens have a legal obligation to pay a debt to it, and before it recovers those debts, the debts have a proper basis in law. The group of Australians who, from time to time, find themselves in need of support through the provision of social security benefits is broad and includes many who are marginalised or vulnerable and ill-equipped to properly understand or to challenge the basis of the asserted debts so as to protect their own legal rights. Having regard to that, and the profound asymmetry in resources, capacity and information that existed between them and the Commonwealth, it is self-evident that before the Commonwealth raised, demanded and recovered asserted social security debts, it ought to have ensured that it had a proper legal basis to do so. The proceeding revealed that the Commonwealth completely failed in fulfilling that obligation.[65]

The pain and suffering[66] from the abysmal failure of governance, ethics, and legal rectitude in the $1.8 billion robodebt catastrophe[67] was ultimately brought to heel by judicial review and class actions. Yet as already mentioned, the much vaunted 'new administrative law' remedial machinery of the 1970s was seriously exposed. Merits review failed because government 'gamed it' by failing to further appeal over 200 adverse rulings that would have made the issue public.[68] Other accountability mechanisms also proved toothless.[69] Holding ADM to account through judicial remedies is rarely viable, though very powerful when it is apt.[70] Judicial review is costly to mount, gameable, and confined to those risks stemming from clear illegality. Robodebt was a superb but very rare exception to the rule, despite the November 2019 settlement victory in the *Amato*[71] test case action, and the sizeable class action compensation settlement subsequently achieved in *Prygodicz*.[72] A test case launched prior to *Amato* was subject to government litigational gaming. That challenge was halted by the simple step of a very belated exercise of the statutory power to waive the 'debt'. The same fate could have befallen *Amato* had the then

---

[65] *Prygodicz (No 2)*, para [7].

[66] As Murphy J wrote in *Prygodicz* at para [23] 'One thing, however, that stands out ... is the financial hardship, anxiety and distress, including suicidal ideation and in some cases suicide, that people or their loved ones say was suffered as a result of the Robodebt system, and that many say they felt shame and hurt at being wrongly branded "welfare cheats"'.

[67] Whiteford, 'Debt by Design'.

[68] Townsend, 'Better Decisions?'. As pointed out in *Prygodicz*. 'The financial hardship and distress caused to so many people could have been avoided had the Commonwealth paid heed to the AAT decisions, or if it disagreed with them appealed them to a court so the question as to the legality of raising debts based on income averaging from ATO data could be finally decided': *Prygodicz (No 2)* para [10].

[69] Carney, 'Robo-debt Illegality'.

[70] Jack Maxwell, 'Judicial Review and the Digital Welfare State in the UK and Australia' (2021) 28(2) *Journal of Social Security Law* 94.

[71] *Amato v The Commonwealth of Australia* Federal Court of Australia, General Division, Consent Orders of Justice Davies, 27 November 2019, File No VID611/2019 (Consent Orders).

[72] *Prygodicz (No 2)*.

government been less stubborn in refusing to pay interest on the waived debt.[73] For its part, the reasons approving the *Prygodicz* settlement makes clear how remote is the prospect of establishing a government duty of care in negligence, much less establishing proof of breach of any duty of care.[74]

Administrative law judicial or merits review redress predicated on an 'after-the-event' interrogation of the *process* of decision-making or the lawfulness (and merits in the case of tribunal review) of the *reasons* for decisions is further undermined by the character of ADM and AI decision-making. This is because neither the decision-making processes followed, nor the thinned down/non-existent reasons generated by the 'new technological analytics'[75] are sufficiently amenable to traditional doctrine.[76] For example, bias arising from the data and code underlying ADM together with biases arising from any human deference to automated outputs, pose evidentiary challenges which may not be capable of being satisfied for the purpose of meeting the requirements of the rule against bias in judicial review.[77] The ability to bend traditional administrative law principles of due process, accountability, and proportionality to remedy the concerns posed by ADM thus appears to be quite limited.[78]

Outranking all of these concerns, however, is that neither merits review nor judicial review is designed to redress *systemic* concerns as distinct from individual grievances. So radical new thinking is called for,[79] such as a greater focus on governmentality approaches to accountability.[80] To understand the gaps in legal and institutional frameworks, the use of ADM systems in administrative settings must be reviewed as a whole – from the procurement of data and design of ADM systems to their deployment.[81] Systemic grievances are not simply a result of purely

---

[73] *Madeleine Masterton v Secretary, Department of Human Services of the Commonwealth* VID73/2019.

[74] *Prygodicz (No 2)*, paras [172]–[183] Murphy J.

[75] The emerging field of explainable AI (XAI) is a prime example which aims to address comprehension barriers and improve the overall transparency and trust of AI systems. These machine learning applications are designed to generate a qualitative understanding of AI decision-making to justify outputs, particularly in the case of outliers: Amina Adadi and Mohammed Berrada, 'Peeking Inside the Black-Box: A Survey on Explainable Artificial Intelligence (XAI)' (2018) 6 *IEEE Access* 52138.

[76] Raso, 'Unity in the Eye of the Beholder?'.

[77] Anna Huggins, 'Decision-Making, Administrative Law and Regulatory Reform' (2021) 44(3) *University of New South Wales Law Journal* 1048.

[78] But see: Makoto Cheng Hong and Choon Kuen Hui, 'Towards a Digital Government: Reflections on Automated Decision-Making and the Principles of Administrative Justice' (2019) 31 *Singapore Academy of Law Journal* 875; Arjan Widlak, Marlies van Eck, and Rik Peeters, 'Towards Principles of Good Digital Administration' in Marc Schuilenburg and Rik Peeters (eds), *The Algorithmic Society* (Abingdon: Routledge, 2020) 67–83.

[79] O'Sullivan, 'Automated Decision-Making and Human Rights', 70–88.

[80] Raso, 'Unity in the Eye of the Beholder?'.

[81] Yee-Fui Ng et al, 'Revitalising Public Law in a Technological Era: Rights, Transparency and Administrative Justice' (2020) 43(3) *University of New South Wales Law Journal* 1041.

'mathematical flaws' in digital systems, as opposed to the product of accountability deficiencies within the bureaucracy and structural injustice.[82]

One possible new direction is through ADM impact statement processes designed to help prevent systemic grievances. An example is Canada's Directive, modelled on the GDPR and largely mimicking administrative law values.[83] While this certainly has merit, it is open to critique as paying but lip service to risk prevention because it relies on industry collaboration and thus has potential for industry 'capture' or other pressures.[84] Other alternatives include a mixture of ex ante and ex post oversight in the form of an oversight board within the administrative agency to circumvent the barrier of a costly judicial challenge,[85] and the crafting of sector-specific legal mechanisms.[86]

There is also theoretical appeal in the more radical idea of turning to a governance frame that incorporates administrative accountability norms as its governance standard. The best known of these are Mashaw's trinity of bureaucratic rationality, moral judgement, and professional treatment, and Adler's additions of managerialism, consumerist, and market logics.[87]

However these innovative ideas presently lack remedial purchase. Incorporation of tools such as broadened impact assessments may give these norms and values some operational purchase, but the limitations of impact assessment would still remain.[88] A research impact framework for AI framed around concepts of public value and social value may hold greater promise.[89]

Self-regulation against industry ethics codes, or those co-authored with regulators, has also proven to be weak reeds. They too are easily 'subsumed by the business logics inherent in the technology companies that seek to self-impose ethical

---

[82] Abe Chauhan, 'Towards the Systemic Review of Automated Decision-Making Systems' (2020) 25(4) *Judicial Review* 285.

[83] Teresa Scassa, 'Administrative Law and the Governance of Automated Decision-Making: A Critical Look at Canada's Directive on Automated Decision-Making' (2021) 54(1) *University of British Columbia Law Review* 251.

[84] Andrew Selbst, 'An Institutional View of Algorithmic Impact Assessments' (2021) 35(1) *Harvard Journal of Law & Technology* 117.

[85] David Freeman Engstrom and Daniel E Ho, 'Algorithmic Accountability in the Administrative State' (2020) 37(3) *Yale Journal on Regulation* 800.

[86] Frederik J Zuiderveen Borgesius, 'Strengthening Legal Protection against Discrimination by Algorithms and Artificial Intelligence' (2020) 24(10) *The International Journal of Human Rights* 1572.

[87] E.g. Jennifer Raso, 'Implementing Digitalization in an Administrative Justice Context' in Joe Tomlinson et al (eds), *Oxford Handbook of Administrative Justice* (Oxford: Oxford University Press, 2021).

[88] Selbst, 'An Institutional View of Algorithmic Impact Assessments'.

[89] Colin van Noordt and Gianluca Misuraca, 'Evaluating the Impact of Artificial Intelligence Technologies in Public Services: Towards an Assessment Framework' (Conference Paper, *Proceedings of the 13th International Conference on Theory and Practice of Electronic Governance*, Association for Computing Machinery) 12–15.

codes',[90] or a form of 'ethics washing'.[91] As Croft and van Rijswijk[92] detailed for industry behemoths such as Google, this inability to curb corporate power is because it is systemic. As James and Whelan recently concluded:

> Codifying ethical approaches might result in better outcomes, but this still ignores the structural contexts in which AI is implemented. AI inevitably operates within powerful institutional systems, being applied to the 'problems' identified by those systems. Digital transformation reinforces and codifies neoliberal agendas, limiting capacities for expression, transparency, negotiation, democratic oversight and contestation ... This can be demonstrated by juxtaposing the AI ethics discourse in Australia with how AI has been implemented in social welfare.[93]

The Australian Human Right Commission (AHRC) Report also delivered underwhelming support,[94] though academic work is continuing to boost the contribution to be made by ethics-based audits.[95]

Consideration of how to mitigate risk of harm to vulnerable recipients of the social services cannot be divorced from meta-level impacts of ADM and AI technology on the character and design of law and social programs, as discussed below.

5.3.2 *The Transformational Power of AI to Shape Social Policy and Law*

Lawyers and social policy designers are rather accustomed to calling the shots in terms of setting normative and procedural standards of accountability (law) and formulating optimally appropriate social service programs (social policy). Digitisation, however, not only transforms the way individual citizens engage with the state and experience state power at the micro-level, but also transforms the nature of government services and modes of governance. The second of these, the transformation of governance by ADM and AI technologies,[96] is perhaps better known than the first.

Public law scholars have begun to recognise that it may not simply remain a question of how to tame ADM by rendering it accountable to traditional administrative law standards such as those of transparency, fairness, and merits review, but rather of how to avoid those values being supplanted by ADM's values and ways of thinking. The concern is that ADM remakes law in its *technological* image rather than the reverse of making ADM conform to the paradigms of the law.[97]

---

90 Selbst, 'An Institutional View of Algorithmic Impact Assessments', 166.
91 Ibid, 188.
92 Croft and van Rijswijk, *Technology: New Trajectories in Law*, ch 4.
93 James and Whelan, '"Ethical" Artificial Intelligence in the Welfare State', 37.
94 Australian Human Rights Commission (AHRC), *Human Rights and Technology: Final Report* (Final Report, 2021) 88–91 <https://tech.humanrights.gov.au/downloads>.
95 Jakob Mökander et al, 'Ethics-Based Auditing of Automated Decision-Making Systems: Nature, Scope, and Limitations' (2021) 27(4) *Science and Engineering Ethics* 44.
96 Fleur Johns, 'Governance by Data' (2021) 17 *Annual Review of Law and Social Science* 4.1.
97 Richard Re and Alicia Solow-Niederman, 'Developing Artificially Intelligent Justice' (2019) 22 (Spring) *Stanford Technology Law Review* 242; Carol Harlow and Richard Rawlings,

The same contest between ADM and existing paradigms is evident in other domains of government services. Contemporary advances in design of social services for instance favours ideas such as personalisation, social investment, and holistic rather than fragmented services.[98] But each of these policy goals is in tension with ADM's design logic of homogenisation and standardisation.[99] Personalisation of disability services through case planning meetings and devolution of responsibility for individual budgets to clients, in place of top-down imposition of standard packages of services, is one example of that tension, as recently exemplified in the NDIS.[100] The mid-2022 roll-out of algorithmic online self-management of employment services (PEPs) to all except complex or more vulnerable clients is another[101] despite introduction of requirement for a digital protection framework under s 159A (7) and (9) of the *Social Security Legislation Amendment (Streamlined Participation Requirements and Other Measures) Act 2022*.

Initiatives across the health and justice systems, such as 'social prescribing' designed to address the contribution of socioeconomic disadvantage to disability and health issues such as by coordinating income support and health

'Proceduralism and Automation: Challenges to the Values of Administrative Law' in Elizabeth Fisher, Jeff King, and Alison Young (eds), *The Foundations and Future of Public Law* (Oxford: Oxford University Press, 2020) 275–98 point out that 'Computerisation is apt to *change the nature of an administrative process*, translating public administration from a person-based service to a dehumanised system where expert systems replace officials and routine cases are handled without human input'.

[98] Australia, *A New System for Better Employment and Social Outcomes* (Final Report, Department of Social Services Reference Group on Welfare Reform to the Minister for Social Services, 2015) <www.dss.gov.au/sites/default/files/documents/02_2015/dss001_14_final_report_access_2.pdf>; Christopher Deeming and Paul Smyth, 'Social Investment after Neoliberalism: Policy Paradigms and Political Platforms' (2015) 44(2) *Journal of Social Policy* 297; Greg Marston, Sally Cowling, and Shelley Bielefeld, 'Tensions and Contradictions in Australian Social Policy Reform: Compulsory Income Management and the National Disability Insurance Scheme' (2016) 51(4) *Australian Journal of Social Issues* 399; Paul Smyth and Christopher Deeming, 'The "Social Investment Perspective" in Social Policy: A Longue Durée Perspective' (2016) 50(6) *Social Policy & Administration* 673.

[99] Jutta Treviranus, *The Three Dimensions of Inclusive Design: A Design Framework for a Digitally Transformed and Complexly Connected Society* (PhD thesis, University College Dublin, 2018) <http://openresearch.ocadu.ca/id/eprint/2745/1/TreviranusThesisVolume1%262_v5_July%204_2018.pdf>; Zoe Staines et al, 'Big Data and Poverty Governance under Australia and Aotearoa/New Zealand's "Social Investment" Policies' (2021) 56(2) *Australian Journal of Social Issues* 157.

[100] Terry Carney, 'Equity and Personalisation in the NDIS: ADM Compatible or Not?' a paper delivered at the Australian Social Policy Conference 25–29 October to 1–5 November 2021 Sydney; Alyssa Venning et al, 'Adjudicating Reasonable and Necessary Funded Supports in the National Disability Insurance Scheme: A Critical Review of the Values and Priorities Indicated in the Decisions of the Administrative Appeals Tribunal' (2021) 80(1) *Australian Journal of Public Administration* 97, 98.

[101] Casey, 'Towards Digital Dole Parole'; Mark Considine et al, 'Can Robots Understand Welfare? Exploring Machine Bureaucracies in Welfare-to-Work' (2022) 51(3) *Journal of Social Policy* 519.

services,[102] or integration of human services and justice systems through justice reinvestment or therapeutic 'problem-solving' courts[103] are two other settings where the same tension arises. In the case of social prescribing, the rigid 'quantification' of eligibility criteria for access to the disability pension, together with strict segregation of social security and health services, compounds the issue. In the second instance, predictive criminal justice risk profiling tools threaten to undermine the central rationale of individualisation and flexibility of justice reinvestment interventions to build capacity and avoid further progression into criminality.[104]

What is able to be built in social policy terms depends in no small part on the available materials from which it is to be constructed. Rule-based materials such as the algorithms and mechanisms of ADM are unsuited to building social programs reliant on the exercise of subjective discretionary choices. Just as the fiscal objective of reducing staff overheads to a minimum led to enactment of rules in place of former discretionary powers in Australian social security law,[105] government policies such as 'digital first' inexorably lead to push back against policies of individualisation and accommodation of complexity. Those program attributes call for expensive professional skills of human caseworkers or the less pricey discretionary judgments of human case administrators. ADM is far less costly than either, so in light of the long reign of neoliberal forms of governance,[106] it is unsurprising that social protection is being built with increasing amounts of ADM and AI,[107] and consequently is sculpted more in the image of that technology than of supposedly favoured welfare policies of personalisation[108] or those of social investment.[109]

There are many possible longer-run manifestations should ADM values and interests gain the upper hand over traditional legal values. One risk is that ADM

---

[102] Alex Collie, Luke Sheehan, and Ashley McAllister, 'Health Service Use of Australian Unemployment and Disability Benefit Recipients: A National, Cross-Sectional Study' (2021) 21(1) *BMC Health Services Research* 1.

[103] Lacey Schaefer and Mary Beriman, 'Problem-Solving Courts in Australia: A Review of Problems and Solutions' (2019) 14(3) *Victims & Offenders* 344.

[104] David Brown et al, *Justice Reinvestment: Winding Back Imprisonment* (Basingstoke: Palgrave Macmillan, 2016).

[105] Carney, *Social Security Law and Policy*.

[106] Rob Watts, '"Running on Empty": Australia's Neoliberal Social Security System, 1988–2015' in Jenni Mays, Greg Marston, and John Tomlinson (eds), *Basic Income in Australia and New Zealand: Perspectives from the Neoliberal Frontier* (Basingstoke: Palgrave Macmillan, 2016) 69–91.

[107] Monique Mann, 'Technological Politics of Automated Welfare Surveillance: Social (and Data) Justice through Critical Qualitative Inquiry' (2020) 1(1) *Global Perspectives* 12991 <https://doi.org/12910.11525/gp.12020.11299>.

[108] Andrew Power, Janet Lord, and Allison deFranco, *Active Citizenship and Disability: Implementing the Personalisation of Support*, Cambridge Disability Law and Policy Series (Cambridge: Cambridge University Press, 2013); Gemma Carey et al, 'The Personalisation Agenda: The Case of the Australian National Disability Insurance Scheme' (2018) 28(1) *International Review of Sociology* 1.

[109] Smyth and Deeming, 'The "Social Investment Perspective" in Social Policy'; Staines et al, 'Big Data and Poverty Governance'.

systems will create subtle behavioural biases in human decision-making,[110] changing the structural environment of decision-making. For example the facility of ADM to ascertain and process facts may lead to lesser scrutiny of the veracity of these facts than would be the case in human decision-making. Abdicating the establishment of fact and the value-judgements underlying factfinding to ADM substitutes digital authority for human authority.[111] This raises questions of accountability where human actors develop automation bias as a result of failing to question outputs generated by an automated system.[112]

Other manifestations are more insidious, including entrenchment of an assumption that data-driven decision-making is inherently neutral and objective rather than subjective and contested, or overlooking the contribution of surveillance capitalism discourse around the business practices that procure and commodify citizen data for a profit.[113] This criticism has been levelled at Nordic governmental digitalisation initiatives. The Danish digital welfare state, for example, has drawn academic scrutiny for an apparently immutable belief that data processing initiatives will create a more socially responsible public sector, overlooking the consequences of extensive data profiling using non-traditional sources such as information from individuals' social networking profiles. The public sector's embrace of private sector strategies of controlling consumers through data suggests a propensity for rule of law breaches through data maximisation, invasive surveillance, and eventual citizen disempowerment.[114]

This is not the place to do other than set down a risk marker about the way ADM and AI may change both the architecture and values of the law as well as of the very policy design of social service programs. That resculpting may be dystopian (less accommodating of human difference and discretions) or utopian in character (less susceptible to chance variability and irrelevant influences known as decisional 'noise'). The reciprocal power contest between the power of AI technology on the one hand and law/social policy on the other is however a real and present concern, as the NDIS example demonstrated.

5.4 TOWARDS AI TRUST AND EMPATHY FOR ORDINARY CITIZENS

Administration of social security payments and the crafting of reasonable and necessary supports under the NDIS are quintessentially examples of how law and government administration impact 'ordinary' citizens. As Raso has observed:

---

[110] Madalina Busuioc, 'Accountable Artificial Intelligence: Holding Algorithms to Account' (2021) 81(5) *Public Administration Review* 825.
[111] Bertolini, 'Is Technology Really Inclusive?'.
[112] Busuioc, 'Accountable Artificial Intelligence'.
[113] Shoshana Zuboff, 'Big Other: Surveillance Capitalism and the Prospects of an Information Civilization' (2015) 30(1) *Journal of Information Technology* 75.
[114] Rikke Frank Jørgensen, 'Data and Rights in the Digital Welfare State: The Case of Denmark' (2021) 26(1) *Information, Communication & Society* 123–38 <https://doi.org/10.1080/1369118X.2021.1934069>.

As public law scholars, we must evaluate how legality or governance functions within administrative institutions in everyday and effectively final decisions. As we develop theories of how it ought to function, we must interrogate how decision making *is* functioning.[115]

It is suggested here that the principal impression to be drawn from this review of Australia's recent experience of rolling out ADM in Raso's 'everyday' domain of the ordinary citizen, is one of failure of government administration. It is argued that the history so far of Australian automation of welfare – most egregiously the robodebt debacle – demonstrates both a lack of government understanding that the old ways of policy-making are no longer appropriate, and that public trust in government has seriously eroded. Automation of welfare in Australia has not only imposed considerable harm on the vulnerable,[116] but has destroyed an essential trust relationship between citizens and government.[117]

Restoring trust is critical. Trust is one of the five overarching themes identified for consultation in February 2022 by the PM&C's Digital Technology Taskforce and in the AHRC's final report.[118] Restoration of trust in the NDIS was also one of the main themes of the recent Joint Parliamentary Committee report on independent assessments.[119] Consequently, if future automation is to retain fidelity to values of transparency, quality, and user interests, it is imperative that government engage creatively with the welfare community to develop the required innovative new procedures. A commitment to genuine co-design and collaborative fine-tuning of automation initiatives should be a non-negotiable first step, as stressed for the NDIS.[120] Ensuring empathy of government/citizen dealings is another.

Emphasising in Chapter 9 about the potential for the automated state, wisely crafted and monitored to realise administrative law values, Cary Coglianese writes that

[i]n an increasingly automated state, administrative law will need to find ways to encourage agencies to ensure that members of the public will continue to have opportunities to engage with humans, express their voices, and receive acknowledgment of their predicaments. The automated state will, in short, also need to be an empathic state.

He warns that '[t]o build public trust in an automated state, government authorities will need to ensure that members of the public still feel a human connection'.

[115] Raso, 'Unity in the Eye of the Beholder?'.
[116] Carney, 'Artificial Intelligence in Welfare'.
[117] Valerie Braithwaite, 'Beyond the Bubble that Is Robodebt: How Governments that Lose Integrity Threaten Democracy' (2020) 55(3) *Australian Journal of Social Issues* 242.
[118] AHRC, *Human Rights and Technology*, 24, 28 respectively.
[119] Joint Standing C'tte on NDIS, *Independent Assessments*, ix, 22, 120, 152.
[120] 'Co-design should be a fundamental feature of any major changes to the NDIS': ibid, 145, para 9.28 and recommendation 2.

This calls for a creative new administrative vision able to honour human connection, because '[i]t is that human quality of empathy that should lead the administrative law of procedural due process to move beyond just its current emphasis on reducing errors and lowering costs'. That vision must also be one that overcomes exclusion of the marginalised and vulnerable.[121] Another contribution to building trust is to be more critical of the push for automated administration in the first place. An American 'crisis of legitimacy' in administrative agencies has been attributed to the way uncritical adoption of ADM leads to the loss of the very attributes that justify their existence, such as individualisation.[122] Framing the NDIS independent assessor episode in this way demonstrated a similar potential deterioration of citizen trust and legitimacy.

Building trust and empathy in social service administration and program design must fully embrace not only the mainstream human condition but also the 'outliers' that AI standardisation excludes.[123] At the program design level this at a minimum calls for rejection of any AI or ADM that removes or restricts inclusion of otherwise appropriate elements of personalisation, subjective human judgement, or exercise of discretion relevant to advancing agreed social policy goals. This extends to AI outside the program itself, including being sensitive to indirect exclusion from discriminatory impacts of poorly designed technological tools such as smartphones.[124]

Half a century ago in the pre-ADM 1970s, the 'new administrative law' of merits review and oversight bodies was touted as the way to cultivate citizens' trust in government administration and provide access to administrative justice for the ordinary citizen, though even then the shortfall of preventive avenues was recognised.[125] Overcoming the ability of government to game first-tier AAT by keeping adverse rulings secret, and arming it with ways of raising systemic issues (such as a form of 'administrative class action') might go a small way to restoring trust and access to justice. But much more creative thinking and work is still to be done at the level of dealing with individual grievances as well.[126]

In short, this chapter suggests that the conversation about the ADM implications for the socioeconomic rights of marginalised citizens in the social services has barely begun. Few remedies and answers currently exist either for program design or for individual welfare administration.

---

[121] Michael D'Rosario and Carlene D'Rosario, 'Beyond RoboDebt: The Future of Robotic Process Automation' (2020) 11(2) *International Journal of Strategic Decision Sciences (IJSDS)* 1; Jennifer Raso, 'AI and Administrative Law' in Florian Martin-Bariteau and Teresa Scassa (eds), *Artificial Intelligence and the Law in Canada* (Toronto: LexisNexis, 2021).

[122] Ryan Calo and Danielle Citron, 'The Automated Administrative State: A Crisis of Legitimacy' (2021) 70(4) *Emory Law Journal* 797.

[123] Treviranus, *The Three Dimensions of Inclusive Design*.

[124] Shari Trewin et al, 'Considerations for AI Fairness for People with Disabilities' (2019) 5(3) *AI Matters* 40.

[125] Jinks, 'The "New Administrative Law"'.

[126] One outstanding question for instance is whether the AHRC Report (AHRC, 'Human Rights and Technology') is correct in thinking that post-ADM merits and judicial review reforms should remain 'technology neutral' or whether more innovative measures are needed.

6

A New 'Machinery of Government'?

The Automation of Administrative Decision-Making

*Paul Miller**

6.1 INTRODUCTION: ADM AND THE MACHINERY OF GOVERNMENT

The machinery of government are those structures, processes, and people that comprise departments and agencies, and through which governments perform their functions. The term is perhaps best known in the context of 'MoG changes' – the frequent adjustments made to the way departments and agencies are structured, responsibilities and staff are grouped and managed,[1] and how agencies are named.[2] For at least the last half century, the defining characteristic of the machinery of government has been public officials (the 'bureaucrats'), structured into branches, divisions, and departments, operating pursuant to delegations, policies and procedures, and providing advice, making and implementing decisions, and delivering services for and on behalf of the government. Characterising governments as a 'machine' is both a metaphor and, like the term 'bureaucracy', can convey a somewhat pejorative connotation: machines (even 'well-oiled machines') are cold, unfeeling, mechanical things that operate according to the dictates of their fixed internal rules and logic.

---

* NSW Ombudsman. This chapter and the presentation given to the 'Money, Power and AI: From Automated Banks to Automated States' conference are edited versions of a report the Ombudsman tabled in the NSW Parliament in 2021 titled *The New Machinery of Government: Using Machine Technology in Administrative Decision-Making*. With appreciation to all officers of the NSW Ombudsman who contributed to the preparation of that report, including in particular Christie Allan, principal project officer, and Megan Smith, legal counsel.

[1] For this reason, machinery of government or 'MoG' has taken on the character of a verb for public servants – to be 'mogged' is to find oneself, through executive order, suddenly working in a different department, or unluckier still, perhaps out of a role altogether.

[2] Machinery of government changes provide an opportunity for government to express its priorities and values, or at least how it wishes those to be perceived – abolishing a department or merging it as a mere 'branch' into another may signal that it is no longer seen as a priority; re-naming a department (like re-naming a ministerial portfolio) provides an opportunity to highlight an issue of importance or proposed focus (e.g., a Department of *Customer Service*).

This chapter examines a change brought about to the machinery of government that is increasingly permeating government structures and processes – the adoption of automated decision-making (ADM) tools to assist, augment, and, in some cases, replace human decision-makers. The 'machinery of government' metaphor has been extended to frame the discussion of this topic for three reasons. First, it more clearly focuses attention on the entire system that underpins any government administrative decision, and in which digital technology may play some role. Second, rather than assuming that new technologies must – because they are *new* – be unregulated, the *role* of new technology within the machinery of government should be considered, and therefore (at least as a starting point) the well-established laws and principles that *already* control and regulate the machinery of government need to be analysed. Finally, this chapter aims to consider whether there might be lessons to be learnt from the past when other significant changes have taken place in the machinery of government. For example, do the changes that are now taking place with the increasing digitisation of government decision-making suggest that we should consider a deeper examination and reform of our mechanisms of administrative review, in a similar way to what happened in Australia in the 1970s and 1980s in response to the upheavals then taking place?

In this chapter, some of the key themes addressed in detail in the NSW Ombudsman's 2021 special report to the NSW Parliament, titled 'The new machinery of government: using machine technology in administrative decision-making'[3] (Machine Technology report), are outlined. This chapter provides a brief context of the need for visibility of government use of ADM tools and the role of the Ombudsman, key issues at the intersection between automation and administrative law and practice, and broad considerations for agencies when designing and implementing ADM tools to support the exercise of statutory functions. The chapter concludes with a question of whether the rise of ADM tools may also warrant a reconsideration of the legal frameworks and institutional arrangements.

6.2 CONTEXT

6.2.1 *The New Digital Age*

We have entered a digital age, and it is widely accepted that governments must transform themselves accordingly.[4] In this context, government digital strategies often refer to a 'digital transformation' and the need for government to become

---

[3] NSW Ombudsman, *The New Machinery of Government: Using Machine Technology in Administrative Decision-Making* (Report, 29 November 2021) <The new machinery of government: using machine technology in administrative decision-making - NSW Ombudsman>.

[4] See for example Australian Government, *Digital Government Strategy 2018–2025* (Strategy, December 2021) <www.dta.gov.au/sites/default/files/2021–11/Digital%20Government%20Strategy_acc.pdf>.

'digital by design' and 'digital by default'.[5] It is unsurprising then that digital innovation has also begun to permeate the machinery of government, changing the ways public officials make decisions and exercise powers granted to them by Parliament through legislation.[6] ADM involves a broad cluster of current and future systems and processes that, once developed, run with limited or no human involvement, and whose output can be used to assist or even displace human administrative decision-making.[7] The technology ranges in complexity from relatively rudimentary to extremely sophisticated.

6.2.2 *Government Use of ADM Tools*

The use of simpler forms of ADM tools in public sector decision-making is not new. However, what is changing is the power, complexity, scale, and prevalence of ADM tools, and the extent to which they are increasingly replacing processes that have, up to now, been the exclusive domain of human decision-making. The Machine Technology report includes case studies of New South Wales (NSW) government agencies using AI and other ADM tools in administrative decision-making functions, including fines enforcement, child protection, and driver license suspensions. Such tools are also used in areas such as policing (at NSW State level) and taxation, social services and immigration (at Australian Commonwealth level). This rise of automation in government decision-making and service delivery is a global phenomenon.[8] Internationally, it has been observed that ADM tools are disproportionately used in areas that affect 'the most vulnerable in society' – such as policing, healthcare, welfare eligibility, predictive risk scoring (e.g., in areas such as recidivism, domestic violence, and child protection), and fraud detection.[9]

As noted by the NSW Parliamentary Research Service, while there has been some international progress on increased transparency of ADM, no Australian jurisdiction

---

[5] See for example the first NSW Government Digital Strategy, NSW *Digital Government Strategy* (Strategy, May 2017) <www.digital.nsw.gov.au/sites/default/files/DigitalStrategy .pdf>; that Strategy has been revised and replaced by NSW Government, *Beyond Digital* (Strategy, November 2019) <www.digital.nsw.gov.au/sites/default/files/Beyond_Digital.pdf>.

[6] See Andrew Le Sueur, 'Robot Government: Automated Decision-Making and Its Implications for Parliament' in Alexander Horne and Andrew Le Sueur (eds), *Parliament: Legislation and Accountability* (Oxford: Hart, 2016) 181.

[7] See Commonwealth Ombudsman, *Automated Decision-Making Better Practice Guide* (Guide, 2019) 5 <www.ombudsman.gov.au/__data/assets/pdf_file/0030/109596/OMB1188-Automated-Decision-Making-Report_Final-A1898885.pdf>.

[8] Including health, criminal justice and education settings. A 2019 survey of US federal agency use of AI found that many agencies have experimented with AI and machine learning: David Freeman Engstrom et al, *Government by Algorithm: Artificial Intelligence in Federal Administrative Agencies* (Report, February 2020) <www-cdn.law.stanford.edu/wp-content/uploads/2020/02/ACUS-AI-Report.pdf>.

[9] See Jennifer Cobbe et al, 'Centering the Rule of Law in the Digital State' (2020) 53(10) *IEEE Computer* 4; Virginia Eubanks, *Automating Inequality: How High-Tech Tools Profile, Police, and Punish the Poor* (New York: St. Martin's Press, 2018).

appears to be working on creating a registry of ADM systems.[10] Additionally, in no Australian jurisdiction do government agencies currently have any general obligation to notify or report on their use of ADM tools. Nor does it appear that they routinely tell people if decisions are being made by or with the assistance of ADM tools. This lack of visibility means that currently it is not known how many government agencies are using, or developing, ADM tools to assist them in the exercise of their statutory functions, or which cohorts they impact. This is a substantial barrier to external scrutiny of government use of ADM tools.

6.2.3 The Risks of 'Maladministration'

Clearly, there are many situations in which government agencies can use appropriately designed ADM tools to assist in the exercise of their functions, which will be compatible with lawful and appropriate conduct. Indeed, in some instances automation may improve aspects of good administrative conduct – such as accuracy and consistency in decision-making, as well as mitigating the risk of individual human bias. However, if ADM tools are not designed and used in accordance with administrative law and associated principles of good administrative practice, then its use could constitute or involve 'maladministration' (for example, unlawful, unreasonable, or unjust conduct).[11] This is where an agency's conduct may attract the attention of the Ombudsman – as its role generally is to oversee government agencies and officials to ensure that they are conducting themselves lawfully, making decisions reasonably, and treating all individuals equitably and fairly. Maladministration can, of course, also potentially result in legal challenges, including a risk that administrative decisions or actions may later be held by a court to have been unlawful or invalid.[12]

---

[10] Daniel Montoya and Alice Rummery, The Use of Artificial Intelligence by Government: Parliamentary and Legal Issues' (e-brief, NSW Parliamentary Research Service, September 2020) 20.

[11] For example, the NSW Ombudsman can generally investigate complaints if conduct falls within any of the following categories set out in section 26 of the Ombudsman Act 1974:

  (a) contrary to law,
  (b) unreasonable, unjust, oppressive, or improperly discriminatory,
  (c) in accordance with any law or established practice but the law or practice is, or may be, unreasonable, unjust, oppressive, or improperly discriminatory,
  (d) based wholly or partly on improper motives, irrelevant grounds, or irrelevant consideration,
  (e) based wholly or partly on a mistake of law or fact,
  (f) conduct for which reasons should be given but are not given,
  (g) otherwise wrong.

  Conduct of the kinds set out above may be said to constitute 'maladministration' (although the NSW Act does not actually use that term).

[12] See example 'Services Australia Centrelink's automated income compliance program (Robodebt)' in NSW Ombudsman, Machine Technology Report, 27.

6.3 ADMINISTRATIVE LAW AND ADM TECHNOLOGIES

There is an important ongoing discussion about the promises and potential pitfalls of the most highly sophisticated forms of AI technology in the public sector. However, maladministration as described above can arise when utilising technology that is substantially less 'intelligent' than many might expect. The case studies in the Machine Technology Report illustrate a range of issues relating to administrative conduct, for example, the automation of statutory discretion, the translation of legislation into code, and ADM governance. Only some aspects of the technologies used in those case studies would be described as AI. In any case, the focus from an administrative law and good conduct perspective is not so much on what the technology *is*, but what it *does*, and the risks involved in its use in the public sector.[13]

Mistakes made when translating law into a form capable of execution by a machine will likely continue to be the most common source of unlawful conduct and maladministration in public sector use of ADM tools. While of course unaided human decision-makers can and do also make mistakes, the ramifications of automation errors may be far more significant. The *likelihood* of error may be higher, as the natural language of law does not lend itself easily to translation into machine code. The *scale* of error is likely to be magnified. The *detection* of error can be more difficult, as error will not necessarily be obvious to any particular person affected, and even where error is suspected, identifying its source and nature may be challenging even for the public authority itself. A machine itself is, of course, incapable of ever doubting the correctness of its own outputs. *Rectifying* errors may be more cumbersome, costly, and time-consuming, particularly if it requires a substantial rewriting of machine code, and especially where a third party vendor may be involved.

6.3.1 *The Centrality of Administrative Law and Principles of Good Administrative Practice*

Some of the broader concerns about use of ADM tools by the private sector, in terms of privacy, human rights, ethics, and so on, also apply (in some cases with greater relevance) to the public sector.[14] However, the powers, decisions, and actions of

---

[13] See further chapters 5–10 of NSW Ombudsman, *Machine Technology Report*; Marion Oswald, 'Algorithm-Assisted Decision-Making in the Public Sector: Framing the Issues Using Administrative Law Rules Governing Discretionary Powers' (2018) 376(2128) *Philosophical Transactions of the Royal Society* A 1 for a discussion of how administrative law or 'old law – interpreted in a new context – can help guide our algorithmic-assisted future'.

[14] Many of these are discussed in Australian Human Rights Commission, *Human Rights and Technology* (Final Report, 1 March 2021).

government agencies and officials are constitutionally different from that of the general private sector.

Public authorities exercise powers that impact virtually all aspects of an individual's life – there is 'scarcely any field of human activity which is not in some way open to aid or hindrance by the exercise of power by some public authority'.[15] The inherently 'public' nature of such functions (such as health, education, and transport) and the specific focus of some government service provision on groups of people likely to experience vulnerability, means that the government's use of ADM tools will necessarily, and often significantly, impact most of society. Recipients of government services – unlike customers of private sector businesses – are also typically unable to access alternative providers or to opt out entirely if they do not like the way decisions are made and services are provided. Most importantly, governments do not just provide services – they also regulate the activity of citizens and exercise a monopoly over the use of public power and coercive force – for example, taxation, licensing, law enforcement, punishment, forms of detention, and so on. It is in the exercise of functions like these, which can affect people's legal status, rights, and interests, that administrative decision-making principles raise particular issues that are unique to the public sector. Governments, by their nature, have a monopoly over public administrative power, but this means that the exercise of that power is controlled through public administrative law. Any use of ADM tools by government agencies must therefore be considered from an administrative law perspective – which is not to disregard or diminish the importance of other perspectives, such as broader ethical[16] and human rights[17] concerns.

This *administrative law* – the legal framework that controls government action – does not necessarily stand in the way of adopting ADM tools, but it will significantly control the purposes to which they can be put and the ways in which they can operate in any particular context. The ultimate aim of administrative law is good government *according to law*.[18] Administrative law is essentially principles-based and can be considered, conceptually at least, to be 'technology agnostic'. This

---

[15] New South Wales Law Reform Commission, *Appeals in Administration* (Report 16, December 1972) 6.

[16] See Madeleine Waller and Paul Waller, 'Why Predictive Algorithms Are So Risky for Public Sector Bodies' (Article, October 2020) <https://ssrn.com/abstract=3716166> who argue that consideration of ethics may be 'superfluous':

> The understanding of 'ethical behaviour' depends on social context: time, place and social norms. Hence we suggest that in the context of public administration, laws on human rights, statutory administrative functions, and data protection provide the basis for appraising the use of algorithms: maladministration is the primary concern rather than a breach of 'ethics': at 4–5, 11.

[17] Of course, although not explicitly couched in 'human rights' terms, a core preoccupation of administrative law and good administrative practice is the protection of fundamental human rights: see Australian Human Rights Commission, *Human Rights and Technology*, 55.

[18] *Corporation of the City of Enfield v Development Assessment Commission* [2000] HCA 5; (2000) 199 CLR 135, 157 at 56.

means that, while the technology used in government decision-making may change, the underlying norms that underpin administrative law remain constant. The essential requirements of administrative law for good decision-making can be grouped into four categories: proper authorisation, appropriate procedures, appropriate assessment, and adequate documentation. Administrative law is more complex than this simple list may suggest, and there are more technically rigorous ways of classifying its requirements.[19] There are, of course, also myriad ways in which administrative decision-making can go wrong – some of the more obvious considerations and risks when ADM tools are used are highlighted below.

6.3.2 *Proper Authorisation*

When Parliament creates a statutory function, it gives someone (or more than one person) power to exercise that function. This person must be a 'legal person', which can be a natural person (a human being) or a legally recognised entity, such as a statutory corporation, legally capable of exercising powers and being held accountable for obligations.[20] Proper authorisation means there must be legal power to make the relevant decision, that the person making the decision has the legal authority to do so, and that the decision is within the scope of decision-making power (including, in particular, within the bounds of any discretion conferred by the power). The requirement for proper authorisation means that statutory functions are not, and cannot be, granted to or delegated to ADM systems,[21]

---

[19] For example, requirements can be grouped according to whether a failure to comply with them gives rise to a right to challenge the decision in the courts by way of judicial review, and if they do the various individual 'grounds' of such review. They can also be grouped broadly by considering whether a failure to comply with them would mean: (a) the decision is invalid (jurisdictional error); (b) there has been some other breach of law (other legal error); or (c) the decision, or its processes, is otherwise wrong (for example, in a way that could result in an adverse finding under section 26 of the *Ombudsman Act 1974* (NSW)).

[20] There have separately been questions raised as to whether the constitutionally entrenched rights of judicial review (Commonwealth of Australia Constitution Act s 75(v)) may be affected by a move towards the automation of administrative decision-making, as those rights refer to relevant orders being 'sought against an officer of the Commonwealth': Yee-Fui Ng and Maria O'Sullivan, 'Deliberation and Automation – When Is a Decision a "Decision"?' (2019) 26 *Australian Journal of Administrative Law* 31–32. On the other hand, it might be that this constitutional provision could ultimately come to limit the ability of the government to adopt fully autonomous machines. In particular, might it be inconsistent with this provision – and therefore constitutionally impermissible – for an agency to put in place autonomous mechanisms in such a way that would result in there being no 'officer of the Commonwealth' against whom orders could be sought for legal (jurisdictional) errors? See Will Bateman and Julia Powles, Submission to the Australian Human Rights Commission, *Response to the Commission's Discussion Paper* (2020) ('Any liability rules which sought to circumvent that constitutional rule (section 75(v)) would be invalid . . .').

[21] Currently, the law recognises as 'legal persons' both individuals and certain artificial persons, such as companies and other legally incorporated bodies. Despite suggestions that AI may one day develop to such a degree that the law might recognise such a system as having legal

but only to a legal subject (a someone) and not a legal object (a something).[22]

However, a person who has been conferred (or delegated) the function may be able to obtain assistance in performing their statutory functions, at least to some extent.[23] This is recognised by the Carltona principle.[24] In conferring a statutory function on an administrator, Parliament does not necessarily intend that the administrator personally undertake every detailed component or step of the function. As a matter of 'administrative necessity', some elements of a function might need to be shared with others who are taken to be acting on the administrator's behalf. The reasoning underlying the Carltona principle appears to be sufficiently general that it could extend to permit at least some uses of ADM tools. However, the principle is based on a *necessity* imperative,[25] and cannot be relied upon to authorise the shared performance of a function merely on the basis that it might be more *efficient* or otherwise desirable to do so.[26] While the Carltona principle may be extended in the future,[27] whether and how that might happen is not clear and will depend on the particular statutory function.[28]

---

personality, this is clearly not the case today. See Will Bateman, 'Algorithmic Decision-Making and Legality: Public Law Dimensions' (2020) 94 *Australian Law Journal* 529–30.

[22] Of course, it is conceivable that legislation could be amended so that something that is now required or permitted to be done by a human administrator is instead to be done in practice by a machine. However, depending on how the legislation is drafted, the proper legal characterisation will not be that the statutory function has *moved* (from the human administrator to the machine) but rather that the *statutory function* itself has changed. For example, a legislative amendment may result in an administrator, whose original statutory function is to perform a certain decision-making task, instead being conferred a statutory function to design, install, maintain, etc. a machine that will perform that task.

[23] However, an administrator cannot abdicate to others those elements of a function where the administrator must form their own opinion: see *New South Wales Aboriginal Land Council v Minister Administering the Crown Lands Act (the Nelson Bay Claim)* [2014] NSWCA 377.

[24] *Carltona Ltd v Commissioner of Works* [1943] 2 All ER 560.

[25] 'Practical necessity' in *O'Reilly v Commissioners of State Bank of Victoria* [1983] HCA 47; (1983) 153 CLR 1 at 12.

[26] *New South Wales Aboriginal Land Council v Minister Administering the Crown Lands Act* [2014] NSWCA 377 at 38.

[27] See Katie Miller, 'The Application of Administrative Law Principles to Technology-Assisted Decision-Making' (2016) 86 *Australian Institute of Administrative Law Forum* 20 at 22. Miller argues that '[t]he need to avoid administrative "black boxes" which are immune from review or accountability may provide a basis for extending the *Carltona* principle to public servants in the context of technology-assisted decision-making to ensure that actions of technology assistants are attributable to a human decision-maker who can be held accountable'.

[28] Given uncertainty around the application of the *Carltona* principle (which is based on an inference as to Parliament's intent), the Commonwealth Ombudsman has suggested that the authority to use machine technology 'will only be beyond doubt if specifically enabled by legislation': Commonwealth Ombudsman, 'Automated Decision-Making Guide', 9. That is, rather than *inferring* that Parliament must have intended that administrators be able to seek the assistance of machines, Parliament could *expressly* state that intention.

The Carltona principle is not the only means by which administrators may obtain assistance, whether from other people or other things, to help them better perform their functions. For example, depending on the particular function, administrators can (and in some cases should, or even must) draw upon others' scientific, medical, or other technical expertise. Sometimes, this input can even be adopted as a component of the administrator's decision for certain purposes.[29] It can be expected that, like the obtaining of expert advice and the use of traditional forms of technology, there will be at least some forms and uses of sophisticated ADM tools that will come to be recognised as legitimate tools administrators can use to assist them to perform their functions, within the implicit authority conferred on them by the statute. However, whether and the extent to which this is so will need to be carefully considered on a case-by-case basis, taking into account the particular statutory function, the proposed technology, and the broader decision-making context in which the technology will be used.

Additionally, if the function is discretionary, ADM tools must not be used in a way that would result in that discretion being fettered or effectively abandoned. By giving an administrator a discretion, Parliament has relinquished some element of control over individual outcomes, recognising that those outcomes cannot be prescribed or pre-ordained in advance by fixed rules. But at the same time, Parliament is also prohibiting the administrator from setting and resorting to its own rigid and pre-determined rules that Parliament has chosen not to fix.[30] This means that exercising a discretion that Parliament has given to an administrator is just as important as complying with any fixed rules Parliament has prescribed. Over time, administrative law has developed specific rules concerning the exercise of statutory discretions. These include the so-called rule against dictation and rules governing (and limiting) the use of policies and other guidance material to regulate the use of discretion. Such rules are best viewed as applications of the more general principle described above – that where a statute gives discretion to an administrator, the administrator must retain and exercise that discretion. Those given a discretionary statutory function must, at the very least, 'keep their minds open for the exceptional case'.[31] Given this principle, some uses of ADM tools in the exercise of discretionary

---

There are already some rudimentary examples of such legislative provisions but, they are not without their own problems. See further chapter 15 of NSW Ombudsman, *Machine Technology Report*.

[29] See, for example, *Commissioner of Victims Rights v Dobbie* [2019] NSWCA 183, which involved legislation requiring a decision-maker to obtain and have regard to a report written by a relevantly qualified person but not being legally bound to accept and act on that assessment.

[30] *NEAT Domestic Trading Pty Limited v AWB Limited* [2003] HCA 35; (2003) 216 CLR 277 at 138.

[31] Ibid at 150 citing, among other authorities *R v Port of London Authority; Ex parte Kynoch Ltd* [1919] 1 KB 176 at 184; *Green v Daniels* [1977] HCA 18; (1977) 51 ALJR 463 at 467 and *Kioa v West* [1985] HCA 81; (1985) 159 CLR 550 at 632–33.

functions may be legally risky. This was the view of the Australian Administrative Review Council, which concluded that, while 'expert systems' might be used to *assist* an administrator to exercise a discretionary function, the exercise of the discretion should not be automated and any expert systems that are designed to assist in the exercise of discretionary functions should not fetter the exercise of that function by the administrator.[32] At least on current Australian authorities, ADM tools cannot be used in the exercise of discretionary functions if (and to the extent that) it would result in the discretion being effectively disregarded or fettered.[33] If the introduction of automation into a discretionary decision-making system has the effect that the administrator is no longer able to – or does not in practice – continue to exercise genuine discretion, that system will be inconsistent with the statute that granted the discretion, and its outputs will be unlawful.[34] In practice, this suggests that discretionary decisions cannot be fully automated by ADM tools.[35]

6.3.3 *Appropriate Procedures*

Good administrative decision-making requires a fair process. Appropriate procedures means that the decision has followed a procedurally fair process, that the procedures comply with other obligations including under privacy, freedom of information, and anti-discrimination laws, and that reasons are given for the decision (particularly where it significantly affects the rights or interests of individuals). Generally, a fair process requires decisions to be made without bias on the part of the decision-maker ('no-bias rule') and following a fair hearing of the person affected ('hearing rule'). ADM tools can introduce the possibility of a different form of bias known as 'algorithmic bias',[36] which arises when a machine produces results that are

---

[32] Administrative Review Council, *Automated Assistance in Administrative Decision Making* (Report No 46, 1 January 2004) <www.ag.gov.au/sites/default/files/2020–03/report-46.pdf> 15–16.

[33] James Emmett SC and Myles Pulsford, *Legality of Automated Decision-Making Procedures for the Making of Garnishee Orders* (Joint Opinion, 29 October 2020) 11 [35] from 'Annexure A – Revenue NSW case study' in NSW Ombudsman, *Machine Technology Report*: 'Subject to consideration of issues like agency (see *Carltona Ltd v Commissioner of Works* [1943] 2 All ER 560) and delegation, to be validly exercised a discretionary power must be exercised by the repository of that power'.

[34] Of course, machines themselves are inherently incapable of exercising discretion. Even if machines could exercise discretion, their doing so would not be consistent with the legislation, which has conferred the discretion on a particular (human) administrator.

[35] See 'Annexure A – Revenue NSW case study' in NSW Ombudsman, *Machine Technology Report* for a detailed case study relating to a NSW Ombudsman investigation where proper authorisation, discretionary decision-making, and the need for a decision-maker to engage in an active intellectual process were key issues.

[36] Algorithmic bias may arise without any intention to discriminate, without any awareness that it is occurring, and despite the best intentions of designers to exclude data fields that record any sensitive attributes or any obvious (to humans) proxies. See examples under 'Algorithmic bias' in NSW Ombudsman, *Machine Technology Report*, 35.

systemically prejudiced or unfair to certain groups of people. Although it is unclear whether the presence of algorithmic bias would necessarily constitute a breach of the no-bias rule, it may still lead to unlawful decisions (based on irrelevant considerations or contravening anti-discrimination laws) or other maladministration (involving or resulting in unjust or improperly discriminatory conduct). Having appropriate procedures also means providing where required, accurate, meaningful, and understandable reasons to those who are affected by a decision, which can be challenging when ADM tools have made or contributed to the making of that decision.

6.3.4 *Appropriate Assessment*

Appropriate assessment means that the decision answers the right question, is based on a proper analysis of relevant material and on the merits, and is reasonable in all the circumstances. Using ADM tools in the exercise of statutory functions means translating legislation and other guidance material (such as policy) into the form of machine-readable code. A key risk is the potential for errors in this translation process, and possibly unlawful decisions being made at scale. Any errors may mean that, even in circumstances where technology can otherwise be used consistently with principles of administrative law, doubts will arise about the legality and reliability of any decisions and actions of the public agency relying upon the automation process.[37] When designing and implementing ADM tools, it is also essential to ensure that its use does not result in any obligatory considerations being overlooked or extraneous considerations coming into play. While the use of automation may enhance the consistency of outcomes, agencies with discretionary functions must also be conscious of the duty to treat individual cases on their own merits.

6.3.5 *Adequate Documentation*

Agencies are required to properly document and keep records of decision-making. In the context of ADM tools, this means keeping sufficient records to enable comprehensive review and audit of decisions. Documentation relating to different 'versions'[38] of the technology, and details of any updates or changes to the system, may be particularly important.

6.4 DESIGNING ADM TOOLS TO COMPLY WITH THE LAW AND FUNDAMENTAL PRINCIPLES OF GOOD GOVERNMENT

To better manage the risks of maladministration in the use of ADM tools, there are at least five broad considerations that government agencies must address when

---

[37] See example 'Lost in translation – a simple error converting legislation into code' in NSW Ombudsman, *Machine Technology Report*, 43.
[38] See Miller, 'Application of Administrative Law Principles', 26.

designing and implementing ADM systems to support the exercise of an existing statutory function.[39] Dealing with those comprehensively will assist compliance with the principles of administrative law and good decision-making practice.

6.4.1 *Putting in Place the Right Team*

Adopting ADM tools to support a government function should not be viewed as simply, or primarily, an information technology project. Legislative interpretation requires specialist skills, and the challenge involved is likely to be especially pronounced when seeking to translate law into what amounts to a different language – that is, a form capable of being executed by a machine.[40] Agencies need to establish a multidisciplinary design team that involves lawyers, policymakers, and operational experts, as well as technicians, with clearly defined roles and responsibilities.[41] It is clearly better for all parties (including for the efficiency and reputation of the agency itself) if ADM tools are designed with those who are best placed to know whether it is delivering demonstrably lawful and fair decisions, rather than having to try to 'retrofit' that expertise into the system later when it is challenged in court proceedings or during an Ombudsman investigation.[42] The task of interpreting a statute to arrive at its correct meaning can be a complex task, and one that can challenge both highly experienced administrative officials and lawyers.[43] Even legal rules that appear to be straightforwardly 'black and white', and therefore appropriate candidates for ADM use, can nonetheless have a nuanced scope and meaning. They may also be subject to administrative law principles – such as underlying assumptions (for example, the principle of legality)[44] and procedural fairness obligations – which would not be apparent on the face of the legislation.

6.4.2 *Determining the Necessary Degree of Human Involvement*

Government agencies using ADM tools need to assess the appropriate degree of human involvement in the decision-making processes – discretionary and otherwise – having regard to the nature of the particular function and the statute in

---

[39] See further chapters 11–15 of NSW Ombudsman, *Machine Technology Report*.

[40] See Bernard McCabe, 'Automated Decision-Making in (Good) Government' (2020) 100 *Australian Institute of Administrative Law Forum* 118.

[41] As far back as 2004, the Administrative Review Council emphasised the need for lawyers to be actively involved in the design of machine technology for government. Administrative Review Council, *Automated Assistance in Administrative Decision Making*.

[42] See Miller, 'Application of Administrative Law Principles', 31.

[43] Anna Huggins, 'Executive Power in the Digital Age: Automation, Statutory Interpretation and Administrative Law' in J Boughey and L Burton Crawford (eds), *Interpreting Executive Power* (Alexandria: The Federation Press, 2020) 117; McCabe, 'Automated Decision-Making', 118.

[44] See the reversal of the onus of proof of the existence of a debt in the initial implementation of the Commonwealth 'Robodebt' system: Huggins, 'Executive Power in the Digital Age', 125.

question. What level of human involvement is necessary? This is not a straightforward question to answer. As noted earlier, any statutory discretion will require that a person (to whom the discretion has been given or delegated) makes a *decision* – including whether and how to exercise their discretion. Given that ADM tools do not have a subjective mental capacity, their 'decisions' may not be recognised by law as a decision.[45] Merely placing a 'human-on-top' of a process will not, of itself, validate the use of ADM tools in the exercise of a discretionary function.[46] The need for a function to be exercised by the person to whom it is given (or delegated) has also been emphasised in Australian Federal Court decisions concerning the exercise of immigration discretions, which have referred to the need for 'active intellectual consideration',[47] an 'active intellectual process',[48] or 'the reality of consideration'[49] by an administrator when making a discretionary decision.[50] The 'reality of consideration' may look different in different administrative contexts, in proportion to the nature of the function being exercised and the consequences it has for those it may affect. However, the principle remains relevant to the exercise of all discretionary functions – some level of genuine and active decision-making by a particular person is required. In a 2022 Federal Court matter, it was held that a minister failed to personally exercise a statutory power as required. The NSW Crown Solicitors Office noted, 'The decision emphasises that, whilst departmental officers can assist with preparing draft reasons, a personal exercise of power requires a minister or relevant decision-maker to undertake the deliberate task by personally considering all

---

[45] *Pintarich v Federal Commissioner of Taxation* [2018] FCAFC 79; (2018) 262 FCR 41. The situation is complicated where legislation purports to deem the output of a machine to be a decision by a relevant human administrator (see chapter 15 in NSW Ombudsman, *Machine Technology Report*).

[46] See for example 'Annexure A – Revenue NSW case study' in NSW Ombudsman, *Machine Technology Report*.

[47] *Navoto v Minister for Home Affairs* [2019] FCAFC 135 at 89.

[48] *Carrascalao v Minister for Immigration and Border Protection* [2017] FCAFC 107; (2017) 252 FCR 352 at 46; *Chetcuti v Minister for Immigration and Border Protection* [2019] FCAFC 112 at 65.

[49] *Minister for Immigration and Border Protection v Maioha* [2018] FCAFC 216; (2018) 267 FCR 643 at 45. In *Hands v Minister for Immigration and Border Protection* [2018] FCAFC 225 at 3, Allsop CJ described this, in the context of decisions made under the *Migration Act 1958* (Cth), as the need for an 'honest confrontation' with the human consequences of administrative decision-making.

[50] Among other things, these cases looked at the amount of time an administrator had between when they received relevant material and the time when they made their decision. In some cases, this time period was shown to have been too short for the administrator to have even read the material before them. The court concluded that there could not have been any 'active intellectual consideration' undertaken in the exercise of the function, and therefore overturned the decisions on the basis that there had been no valid exercise of discretion. *Carrascalao v Minister for Immigration and Border Protection* [2017] FCAFC 107; (2017) 252 FCR 352; *Chetcuti v Minister for Immigration and Border Protection* [2019] FCAFC 112.

relevant material and forming a personal state of satisfaction.'[51] What matters is not just that there is the required degree of human involvement *on paper* – there must be that human involvement *in practice*.

When designing and implementing ADM tools, government agencies need to also consider how the system will work in practice and over time, taking into consideration issues like natural human biases and behaviour and organisational culture. They must also recognise that those who will be making decisions supported by ADM tools in future will not necessarily be the people who were involved in its original conception, design, and implementation. The controls and mitigations that are needed to avoid 'creeping control' by ADM tools will need to be fully documented so they can be rigorously applied going forward.

There are several factors that are likely to be relevant to consider in determining whether there is an appropriate degree of human involvement in an ADM system. One is *time* – does the process afford the administrator sufficient time to properly consider the outputs of the tool and any other relevant individual circumstances of the case(s) in respect of which the function is being exercised? Does the administrator take this time in practice? *Cultural acceptance* is also important, particularly as it can change over time. Are there systems in place to overcome or mitigate automation-related complacency or technology bias, to scrutinise and raise queries about the output of the ADM tool, and to undertake further inquiries? If the administrator considers it appropriate, can they reject the output of the ADM tool? Is the authority of the administrator to question and reject the outputs respected and encouraged? Does it happen in practice?

Some other factors[52] relevant to active human involvement include: an administrator's access to source material used by the ADM tool and other relevant material to their decision, the seniority and experience of the administrator in relation to the type of decision being made, whether the administrator is considered responsible for the decisions they make, and whether the administrator can make or require changes to be made to the ADM tool to better support their decision-making. Finally, an appreciation of the decision-making impact including a genuine understanding of what their decision (and what a different decision) would mean in reality, including for the individuals who may be affected by the decision, is also

---

[51] NSW Crown Solicitors Office, *Administrative Law Alert: 'Sign here': A Word of Warning about Briefs to Ministers Exercising Statutory Power Personally to Make Administrative Decisions* (Web Page, April 2022) <www.cso.nsw.gov.au/Pages/cso_resources/cso-alert-ministers-statutory-power-administrative-decisions.aspx> citing *McQueen v Minister for Immigration, Citizenship, Migrant Services and Multicultural Affairs (No 3)* [2022] FCA 258.

[52] See further chapter 13 in NSW Ombudsman, *Machine Technology Report* for a more comprehensive list of considerations. Also see 'What Does the GDPR Say about Automated Decision-Making and Profiling?', *Information Commissioner's Office (UK)* (Web Page) <https://ico.org.uk/for-organisations/guide-to-data-protection/guide-to-the-general-data-protection-regulation-gdpr/automated-decision-making-and-profiling/what-does-the-gdpr-say-about-automated-decision-making-and-profiling/#id2>.

likely to be relevant.[53] It is particularly important that the relevant administrator, and others responsible for analysing or working with the outputs of the technology, has a sufficient understanding of the technology and what its outputs actually *mean* in order to be able to use them appropriately.[54] This is likely to mean that comprehensive training, both formal and on-the-job, will be required on an ongoing basis.

6.4.3 *Ensuring Transparency Including Giving Reasons*

In traditional administrative decision-making, a properly prepared statement of reasons will promote accountability in at least two ways, which can be referred to as explainability and reviewability. The former enables the person who is affected by the decision to understand it, and provides a meaningful justification for the decision. The latter refers to the manner and extent to which the decision, and the process that led to the decision, can be reviewed. A review may be by the affected persons themselves, or by another person or body, such as an Ombudsman or a court, to verify that it was lawful, reasonable, and otherwise complied with norms of good decision-making. With ADM, these two aspects of accountability tend to become more distinct.

Agencies need to ensure appropriate transparency of their ADM tools, including by deciding what can and should be disclosed about their use to those whose interests may be affected. An explanation of an automated decision might include information about the ADM tool's objectives, data used, its accuracy or success rate, and a meaningful and intelligible explanation of how the technology works to an ordinary person. When a human makes a decision, the reasons given do not refer to brain chemistry or the intricate process that commences with a particular set of synapses firing and culminates in a movement of the physical body giving rise to vocalised or written words. Likewise, explaining how an ADM tool works in a technical way, even if that explanation is fully comprehensive and accurate, will not necessarily satisfy the requirement to provide 'reasons' for its outputs. Reasons must be more than merely accurate – they should provide a meaningful and intelligible 'explanation'[55] to the person who is to receive them. Generally, this means they should be in plain English, and provide information that would be intelligible to a person with no legal or technical training. Of course, the statement of reasons should also include the usual requirements for decision notices, including details of how the decision may be challenged or reviewed, and by whom. If a review is requested or required, then further 'reasons' may be needed, which are

---

[53] *Hands v Minister for Immigration and Border Protection* [2018] FCAFC 225; (2018) 267 FCR 628 at 3.

[54] See further Counsel's advice at 'Annexure A – Revenue NSW case study' in NSW Ombudsman, *Machine Technology Report* and refer to Michael Guihot and Lyria Bennett Moses, *Artificial Intelligence, Robots and the Law* (Toronto: LexisNexis, 2020), 160.

[55] Guihot and Moses, 'Artificial Intelligence', 151–59.

more technical and enable the reviewer to 'get under the hood' of the ADM tool to identify any possible error.

Although provision of computer source code may not be necessary or sufficient as a statement of reasons, there should be (at least) a presumption in favour of proactively publishing specifications and source code of ADM technology used in decision-making. A challenge here may arise when government engages an external provider for ADM expertise.[56] Trade secrets and commercial-in-confidence arrangements should not be more important than the value of transparency and the requirement, where it exists, to provide reasons. Contractual confidentiality obligations negotiated between parties must also be read as being subject to legislation that compels the production of information to a court, tribunal, or regulatory or integrity body.[57] As a minimum, agencies should ensure that the terms of any commercial contracts they enter in respect of ADM technology will not preclude them from providing comprehensive details (including the source code and data sets) to the Ombudsman, courts, or other review bodies to enable them to review the agency's conduct for maladministration or legal error.

6.4.4 Verification, Testing, and Ongoing Monitoring

It is imperative both to test ADM tools before operationalising and to establish ongoing monitoring, audit, and review processes. Systems and processes need to be established up front to safeguard against inaccuracy and unintended consequences, such as algorithmic bias.[58] Agencies need to identify ways of testing that go beyond whether the ADM tool is performing according to its programming to consider whether the outputs are legal, fair, and reasonable. This means the costs of these ongoing testing requirements, governance processes, ongoing maintenance of the system, and training needs of the staff need to be factored in from the outset when evaluating the costs and benefits of moving to an automated system. Ignoring or underestimating these future costs and focusing only on apparent up-front cost-savings (by simplistically comparing an ADM tool's build and running costs against the expenses, usually wages, of existing manual processes) will present an inflated

---

[56] See eg, *O'Brien v Secretary, Department Communities and Justice* [2022] NSWCATAD 100. In that case a social housing tenant had applied for information about how government rental subsidies were calculated. The information sought included confidential developer algorithms and source code for an application created for the relevant government department by an external ADM tool provider. The Tribunal held that the information was not held by the department (and therefore not required to be made available to the applicant).

[57] *Smorgon v Australia and New Zealand Banking Group Limited* [1976] HCA 53; (1976) 134 CLR 475 at 489.

[58] There are various examples that demonstrate the need to verify and validate machine technology at the outset and periodically after implementation. See further chapter 14 in NSW Ombudsman, *Machine Technology Report*.

picture of the financial benefits of automation. It also ignores other qualitative considerations, such as decision-making quality and legal risks.

6.4.5 *The Role of Parliament in Authorising ADM Tools*

If the implementation of ADM tools would be potentially unlawful or legally risky, this raises the question: can and should the relevant statute be amended to expressly authorise the use of ADM tools? Seeking express legislative authorisation for the use of ADM tools not only reduces the risks for agencies, but gives Parliament and the public visibility of what is being proposed, and an opportunity to consider what other regulation of the technology may be required. There is a growing practice, particularly in the Australian Commonwealth Parliament, of enacting provisions that simply authorise, in very general terms, the use of computer programs for the purpose of certain statutory decisions. A potential risk of this approach is complacency, if agencies mistakenly believe that such a provision, of itself, means that the other risks and considerations related to administrative law and good practice (see Section 6.3) do not need to be considered. Perhaps more importantly, this approach of legislating only to 'authorise' the use of ADM tools in simple terms seems to be a missed opportunity. If legislation is going to be introduced to enable the use of ADM tools for a particular statutory process, that also presents an opportunity for public and Parliamentary debate on the *properties* that the process should be required to exhibit to meet legal, Parliamentary, and community expectations of good administrative practice. Whether or not these properties are ultimately prescribed as mandatory requirements in the legislation itself (or some other overarching statutory framework), they can guide comprehensive questions that should be asked of government agencies seeking legislative authorisation of ADM tools, as illustrated below.

- **Is It *Visible*?**

  What information does the public, and especially those directly affected, need to be told regarding the involvement of the ADM tool, how it works, its assessed accuracy, testing schedule etc? Are the design specifications and source code publicly available – for example as 'open access information' under freedom of information legislation? Is an impact assessment required to be prepared and published?[59]

- **Is It *Avoidable*?**
  Can an individual 'opt out' of the automation-led process and choose to have their case decided through a manual (human) process?

---

[59] A number of commentators have proposed 'algorithmic impact assessment' processes be undertaken similar to environment or privacy impact assessments: see, for example Michele Loi, Algorithm Watch, *Automated Decision Making in the Public Sector: An Impact Assessment Tool for Public Authorities* (Report, 2021); Nicol Turner Lee, Paul Resnick, and Genie Barton, Brookings, *Algorithmic Bias Detection and Mitigation: Best Practices and Policies to Reduce Consumer Harms* (Report, 22 May 2019).

- **Is It *Subject to Testing*?**
What testing regime must be undertaken prior to operation, and at scheduled times thereafter? What are the purposes of testing (eg compliance with specifications, accuracy, identification of algorithmic bias)? Who is to undertake that testing? What standards are to apply (eg randomised control trials)? Are the results to be made public?

- **Is It *Explainable*?**
What rights do those affected by the automated outputs have to be given reasons for those outcomes? Are reasons to be provided routinely or on request? In what form must those reasons be given and what information must they contain?

- **Is It *Accurate*?**
To what extent must the predictions or inferences of the ADM tool be demonstrated to be accurate? For example, is 'better than chance' sufficient, or is the tolerance for inaccuracy lower? How and when will accuracy be evaluated?

- **Is It *Subject to Audit*?**
What audit records must the ADM tool maintain? What audits are to be conducted (internally and externally), by whom and for what purpose?

- **Is It *Replicable*?**
Must the decision of the ADM tool be replicable in the sense that, if exactly the same inputs were re-entered, the ADM tool will consistently produce the same output, or can the ADM tool improve or change over time? If the latter, must the ADM tool be able to identify why the output now is different from what it was previously?

- **Is It *Internally Reviewable*?**
Are the outputs of the ADM tool subject to internal review by a human decision maker? What is the nature of that review (eg full merits review)? Who has standing to seek such a review? Who has the ability to conduct that review and are they sufficiently senior and qualified to do so?

- **Is It *Externally Reviewable*?**
Are the outputs of the ADM tool subject to external review or complaint to a human decision maker? What is the nature of that review (eg for example, merits review or review for error only)? Who has standing to seek such a review? If reviewable for error, what records are available to the review body to enable it to thoroughly inspect records and detect error?

- **Is It *Compensable*?**
Are those who suffer detriment by an erroneous action of the ADM tool entitled to compensation, and how is that determined?

- **Is It *Privacy Protective and Data Secure*?**
What privacy and data security measures and standards are required to be adhered to? Is a privacy impact assessment required to be undertaken and published? Are there particular rules limiting the collection, use and retention of personal information?

The properties suggested above are not exhaustive and the strength of any required properties may differ for different technologies and in different contexts. For example, in some situations, a process with a very strong property of *reviewability* may mean that a relatively weaker property of *explainability* will be acceptable.

6.5 CONCLUSION

Appropriate government use of ADM tools starts with transparency. The current lack of visibility means that it is not well known how many government agencies in NSW are using or developing ADM tools to assist in the exercise of administrative functions or what they are being used for. Nor is it possible to know who is impacted by the use of ADM tools, what validation and testing is being undertaken, whether there is ongoing monitoring for accuracy and bias, and what legal advice is being obtained to certify conformance with the requirements of administrative law.

Much of this chapter has focussed on how existing laws and norms of public sector administrative decision-making may control the use of ADM tools when used in that context. However, there are likely to be, at least initially, significant uncertainties and potentially significant gaps in the existing legal framework given the likely rapid and revolutionary changes to the way government conducts itself in the coming years. Government use of ADM tools in administrative decision-making may warrant a reconsideration of the legal frameworks, institutional arrangements, and rules that apply. It may be, for example, that existing administrative law mechanisms of redress, such as judicial review or complaint to the Ombudsman, will be considered too slow or individualised to provide an appropriate response to concerns about systemic injustices arising from algorithmic bias.[60] Modified frameworks may be needed – for example, to require the proactive external testing and auditing of systems, rather than merely reactive individual case review. If a statute is to be amended to specifically authorise particular uses of ADM tools, this creates an opportunity for Parliament to consider scaffolding a governance framework around that technology. That could include stipulating certain properties the system must exhibit in terms of transparency, accuracy, auditability, reviewability, and so on.

However, an open question is whether there is a need to consider more generally applicable legal or institutional reform, particularly to ensure that ADM tools are subject to appropriate governance, oversight, and review when used in a government

---

[60] See Jennifer Raso, 'AI and Administrative Law' in Florian Martin-Bariteau and Teresa Scassa (eds), *Artificial Intelligence and the Law in Canada* (Toronto: LexisNexis Canada, 2021); Joel Townsend, 'Better Decisions? Robodebt and the Failings of Merits Review' in Janina Boughey and Katie Miller (eds), *The Automated State: Implications, Challenges and Opportunities* (Alexandria: The Federation Press, 2021), 52, 56 (discussing the limits of existing merits review systems to address high volume, technology-assisted decision-making).

context.[61] There may be precedent for this approach. The machinery of Australia's modern administrative law – the administrative decisions tribunals, Ombudsman institutions, privacy commissions, and (in some jurisdictions) codified judicial review legislation – was largely installed in a short period of intense legislative reform, responding to what was then the new technology of modern government.[62] Ombudsman institutions (and other bodies which perform similar and potentially more specialised roles, including, for example, human rights commissions, anti-discrimination bodies, or freedom of information (FOI) and privacy commissions) have proven useful in many areas where traditional regulation and judicial enforcement are inadequate or inefficient. Ombudsman institutions also have the ability to not only respond reactively to individual complaints but also to proactively inquire into potential systemic issues, and to make public reports and recommendations to improve practices, policies, and legislation.[63] This ability to act proactively using 'own motion' powers may become increasingly relevant in the context of government use of ADM tools, partly because it seems less likely that complaints will be made about the technology itself – including if complainants are unaware of the role played by technology in the relevant decision. Rather, when people complain to bodies like the Ombudsman, the complaint is usually framed in terms of the outcome and impact on the individual. It must also be recognised that, if Ombudsman institutions are to perform this oversight role, there will be a need for capability growth. At present, it is likely they lack the in-house depth of technical skills and resources needed for any sophisticated deconstruction and interrogation of data quality and modelling, which may, at least in some cases, be required for effective scrutiny and investigation of ADM tools.[64]

---

[61] See for example Cobbe et al, 'Centering the Rule of Law', 15 ('Given the limitations of existing laws and oversight mechanisms, ... as well as the potential impact on vulnerable members of society, we argue for a comprehensive statutory framework to address public sector automation.'); Bateman, 'Public Law Dimensions', 530 ('Attaining the efficiency gains promised by public sector automation in a way that minimizes legal risk is best achieved by developing a legislative framework that governs the exercise and review of automated statutory powers in a way which protects the substantive values of public law. Other jurisdictions have made steps in that direction, and there is no reason Australia could not follow suit.'); see also Terry Carney, 'Robo-debt Illegality: The Seven Veils of Failed Guarantees of the Rule of Law?' (2019) 44(1) *Alternative Law Journal* 4.

[62] Robin Creyke, 'Administrative Justice – Towards Integrity in Government' (2007) 31(3) *Melbourne University Law Review* 705.

[63] Cf Simon Chesterman, *We, the Robots? Regulating Artificial Intelligence and the Limits of the Law* (Cambridge: Cambridge University Press, 2021), 220–22 (suggesting the establishment of 'an AI Ombudsperson').

[64] Cf Cary Coglianese and David Lehr, 'Regulating by Robot: Administrative Decision Making in the Machine-Learning Era' (2017) 105 *The Georgetown Law Journal* 1190 (suggesting oversight approaches including 'the establishment of a body of neutral and independent statistical experts to provide oversight and review, or more likely a prior rule making process informed by an expert advisory committee or subjected to a peer review process').

7

A Tale of Two Automated States

Why a One-Size-Fits-All Approach to Administrative Law Reform to Accommodate AI Will Fail

José-Miguel Bello y Villarino

7.1 INTRODUCTION: TWO TALES OF THE AUTOMATED STATE

In his 1967 book, which partially shares its title with this edited collection (*The Automated State: Computer Systems as a New Force in Society*),[1] Robert McBride anticipated that public authorities would be able to do 'more' thanks to the possibility of storing more detailed data combined with the increasing capacity of machines to process that data. He conjectured that this would create new legal problems. Fast forward half a century and the Automated State may (really) be on the brink of happening. AI can essentially change the state and the way it operates – note the 'essentially'.

Public authorities, employing (or assisted by) machines to a large scale, could do more. What this 'more' is, is a matter of discussion,[2] but, broadly speaking, it can mean two ideas: (i) doing things that humans could do, but more efficiently or to a larger scale; or (ii) doing things that could not be done before, at all or at a reasonable cost.[3] Therefore, the rules that regulate the action of public authorities need to be adapted. This chapter deals with the normative question of the type of regulatory reform that we should aim for.

It can be anticipated that changes within the immediate horizon – three to five years – will be marginal and starting at the points of least resistance, that is, in tasks

---

[1] Robert McBride, *The Automated State: Computer Systems as a New Force in Society* (Chilton Book Company, 1967).

[2] WG de Sousa et al, 'How and Where Is Artificial Intelligence in the Public Sector Going? A Literature Review and Research Agenda' (2019) 36 *Government Information Quarterly* 101392; BW Wirtz, JC Weyerer, and C Geyer, 'Artificial Intelligence and the Public Sector – Applications and Challenges' (2019) 42 *International Journal of Public Administration* 596–615.

[3] K Gulson and J-M Bello y Villarino, 'AI in Education' in Regine Paul, Emma Carmel, and Jennifer Cobbe (eds), *Handbook on Public Policy and Artificial Intelligence* (Edward Elgar, forthcoming 2023).

currently done by humans that could be easily automated. In these cases, the preferred regulatory option is likely to be the creation of some *lex specialis* for the situations when public authorities are using AI systems. This approach to automating the state and the necessary changes to the administrative law are explored in the following section (Section 7.2).

The much bigger challenge for the regulation of the Automated State will come from structural changes in the way we design policy and decide on policy options. This is best illustrated with one example already in the making: digital twins, data-driven copies of existing real-life environments or organisms. Although the attention has primarily focused on digital twins of living organisms,[4] promising work is being undertaken in other types of real-life twins, such as factories or cities. One leading example is the work in Barcelona (Spain) to create a digital twin that will help make decisions on urban policy, such as traffic management or planning.[5]

According to some reports, when one of the key planning initiatives of the local government – the *superilles*, which involved the creation of limited-traffic city-block islands – was run through the system to see the effects with and without its implementation, it showed that there was close to no improvement on air pollution levels, one of the drivers for the creation and implementation of the initiative.[6] In other words, the intervention failed to achieve one of its main goals. Does this matter for administrative law?

Section 7.3 considers these policy-oriented types of AI systems. The systems used to design policy and make decisions among policy options open the door to an intrinsically different automated state which may require completely new tools and approaches to regulate it. Although the word 'automated' could be misleading – it is better described by the periphrastic 'AI-driven decision support system for policy design and creation' – the outputs of these systems are within the scope of administrative law. They are part of processes that eventually generate administrative acts or decisions and, as such, can be the object of challenges on legal grounds in many jurisdictions.

A key part of that discussion is the problem of translating into law a procedure for legal administrative accountability for 'objectives' (a particular type of input for those AI systems) and 'insights' (outputs). AI systems are often developed to optimise a number of objectives set by humans or to autonomously find insights and interesting relations among the data fed into it. When these types of AI systems are used on data held by public authorities for policy-making purposes, they generate immediate

---

4   S Scoles, 'A Digital Twin of Your Body Could Become a Critical Part of Your Health Care' (10 February 2016) *Slate*; J Corral-Acero et al, 'The "Digital Twin" to Enable the Vision of Precision Cardiology' (2020) 41 *European Heart Journal* 4556–64.

5   J Argota Sánchez-Vaquerizo, 'Getting Real: The Challenge of Building and Validating a Large-Scale Digital Twin of Barcelona's Traffic with Empirical Data' (2022) 11 *ISPRS International Journal of Geo-Information* 24.

6   A Hernández Morales, 'Barcelona Bets on "Digital Twin" as Future of City Planning' (18 May 2022) *Politico*.

challenges to administrative law: how do we regulate policy-making that is meant not to be about discretionary choices, but about data-driven optimisation?

Concepts such as 'arbitrariness' or 'discretion' mean very different things in regard to public authorities' decisions which are an application of the law to individuals or groups, covered in Section 7.2,[7] and for decisions about how to best use public resources at a policy level, explored in Section 7.3.[8] Distinguishing between legitimate political (or policy) choices and unreasonable decisions will be challenging if at a given stage of the decision-making process there is a system that is considering one option preferable to another according to the parameters built into that system.

This type of problem may still be incipient. The technology may still be very far from reliable, but if we reach a point when some policies can be shown to be Pareto superior to others (i.e., not one of the indicators considered in the policy is worse-off, but at least one is improved), is the choice of the Pareto inferior option still legitimate or fair? Will it be legal? How much deference should then be given to the choices of decision-makers?

To solve some of these questions in Section 7.4, I suggest some preparatory work for this scenario. I develop some heuristics – or rules of thumb – to distinguish between both tales of the Automated State. On that basis, I explore whether democratic and liberal societies can create a new type of administrative law that can accommodate divergence of views and still ensure that the margin of discretion of policy choices is adjusted to this new reality.

7.2 THE ADMINISTRATIVE LAW OF AI SYSTEMS THAT REPLACE BUREAUCRATS

The use of AI for automating work currently done by humans – or creating systems that facilitate the performance of those tasks by humans – can be directly linked to previous investments by governments in information systems. These were generally associated with attempts to update the ways public organisations operated to enhance efficiency and policy effectiveness.[9] Those AI systems, if used for fully automated administrative tasks, could be 'isolated from the organisational setting they originated from'[10] and, therefore even legally considered as 'individual artificial bureaucrats'.[11]

---

[7] See, for example, the discussion about discretion in different levels of bureaucracy in JB Bullock, 'Artificial Intelligence, Discretion, and Bureaucracy' (2019) 49 *The American Review of Public Administration* 751–61.

[8] See also the discussion in Chapter 10 in this book.

[9] See A Cordella and N Tempini, 'E-Government and Organizational Change: Reappraising the Role of ICT and Bureaucracy in Public Service Delivery' (2015) 32 *Government Information Quarterly* 279–86 at 279, and the references therein.

[10] Ibid, 281.

[11] JB Bullock and K Kim, 'Creation of Artificial Bureaucrats' (Lisbon, Portugal (Online), 2020), 8.

In this context, the main consideration is that the system should be able to do its job properly. This view, therefore, naturally places the accent on testing the AI systems beforehand, particularly for impartiality and standardisation. This is something we are relatively familiar with and not conceptually dissimilar to the way Chinese imperial mandarins were subject to excruciating exams and tests before they could work for the emperor, or to the way the Spanish and French systems (and the countries in their respective areas of influence) still see the formalised gruelling testing of knowledge as a requisite to access a 'proper' bureaucrat position.

Therefore, administrative rules for the use of these AI systems are likely to focus on the systems themselves. As mentioned, the regulatory approach will then most likely emphasise ensuring that they are fit for purpose before starting operation, which is a type of legal reform already observed in several jurisdictions.

Commonly cited examples are the mechanisms already in place in Canada,[12] which focus on the risks of AI systems employed by public authorities; the proposed general approach in the European Union,[13] which expands to high-risk systems in the public and private sector; or the light-touch intervention model, which creates some pre-checks for the use of certain AI systems by the public authorities, such as the recently introduced rules in the state of New South Wales in Australia[14] – although with no concrete consequences, in this case, if the pre-check is not done properly.

Generally speaking, these approaches place the stress on the process (or its automated part) and not on the outputs. It is the system itself that must meet certain standards, defined on the basis of actual standards or specifications (in the EU case as described in article 9 of the proposal) or an impact assessment of some kind (Canada model) or the considerations of 'experts' (New South Wales, Australia model). At a higher level, this makes sense if what we are concerned about is the level of risk that could be generated by the system. The question here is 'how bad can it go?', and the law mandates to undertake that check beforehand.

In my opinion, this deviates from the views of administrative law that see the action of the public authorities as a materialisation of values such as equality and fairness.[15] Instead, this Weberian machine bureaucracy would stress impartiality and standardisation,[16] values more intrinsically attached to procedural elements.[17]

---

[12] Treasury Board of Canada, *Directive on Automated Decision-Making* (2019).

[13] European Commission, *Proposal for a Regulation of the European Parliament and of the Council Laying Down Harmonised Rules on Artificial Intelligence (Artificial Intelligence Act) and Amending Certain Union Legislative Acts* (Proposal, 21 April 2021), see also Chapter 1 in this book.

[14] Digital.NSW, NSW Government, *NSW AI Assurance Framework* (Report, 2022).

[15] S Verba, 'Fairness, Equality, and Democracy: Three Big Words' (2006) 73 *Social Research: An International Quarterly* 499–540.

[16] TM Vogl et al, 'Smart Technology and the Emergence of Algorithmic Bureaucracy: Artificial Intelligence in UK Local Authorities' (2020) 80 *Public Administration Review* 946–61 at 946.

[17] See also discussion in Chapter 12 in this book.

In the classic model of Peters, in which the public administration is a manifestation of a combination of societal, political, and administrative cultures,[18] the direct connection here is to the administrative culture, and only collaterally to societal or political elements. That type of Automated State does not need to be fair, it needs to be accurate. The fairness is meant to be embedded in the policy it implements and the legitimacy of outputs depends on whether the process correctly implements the policy.

However, as this approach incorporates elements of risk-based regulatory techniques, outputs are indeed considered in the process of conformity checks. Normally, most of these regulations of the use of AI in administrative law settings will mandate, or make a reference to, some kind of cost–benefit analysis of the social utility of the deployment and use of the system, in the way described by Sunstein.[19] The test to start employing automated systems in this context is one that compares an existing procedure in which humans participate against the efficiency, savings, reliability, risks of mistakes and harms, and other social and cultural aspects of the automated systems.

Probably the only real complication from a regulatory point of view for these systems is the decision to shift from one model to another. I have considered this problem with Vijeyarasa in relation to the VioGén, a computer-based system used for the assessment of the level risk of revictimisation of victims of gender-based violence in Spain.[20] If an AI-based system is considered to be ready to deliver an output better than a human qualitative assessment or one based on traditional statistics, what is the degree of outperformance compared to humans, or the level of reassurance necessary to make that shift, and how much capacity should be left to bureaucrats to override the system's decisions? These are not easy questions, but they are not difficult to visualise: should the standard for accepting automation be performing better than an average bureaucrat? Better than the bureaucrats with the best track records? Or when the risk of expected errors is considered as reduced as possible? At similar levels of performance, should cost be considered?

These are decisions that administrative law could explicitly leave to the discretion of bureaucrats, establish *ex ante* binding rules or principles, or leave it to the judiciary to consider it if a complaint is made. Again, not easy questions, but decisions that could be addressed within the principles that we are familiar with. In the end, the reasoning is not that dissimilar from a decision to externalise to a private provider a service hitherto delivered by the state.

[18] BG Peters, *Politics of Bureaucracy*, 5th ed (Routledge, 2002) 35.
[19] CR Sunstein, *The Cost–Benefit Revolution* (MIT Press, 2019).
[20] J-M Bello y Villarino and R Vijeyarasa, 'International Human Rights, Artificial Intelligence, and the Challenge for the Pondering State: Time to Regulate?' (2022) 40 *Nordic Journal of Human Rights* 194–215 at 208–9.

To be clear, I am not suggesting that there is anything intrinsically wrong with focusing our (regulatory) attention on these issues. I believe, however, that this view encompasses a very narrow understanding of what AI systems could do in the public sector and the legal problems it can create. This approach is conceptualised in terms of efficiency and the hope that AI can finally deliver the (so far) unmet promise of the productivity revolution that was expected from the massive incorporation of computers in the public officials' desks.[21]

From that perspective AI could be a key element of *that* Automated State. AI systems could be optimised to limit the variance between decisions with similar or equal relevant attributes. Consequently, AI-driven systems could be the best way to reach a reasonable level of impartiality, while fulfilling mundane tasks previously performed by humans.

Obviously, this cannot happen without maintaining or improving the rights of those individually or collectively affected by these automated decisions. Administrative law would need to ensure that the possible mistakes of these 'approved and certified' systems can be redressed. The legal system must allow affected parties to challenge outputs that they believe do not correctly implement policy. This could be, at least, on the basis of a possible violation of any relevant laws for that policy or a lack of coherence with its objectives, or with other relevant rights of the person or entity affected by the output of the system.

Therefore, the only need for reforms (if any) for administrative law in *this* Automated State is to (i) create a path to pre-validate the system; (ii) create guidance or determine when to change to such a system; and (iii) enable parties affected by its outputs to complain and challenge these decisions.

Other chapters in this book look at this third point in more detail, but I see it as requiring affected parties to go 'deeper' into the automated (or machine-supported) decision. The affected party, alone or in conjunction with others affected by the same or similar decisions from that system, need to be able to – at least – (i) explore why their decision can be distinguished from similar cases deserving a different administrative response; (ii) be able to raise new distinguishing factors (attributes) not considered by the system; and (iii) challenge the whole decision system on the basis of the process of pre-certification of the system and its subsequent monitoring as the system learns.

Generally speaking, the type of legislative reform necessary to accommodate this change will not create excessive friction with the approaches to administrative law

---

[21] There is a societal expectation that AI-driven systems can materialise the productivity jump that computers did not bring, and respond to Nobel Prize laureate Robert Solow's quip that 'you can see the computer age everywhere but in the productivity statistics'. 'Why a Dawn of Technological Optimism Is Breaking' (16 January 2021) *The Economist*; 'Paradox Lost' (11 September 2003) *The Economist*.

already in place in civil and common law systems.[22] Essentially, the only particularity is to be sure that the rights of the parties affected by administrative decisions do not get diluted because the administrative decision comes from a machine. The right to receive a reply, or to an intelligible explanation, or to appeal a decision considered illegal should be adapted, but not substantially changed.

Perhaps the concept of the 'organ' in civil law systems and the allocation of responsibility to the organ, which in practice makes administrative law a distinct area of law, with a different logic from the civil/criminal dichotomy still dominating the common law system,[23] could make the transition easier in civil law systems. The organ, not the bureaucrats or their service, is responsible for its outputs. However, certain rules about the burden of proof and the deference towards the state in continental systems could make it more difficult to interrogate the decision-making process of a machine.

Finally, in terms of administrative law, it is even possible to envisage a machine-driven layer of supervision or control that could monitor human action, that is, using AI to supervise the activity of public officials. One could imagine a machine-learning system which could continuously check administrative outputs created by human bureaucrats alerting affected parties and/or bureaucrats when it detects decisions that do not appear to align with previous practice or with the application of the normative and legal framework. Such an Automated State could even increase the homogeneity and predictability of administrative procedures and their alignment with the regulatory regime,[24] therefore increasing trust in the public system.

In this scenario, the Automated State will not (for the time being) replace humans, but work alongside them and only reveal itself when there is a disparity of criteria between the output of the human bureaucrat and the automatic one. The existence of this Automated State cohabiting with a manual one may require different administrative rules for human-made decisions. When decisions diverge, possible options may involve an obligation to notify affected parties of this divergence and, perhaps, granting them an automatic appeal to other administrative entities, or requiring reconsideration by the decision-maker, or imposing on the human decision-maker an obligation of more detailed and explicit motivations. In this state of automation, the human administrative decision will not be fully acceptable unless it aligns with the expected one from the Automated State. And, yet, we can still address these situations with a *lex specialis* for the automated decision, remaining within the logic and mechanisms of 'traditional' administrative law.

---

[22] Ombudsman New South Wales, *The New Machinery of Government: Using Machine Technology in Administrative Decision-Making* (Report, 2021).

[23] JAS Pastor, 'La teoría del órgano en el Derecho Administrativo' (1984) *Revista española de derecho administrativo* 43–86.

[24] Cordella and Tempini, 'E-Government and Organizational Change', 280.

Having now covered the easier of the two transitions, it is now the time to consider the other Automated State, the one that liberal-democratic legal systems could find most difficult to accommodate. The tale of the Automated State that designs or evaluates policy decisions.

7.3 REGULATING THE UNSEEN AUTOMATED STATE

As noted in the Introduction, AI can be harnessed by public authorities in ways that have not been seen before. The idea of a digital twin, for example, alters the logic behind the discretion in the decision of public authorities, as it makes possible to envisage both states of a world, with and without a decision.

If we take another step in the same direction, one could even assume that in the future the design and establishment of policy itself could be delegated to machines (cyber-delegation).[25] In this scenario, AI systems could be monitoring opportunities among existing data to suggest new policies or the modification of existing regulations in order to achieve certain objectives as defined by humans or other AI systems.

Yet, for the purpose of this chapter, we will remain at the level of the foreseeable future and only consider systems that may contribute to policy determination. The discussion below also assumes that the systems are correctly designed and operate as they are expected.

This type of automation of the state involves expert systems that are considered to provide higher levels of confidence about choices in the policy-making process. This view of the Automated State sees AI systems as engineered mechanisms 'that generate[...] outputs such as content, forecasts, recommendations or decisions for a given set of human-defined objectives', in line with current thinking in the global standardisation process.[26]

This corresponds to existing observations in governance theory that note that 'the transfer of governmental decision-making authority to outside actors occurs along a continuum'.[27] A public authority generally decides on policy through an output generated by one of its employees (elected or appointed) or a committee of them. How to reach that policy decision could be left to the employees of that public authority, reached through a system of consultation, or fully deferred to a committee of experts.

Regardless of how the decision is reached, the essential element is that the decision process is oriented towards the achievement of an implicit or explicit set of human-defined objectives. Achieving these objectives is the raison d'être of the policy decision, even if, from a social point of view, the ultimate motivation, and,

---

[25] Gulson and Bello y Villarino, 'AI in Education'.

[26] 'ISO/IEC 22989:2022(en)' (2022) sec. 3.1.4.

[27] M Shapiro, 'Administrative Law Unbounded: Reflections on Government and Governance Symposium: Globalization, Accountability, and the Future of Administrative Law' (2000) 8 *Indiana Journal of Global Legal Studies* 369–78 at 371–72.

therefore, the legitimacy of the decision to set these precise objectives, may have been spurious (e.g., to unjustifiably favour a certain service provider over others). If the advice to the decision-maker is assisted by an AI system, however, that objective needs to be explicit as it is what the system will try to achieve and optimise in relation to other factors.

Allow me, however, to explain the consequences of this statement, before exploring these objectives. The state, as an agent, does not act on its own behalf. The existence of the modern liberal state is based on the founding principle that it does not act on its own interest, but as a human creation for the benefit of its society. The human-defined objectives are the reason for its existence, the state being a tool to achieve them.

Leaving aside if this is actually the case – diverging from those who see the state as better described as a mechanism for preservation of certain parts of that society or more theoretical discussions about the role of the state – in this section I assume that decision-makers are honest about those objectives or boundary conditions.[28] As noted in the previous sections, what matters for systems that merely apply policy to reach outputs is to correctly reflect that policy in those outputs. Broader objectives such as fairness through redistribution, or equality of opportunities must be embedded in the policy design, the outputs just being the automated application of that policy. Here, the policy is what is being created by the Automated State, so the system will design or propose a policy that optimises those objectives.

In societies that democratically elect its decision-makers, one can assume that some of these objectives can come from different sources, such as:

1. Those determined by basic legal norms that constrain the action of public authorities. This is the case, for example, of constitutional rules, such as 'no discrimination on grounds of age or socioeconomic grounds', or a mandate to redress inequality derived from socioeconomic grounds or a 'right to access a no-fee system of quality education until the age of 16'.[29]
2. Those determined by the objectives hierarchically established at higher levels of decision-making. For example, one could consider the programme from a central government, or the priorities established at the ministerial level – and the principles explicated therein – as a restriction to the action of lower hierarchical levels, especially when materialised in formal directives. For example, in the fiscal context, one objective could

---

[28] That is, not cheating the process, for example, through entering into the automated system a series of acceptable objectives until they reach a desired output for other reasons, that is, their real hidden objectives.

[29] For a sample of countries having the right of education in their constitutions, see S Edwards and AG Marin, *Constitutional Rights and Education: An International Comparative Study* (2014).

be increasing the fight against fraud or, in the education context, improving the standardised results of students from disadvantage backgrounds.
3. Those that are determined by the specific decision-maker (organ or individual), who is formally in charge of making that decision. For example, in the tax context it could be accepting that more exhaustive detection of fraud would be at the cost of more administrative complaints from honest taxpayers that would be incorrectly identified. In the education context it could be a limit in the amount of resources that could be allocated to improving educational standards overall.

In all three cases the objective is the key element for the development of policy. An Automated State in which AI systems are designed to optimise these objectives will, in principle, derive its legitimacy and legality from these objectives. More importantly, the sequence of objectives listed above can be seen as hierarchical, with policymakers assisted by these AI systems bound by the objectives established by the superior levels. As an example, a decision-maker on the lowest level of hierarchy who sets the level of expenditure at this lowest level (district, local council, federated state, or national level) for public (government paid) education could not accept any recommendations from the Automated State that could suggest as optimal interventions those expected to deliver a significant improvement for overall academic standards for 99.9 per cent of the students of that administrative level, but would not offer free education for the 0.1 per cent living in the most remote communities if there is a constitutional mandate to offer free education for all. A proposal that would involve the exclusion of even one person would not be acceptable. Similarly, an option that improves the academic results for all at a given cost, but forces students from the most deprived backgrounds to separate from their families would be a violation of a tier 1 objective, and, therefore, not acceptable either. A correct design of the AI system producing the recommendation should not even generate these options.

Obviously, not all objectives follow this neat hierarchical structure. Sometimes the systems could offer recommendations for policy options that are seen as trade-offs between objectives at the same level. Some other times, there could be enough flexibility in the language of the boundary conditions that, at least formally speaking, it would not require to build those boundary conditions into the system. This would allow systems to generate some proposals that would not be accepted under a stricter objective or a different reading of the wording of the objective.

For example, a system may be allowed by humans to suggest an education policy that is expected to achieve a significant improvement for 99.9 per cent of the students. In this case policymakers tasked with creating a policy to improve standardised scores may decide to allow systems to consider this option, if they knew that they could meet the formal requirement of providing free education for all students through other means or policies. That could for example involve providing untested remote self-learning program to students for free. This would be feasible in policy settings where the boundary condition is just 'providing non-fee education' without qualification of '(proved) quality'.

As we know, it is not unusual for general mandates to be unqualified, particularly at the constitutional level, and see the qualifications being derived by interpretation from other sources (human rights principles or meaningful interpretations from high-ranking courts). In any case, it is how humans decide to translate those mandates into the system objectives what matters here.

Yet, this kind of problem may still not be that different from what systems of administrative control are facing today. The level of discretion is still added into the systems by humans and this concrete human choice (the decision to place other options within the scope of analysis) is still the one that could be controlled by courts, Ombudsman, or any other systems of administrative checks.

A second type of problem appears when the system is showing that certain options are superior to others, but benefit some groups of people differently. For example, a system that is expected to improve the results of all students, but improve the results of students from advantaged socioeconomic backgrounds by 10 per cent and those from disadvantaged backgrounds by the same 10 per cent would not be generated as a recommendation by a system which is requested to produce only options that are also expected to redress inequality. However, the same system could recommend the next best option at the same cost, which is expected to improve the results of the first group by 7 per cent and the second by 9 per cent, as this option does address inequality, which was a requirement set by humans to the system.

Favouring the latter proposal may seem absurd from a (human) rational point of view. The first suggestion is clearly superior as it would see all students being better off overall in terms of academic performance. Yet, only the second system would meet the objectives manifested in boundary conditions. A correctly built system would respect the hierarchy of objectives. Given that redressing inequality is more likely to be a constitutional or general mandate and, therefore, trump improving results – which is more likely to be an objective set at a lower hierarchical level – the first option would never be offered as a suggestion to the policymaker.

In this case, a better approach would be to allow the Automated State to present the first option to policymakers as far as the expected outputs are clear and the violation of the boundary condition is explicit. This would allow policymakers to simultaneously intervene in other ways to redress inequality. AI systems do not live in a policy vacuum, so it is important to design them and use them in a way that allows for a broader human perspective.

A third type of problem could occur when the system is designed with an added level of complexity, presenting the options in terms of trade-offs between different objectives at the same level.[30] For example, the choice could be offered to the

---

[30] Gradient Institute, *Practical Challenges for Ethical AI* (Report, 2019) 8.

decision-maker as policies that are expected to deliver overall improvements of educational standards, for all students, with a bigger gain for those from disadvantaged backgrounds (i.e., meeting all the boundary conditions and objectives), but expressed in terms of cost (in monetary units) and levels of overall improvement. Then it would be up to the decision-maker to decide which option of the many possible ones would be preferred. In this case, the main problem is one of allocation of resources, so this could initially be left to human discretion. However, as public resources are limited, if different AI systems are used to automate policy-making, setting a limit for one of these trade-offs would affect the level of trade-offs for other recommendation systems operating in other policy areas.

This could be intuitively grasped in the tax context. Imagine a public authority tasked with maximising tax revenue at the lowest cost within the legal boundaries. The system assessing anti-fraud policy may recommend an optimal level of investment in anti-fraud and establish the identified taxpayers that should be checked. Other system may be used to recommend possible media campaigns promoting compliance. This other system may suggest an optimal level of investment and the type of campaigns expected to give the highest return. Yet, it is possible that the level of resources available may not be enough to follow both suggestions. A broader system could be created to optimise both systems considered together, but what could not be done is considering each of the systems in isolation.

Looking together at these three types of problems gives us an idea about how this Automated State is different. For the systems discussed in Section 7.2, those that replace humans, I indicated that the most promising regulatory approach is the one that focuses on the systems and the testing beforehand and then shifts to monitoring of the outputs. As the bulk of the effects of each automated decision will be centred around a limited (even if large) number of individuals, the affected parties will have an incentive to raise their concerns about these decisions. This could allow for a human (administrative or judicial) review of these decisions according to the applicable rules. The automated outputs could be compared with what humans could do, according to the applicable administrative law, in those circumstances. This process would confirm or modify the automated decision and the automated systems could be refined to learn from any identified errors.

However, for the systems discussed in Section 7.3, that are used to do things that humans cannot do, especially in terms of policy design or supervision, it is impossible to proceed in such a way. Any challenge of a concrete decision could not be compared with what a human could do. Any disagreement about the reliability of the system would be too complex to disentangle.

Yet, there are aspects of the process that would still need to meet societal standards about adequate use of resources, fulfilment of superior principles of the state, or, more generally, the need to meet the state's positive obligations to protect human rights, remove inequalities, and redress violations of rights of individuals or groups.

At the very least there are three elements regarding how humans interact with the systems that generate the outputs that could be considered.

First, humans must test the systems. To grant some legal value to the recommendations of these systems – for example, to demand more from policymakers that deviate from their recommendations – this type of Automated State must be tested in real-life, real-time conditions. In the next section I explain in more detail what I mean by this point. Suffice to note here that systems tested only against data from the past may not perform well in the future and their legal usefulness as a standard for the behaviour of policymakers may therefore be undermined.

Second, humans must set the objectives that the system is meant to optimise (and suggest ways to achieve) and the boundaries that the suggestions are not meant to trespass. Which objectives and boundaries are incorporated into the system and how they are hierarchically placed and balanced can be explained and the legality of those choices controlled.

Third, humans must translate automated suggestions into policy. The example of the AI system used for assessing quality of teaching in the United States discussed in Chapter 10 of this book[31] is a perfect example of this point. Even if we trusted that the system was correctly evaluating the value of a teacher in terms of improvement of the results of their students, the consequence attached to those findings is what really matters in the legal sphere. Policymakers using such a system to assess quality of teaching could decide to fire the lowest performing teachers – as it was the case in Houston – or to invest more in the training of those teachers.

7.4 PREPARING FOR THE TWO TALES OF THE AUTOMATED STATE

In the previous sections, I discussed the two different tales of the Automated State and the distinct legal implications that each tale involves. This, however, was an oversimplification. Going back to the VioGén system presented above, one can today see a system of implementation, typical of the first tale of the Automated State, as it assesses each individual woman based on their risk of revictimisation. The suggested assessment, if accepted by the human decision-maker, automatically triggers for that victim the implementation of the protection protocol linked to her level of risk. Yet, VioGén could easily become a policy design tool. For example, it could be repurposed to collate all data for all victims and redeveloped into a system that allocates resources between women (e.g., levels of police surveillance, allocation of housing, allocations of educational programmes, suggestions about levels of monitoring of restraining orders for those charged with gender-based violence). If we consider every automated system a potential policy tool, we may be moving towards an excessive degree of administrative control of policy-making. As policymakers will

---

[31] *Houston Federation of Teachers Local 2415 et al v Houston Independent School District*, 251 F. Supp. 3d 1168 (2017).

have much more and richer data, administrative law could be used to question virtually any policy decision.

At the other extreme, one could think that it could be better to revert to almost complete deference to the discretion of policymakers. If we think of policy-making as a black box driven by criteria of opportunity or the preferences of high-ranking elected officials it is difficult to justify the need for a new type of administrative law for these situations, even if the policymakers are better placed to assess the consequences of their decisions. One can, for example, imagine the decision of a public authority to approve a new urban planning policy after a number of houses are destroyed by floods. The new policy may be so different to previous practice that its effects in case of another flood cannot be assessed by an AI-driven recommendation system. The system, however, can suggest several minor modifications that are expected to be enough to avoid a repetition of the situation. In this case the ultimate purpose of the new policy may be to increase resilience of the housing in case of new floods, but the real value of the initiative is to convey that public authorities are seen as reacting to social needs.

The expected evolution of the first type of the Automated State could also support deferring to the discretion of policymakers and ignoring the new tools of the Automated State from an administrative law perspective. As more decision-making is automated at the level of implementation, a reduction of variance should be expected. The effect in the world of these outputs could then be analysed in real time and the outputs will speak for the policies they implement. Public office holders would then be accountable if they fail to modify policies that are generating undesirable outputs. The effects of a change in policy that is implemented through fully automated means will be the basis to judge that policy. Policy design will not only refer to 'design', but also the choice and design of the automated tools that implement it.

In my view, none of these options are reasonable, so it is necessary to start developing new principles that acknowledge the legal relevance of these new tools in policy-making, without separating ourselves excessively from the process. The absolute deference to policymakers choices, even if tempting, would be a reversal of the positive 'erosion of the boundaries separating what lies inside a government and its administration and what lies outside them' or, in other words, of the transition from 'government' to 'governance'.[32]

A way to illustrate this latter point would be to consider the French example, and its evolution from a black-box State to an *administré*-centred one.[33] This transition, induced – according to a leading French scholar – by Scandinavian-, German-, and EU-driven influences, has forced administrative law to go beyond traditional rights

---

[32] Shapiro, 'Administrative Law Unbounded', 369.
[33] P Gérard, 'L'administré dans ses rapports avec l'État' (2018) 168 *Revue française d'administration publique* 913–23.

in French law (to an intelligible explanation, to receive a reply, to appeal a decision considered illegal) into a regime where the *administré* can be involved in the decision-making process and is empowered vis-à-vis the State.[34] It is not just the output, but also the logic behind the process that matters.

If the reasons for policy decisions matter, how can we then use the Automated State to demand better accountability for those decisions? Trusting this Automated State blindly or inextricably binding decision-makers to its decisions does not appear to be a good option, even if we have tested the AI systems according to the most stringent requirements. My suggestion is to develop a few principles or heuristics that could guide us in the process of reform of administrative law.

The first – and most essential from my point of view in a technology without historic track record of performance – is that systems designed to make predictions about impacts of public actions in the future need to have been tested in real conditions. This Automated State could only be relied upon for the purpose of legal assessments of policy decisions, if the predictions or suggestions of its systems have been proven to be reliable over a given number of years before the date of the decision.

Systems that are 'refined' and reliable when tested against the past cannot be a legal basis to contest policy decisions. Only real-life experiments for policy design without 'the benefit of hindsight' should matter. In these cases, deference should be paid to policymakers to the same degree as before. However, for learning and testing processes an adequate record of use should be kept – that is, systematically recording how the system was used (for testing purposes) in real-time conditions.

Secondly, we should be flexible about setting boundaries and objectives. Administrative rules should not impose designs that are excessively strict in terms of hierarchy of objectives, as some of the objectives can be addressed by different policies at the same time, not all covered by the automated systems. For those cases, the systems should be designed to allow for the relaxation of the boundary conditions (objectives) in a transparent manner, so policymakers can assess the need for other interventions. In the example above about the education systems, a rigid translation of legal principles into data could blindside us to policy options that could be adapted further to respect legal boundaries or even be the reason to adapt those boundaries.

Finally, decisions that deviate from those suggested by legally reliable automated systems should be (i) motivated by decision-makers in more detail than traditionally required; and (ii) the selected (non-recommended/Pareto-inferior) policy should be also assessed with the relevant AI systems before implementation. The results of that assessment, the policymaker motivation, and all connected information should be made – in normal circumstances – publicly available. This would allow the improvement of systems, if necessary (e.g., incorporating other considerations),

---

[34] Ibid.

and allow better administrative or judicial control of the decision in the future. Guidance could be extracted from decisions that override recommendations of environmental impact assessment, where an administrative culture that relied on discretion rather than law – for example in the English context[35] – has traditionally been an obstacle to the effective judicial control of those decisions. Discretion should be accepted as an option as far as it is explicitly justified and, hopefully, used for developing better automated systems.

[35] J Alder, 'Environmental Impact Assessment – The Inadequacies of English Law' (1993) 5 *Journal of Environmental Law* 203–20 at 203.

8

The Islamophobic Consensus

Datafying Racism in Catalonia

Aitor Jiménez and Ainhoa Nadia Douhaibi

8.1 INTRODUCTION

Catalonia is home to the largest Muslim communities of the Iberian Peninsula: a roughly 8 per cent of its population (617,453 out of 7,739,758) follows the Islamic tradition. Despite the neofascist natalist rhetoric of far-right parties speaking about a 'great replacement' (Aduriz, 2022), the number of Muslim students is consistent with the total number of Muslims. There are 1,337,965 non-tertiary education students in Catalonia,[1] approximately 101,721 of them are Muslims (7.60 per cent).[2] However, here the statistical consistencies end. The majority of Muslims work in precarious jobs or do not have jobs at all. Roughly 20 per cent of the migrant population is unemployed, compared to 8.19 per cent of general population in Catalonia.[3] They live in impoverished and deprived zones with less access to public resources and green areas. Traditionally migrant neighbourhoods such as la Barceloneta, el Raval, or Poblenou in Barcelona are among the most affected by the touristification and gentrification unleashed by foreign investment firms.[4] With scarce jobs, skyrocketing rents, and living costs, thousands of families are forced to live in slums and industrial areas with extremely poor living conditions, and are exposed to violent evictions and fatal accidents.[5] But the socioeconomic is just one of the areas where Muslim population face discrimination.

---

[1] Institut d'Estadística de Catalunya (Idescat), *Prison Population, by Nationality and Geographical Origin* (Report, 2022) <www.idescat.cat/pub/?id=aec&n=881&lang=es>.

[2] Observatorio Andalusí, *Estudio Demográfico de la Población Musulmana* (Report, 2021).

[3] Instituto Nacional de Estadística (INE), *Tasas de paro por nacionalidad, sexo y comunidad autónoma* (Report, 2022) <www.ine.es/jaxiT3/Datos.htm?t=4249>.

[4] A López-Gay, A Andújar-Llosa, and L Salvati, 'Residential Mobility, Gentrification and Neighborhood Change in Spanish Cities: A Post-Crisis Perspective' (2020) 8(3) *Spatial Demography* 351–78.

[5] Plataforma Anti-desahucios, *Emergencia habitacional, pobreza energética y salud* (Report, 2020) <https://pahbarcelona.org/wp-content/uploads/2021/01/Informe-Emergencia-Habitacional-Pobreza-Energetica-Salud-Barcelona-2017-2020-CAST.pdf>.

Muslim communities are targeted in relation to their beliefs, culture, and ways of socialising. Despite their demands, 90 per cent of Muslim students do not enjoy the same right to religious class in the public education system as their Christian-Catholic counterparts. Muslim communities often face fierce resistance from far-right organisations and public officers against their attempts of setting up and/or building mosques.[6] However, the situation is even worse within the welfare and the punitive systems. People of migrant origin, especially those from countries with Muslim majorities, are disproportionally present in the prison system. Despite being just 3.1 per cent of the population, people of Maghrebian background represent 16 per cent of the incarcerated population in Catalonia.[7] As has been pointed out by a large number of academics and activists, this is not a matter of rampant criminality among a very specific and identifiable segment of population, but the consequence of racial profiling among police agencies and social services who disproportionately target those produced as 'enemies'.[8] These episodes of discrimination are not accidental, but rather functional elements of what we conceptualised as the *Islamophobic Consensus*.

From the early days of inquisition to the latest developments in automation the social construction of the Muslim as a social enemy has helped to shape both the Spanish identity and the Spanish state's surveillance and repressive apparatuses. The subjectification of Muslims as a threat ranges from labelling them as job-stealers, and herein as a risk to the working class, to them being the ultimate enemy, the terrorist.[9] This racialisation process operates not only in relation to newcomers, but also towards the second and third generation of Muslims. As Suhaymah Manzoor-Khan has recently pointed out,[10] the pernicious characteristics attributed to the 'Muslim culture' rapidly evolved into a racially inherited condition that passes through generations.

The second decade of the twenty-first century has witnessed the proliferation of heavily racialised surveillance and carceral geographies. As the anti-immigrant raids in the United Kingdom, the United States, and Australia show, bordering

6 Observatorio Andalusí, *Estudio Demográfico de la Población Musulmana*; United Nations Special Rapporteur on Freedom of Religion or Belief, *Countering Islamophobia/Anti-Muslim Hatred to Eliminate Discrimination and Intolerance Based on Religion or Belief* (Report A/HRC/46/30, 2021) <https://documents-dds-ny.un.org/doc/UNDOC/GEN/G21/086/49/PDF/G2108649.pdf?OpenElement>.
7 Institut d'Estadística de Catalunya (Idescat), *Prison Population, by Nationality and Geographical Origin*.
8 SOS Racisme, *(In)Visibles. L'estat del racisme a Catalunya* (Report, 16 March 2022) <https://ec.europa.eu/migrant-integration/library-document/invisibles-state-racism-catalonia_en>; A Douhaibi and S Amazian, *La radicalización del racismo Islamofobia de Estado y prevención antiterrorista* (Oviedo: Editorial Cambalache, 2019).
9 D Kumar, *Islamophobia and the Politics of Empire: Twenty Years after 9/11* (London: Verso, 2021).
10 S Manzoor-Khan, *Tangled in Terror Uprooting Islamophobia* (London: Pluto, 2022).

technologies extend now to every territory, every street, and every working place.[11] The 'exceptional' and 'temporary' powers to surveil and to punish delegated to public authorities in order to fight the 'war on terror' are now well-established practices affecting every area of the public life. In Catalonia, entire Muslim communities and mosques are targeted and surveilled by an expanding 'preventive' sociotechnical system.[12] An army of educators, social workers, and police officers are now entrusted with gathering information from endless data points, and to report to their civil and police superiors the most subtle changes in individual and collective behaviour. For instance, teachers are taught by police agencies that the everyday manifestations of religiosity such as the adoption of 'Islamic' dress codes or collective prayer could could be indicators of 'radicalisation'. This information is used to terrorise vulnerable communities who are routinely threatened with criminalisation, family separation, and even deportation.

The system to prevent terrorism envisaged by the Spanish multiagency initiative on national security operates as a self-fulfilling prophecy mechanism. The risk assessments tools may flag as a threatening symbol of radicalisation of mundane and often contradictory facts. For instance, either exercising too much or having an absolute sedentary life may induce vigilantes to believe that a young Muslim is up to something.[13] In the same vein, young Muslims following severe religious routines may signal fundamentalist tendencies, but also not following religious mandates may be, in the eyes of the police services, a worrying nihilistic symptom of latent lone-wolf tendencies. These instruments and the way they look, and produce Muslims have a profound impact on the lives of thousands. Are these individuals appropriate candidates for welfare benefits? Will they be subject of an investigation either by social services or by any of the multiple police agencies? Will they be released on parole? Will they remain in prison? Will they be processed under terrorism charges? A vast sociotechnical assemblage of analogical and digital technologies controls the lives of thousands of Muslim people in Catalonia.

However, these control and disciplinary technologies are not only aimed at limiting, cancelling, and governing subaltern people. Drawing on the structural comprehension of racism pinpointed by Eduardo Bonilla Silva,[14] we argue that these technologies are part of what here is coined as the *Islamophobic Consensus*, that is, the Southern European iteration of racial neoliberalism. A system of

---

[11] S Mezzadra and B Neilson *Border as Method, or the Multiplication of Labor* (Durham: Duke University Press, 2013).

[12] JC Aguerri and D Jiménez-Franco, 'On Neoliberal Exceptionalism in Spain: A State Plan to Prevent Radicalization' (2021) 29(4) *Critical Criminology* 817–35.

[13] CITCO, Ministerio del Interior – Secretaría de Estado de Seguridad, *Plan Estratégico Nacional de Lucha Contra la Radicalización Violenta (PEN-LCRV)* (Report, 2015) <www .interior.gob.es/documents/642012/5179146/PLAN+DEFINITIVO+APROBADO.pdf/ f8226631-740a-489a-88c3-fb48146ae20d>.

[14] E Bonilla-Silva, *Racism without Racists: Color-Blind Racism and the Persistence of Racial Inequality in the United States* (Lanham: Rowman & Littlefield Publishers, 2006).

domination intended to reinforce structural gender, racial, and class inequalities, through a sociotechnical system encompassing all sorts of surveillance, repressive legal, political, economic, educational, and military instruments. Some may argue that the Spanish surveillance state has not reached full or high degrees of datafication or digitalisation as it may have been the case in countries such as the Netherlands.[15] And, perhaps, the digitalisation in Spain will never reach this level, given the characteristics of Southern European countries. However, as this chapter hypothesises, the vast surveillance apparatus deployed for gathering data of vulnerable populations, and the extensive use of actuarial and automated methods is leading to a form of datafied surveillance state.[16]

This chapter has two objectives. First, to point to the necessity of building a non-Anglocentric theoretical framework from which to study the ideological and sociological fundamentals in which datafied forms of societal oppression stand. As we further develop, the datafication techniques underpinning contemporary automated governmentalities build on long-term historical, epistemological, and ideological processes. In the case of Southern Europe these techniques can be traced back to the sixteenth century genocidal biopolitics deployed against Muslims, Jews, Roma, and Indigenous peoples.[17] We aim to fill an important gap in race, sociolegal, and critical data studies. Despite Spain and Catalonia's long and influential history of surveillance and racial oppression, its institutional surveillance apparatuses remain largely unknown and understudied. As the chapter demonstrates, the data surveillance state does not rely on the same technologies, focus on the same subjects, and pursue the same objectives in every context. On the contrary, it draws on contextual genealogies of domination, specific socioeconomic structures, and distinctive forms of distributing power. The second objective is to provide an empirical analysis on the ways the Islamophobic Consensus[18] is being operationalised in Catalonia, and with it to expose the overlapped racist mechanisms governing the lives of racialised black and brown young adults.

Drawing on empirical and archival research, the first part of the chapter analyses the surveillance-governmental apparatus deployed over Islamic communities in Catalunya. The second part of the chapter frames the ideological, epistemological, and historical fundamentals of the Southern European way to racial neoliberalism,

---

[15] A Rachovitsa and N Johann, 'The Human Rights Implications of the Use of AI in the Digital Welfare State: Lessons Learned from the Dutch SyRI Case' (2022) 22(2) *Human Rights Law Review* 1.

[16] P Alston, *Report of the Special Rapporteur on Extreme Poverty and Human Rights* (Report, 2019).

[17] I Cortés, *Sueños y sombras sobre los gitanos. La actualidad de un racismo histórico* (Barcelona: Bellaterra, 2021); S Castro-Gómez, *La hybris del punto cero: ciencia, raza e ilustración en la Nueva Granada (1750–1816)* (Bogotá: Editorial Pontificia Universidad Javeriana, 2010).

[18] KA Beydoun, 'Islamophobia, Internationalism, and the Expanse Between' (2021) 28 *Brown Journal of World Affairs* 101; Kumar, *Islamophobia and the Politics of Empire: Twenty Years after 9/11*.

here labelled as the Islamophobic Consensus. Drawing on surveillance and critical race studies, we synthesise the defining features that distinguish this model of domination from other iterations of neoliberal racism. The section continues examining two dimensions of the Islamophobic Consensus: Islamophobia as an epistemology of domination and Islamophobia as a governmentality.

8.2 DATAFYING ISLAMOPHOBIA

Since 2016, Catalonia has been implementing the *Catalan Protocol for prevention, detection and intervention in processes of Violent Extremism* or PRODERAE in schools, local police stations, prisons, and social services. PRODERAE is part of the wider Special Counter Terrorism Policing Operational Program. Despite its relevance (and the persistent requests of the authors through official channels) most details of the PRODERAE remain unavailable to the public and hence hidden from democratic scrutiny due to 'security reasons'.[19] However, a leak allowed us to get access to some documents and to a non-official recording of the PRODERAE training. On 18 May 2022, upon the requirement of the Catalan parliamentary group of the Candidatura d'Unitat Popular, we also obtained information on the training given on these instruments to public servants across different services. Specifically, the scarce data provided by the Catalan authorities accounts for the number of attendees and the number of courses given. We have crossed this documentation with the PRODERAE antecedent, the PRODERAI-CE *Protocol de prevenció, detecció i intervenció de processos de radicalització islamista- Centres Educatius* [Protocol for the prevention, detection and intervention of Islamist radicalization processes – Education centres] widely used over young Muslims. While not fully accurate, this analysis could provide a glimpse into the racist governmental strategies deployed over Muslim population in Catalonia.

Both instruments evaluate and assess the risk to individuals based on different elements such as their individual behaviour, the social, economic, professional, and educational contexts, or the ways they engage with beliefs, politics, and religion. In this regard the instruments used in Catalonia are similar to other predictive and preemptive tools used in the European context, such as the Dutch *Violent Extremism Risk Assessment*[20] and the British *Structured Professional Guidelines for Assessing Risk of Extremist Offending.*[21] Like the infamous British Prevent strategy,[22]

[19] A Douhaibi and V Almela, 'Vigilància de Frontera a plicadaa les Escoles' (29 November 2017) *La Directa* 443.s.
[20] 'Violent Extremism Risk Assessment Revised', *Dutch Ministry of Justice and Security* (Web Page) <www.vera-2r.nl/>.
[21] UK Ministry of Justice, *The Structural Properties of the Extremism Risk Guidelines (ERG22+): A Structured Formulation Tool for Extremist Offenders* (Report, 2019).
[22] UK Government, *Statutory Guidance Revised Prevent Duty Guidance: For England and Wales* (Report, 2021) <www.gov.uk/government/publications/prevent-duty-guidance/revised-prevent-duty-guidance-for-england-and-wales>.

the model proposed by the Spanish and Catalan authorities establishes a comprehensive although distributed surveillance regime over the population under risk of radicalisation (the entire Muslim community).

The PRODERAI-CE differentiates four areas from which the risk of a given subject will be evaluated: personal development, school context, family context, and social context. To obtain information the system relies on a vast array of agents, technologies, and points of data extraction that amalgamate under the securitarian prism – members of the community, educators, social workers, police officers, and intelligence services. To that end, the Catalan government has deployed considerable efforts and resources in providing training on the use of these tools to educators (3,118 since 2018), officers of the criminal justice system (CJS) including lawyers and social workers (2,013 since 2015), and police officers (30,902 since 2015). This has resulted in 667 thorough investigations of which 250 were conducted by police intelligence services. Herein, the boundaries between welfare and policing, street surveillance and cyberwarfare blurry in a diffuse although perceptible regime of racialised social control.

Among the factors related to personal development the instruments evaluate negatively 'the difficulty of managing emotions', 'the difficulty of building a multiple identity', the 'proximity to radicalised peer groups', and 'low expectations of success'.[23] Elements such as the dress code (hijab, niqab), personal appearance (beard), as well as dietary and leisure habits (halal, alcohol consumption), are surveilled with special interest. In the same vein public servants are instructed to follow closely religious beliefs and political attitudes towards specific issues. Besides the above elements, school educators are asked to pay special attention to 'the lack of bonds between peers' and 'the difficulty of (the teacher) establishing bonds with students',[24] as these elements are considered risk indicators.

With regard to the family environment, 'low family participation and involvement in school activities' and 'the [lack of] sense of belonging' are also considered as elements to consider in measuring potential radicalisation processes.[25] In terms of social context, the instruments evaluate negatively 'the influence of social networks', or if the individual belongs to 'socioeconomically disadvantaged contexts'. Another element that may trigger an alarm is the 'lack of attachment to the social environment'.[26] The information collected by public servants is transferred to the Territorial Evaluation and Monitoring Board where police officers and education inspectors will decide the feasibility of the indicated risk. This could eventually lead to further investigation, wiretapping, raids, detentions, and deportations.

---

[23] Generalitat de Catalunya, Departament d'Ensenyament, Protocol de Prevenció, detecció i intervenció de processos de radicalització als centres educatius (PRODERAI CE) 2016, 7–13 <http://educacio.gencat.cat/documents/PC/ProjectesEducatius/PRODERAI-CE.pdf>.

[24] Ibid, 13–20.

[25] Ibid, 20–24.

[26] Ibid, 24–28.

Given the opacity, secrecy, and the lack of transparency[27] guiding the Spanish and Catalan authorities' operations with regard to cases of alleged radicalisation, it is utterly difficult for researchers, activists, and even politicians to access critical information. What data gathering tools, both analogical and digital, are currently being used? How is the data gathered across services being stored, processed, analysed, and by whom? Are these data sets feeding ADM systems used in the public sector? Who is entrusted with overseeing these data-intensive tasks? Had these instruments and technological tools passed any form of auditing and impact assessment? We have asked Spanish and Catalan authorities these and other questions, but have not received any response whatsoever. However, we can infer some of this information from: (1) The documentation related to RisCanvi, the risk assessment tool used in the Catalan prison system to assess the potential recidivism of inmates in order to determine paroles, and (2) the well documented usage of tools for preventing 'radicalisation' in the United Kingdom and the Netherlands.

RisCanvi is an automated tool used by prison authorities, psychologists, criminologists, and social workers in the Catalan prison system. So far only one official report has been published,[28] which is consistent with the lack of transparency in other instruments and areas; however, the report and several academic works published by its designers gives a glimpse of the system. The tool provides a recidivism risk score that helps professionals to decide whether inmates can be paroled. For that it takes into account forty-five variables, encompassing behavioural, sociodemographic, biographical, educational, economic and social data. For instance, the system will measure whether an inmate belongs to a vulnerable group, their criminal history (and that of their peers), addictions, sexual behaviour, and so on. While necessarily overseen by humans, officers rarely disagree with the 'algorithmic score' (1 per cent) which given the 82 per cent false-positive rate[29] leads to a situation of unfairness. The weight of each variable in the final score has not been revealed, however given the known items we can infer that a potential automated discrimination may be taking place. For instance, the tool negatively weighs a vulnerable economic situation, employment status, the criminal history of family and peers among others. Items like these have been used in other tools[30] as proxies to punish race and poverty, reinforcing social prejudices against vulnerable collectives. In addition, RisCanvi has been built upon historical data gathered by the prison system, the fact which raises important problems. As we have demonstrated

---

[27] On opacity and lack of transparency see also Chapters 2, 4, 10, and 11 in this volume.

[28] As has been criticised in LISA News, '¿Es posible predecir la reincidencia de los presos?' (16 February 2022, Web Page) <www.lisanews.org/actualidad/es-posible-predecir-reincidencia-de-presos-espana/>.

[29] LM Garay, 'Errores conceptuales en la estimación de riesgo de reincidencia' (2016) 14 *Revista Española de Investigación Criminológica* 1–31.

[30] BE Harcourt, 'Risk as a Proxy for Race: The Dangers of Risk Assessment' (2015) 27(4) *Federal Sentencing Reporter* 237–43.

elsewhere,[31] classism and racism run rampant across the Spanish and Catalan criminal justice systems. Racialised and poor subjects are more likely to be stopped, detained, arrested, and processed. Hence, the 'dirty' data set[32] feeding the system nurture a discriminatory feedback loop.

Britain's Violent Extremism Preventing Program, popularly known as Prevent, is part of United Kingdom's national counter-terrorism strategy CONTEST. It was launched in 2006 by the then governing UK Labour Party.[33] Its reach has expanded from police and prisons, to child care, elementary and high schools, tertiary education institutions, and even the National Healthcare System (NHS). The Extremism Risk Guidelines 22+ (known as ERG 22+) developed by 'Her Majesty's Prison and Probations Service' in 2011 is the inductive instrument that gathers the 'radicalisation signals' and backs-up the program with the risk assessment framework. The ERG22+ is presented as 'a structured professional judgement (SPJ) tool that assesses individuals along 22 factors that are grouped into three domains; Engagement, Intent and Capability'.[34] This has been replicated in the PRODERAE-PRODERAI-CE training, which uses terminology such as 'identity, meaning and belonging', 'us and them thinking', 'overidentification with a group, cause or ideology', 'the need to redress justice', or 'the need to defend against threats'.

Many scholars have highlighted how the UK's automated tools associate Muslims with terrorism, putting the entire Muslim population on the spot.[35] Moreover, recent research highlights community surveillance is becoming universal surveillance.[36] For instance, NHS' public servants are now legally obliged to comply with their policing tasks, not only over 'suspicious communities', but also have to look for unpredicted new patterns of extremism in the entire patient population.[37]

---

[31] Douhaibi and Amazian, *La radicalización del racismo Islamofobia de Estado y prevención antiterrorista*; A Jiménez and E Cancela, 'Surveillance Punitivism: Colonialism, Racism, and State Terrorism in Spain' (2021) 19(3) *Surveillance & Society* 374–78.

[32] R Richardson, JM Schultz, and K Crawford, 'Dirty Data, Bad Predictions: How Civil Rights Violations Impact Police Data, Predictive Policing Systems, and Justice' (2019) 94 *NYUL Review Online* 15.

[33] A Kundnani, Institute of Race Relations, *Spooked! How Not to Prevent Violent Extremism* (Report, 2009).

[34] UK Ministry of Justice, *The Structural Properties of the Extremism Risk Guidelines (ERG22+): A Structured Formulation Tool for Extremist Offenders*, 3.

[35] Manzoor-Khan, *Tangled in Terror Uprooting Islamophobia*; C Heath-Kelly, 'Algorithmic Autoimmunity in the NHS: Radicalisation and the Clinic' (2017) 48(1) *Security Dialogue* 29–45; T Younis and S Jadhav, 'Islamophobia in the National Health Service: An Ethnography of Institutional Racism in PREVENT's Counter-Radicalisation Policy' (2020) 42(3) *Sociology of Health & Illness* 610–26.

[36] Heath-Kelly, 'Algorithmic Autoimmunity in the NHS: Radicalisation and the Clinic'; Younis and Jadhav, 'Islamophobia in the National Health Service: An Ethnography of Institutional Racism in PREVENT's Counter-Radicalisation Policy'.

[37] Heath-Kelly, 'Algorithmic Autoimmunity in the NHS: Radicalisation and the Clinic'.

In fact, as Heath-Kelly[38] points out the implementation in the national healthcare and education systems belongs to modalities of calculation derived from automated and big data tools that enable mass surveillance methods. She even argues that this kind of surveillance inductively produces the terrorist profile.[39] Consequently, the outcome of this approach is the production of Islamophobic data associated with Muslim (pre)criminality. Even if the cases are dismissed, the details of the people that flagged the alert remain in the UK's police database for seven years.[40] 'Prevent' has been the target of profound critique in numerous reports from antiracist and anticolonial grassroots movements (Islamic Human Rights Commission, Cage UK), as well as international human rights organisations such as the Transnational Institute and Amnesty International.[41] One of the last reports not only pointed to its Islamophobic and discriminatory nature, but also to its ineffectiveness.[42] Despite the wide critique, the UK Home Office has only expressed that they 'can find no evidence to support these claims'.[43]

Despite the limited information available, the PRODERAE and PRODERAI show important theoretical and operational flaws worth highlighting. First and foremost, both instruments are aimed at preventing radicalisation. However, there is a striking lack of theoretical consensus on its definition.[44] Radicalisation takes shape when protocols such as PRODERAE are applied. It is thus a tool for producing 'dangerous subjects'. The second problem is that many of the hidden indicators are expressions of religious practice. Changing the dressing code or adopting a more visibly Muslim expression, as wearing a hijab, putting henna on their hands, respecting prayer hours, demanding a halal menu, speaking or expressing opinions based on Islamic precepts or even expressing social discontent or pointing out Islamophobic or racist practices can all be indicators of radicalisation.

The tools analysed are embedded in vagueness and abstraction, if not falling in blatant contradictions. Factors and indicators that guide their implementation are left to the arbitrary interpretation of public officers. For instance, playing too many violent video games may indicate 'military training', although not playing video games at all may be a symptom of rejection of 'westernisation', in consequence both

---

[38] Ibid, 30.

[39] Ibid, 39.

[40] Manzoor-Khan, *Tangled in Terror Uprooting Islamophobia*; A Kundnani, *The Muslims Are Coming!: Islamophobia, Extremism, and the Domestic War on Terror* (London: Verso, 2014).

[41] Amnesty International & Open Society Foundation, *A Human Rights Guide for Researching Racial and Religious Discrimination in Counter-Terrorism in Europe* (Report, 2021) <www.amnesty.org/en/wp-content/uploads/2021/05/EUR0136062021ENGLISH.pdf>.

[42] J Holmwood and L Aitlhadj, *The People's Review of Prevent* (Report, February 2022).

[43] HM Government, Prevent Strategy, Presented to Parliament by the Secretary of State for the Home Department by Command of Her Majesty June 2011, 28, <https://assets.publishing.service.gov.uk/government/uploads/system/uploads/attachment_data/file/97976/prevent-strategy-review.pdf>.

[44] A Kundnani, 'Radicalization: The Journey of a Concept' (2012) 54(2) *Race & Class* 3–25; Manzoor-Khan, *Tangled in Terror Uprooting Islamophobia*.

playing and not playing video games become a cause of suspicion. In the same vein, many of the 'radicalisation symptoms' indicated by the tools, such as troubles in navigating multiple identities, swift changes in appearance, friends, and habits, are most often processes inherent to the personal development of teenagers and young adults, and not 'strange' or 'deviated' as the tools make them to be. These tools embrace a hyper individualistic approach making individuals responsible for the consequences of complex socio-structural problems. For instance, individuals are accused of separatism and cultural isolation, ignoring the endemic economic crisis that, along with the racial division of labour, nurtures a growing racialised geography and school segregation. To illustrate, the chances of being flagged as a risky subject dramatically rise when students rely too much on 'cultural and religious' peers, because as the document states 'the school has difficulties in promoting an inclusive environment'.[45] The tools, far from helping the school to better understand these difficulties, seem to present them as elements of suspicion. As we can see, the pernicious consequences of the racial neoliberal project are datafied and hidden under an aura of false technological neutrality, just to be weaponised against its victims.

Finally, as multiple scholars have warned, predictive and preemptive tools used across the public sector (welfare, CJS, policing, and surveillance) entail considerable risks especially for already vulnerable and racialised populations.[46] This has been demonstrated in recent scandals involving classist and racist sociotechnical systems deployed in Australia, the United Kingdom, and the Netherlands, to name a few. It was Bernard Harcourt who famously stated that these technologies can 'create a vicious circle, a kind of self-fulfilling prophecy'[47] contributing to 'reinforce[ing of] stigmatisation, significantly undermining living conditions of certain population groups and restricting the possibilities of insertion of the individuals belonging to them'.[48] Some have rightfully described the plans to prevent radicalisation in Spain as an example of neoliberal exceptionalism.[49] A system that 'employs surveillance technologies and situational crime control measures and that minimises or curtails a variety of social welfare programs' against vulnerable people, producing it as dangerous population and criminalising it accordingly. Far from preventing any potential harm, the datafication processes triggered by tools like the ones analysed increase the occurrence of racial pre-criminality and reinforce the socially harmful policies. Our aim in the following sections is to contextualise the ongoing actuarial and

[45] Generalitat de Catalunya, PRODERAI-CE, 14.
[46] See e.g. Chapter 5 in this book. Richardson et al, 'Dirty Data, Bad Predictions: How Civil Rights Violations Impact Police Data, Predictive Policing Systems, and Justice'; P Alston, *Report of the Special Rapporteur on Extreme Poverty and Human Rights.*
[47] BE Harcourt, *Against Prediction* (Chicago: University of Chicago Press, 2007) 30.
[48] JA Brandariz García, 'La difusión de las lógicas actuariales y gerenciales en las políticas punitivas' (2014) 2 *InDret* 4, 18.
[49] JC Aguerri and D Jiménez-Franco, 'On Neoliberal Exceptionalism in Spain: A State Plan to Prevent Radicalization'.

datafication processes within a longer history of Islamophobia that far predates contemporary forms of datafied governance.

8.3 SOUTHERN EUROPEAN NEOLIBERALISM FUNDAMENTALS

Multiple local organisations and antiracist grassroots movements such as the Asociación Musulmana por los Derechos Humanos [The Islamic Association for Human Rights],[50] SOS Racisme Catalunya[51] have denounced how institutional, political, and social Islamophobia narratives run rampant in Southern Europe. They are not alone in their criticism. Higher supranational instances have also pointed in the same direction. For instance, the UN Special Rapporteur on freedom of religion or belief released in 2021, a report on anti-Muslim racism informing how government-driven securitisation processes severely affect Muslim rights to freely exercise their religion, with intelligence services surveilling mosques, and governments such as the French restricting the ability of Muslim communities to stabilising charitable institutions.[52] However, these efforts can do little against the Islamophobic narrative deployed at every institutional and social level. In the media, a wide variety of actors, from so-called liberal philosophers to well-known white feminist writers have contributed to the production of the Islamic other[53] with labels such as 'backwards', 'antimodern', 'violent patriarchal', and 'dangerous'.[54] As the report highlights, these stereotyped narratives promoted by 'prominent politicians, influencers, and academics' who 'advance discourses online on both social networks and blogs that Islam is innately antithetical to democracy and human rights, particularly gender equality, often propagating the trope that all Muslim women are oppressed'. Sociologist Sara Farris has coined this ideological, neoliberal political-economy convergence as *Feminacionalism*.[55] Despite meaningful divergencies in other political arenas, neoliberal politicians, right- and far-right nationalist parties and feminist bureaucrats, or 'femicrats' seem to agree on the intrinsic dangers of Islam in general and male Muslims in particular.

Politically, far-right parties cashed the endless succession of crises caused by financial capitalism, becoming key political actors in Spain (third political party),

---

[50] 'It's for your safety. Institutional machinery of Islamophobia', *Asociación Musulmana de Derechos Humanos* (Video, 2021).

[51] SOS Racisme, *(In)Visibles. L'estat del racisme a Catalunya*.

[52] United Nations Special Rapporteur on Freedom of Religion or Belief, *Countering Islamophobia/Anti-Muslim Hatred to Eliminate Discrimination and Intolerance Based on Religion or Belief*, 9.

[53] H Bouteldja, *Whites, Jews and Us: Toward a Politics of Revolutionary Love* (Cambridge: MIT Press, 2016).

[54] S Ahmed and J Matthes, 'Media Representation of Muslims and Islam from 2000 to 2015: A Meta-analysis' (2017) 79(3) *International Communication Gazette* 219–44.

[55] Sara Farris, *In the Name of Women's Rights: The Rise of Femonationalism* (Durham: Duke University Press, 2017).

Portugal (third political party), Greece (formerly third political party), Italy (first political party). The most impoverished and discriminated segments of populations were used by the far-right as a scapegoat of the 2008 and 2021 crises, and accused of stealing jobs, being responsible for an inexistent wave of criminality, and the destruction of moral values and social coexistence. Rising neofascist political parties such as Vox in Spain (a spin-off of the conservative Popular Party) have, for instance, proposed to reverse the already granted Spanish citizenship to 'dubious migrants' stating that '[c]itizenship is a privilege'.[56] These discriminatory discourses permeate the political landscape across the political spectrum due to the modern transhistorical persistence of what Edward Said described as Orientalism.[57] Islamophobia is indeed one of the defining features of the Southern European iteration of racial neoliberalism. Although sharing some common traits with its Global North counterparts, Southern European racial neoliberalism emerges from a different genealogy and is built upon different socioeconomic and ideological structures, presenting thus its own characteristics.[58] While the main objective of the chapter is to focus on the Islamophobic Consensus, it is worth highlighting some distinguishable elements of Southern European neoliberalism.

First, Southern European racial neoliberalism does not stick to a single ideology, policy, technology, and regulation, nor univocally attached to exclusive forms of domination. Instead, it is composed by a baroquian[59] multilayered structure encompassing traditional and latest technological developments (including ADM and AI) with colonial and postcolonial practices of racialised governmentality developed through centuries of colonialism. These proto-racist[60] dynamics defined by pre- and capitalist cultural and religion discrimination practices, still inform the performativity of the Spanish racial formation. For instance, the colour-line created during the slave economy still works as a racialising technology in the current welfare, migration, and criminal policies.[61] As Deepa Kumar stated: 'While race is dynamic, contingent, and contextual, the ideology of Islamophobia attempts to fix what it means to be Muslim and to create a reified Muslim whose behaviour can be predicted, explained, and controlled.'[62] Because of the above, racial politics, deeply bound with the legacies of coloniality, operate with significant differences from

---

[56] 'Contreras explica por qué y cómo quiere reforzar VOX la concesión de la nacionalidad española', *Vox Parliamentary Group* (Media Release, 15 February 2022) <www.voxespana .es/grupo_parlamentario/actividad-parlamentaria/proposiciones-de-ley/vox-ley-nacionalidad-espanola-20220215>.

[57] EW Said, *Orientalism* (New York: Vintage, 1979).

[58] E Tastsanis, 'The Social Determinants of Ideology: The Case of Neoliberalism in Southern Europe' (2009) 35(2) *Critical Sociology* 199.

[59] B Echeverría, *La modernidad de lo barroco* (México DF: Ediciones Era, 2000).

[60] Cedric Robinson, *Black Marxism: The Making of the Black Radical Tradition*, 1st ed (London: Zed Books, 1983).

[61] Jiménez and Cancela, 'Surveillance Punitivism: Colonialism, Racism, and State Terrorism in Spain'.

[62] Kumar, *Islamophobia and the Politics of Empire: Twenty Years after 9/11*.

other countries in the Global North. For instance, Romani people, an extremely diverse and historically oppressed minority,[63] is also celebrated as quintessential of the Spanish and Catalan popular cultures. As the global success of the Catalan singer Rosalia stresses (see, for instance, her video 'Málamente'), folklorised values and aesthetics associated with Romani people are appropriated by individuals and institutions and commodified, while Romani people are discriminated at every level.[64]

Secondly, the public sector plays a key role in the societal, economic, and political dimensions. It controls significant aspects of key ideological apparatuses such as schools and media. It holds a vast influence over the workforce through direct employment of relatively significant segments of population.[65] Unlike other polities such as the United States, Southern European countries have not fully privatised their criminal justice systems, retaining much of the organisational, operational, and designing sovereignty over these areas.

Thirdly, the privatisation of democracy described by Basque philosopher Jule Goikoetxea[66] as the hijack of public institutions and common assets by corporations and private interests, and the perceptible sacrifice of social rights for the sake of the capitalist class has not fully impacted the entire population. As a plethora of feminist researchers demonstrate, women, especially those belonging to racialised communities, have disproportionally paid a heavy price containing what would have been otherwise a societal tragedy.[67] They have disproportionately sustained the family structures that have safeguarded the well-being of entire families, especially taking care of dependents. In the following section we will focus on two dimensions of what we identify as the Southern European path to neoliberal racism, what here is called the Islamophobic Consensus: Islamophobia as a racialised epistemic formation, and as a form of governmentality.

8.3.1 *Islamophobia as an Epistemic Formation*

During his courses in the College du la France (1977–1978) French philosopher Michel Foucault described how the western European states slowly switched their object and subject of governance from the vagueness of kingdoms and nations to the scientific and measurability of territories and population. The rise of governmentality and the birth of biopolitics placed life as something to govern, to manage, to

[63] Cortés, *Sueños y sombras sobre los gitanos. La actualidad de un racismo histórico.*
[64] Ibid.
[65] J Goikoetxea, *Privatizing Democracy* (Oxford: Peter Lang, 2017).
[66] Ibid.
[67] P Moré, 'Cuidados y crisis del coronavirus: el trabajo invisible que sostiene la vida' (2020) 29(3) *Revista Española de Sociología (RES)* 737–45.

commodify, and reproduce.[68] In his landmark book *The Taming of Chance*, Ian Hacking explained how during 1860–1882 the expansionist Prussian State developed one of the most powerful statistical apparatuses of the era.[69] One of its most unsettling results was the emergence of a distinguishable and previously inexistent population within Prussia: the Jews. Under the Enlightened Prussian direction, racialisation of German Jews started through the act of being counted and measured as a category separated from *true* Germans of the Empire and a dangerous population to be controlled, to be governed.

A new interest for counting and measuring bodies, goods, commodities grew as a consequence of the expansion of new governmental techniques.[70] This led to a transformation in the way decision, policies, and laws were produced, and how they were re-centred to producing and managing territories and population under a securitarian regime. How many people, of what kind, creed, were born and deceased? How many apples were picked? How much gold, iron, how many roads? Numbers became the glorified signature and evidence of a scientifically based knowledge. Nature was subjected to the apprehension of its intuited regularities, so did societies. Natural and social phenomena were no longer discernible through the lens of mechanicist eternal laws in motion. Instead, they were the result of complex interactions between a nearly endless succession of events determined by chance and apprehensible through mathematical probabilistic models . . . if enough data was available.[71] That was the first step towards the dethroning of law as the inspiring principle of the state and its substitution by the actuarial dispositives, or as Alain Supiot[72] put it, 'the beginning of the governance by numbers'.

However, as Aimé Césaire explains in his powerful work *Discourse on Colonialism*,[73] almost all major institutionalised crime against the 'white man' had already been practised in the colonial laboratory against non-Europeans. The very first to be counted, numbered and managed, to be commodified, to be produced and reproduced, to be scientifically governed and datafied were not white subjects of the metropolises, but racialised dominated subjects. The first systematic censuses were undertaken not in European metropolises as Hacking mentioned, but in Al-Andalus, Peru, and Mexico, where Whites, Catholics, Moriscos, Jews, and Converses (to name some of the endless racial categories) were counted in order

---

[68] M Foucault, *Security, Territory, Population: lectures at the Collège de France, 1977–78* (Berlin: Springer, 2007).

[69] I Hacking, *The Taming of Chance* (Cambridge: Cambridge University Press, 1990).

[70] C Rosenthal, *Accounting for Slavery* (Cambridge: Harvard University Press, 2018).

[71] WHK Chun, *Discriminating Data: Correlation, Neighborhoods, and the New Politics of Recognition* (Cambridge: MIT Press, 2021); I Hacking, 'Biopower and the Avalanche of Printed Numbers' in Vernon W Cisney and Nicolae Morar (eds), *Biopower: Foucault and Beyond* (Chicago: The University of Chicago Press, 2015) 65–80.

[72] A Supiot, *Governance by Numbers: The Making of a Legal Model of Allegiance* (London: Bloomsbury, 2017), vol. 20.

[73] Originally published as *Discours sur le colonialisme* (Editions Présence Africaine, 1955).

to inform political, economic, ecclesiastic, and social decisions.[74] The will to exploit and colonise lands and peoples fuelled much of the sociotechnical developments nowadays considered modern science. An army of colonial scientists swarmed the colonies measuring forests and lakes, mines, and dunes. Counting bodies, scrutinising eyes, arms, and craniums. Evaluating the fertility of the land and of the women's wombs.[75]

Fifteenth century Iberian Peninsula's politics and heated intellectual debates testify to the interconnected genealogy of the birth of the colonial enterprise, racial capitalism, and population control technologies.[76] The most renowned intellectuals of the time, gathered around the School of Salamanca, demanded a shift from medieval politics cantered in aristocratic factions and vague notions of territory, towards the government of the population. As has been stated the School of Salamanca advanced much of the early capitalist political economy, and, as we are just now starting to unveil, they also set the grounds for the ideological justification of opprobrious forms of human exploitation.[77] For instance, the commonly cited theological debates of Valladolid allegedly discussing whether Indigenous people had souls were not a backward Byzantine debate, as it has often been depicted. They were instead highly sophisticated negotiations between colonial factions arguing whether 'Indians' and 'Moros' were to be massacred, enslaved, or included within the political body of the empire.[78]

Accordingly, the state governmental strategies switched from regarding the population as a passive element, to contemplating it as an active resource that needed to be governed and mobilised. The new morals demanded mechanisms for counting, controlling, multiplying, governing, and mobilising the population along the States' needs. But also, to control, regulate, and punish its 'ill' and 'impure' elements. For that, the Spanish colonial State developed sophisticated technologies of power aimed at producing racialised subjects ready to be governed and exploited in the mines, plantations, and endless public and private operations.[79] For instance, the

---

[74] E Martín-Corrales, *Muslims in Spain, 1492–1814: Living and Negotiating in the Land of the Infidel* (Leiden: Brill, 2020).

[75] AH Reggiani, *Historia mínima de la eugenesia en América Latina* (México DF: El Colegio de México, 2019); Castro-Gómez, *La hybris del punto cero: ciencia, raza e ilustración en la Nueva Granada (1750–1816)*.

[76] R Grosfoguel, 'Epistemic Islamophobia and Colonial Social Sciences' (2010) 8(2) *Human Architecture: Journal of the Sociology of Self-Knowledge* 29–38.

[77] AJ Bohrer, 'Just Wars of Accumulation: The Salamanca School, Race and Colonial Capitalism' (2018) 59(3) *Race & Class* 20–37.

[78] Grosfoguel, 'Epistemic Islamophobia and Colonial Social Sciences'; D Montañez Pico, 'Pueblos sin religión: la falacia de la controversia de Valladolid' (2016) 18(36) *Araucaria* 87–110.

[79] DB Rood, *The Reinvention of Atlantic Slavery: Technology, Labor, Race, and Capitalism in the Greater Caribbean* (Oxford: Oxford University Press, 2017); IB Guerra, 'Moriscos, esclavos y minas: comentario al memorial de Juan López de Ugarte o sobre cómo introducir a los moriscos en la labor de minas' (2010) 23 *Espacio Tiempo y Forma. Serie III, Historia Medieval*.

consideration of humans as a resource to be controlled appears as early as 1499 in a document signed by the Catholic Monarchs. There, the 'gitanos', traditionally nomadic and thus unfixed to a specific sovereign, were regarded as an unproductive and dangerous population. Those 'gitanos' with no profession should be physically punished or vanished from the territory, claimed the norm.[80]

A thick network of legal measures plagued the Spanish Empire, underpinning a profoundly racialised epistemology of power. That is a system of knowledge designed to produce dominated political subjectivities bound to inherited tasks considered to be of inferior status.[81] The infamous statutes of 'pureza de sangre' [*purity of blood*] are a well-known example of it. Designed by one of the most advanced political bodies of European modernity: the Inquisition, they consisted of a decentralised and granular system of population classification articulated through parishes and churches, entrusted with certifying the alleged Christian blood purity of a family's genealogy.[82] Those unable to prove their intergenerational purity (more likely conversos, Jewish, and Muslims) were prohibited from accessing positions of social, political, military, religious, and economic relevance.[83] Along with the 'estatutos de limpieza de sangre', endless instruments were deployed to expel 'indios', 'negros', 'mulatos', 'moros', 'mestizos', 'gitanos', and anything in between, from the most socially rewarded and profitable activities.[84] Unlike other previous forms of domination, the new technologies of power configured an inferior subjectivity with hereditary, collective, and functional character. It sought to target and mark entire populations, for exploitation and control. Legalised social status fixations, and consequently the impossibility of social progress for Blacks, Roma, Jews, Muslims, and converts, lies at the very foundations of the Spanish nation-state.

8.3.2 *Islamophobia as a Governmentality Strategy*

As we have briefly seen, Spanish historiography is plagued with examples of racialised governmental technologies. However, for the purpose of this analysis it is worth highlighting two (relatively) recent developments. The first Spanish Immigration law (1985) turned the Muslim Arab-Amazigh population living in the peninsula into

---

[80] J Ramirez, *Libro de las Bulas y Pragmáticas de los Reyes Católicos* (Madrid: Instituto de España, 1973), vol. 1.

[81] Castro-Gómez, *La hybris del punto cero: ciencia, raza e ilustración en la Nueva Granada* (1750–1816).

[82] J Irigoyen-García, *The Spanish Arcadia: Sheep Herding, Pastoral Discourse, and Ethnicity in Early Modern Spain* (Toronto: University of Toronto Press, 2013).

[83] H Kamen, *The Spanish Inquisition: A Historical Revision* (New Haven: Yale University Press, 2014).

[84] A Quijano, 'Colonialidad del poder y clasificación social' (2015) 2(5) *Contextualizaciones Latinoamericanas*; S Rivera Cusicanqui, *Pueblos Originarios y Estado* (Buenos Aires: Instituto Nacional de la Administración Pública de Argentina, 2008); JC Mariátegui, *7 ensayos de interpretación de la realidad peruana* (Caracas: Ayacucho, 1978).

'illegal immigrants'. The colonial dominion of the Spanish state over north African territories lasted until the late 1970s, when Sahara gained independence, with several enclaves, such as Ceuta and Melilla, still controlled by Spain. Former (post)colonial subjects, living in Spanish territories for years, overnight were denied any recognition of residency and citizenship. In other words, they became the new other and were expelled from the symbolic and material benefits of their political community.[85] This measure responded to the forthcoming integration of Spain in the European Union (and therefore, becoming one of the southern borders of Europe) and the new role of the Spanish state, switching from migrant-sender to a migrant-receiving country.[86] The country was transitioning towards neoliberal way of managing subaltern and racialised people locating the dominated within a racially hierarchised labour system. The aim was to prevent them from equal access to the best remunerated jobs through a set of formal and informal mechanisms, that began with the production of differentiated categories in citizenship and residency with different access to rights and work permits, as well as by not recognising foreign degrees certificates, thus deploying discriminatory practices in hiring.[87] The new racial division of labour was especially perceptible in global hubs such as Catalonia. On the one hand, migrants from European Union member countries were rebranded as expats, and accepted as designers, executives, teachers, and scientists. On the other hand, the African and Latin American precarious subaltern were funnelled to the agricultural and construction sectors, both characterised by the poor if not nonexistent labour political and social rights.

The second wave of Islamophobic legislation came enshrined in the wide context of the US-led war on terror. The 2004 Madrid terrorist attack accelerated the neoliberal punitive turn with multiple counter-terrorist policies specifically designed to fight the 'jihadist' threat.[88] The new measures steadily increased policing and judicial powers, and more importantly, validated a securitarian narrative by which entire populations become suspicious. The concept of terrorism itself also shifted to encompass a wide range of activities and behaviours ranging from the mundane, to political and civil activism, the expression of solidarity with international causes or the contentious self-indoctrination. The framing served the purpose of institutionalising racially defined securitarian spaces turning the rhetoric of prevention as political common sense. Herein it becomes *normal* aligning hard and soft State power (police and welfare surveillance) to surveil neighbourhoods framed as

---

[85] S Amazian, SOS Racisme, *Islamofobia Institucional y Securitización* (Report, 2021) <www
.sosracisme.org/wp-content/uploads/2021/07/InformeIslamofobia_01072021_INTERACTIVO_
CAST_.pdf>.

[86] C Fernández Bessa, *El dispositiu de deportació. Anàlisi criminològica de la detenció, interna-
ment i expulsió d'immigrants en el context espanyol.* Universitat de Barcelona (Doctoral Thesis),
(2016) 54.

[87] Douhaibi and Amazian, *La radicalización del racismo Islamofobia de Estado y prevención
antiterrorista.*

[88] Ibid.

dangerous environments, immersed in 'radicalising' atmospheres. It was during this last period when welfare and police surveillance, everyday stop and frisk, arrests and extrajudicial killings fuelled a climate of unrest and repression for many communities while reinvigorating the transhistorical moral panic of the 'Moros'.[89]

To sum, while it is true that Islamophobia as governmentality builds on fictional beliefs that have become western 'common sense', it will be a mistake to consider it just a set of discriminatory narratives. The Islamophobic Consensus operates under the code of a colour-blind racism and defends, reinforces, and produces an unequal distribution of goods and assets, that disproportionally benefits the *right kind* of citizens while punishes the others. In other words, the Islamophobic governmental apparatus was designed to legitimise and to justify very material relations of exploitation (Kumar, 2021).[90]

8.4 CONCLUSION

In 2017 a series of attacks shocked Catalonia. A van was driven in the centric Rambla of Barcelona, killing fourteen people and injuring hundreds. Hours later in Cambrils (Catalonia), another woman was killed, and several others injured. According to the PRODERAE and PRODERAV tools, one of the most relevant factors in any type of radicalisation relates to the perceived sense of belonging and connection with a territory. However, a social educator from Ripoll, the hometown of the young adults who committed the attacks, said: '[t]hese boys were integrated; they spoke perfect Catalan and they became terrorists'. The attacks demonstrated the uselessness of the protocols, indicators, and criteria for detecting radicalisation. As we have seen, the PRODERAI/PRODERAEV are preventive actuarial methods aimed at measuring and preventing radicalisation. For that, the instruments draw on classic social risk factors (personal development, school context, family context, social context) along with other 'radicalisation indicators' inaccessible to the public. The concealment of these indicators from public knowledge hinders social and political opposition, precisely because it hides the explicitly Islamophobic character of the automated tools used. However, the problem will not be solved just by making these sociotechnical systems more transparent and accountable.

As we have demonstrated, the digital and analogue technologies used to control, surveil, and punish young Muslims are not ends by themselves, but rather they mean for reinforcing a socially harmful system of oppression rooted in the darkest moments of the global European domination. The Islamophobic Consensus, that is, the Southern European iteration of neoliberal racism, stands on centuries of eurocentrism and white suprematism articulated through intricate institutional,

---

[89] S Amazian, *SOS Racisme*; S Cohen, *Folk Devils and Moral Panics* (London: Routledge, 2011).

[90] Kumar, *Islamophobia and the Politics of Empire: Twenty Years after 9/11*.

legal, political, and economic developments transcending regional and national boundaries. Similarly, today's astonishing data gathering, data management and data analysis capabilities, and the 'magic' behind predictive automated tools are not spontaneous outputs but the result of centuries of training, experimentation, and scientific developments. From the early colonial censuses and regulations designed to protect the healthy Christian population from depraved Muslims and Jews to more recent forms of predictive policing and digital surveillance, numbers, statistics, and dozens of other governmental tools have served the interests of the powerful.

There are no shortcuts, neither technical, legal nor magical solutions for a global problem rooted in centuries of oppression, domination, genocide, and deprivation. No solution will come from a political party, a corporation, a new legal instrument (either National or Universal). The long history of struggles against colonialism, racism, and fascisms demonstrates that the perversity of domination extends from the most obscene and crude forms of domination to highly sophisticated and subtle alienation. To fight such massive structures we need, undoubtedly, powerful communities, and meaningful relations, let alone the energising voices of empowered singers such as Huda who reminds us to *Keep It Halal*. But we also need adequate epistemic tools to be able to think politically and historically about the events surrounding us. Hopefully, this chapter could help radical researchers and other folks in such endeavour.

PART III

Synergies and Safeguards

9

Law and Empathy in the Automated State

*Cary Coglianese**

9.1 INTRODUCTION

Because the future knows no bounds, the future of administrative law is vast. In the near term, administrative law in the United States will undoubtedly center around how the US Supreme Court decides cases raising core administrative law issues such as the nondelegation doctrine and judicial deference to agencies' statutory interpretation. But over the longer term, new issues will confront the field of administrative law as new changes occur in government and in society. One major change on the horizon will be an increasingly automated administrative state in which many governmental tasks will be carried out by digital systems, especially those powered by AI and ADM tools.

Administrative agencies today undertake a range of activities – granting licenses, issuing payments, adjudicating claims, and setting rules – each of which traditionally has been executed by government officials. But it is neither difficult nor unrealistic to imagine a future in which members of the public, when they interact with the government, increasingly find themselves interacting predominantly with digital systems rather than human officials. Even today, the traditional administrative tasks for which human beings have long been responsible are increasingly augmented by computer systems. Few people today think twice about using government websites to apply for unemployment benefits, register complaints, or file paperwork, rather than visiting or making phone calls to government offices. The federal government in the United States has even created an online portal – USA. gov – that provides its users with easy access to the panoply of resources and digital

* This chapter is a modified and edited version of the essay Cary Coglianese, 'Administrative Law in the Automated State' (Summer 2021) 150(3) *Dædalus* 104 <www.amacad.org/publication/administrative-law-automated-state>. The author thanks Lavi Ben Dor for research assistance and Richard Berk, Amanda Greene, and Mark Tushnet for helpful comments on an earlier draft.

application processes now available to the public via an extensive network of state and federal government websites.

The transition to this online interaction with government over the last quarter-century foreshadows what will likely be a deeper and wider technological transformation of governmental processes over the next quarter-century. Moving beyond the digitization of front-end communication with government, the future will likely feature the more extensive automation of back-end decision-making, which today still often remains firmly in the discretion of human officials. But we are perhaps only a few decades away from an administrative state that will operate on the basis of automated systems built with ADM and AI tools, much like important aspects of the private sector increasingly will. This will lead to an administrative state characterized by what I have elsewhere called *algorithmic adjudication* and *robotic rulemaking*.[1] Instead of having human officials make discretionary decisions, such as judgments about whether individual claimants qualify for disability benefits, agencies will be able to rely on automated systems to make these decisions. Claims-processing systems could be designed, for example, to import automatically a vast array of data from electronic medical records and then use an AI system to process these data and determine whether claimants meet a specified probability threshold to qualify for benefits.[2]

If many of the tasks that government currently completes through decision-making by human officials come to be performed entirely by ADM tools and computer systems, how will administrative law respond to this transformation to an automated state? How *should* it?

Most existing administrative law principles can already accommodate the widespread adoption of automation throughout the administrative state. Not only have agencies already long relied on a variety of physical machines that exhibit automaticity, but an automated state – or at least a *responsible* automated state – could be thought of as the culmination of administrative law's basic vision of government that relies on neutral public administration of legislatively delegated authority. Administrative law will not need to be transformed entirely to operate in an era of increasing automation because that automation, when responsibly implemented, will advance the democratic principles and good governance values that have provided the foundation for administrative law.

Nevertheless, even within an otherwise responsible automated state, an important ingredient of good governance could increasingly turn out to be missing: human empathy. Even bureaucracies comprising human officials can be cold and sterile, but an era of extreme automation could present a state of crisis in human care – or,

---

[1] See Cary Coglianese and David Lehr, 'Regulating by Robot: Administrative Decision Making in the Machine-Learning Era' (2017) 105(5) *The Georgetown Law Journal* 1147 at 1171.

[2] See Cary Coglianese and David Lehr, 'Transparency and Algorithmic Governance' (2019) 71 (1) *Administrative Law Review* 1 at 9.

more precisely, a crisis in the lack of such care. In an increasingly automated state, administrative law will need to find ways to encourage agencies to ensure that members of the public will continue to have opportunities to engage with humans, express their voices, and receive acknowledgment of their predicaments. The automated state will, in short, also need to be an empathic state.

9.2 IMPLEMENTATION OF THE AUTOMATED STATE

The information technology revolution that launched several decades ago shows few signs of abating. Technologists today are both revealing and reaching new frontiers with the use of advanced AI technologies, also referred to as machine learning or predictive analytics. These terms – sometimes used interchangeably – encompass a broad range of tools that permit the rapid processing of large volumes of data that can yield highly accurate forecasts and thereby facilitate the automation of many distinct tasks. In the private sector, AI innovations are allowing the automation of a wide range of functions previously handled by trained humans, such as the reading of chest X-rays, the operation of automobiles, and the granting of loans by financial institutions.

Public administrators have taken notice of these AI advances in the private sector. Some advances in the business world even have direct parallels to governmental tasks. Companies such as eBay and PayPal, for example, have developed their own highly successful automated online dispute resolution tools to resolve complaints without the direct involvement of human employees.[3] Overall, government officials see in modern data analytics the possibility of building systems that could automate a variety of governmental tasks, all with the potential to deliver increased administrative efficiency, speed, consistency, and accuracy.

The vision of an automated administrative state might best be exemplified today by developments in the Republic of Estonia, a small Baltic country that has thoroughly embraced digital government as a mark of distinction. The country's e-Estonia project has transformed the nation's administration by digitizing and securely storing vast amounts of information about individuals, from their medical records to their employment information to their financial statements.[4] That information is cross-linked through a digital infrastructure called X-Road, so that a person's records can be accessed instantly by any entity that needs them, subject to limits intended to prevent wrongdoing. This widespread digitization has

---

[3] See Benjamin H Barton and Stephanos Bibas, *Rebooting Justice: More Technology, Fewer Lawyers, and the Future of Law* (New York: Encounter Books, 2017) 111–15.

[4] See Nathan Heller, 'Estonia, the Digital Republic' (11 December 2017) *The New Yorker* <www.newyorker.com/magazine/2017/12/18/estonia-the-digital-republic> and Republic of Estonia, Ministry of Economic Affairs and Communications, *Report of Estonia's AI Taskforce* (Report, 2019) <https://f98cc689–5814-47ec-86b3-db505a7c3978.filesusr.com/ugd/7df26f_486454c9f32340b28206e140350159cf.pdf>.

Cary Coglianese

facilitated the automation of a range of government services: Individuals can easily vote, apply for a loan, file their taxes, and complete other administrative tasks without ever needing to interact with a human official, simply by transferring their digital information to complete forms and submit requests. By automating many of its bureaucratic processes, Estonia has saved an estimated 2 percent of its GDP each year. The country is even exploring the use of an automated "judge" to resolve small claims disputes.[5]

Other countries such as Denmark and South Korea are also leading the world in the adoption of so-called e-government tools.[6] The United States may not have yet achieved quite the same level of implementation of automated government, but it is certainly not far behind. Federal, state, and local agencies throughout the United States have not only embraced web-based applications – such as those compiled on the USA.gov website – but have begun to deploy the use of AI tools to automate a range of administrative decision-making processes. In most of these cases, human officials remain involved to some extent, but a significant amount of administrative work in the United States is increasingly conducted through digital systems.

Automation helps federal, state, and local governments navigate challenging resource-allocation decisions in the management of public programs. Several state governments in the United States have implemented AI and ADM tools to help make decisions about the award of Medicaid and other social benefits, seeking to speed up and improve the consistency of claims processing.[7] Similarly, the federal Social Security Administration uses automated tools to help support human appeals judges' efforts to provide quality oversight of an agency adjudicatory process that handles as many as 2.5 million disability benefits claims each year.[8]

Municipalities rely on automated systems when deciding where to send health and building inspectors.[9] Some local authorities use such systems when making

---

5   See Eric Niler, 'Can AI Be a Fair Judge? Estonia Thinks So', *Wired* (Web Page, 25 March 2019) <www.wired.com/story/can-ai-be-fair-judge-court-estonia-thinks-so/>.

6   See United Nations Department of Economic and Social Affairs, *E-Government Survey 2020: Digital Government in the Decade of Action for Sustainable Development* (Report, 2020) <https://publicadministration.un.org/egovkb/Portals/egovkb/Documents/un/2020-Survey/ 2020%20UN%20E-Government%20Survey%20(Full%20 Report).pdf>.

7   See Cary Coglianese and Lavi M Ben Dor, 'AI in Adjudication and Administration' (2021) 86 *Brooklyn Law Review* 791 <https://papers.ssrn.com/sol3/papers.cfm?abstract_id=3501067>.

8   See David Freeman Engstrom et al, *Government by Algorithm: Artificial Intelligence in Federal Administrative Agencies* (Report, 2020) <www-cdn.law.stanford.edu/wp-content/uploads/2020/ 02/ACUS-AI-Report.pdf>.

9   See G Cherry, 'Google, U-M to Build Digital Tools for Flint Water Crisis' *University of Michigan News* (3 May 2016) <https://news.umich.edu/google-u-m-to-build-digital-tools-for- flint-water-crisis/>; City of Chicago, 'Food Inspection Forecasting: Optimizing Inspections with Analytics' *City of Chicago* (Web Page) <https://chicago.github.io/food-inspections-evalu ation/>; Robert Sullivan, 'Innovations in Identifying People Who Frequently Use Criminal Justice and Healthcare Systems' *Policy Research Associates* (Web Page, 16 May 2018) <www .prainc.com/innovations-identification-cj-healthcare/>; Harvard Kennedy School, Data-Smart City Solutions, 'A Catalogue of Civic Data Use Cases: How Can Data and Analytics Be Used to

choices about where and when to deploy social workers to follow up on allegations of child abuse and neglect.[10] Federal agencies, meanwhile, have used AI and ADM systems to analyze consumer complaints, process reports of workplace injuries, and evaluate public comments on proposed rules.[11]

Criminal law enforcement agencies throughout the United States also rely on various automated tools. They have embraced tools that automate deployment of officer patrols based on predictions of locations in cities where crime is most likely to occur.[12] Many law enforcement agencies have also widely used automated facial recognition tools for suspect identification or security screenings.[13]

Regulatory agencies similarly have deployed automated tools for targeting auditing and enforcement resources. States have employed data analytics to detect fraud and errors in their unemployment insurance programs.[14] The federal Securities and Exchange Commission and the Internal Revenue Service have adopted AI tools to help detect fraudulent behavior and other wrongdoing.[15]

In these and other ways, public authorities across the United States have already made considerable strides toward an increasingly automated state. Over the next several decades, governmental use of automation driven by AI tools will surely spread still further and is likely to lead to the transformation of or phasing out of many jobs currently performed by government employees.[16] The future state that administrative law will govern will be one of increasingly automated administration.

Enhance City Operations?' *Data-Smart City Solutions* (Web Page, 9 October 2019) <https://datasmart.ash.harvard.edu/news/article/how-can-data-and-analytics-be-used-to-enhance-city-operations-723>; and University of Pennsylvania, 'Uses in Government' *University of Pennsylvania Carey Law School* (Web Page) <www.law.upenn.edu/institutes/ppr/optimizing-government-project/government.php#municipal>.

[10] Dan Hurley, 'Can an Algorithm Tell When Kids Are in Danger?' *The New York Times Magazine* (New York, 2 January 2018) <www.nytimes.com/2018/01/02/magazine/can-an-algorithm-tell-when-kids-are-in-danger.html>.

[11] See Coglianese and Ben Dor, 'AI in Adjudication'.

[12] See Tim Lau, 'Predicting Policing Explained' *Brennan Center for Justice* (Web Page, 1 April 2020) <www.brennancenter.org/our-work/research-reports/predictive-policing-explained>.

[13] See Shirin Ghaffary and Rani Molla, 'Here's Where the U.S. Government Is Using Facial Recognition Technology to Surveil Americans' *Vox* (Web Page, 10 December 2019) <www.vox.com/recode/2019/7/18/20698307/facial-recognition-technology-us-government-fight-for-the-future>.

[14] See Tod Newcombe, 'Aiming Analytics at Our $3.5 Billion Unemployment Insurance Problem' *Government Technology* (Web Page, March 2017) <www.govtech.com/data/Aiming-Analytics-at-Our-35-Billion-Unemployment-Insurance-Problem.html>.

[15] See David Freeman Engstrom and Daniel E Ho, 'Algorithmic Accountability in the Administrative State' (2020) 37(3) *Yale Journal on Regulation* 800 at 815–19; and Richard Rubin, 'AI Comes to the Tax Code' *The Wall Street Journal* (26 February 2020) <www.wsj.com/articles/ai-comes-to-the-tax-code-11582713000>.

[16] Partnership for Public Service and IBM Center for the Business of Government, *More Than Meets AI: Assessing the Impact of Artificial Intelligence on the Work of Government* (Report, February 2019) <https://ourpublicservice.org/wp-content/uploads/2019/02/More-Than-Meets-AI.pdf>.

9.3 US ADMINISTRATIVE LAW AND THE AUTOMATED STATE

Can administrative law accommodate an automated state? At first glance, the prospect of an automated state might seem to demand a fundamental rewriting of administrative law. After all, administrative law developed to constrain the discretion of human officials, to keep their work within the bounds of the law, and to prevent the kinds of principal-agent problems that can arise in the relationships between human decision-makers. Moreover, one of administrative law's primary tenets – that governmental processes should be transparent and susceptible to reason-giving – would seem to stand as a barrier to the deployment of the very AI tools that are driving the emerging trends in automation.[17] That is because the algorithms that commonly drive AI and ADM tools – sometimes referred to as "black box" algorithms – have properties that can make them opaque and hard to explain. Unlike traditional statistical algorithms, in which variables are selected by humans and resulting coefficients can be pointed to as explaining specified amounts of variation in a dependent variable, the algorithms that drive AI systems effectively discover their own patterns in the data and do not generate results that associate explanatory power to specific variables. Data scientists can certainly understand and explain the goals and general properties of these "machine learning" algorithms, but overall these algorithms have a degree of autonomy – hence their "learning" moniker – that can make it more difficult to explain precisely why they reach any specific forecast that they do. They do not usually provide any basis for the kind of causal statements often used to justify administrative decisions (such as "X is justified because it causes Y").

As a result, transparency concerns are reasonable when considering a future of an automated state based on AI systems. But on even a modest degree of additional reflection, these concerns would appear neither to act as any intrinsic barrier in the United States to the reliance on AI automation nor necessarily to demand any fundamental transformation of US administrative law to accommodate an automated state. Administrative law has never demanded anything close to absolute transparency nor required meticulous or exhaustively detailed reasoning, even under the arbitrary and capricious standard of Section 706 of the Administrative Procedure Act.[18] Administrative agencies that rely on AI systems should be able to satisfy any reason-giving obligations under existing legal principles by explaining in general terms how the algorithm underlying the AI system was designed to work and demonstrating that it has been validated to work as designed by comparing its results to those generated by the status quo process. An adequate explanation could involve merely describing the type of AI algorithm used, disclosing the objective it was

---

[17] Such tenets are reflected in both the notion of due process as well as the general standard that
    agency action should not be arbitrary and capricious.
[18] See Coglianese and Lehr, 'Transparency and Algorithmic Governance', 26–29.

established to meet, and showing how the algorithm processed a certain type of data to produce results that were shown to meet its defined objective as well as or better than current processes.

Such an explanation would, in effect, mirror the kinds of explanations that administrators currently offer when they rely on physical rather than digital machines. For example, in justifying the imposition of an administrative penalty on a food processor for failing to store perishable food at a cool temperature, an administrator need not be able to explain exactly how a thermometer works, just that it reports temperatures accurately. Courts have long treated instrument validation for physical machines as a sufficient basis for agency actions grounded on such instruments. Moreover, they have typically deferred to administrators' expertise in cases in which government officials have relied on complex instruments or mathematical analyses. In fact, the US Supreme Court in *Baltimore Gas & Electric Co. v Natural Resources Defense Council* called upon courts to be their "most deferential" when an administrative agency is "making predictions, within its area of special expertise, at the frontiers of science."[19] More recently, the Supreme Court noted in *Marsh v Oregon Natural Resource Council* that whenever an agency decision "requires a high degree of technical expertise," we must defer to "the informed discretion of the responsible agencies."[20] Lower courts have followed these instructions and in various contexts have upheld agencies' reliance on complex algorithms and statistical tools (even if not truly AI ones).

It is difficult to see the US Supreme Court gaining any more confidence in judges' ability to provide independent technological assessments when technologies and statistical techniques grow still more complex in an era of AI. Unless the Court should gain a new source of such confidence and abandon the postures it took in *Baltimore Gas & Electric* and *Marsh*, nothing in administrative law's reason-giving requirements would seem to serve as any insuperable barrier to administrative agencies' more extensive reliance on systems based on AI tools, such as machine learning or other advanced predictive techniques, even if they are properly characterized today as black box models. That portrayal of AI tools as a black box also appears likely to grow less apt in the coming decades, as data scientists are currently working extensively to develop advanced techniques that can better explain the outputs such complex systems generate.[21] Advances in "explainable" AI techniques likely will only make automation even more compatible with long-standing administrative law values.

Of course, all of this is not to say that agencies will or should always receive deference for how they design or operate their systems. Under the standard articulated in *Motor Vehicle Manufacturers Association v State Farm Insurance Co.*,

---

[19]   462 US 87, 103 (1983).
[20]   490 US 360, 371 (2011), quoting *Kleppe v Sierra Club*, 427 US 390, 412 (1976).
[21]   See Coglianese and Lehr, 'Transparency and Algorithmic Governance', 49–55.

agencies will still need to provide basic information about the purposes behind their automated systems and how they generally operate.[22] They will need to show that they have carefully considered key design options. And they will likely need to demonstrate through accepted auditing and validation efforts that these systems do operate to produce results as intended.[23] But all this is to say that it will almost certainly be possible for agencies to provide the necessary information to justify the outcomes that their systems produce. In other words, long-standing administrative law principles seem ready and fit for an automated age.

9.4 AI AND GOOD GOVERNANCE IN AN AUTOMATED STATE

In important respects, a shift to automated administration could even be said to represent something of an apotheosis of the principles behind administrative law. Much of administrative law has been focused on the potential problems created by the discretion that human officials exercise under delegated authority. By automating administration, these problems can be mitigated, and the control of human discretion may be enhanced by the literal hardwiring of certain governmental tasks.[24]

Automation can advance two major themes that have long characterized much of US administrative law: One theme centers on keeping the exercise of administrative authority democratically accountable, while the other seeks to ensure that such authority is based on sound expert judgment. The reason-giving thrust behind the Administrative Procedure Act's arbitrary and capricious standard, for example, reflects both of these themes. Reasoned decision-making provides a basis for helping ensure that agencies both remain faithful to their democratic mandates and base their decisions on sound evidence and analysis. Likewise, the institutionalized regimen of White House review of prospective regulations both facilitates greater accountability to a democratically elected president and promotes expert agency decision-making through the benefit-cost analysis that it calls on agencies to conduct.[25]

In the same vein, in approving judicial deference to agencies' statutory interpretations, it is hardly a coincidence that the US Supreme Court's widely cited decision in *Chevron v Natural Resources Defense Council* stressed both reasons of democratic

---

[22] 463 US 29 (1983).

[23] Validation, which should take place before abandoning the status quo of a human-based process, could involve testing the algorithm on randomly selected cases that are also, in tandem, decided by humans following normal procedures. Closer scrutiny could be provided by panels of human experts of discrepancies between the results of digital systems and the initial human decision-makers.

[24] Cary Coglianese and Alicia Lai, 'Algorithm vs. Algorithm' (2022) 72(6) *Duke Law Journal* 1281.

[25] This regulatory review regimen is outlined in Office of the President, 'Executive Order 12866' (1993) 58(190) *Federal Register* 837–66.

accountability and substantive expertise.[26] It highlighted how agencies are situated within a "political branch of the Government" as well as how they simultaneously possess "great expertise" – and thus are better suited than courts to make judgments about the meaning of ambiguous statutory terms.[27] Although the future of the *Chevron* doctrine itself appears uncertain at best, the Court's underlying emphasis on accountability and expertise is unlikely to disappear, as they are inherent qualities of administrative governance.

Both qualities can be enhanced by AI and ADM. It is perhaps most obvious that automation can contribute to the goal of expert administration. When automated systems improve the accuracy of agency decision-making – which is what makes AI and other data analytic techniques look so promising – this will necessarily promote administrative law's goal of enhancing agency expertise. AI promises to deliver the state of the art when it comes to expert governing. When the Veterans Administration (VA), for example, recently opted to rely on an AI system to predict which veterans were at a higher risk of suicide (and thus in need of more urgent care), it did so because this analytic system was smarter than even experienced psychiatrists.[28] "The fact is, we cannot rely on trained medical experts to identify people who are truly at high risk [because they are] no good at it," noted one VA psychiatrist.[29]

Likewise, when it comes to administrative law's other main goal – democratic accountability – ADM systems can also advance the ball. The democratic advantages of automation may seem counterintuitive at first: Machine-based governance would hardly seem consistent with a Lincolnesque notion of government by "the people." But the reality is that automated systems themselves still demand people who can design, test, and audit such systems. As long as these human designers and overseers operate systems in a manner consistent with the parameters set out for an agency in its governing statute, AI and ADM systems themselves can prevent the kind of slippage and shirking that can occur when agencies must rely on thousands of human officials to carry out major national programs and policies. Even when it comes to making new rules under authority delegated to it by Congress, agencies could very well find that automation promotes democratic accountability rather than impedes it. Some level of accountability will be demanded by the properties of AI tools themselves. To function, the algorithms that drive these tools depend not merely on an "intelligible principle" to guide them; they need a principle that can

---

[26] 467 US 837 (1984). As a formal matter, the Court grounded *Chevron* deference in an explicit or implicit delegation of clarifying or gap-filling authority to the agency. See Cary Coglianese, '*Chevron*'s Interstitial Steps' (2017) 85(5) *The George Washington Law Review* 1339 at 1347–51.

[27] 467 US 837, 865 (1984).

[28] Benedict Carey, 'Can an Algorithm Prevent Suicide?' *The New York Times* (23 November 2020) <www.nytimes.com/2020/11/23/health/artificial-intelligence-veterans-suicide.html>.

[29] Ibid.

be precisely specified in mathematical terms.[30] In this way, automation could very well drive the demand for still greater specification and clarity in statutes about the goals of administration, more than even any potential judicial reinvigoration of the nondelegation doctrine might produce.

Although oversight of the design and development of automated systems will remain important to ensure that they are created in accord with democratically affirmed values, once operating, they should pose far fewer possibilities for the kinds of problems, such as capture and corruption, that administrative law has long sought to prevent. Unlike human beings, who might pursue their own narrow interests instead of those of the broader public, AI and ADM tools will be programmed to optimize the objectives defined by their designers. As long as these designers are accountable to the public, and as long as the system objectives are defined in non-self-interested ways that comport with relevant legislation, then the AI tools themselves pose no risk of capture and corruption. In an important sense, they will be more accountable in their execution than even human officials can be when it comes to implementing law.

This is not to suggest that automated systems will amount to a panacea nor that their responsible development and use will be easy. They can certainly be used in legally and morally problematic ways. Furthermore, their use by agencies will still be subject to constraints beyond administrative law – for instance, legal constraints under the First Amendment or the Equal Protection Clause that apply to all governmental actions. In fact, equality concerns raised by the potential for AI bias may well become the most salient legal issue that automated systems will confront in the coming years. Bias obviously exists with human decision-making, but it also is a concern with AI tools, especially when the underlying data used to train the algorithms driving these tools already contain human-created biases. Nevertheless, absent an independent showing of animus, automated systems based on AI may well withstand scrutiny under equal protection doctrine, at least if that doctrine does not change much over time.[31]

Governmental reliance on AI tools would be able to avoid actionable conduct under equal protection analysis even if an administrator elected to use data that included variables on race, gender, or other protected classifications. As long as the objective the AI tool is programmed to achieve is not stated in terms of such protected classifications, it will be hard, if not impossible, to show that the tool has used any class-based variables as a determinative basis for any particular outcome. The outcomes these AI tools generate derive from effectively autonomous mathematical processes that discern patterns among variables and relationships between different variables. Presumably, AI tools will seldom if ever support the

---

[30] For a discussion of the intelligible principle doctrine, see Cary Coglianese, 'Dimensions of Delegation' (2019) 167(7) *University of Pennsylvania Law Review* 1849.
[31] See *Washington v Davis*, 426 US 229, 239 (1976).

kind of clear and categorical determinations based on class-related variables that the US Supreme Court has rejected, where race or other protected classes have been given an explicit and even dispositive weight in governmental decisions.[32] Even when processing data on class variables, the use of AI tools might well lead to better outcomes for members of a protected class overall.[33]

Moreover, with greater reliance on AI systems, governments will have a new ability to *reduce* undesired biases by making mathematical adjustments to their models, sometimes without much loss in accuracy.[34] Such an ability will surely make it easier to tamp out biases than it is to eliminate humans' implicit biases. In an automated state of the future, government may find itself less prone to charges of undue discrimination.

For these reasons, it would appear that long-standing principles of administrative law, and even constitutional law, will likely continue to operate in an automated state, encouraging agencies to act responsibly by both preserving democratic accountability and making smarter, fairer decisions. This is not to say that existing principles will remain unchanged. No one should expect that any area of the law will stay static over the long term. Given that some scholars and observers have already come to look critically upon governmental uses of AI and ADM tools, perhaps shifting public attitudes will lead to new, potentially more demanding administrative law principles specifically targeting the automated features of the future administrative state.[35]

While we should have little doubt that norms and best practices will indeed solidify around how government officials ought to use automated systems – much as they have developed over the years for the use of other analytic tools, such as benefit-cost analysis – it is far from clear that the fundamentals of administrative law will

---

[32] See *Fisher v University of Texas at Austin*, 133 S. Ct 2411 (2013); *Grutter v Bollinger*, 539 US 306 (2003); *Gratz v Bollinger*, 539 US 244 (2003); and Coglianese and Lehr, 'Regulating by Robot'.

[33] For an accessible account of technical aspects of algorithmic fairness, see Michael Kearns and Aaron Roth, *The Ethical Algorithm: The Science of Socially Aware Algorithm Design* (Oxford: Oxford University Press, 2019) 57–93. For a cogent discussion of how digital algorithms can generate results more fair than human processes, see Sandra G Mayson, 'Bias In, Bias Out' (2019) 128(8) *Yale Law Journal* 2218 at 2277–81.

[34] See, for example, Richard A Berk, Arun Kumar Kuchibhotla, and Eric Tchetgen, 'Improving Fairness in Criminal Justice Algorithmic Risk Assessments Using Conformal Prediction Sets' (2023) 0(0) *Sociological Methods & Research* <https://doi.org/10.1177/00491241231155883>, arXiv:2008.11664 [stat.AP]; James E Johndrow and Kristian Lum, 'An Algorithm for Removing Sensitive Information: Application to Race-Independent Recidivism Prediction' (2019) 13(1) *The Annals of Applied Statistics* 189; and Jon Kleinberg et al, 'Discrimination in the Age of Algorithms' (2018) 10 *Journal of Legal Analysis* 113.

[35] See, for example, Danielle Keats Citron, 'Technological Due Process' (2008) 85(6) *Washington University Law Review* 1249; and Karen Yeung, 'Algorithmic Regulation: A Critical Interrogation' (2018) 12(4) *Regulation and Government* 505.

change dramatically in an era of automated governance.[36] Judges, after all, will confront many of the same difficulties scrutinizing AI tools as they have confronted in the past with respect to other statistical and technical aspects of administration, which may lead to continued judicial deference as exemplified in *Baltimore Gas & Electric*.[37] In addition, rather than public attitudes turning against governmental use of AI and ADM tools, it may just as easily be expected that public expectations will be shaped by widespread acceptance of AI in other facets of life, perhaps even leading to affirmative demands that governments use ADM tools rather than continuing to rely on slower or less reliable processes.[38] Cautious about ossifying automated governance, judges and administrative law scholars might well resist the urge to impose new doctrinal hurdles on automation.[39] They may also conclude, as would be reasonable, that existing doctrine contains what is needed to ensure that government agencies use automated systems responsibly.

As a result, if government agencies wish to expand the responsible use of properly trained, audited, and validated automated systems that are sufficiently aligned with legislative mandates and improve agencies' ability to perform key tasks, it seems they will hardly need any transformation of traditional administrative law principles to accommodate these innovations. Nor will administrative law need to adapt much, if at all, to ensure that kind of responsible use of automated governance. Overall, an automated state could conceivably do a better job than ever before of fulfilling the vision of good governance that has long animated administrative law.

9.5 CONCLUSION: THE NEED FOR HUMAN EMPATHY

Still, even if the prevailing principles of administrative law can deal adequately with public sector use of AI tools, something important could easily end up getting lost in an automated state. Such an administrative government might be smarter, more democratically accountable, and even more fair. But it could also lack feeling, even

---

[36] For example, norms will surely develop about how agencies should document their choices in designing algorithmic systems. See, for example, Timnit Gebru et al, 'Datasheets for Datasets' (2020) <https://arxiv.org/abs/1803.09010>.

[37] Channeling Voltaire, if *Baltimore Gas & Electric* did not exist, courts might still find it necessary to invoke its deference. See Adrian Vermeule, *Law's Abnegation: From Law's Empire to the Administrative State* (Cambridge: Harvard University Press, 2016).

[38] Cary Coglianese and Kat Hefter, 'From Negative to Positive Algorithm Rights' (2022) 30 *William & Mary Bill of Rights Journal* 883–923.

[39] As Steven Appel and I have noted elsewhere, 'it is not hard to imagine a time in the near future when the public actually comes to expect their public servants to rely on such technologies. As complex machine-learning algorithms proliferate in the private sector, members of the public may well come to expect similar accuracy and automated services from their governments'. Steven M Appel and Cary Coglianese, 'Algorithmic Governance and Administrative Law' in Woodrow Barfield (ed), *Cambridge Handbook on the Law of Algorithms: Human Rights, Intellectual Property, Government Regulation* (Cambridge: Cambridge University Press, 2021) 162, 165.

more than sterile bureaucratic processes do today. Interactions with government through smartphones and automated chats may be fine for making campground reservations at national parks or even for filing taxes. But they run the risk of leaving out an important ingredient of good governance – namely, empathy – in those circumstances in which government must make highly consequential decisions affecting the well-being of individuals. In such circumstances, empathy demands that administrative agencies provide opportunities for human interaction and for listening and expressions of concern. An important challenge for administrative law in the decades to come will be to find ways to encourage an automated state that is also an empathic state.

A desire for empathy, of course, need not impede the development of automation.[40] If government manages the transition to an automated state well, it is possible that automation can enhance the government's ability to provide empathy to members of the public, but only if government officials are sufficiently attentive to the need to do so. This need will become even greater as the overall economy moves toward greater reliance on AI and ADM systems. Society will need to value and find new ways to fulfill those tasks involving empathy that humans are good at providing. The goal should be, as technologist Kai-Fu Lee has noted, to ensure that "while AI handles the routine optimization tasks, human beings ... bring the personal, creative, and compassionate touch."[41]

Already, public administration experts recognize that this is one of the great potential advantages of moving to an automated state. It can free up government workers from drudgery and backlogs of files to process, while leaving them more time and opportunities to connect with those affected by agency decisions.[42] A recent report jointly issued by the Partnership for Public Service and the IBM Center for Business and Government explains the importance of this shift in what government employees do:

[40] Notably, technologists are even exploring the possibility of building empathy into automated tools. See, for example, Pascale Fung et al, 'Towards Empathetic Human–Robot Interactions' in Alexander Gelbukh (ed), *Computational Linguistics and Intelligent Text Processing* (New York: Springer International Publishing, 2018).

[41] Kai-Fu Lee, *AI Superpowers: China, Silicon Valley, and the New World Order* (Boston: Houghton Mifflin Harcourt, 2018) 210.

[42] The advent of an automated administrative state will unquestionably lead to changes in the government labor force, much as the expanded use of AI in the private sector will lead to changes in the labor market more generally. David Autor and Anna M Salomons, 'Is Automation Labor-Displacing? Productivity Growth, Employment, and the Labor Share' (2018) *Brookings Papers on Economic Activity*; and David Autor, David Mindell, and Elisabeth Reynolds, MIT Work of the Future, *The Work of the Future: Building Better Jobs in an Age of Intelligent Machines* (Report, 2020) <https://workofthefuture.mit.edu/wp-content/uploads/2021/01/2020-Final-Report4.pdf>. The shift to a government workforce increasingly organized around empathy harkens to a broader shift from a manufacturing economy to service economy, or perhaps still further to a "sharing" economy. See Cary Coglianese, 'Optimizing Regulation for an Optimizing Economy' (2018) 4(1) *University of Pennsylvania Journal of Law and Public Affairs* 1 at 3–4.

Many observers who envision greater use of AI in government picture more face-to-face interactions between agency employees and customers, and additional opportunities for more personalized customer services. The shift toward employees engaging more with agency customers is expected to be one of several possible effects of automating administrative tasks. Relieved of burdensome paperwork, immigration officers could spend more time interacting with visa applicants or following up on individual immigration cases. Scientists could allot more of their day to working with research study participants. And grants managers could take more time to learn about and support individual grantees. On average, federal employees now spend only 2 percent of their time communicating with customers and other people outside their agencies, or less than one hour in a workweek, according to one study. At the same time, citizens want government to do better. The experiences customers have with companies is driving demand for personalized government services. In a survey of more than 6,000 people from six countries, including the United States, 44 percent of respondents identified personalized government services as a priority.[43]

Not only does a substantial portion of the public already recognize the need for empathic, personalized engagement opportunities with government, but as private sector organizations invest more in personalized services, this will only heighten and broaden expectations for similar empathy from government. We already know from extensive research on procedural justice that the way the government treats members of the public affects their sense of legitimacy in the outcomes they receive.[44] To build public trust in an automated state, government authorities will need to ensure that members of the public still feel a human connection. As political philosopher Amanda Greene has put it, "government must be seen to be sincerely caring about each person's welfare."[45]

Can administrative law help encourage empathic administrative processes? Some might say that this is already a purpose underlying the procedural due process principles that make up administrative law. *Goldberg v Kelly*, after all, guarantees certain recipients of government benefits the right to an oral hearing before a neutral decision-maker prior to the termination of their benefits, a right that does afford at least an opportunity for affected individuals to engage with a theoretically empathic administrative judge.[46] But the now-canonical test of procedural due process reflected in *Mathews v Eldridge* is almost entirely devoid of attention to

[43] Partnership for Public Service and IBM Center for the Business of Government, *More Than Meets AI*, 8.

[44] Allen E Lind and Tom Tyler, *The Social Psychology of Procedural Justice* (New York: Springer International Publishing, 1988).

[45] Amanda Greene, Centre for Public Impact, 'Competence, Fairness, and Caring: The Three Keys to Government Legitimacy' (Web Page, 27 February 2018) <www .centreforpublic impact.org/the-three-keys-government-legitimacy/>.

[46] 397 US 254 (1970). See Lucie E White, 'Subordination, Rhetorical Survival Skills, and Sunday Shoes: Notes on the Hearing of Mrs. G.' (1990) 38(1) *Buffalo Law Review* 1.

the role of listening, caring, and concern in government's interactions with members of the public.[47] *Mathews* defines procedural due process in terms of a balance of three factors: (1) the affected private interests; (2) the potential for reducing decision-making error; and (3) the government's interests concerning fiscal and administrative burdens. AI automation would seem to pass muster quite easily under the *Mathews* balancing test. The first factor – the private interests at stake – will be external to AI, but AI systems would seem always to fare well under the second and third factors. Their great promise is that they can reduce errors and lower administrative costs.

This is where existing principles of administrative law will fall short in an automated state and where the need for greater vision will be needed. Hearing rights and the need for reasons are about more than just achieving accurate outcomes, which is what the *Mathews* framework implies. On the contrary, hearings and reason-giving might not be all that good at achieving accurate outcomes, at least not as consistently as automated systems. A 2011 study showed that, among the fifteen most active administrative judges in one office of the Social Security Administration, "the judge grant rates ... ranged ... from less than 10 percent being granted to over 90 percent."[48] The study revealed, for example, that three judges in this same office awarded benefits to no more than 30 percent of their applicants, while three other judges awarded to more than 70 percent.[49] Other studies have suggested that racial disparities may exist in Social Security disability awards, with certain Black applicants tending to receive less favorable outcomes than white applicants.[50] Against this kind of track record, automated systems promise distinct advantages when they can be shown to deliver fairer, more consistent, and even speedier decisions.

But humans will still be good at listening and empathizing with the predicaments of those who are seeking assistance or other decisions from government, or who otherwise find themselves subjected to its constraints.[51] It is that human quality of empathy that should lead the administrative law of procedural due process to move beyond just its current emphasis on reducing errors and lowering costs.

[47] 424 US 319 (1976).
[48] TRAC Social Security Administration, 'Social Security Awards Depend More on Judge Than Facts', *TRAC Social Security Administration* (Web Page, 4 July 2011) <https://trac.syr.edu/tracreports/ssa/254/>. The Social Security Administration sharply disputed aspects of this study.
[49] Ibid.
[50] See, for example, U.S. General Accounting Office, *Racial Difference in Disability Decisions Warrants Further Investigation* B-247327 (Report, 1992) <www.gao.gov/assets/160/151781.pdf>; and Erin M Godtland et al, 'Racial Disparities in Federal Disability Benefits' (2007) 25(1) *Contemporary Economic Policy* 27.
[51] For a discussion of the importance of empathy in the exercise of regulatory authority, see Cary Coglianese, University of Pennsylvania Law School, *Listening, Learning, and Leading: A Framework for Regulatory Excellence* (Report, 2015) 23–25 <www.law.upenn.edu/live/files/4946-pprfinalconvenersreport.pdf>.

To some judges, the need for an administrative law of empathy may lead them to ask whether members of the public have a "right to a human decision" within an automated state.[52] But not all human decisions are necessarily empathic ones. Moreover, a right to a human decision would bring with it the possibility that the law would accept all the flaws in human decision-making simply to retain one of the virtues of human engagement. If automated decisions turn out increasingly to be more accurate and less biased than human ones, a right to a decision by humans would seem to deny the public the desirable improvements in governmental performance that AI and ADM tools can deliver.

Administrative law need not stand in the way of these improvements. It can accept the use of AI and ADM tools while nevertheless pushing government forward toward additional opportunities for listening and compassionate responses.[53] Much as the US Supreme Court in *Goldberg v. Kelly* insisted on a pretermination hearing for welfare recipients, courts in the future can ask whether certain interests are of a sufficient quality and importance to demand that agencies provide supplemental engagement with and assistance to individuals subjected to automated processes. Courts could in this way seek to reinforce best practices in agency efforts to provide empathic outreach and assistance.

In the end, if administrative law in an automated state is to adopt any new rights, society might be better served if courts avoid the recognition of a right to a human decision. Instead, courts could consider and seek to define a right to human *empathy*.

---

[52] For an excellent treatment of this question, see Aziz Z Huq, 'A Right to a Human Decision' (2020) 106(3) *Virginia Law Review* 611.

[53] Sometimes the compassionate response may even call for overriding an automated decision: that is, to have a human official exhibit mercy and reach a different decision on an individual basis. After all, automated systems themselves will still result in errors, and joint human-machine systems may well at times do better to reduce errors than either humans or machines operating separately. The challenge, though, will be to ensure enough structure around the discretion to override automated outcomes, lest human exceptions come to swallow automated rules. See Cary Coglianese, Gabriel Scheffler, and Daniel E Walters, 'Unrules' (2021) 73(4) *Stanford Law Review* 885. One solution might be to create AI tools specifically designed to help with this very problem. If an automated system generates not only an outcome but also an estimate of confidence in that outcome, humans may be guided to go beyond empathic listening and deliver merciful exceptions only in those instances where a system's estimated confidence is sufficiently low.

10

Sorting Teachers Out

Automated Performance Scoring and the Limit of Algorithmic Governance in the Education Sector

Ching-Fu Lin[*]

10.1 INTRODUCTION

Big data is increasingly mined to train ADM tools, with consequential reverberations. Governments are among the primary users of such tools to sort, rank, and rate their citizens, creating a data-driven infrastructure of preferences that condition people's behaviours and opinions. China's social credit system, Australia's robo-debt program,[1] and the United States' welfare distribution platform are prime examples of how governments resort to ADM to allocate resources and provide public services.[2] Some commentators point to the rule of law deficits in the automation of government functions;[3] others emphasize how such technologies systematically exacerbate inequalities;[4] and still others argue that a society constantly being scored, profiled, and predicted threatens due process and justice generally.[5] In contemporary workplaces, algorithmically powered tools have also been widely

[*] The author would like to thank Monika Zalnieriute, Lyria Bennett Moses, Zofia Bednarz, and participants for their valuable comments at the conference on Money, Power, and AI: From Automated Banks to Automated States, co-held by Centre for Law, Markets and Regulation, Australian Institute of Human Rights, ARC Centre of Excellence for Automated Decision-Making and Society, Allens Hub for Technology, Law and Innovation, University of New South Wales (UNSW), Sydney, Australia in November 2021. The author is also grateful to Yu-Chun Liu, Kuan-Lin Ho, Da-Jung Chang, and Yen-Yu Hong for their excellent research assistance. All errors remain the author's sole responsibility. The author can be reached via chingfulin@mx.nthu.edu.tw.
[1] On Australia's robo-debt see Chapter 5 in this book.
[2] Han-Wei Liu et al, "Rule of Trust": Powers and Perils of China's Social Credit Megaproject' (2018) 32(1) *Columbia Journal of Asian Law* 1–36.
[3] Monika Zalnieriute et al, 'The Rule of Law and Automation of Government Decision-Making' (2019) 82(3) *Modern Law Review* 425–55.
[4] Virginia Eubanks, *Automating Inequality: How High-Tech Tools Profile, Police, and Punish the Poor* (New York: St. Martin's Press, 2018).
[5] Danielle K Citron and Frank Pasquale, 'The Scored Society: Due Process for Automated Predictions' (2014) 89(1) *Washington Law Review* 1–33.

adopted in business practices for efficiency, productivity, and management purposes.[6] Camera surveillance, data analysis, and ranking and scoring systems are
algorithmic tools that have given employers enormous power over the employed,
yet their use also triggers serious controversies over privacy, ethical concerns, labour
rights, and due process protection.[7]

Houston Federation of Teachers v Houston Independent School District presents
yet another controversial example of government 'algorithmization' and the power
and perils of automated ranking and rating, targeting at a specific profession –
teachers. The case concerns the implementation of value-added models (VAMs)
that algorithmically link a teacher's contributions to students' growth on standardized tests and hold teachers accountable through incentives such as termination,
tenure, or contract nonrenewal. The Houston Independent School District refused
to renew more than 200 teachers' contracts in 2011 based on low value-added
scores. The VAM is proprietary and is not disclosed to those affected, precluding
them from gaining an understanding of the internal logic and decision-making
processes at work, thereby causing serious harm to due process rights. Similar
practices prevail across the United States following the enactment of the 2002
No Child Left Behind Act and the 2011 Race to the Top Act, in conjunction with
other federal policy actions. Interestingly, until the 2017 summary judgment
rendered by the Court in *Houston Federation of Teachers v Houston Independent
School District*, which ruled in favour of the affected teachers, federal constitutional
challenges against the use of VAMs for termination or nonrenewal of teachers'
contracts were generally rejected. Yet, the case has received little attention, as it was
subsequently settled.

The growing algorithmization of worker performance evaluation and workplace
surveillance in the name of efficiency and productivity is not limited to specific
industry sectors or incomes, and it has been implemented so rapidly that regulators
struggle to catch up and employees suffer in an ever-widening power asymmetry.
Algorithmically powered workplace surveillance and worker performance evaluation effectively expand employers' capacity of control by shaping expectations
and conditioning the behaviours of employees, which may further distort the nature
of the relationship between the employer and the employed. Furthermore, such
algorithmic tools have been widely criticized to be neither reliable nor transparent
and also prone to bias and discrimination.[8] Hence, the prevalent use of algorithmic

---

[6] See e.g., Anne Fisher, 'An Algorithm May Decide Your Next Pay Raise' (14 July 2019) *Fortune*.
[7] Saul Levmore and Frank Fagan, 'Competing Algorithms for Law: Sentencing, Admissions, and
     Employment' (2021) 88(2) *University of Chicago Law Review* 367–412.
[8] See e.g., James A Allen, 'The Color of Algorithms: An Analysis and Proposed Research Agenda
     for Deterring Algorithmic Redlining' (2019) 46(2) *Fordham Urban Law Journal* 219–70;
     Estefania McCarroll, 'Weapons of Mass Deportation: Big Data and Automated Decision-
     Making Systems in Immigration Law' (2020) 34 *Georgetown Immigration Law Journal* 705–
     31; and Sarah Valentine, 'Impoverished Algorithms: Misguided Governments, Flawed
     Technologies, and Social Control' (2019) 46(2) *Fordham Urban Law Journal* 364–427.

worker productivity and performance evaluation systems poses serious economic, social, legal, and political ramifications.

This chapter therefore asks critical questions that remain unanswered. What are the normative ramifications of this case? How can due process protection – procedural or substantive – be ensured under the maze of crude algorithmic worker productivity and performance evaluation systems such as the VAM, especially in light of the black box problems?[9] Can judicial review provide a viable form of algorithmic governance? How are such ADM tools reshaping professions like education? Does the increasingly blurred line between public and private authority in designing and applying these algorithmic tools pose new threats? Premised upon these scholarly and practical inquiries, this article seeks to examine closely the case of *Houston Federation of Teachers v Houston Independent School District*, analyze its ramifications, and provide critical reflections on ways to harness the power of automated governments.

10.2 THE CONTESTED ALGORITHMIZATION OF WORKER PERFORMANCE EVALUATION

Recently, organizations have increased their use of algorithmically powered tools used for worker productivity monitoring and performance evaluation. With the help of camera surveillance, data analysis, and ranking and scoring systems,[10] such tools have given employers significant power over their employees. Growing power asymmetry thereby disrupts the labour market and redefines the way people work. Amazon notoriously uses a combination of AI tools to recruit, monitor, track, score, and even automatically fire its employees and contractors, and these second-by-second measurements have raised serious concerns regarding systematic bias, discrimination, and human rights abuse.[11] Specifically, Amazon uses AI automated tracking systems to monitor and evaluate its delivery drivers, who are categorized as 'lazy' if their movements are too slow and receive warning notifications if they fail to meet the required workloads.[12] The system can even generate an automated order to

9 Han-Wei Liu et al, 'Beyond *State v. Loomis*: Artificial Intelligence, Government Algorithmization, and Accountability' (2019) 27(2) *International Journal of Law and Information Technology* 122–41; Jenna Burrel, 'How the Machine "Thinks": Understanding Opacity in Machine Learning Algorithms' (2016) 3(1) *Big Data & Society* 1–12.
10 David Leonhardt, 'You're Being Watched' (15 August 2022) *The New York Times*.
11 Jeffrey Dastin, 'Amazon Scraps Secret AI Recruiting Tool that Showed bias against Women' (11 October 2018) *Reuters*; Victor Tangermann, 'Amazon Used an AI to Automatically Fire Low-Productivity Workers' (26 April 2019) *Futurism*; Annabelle Williams, '5 Ways Amazon Monitors Its Employees, from AI Cameras to Hiring a Spy Agency' (6 April 2021) *Business Insider*.
12 Yuanyu Bao et al, 'Ethical Disputes of AI Surveillance: Case Study of Amazon', in *Proceedings of the 7th International Conference on Financial Innovation and Economic Development* (2022), 1339.

lay off an employee without the intervention of a human supervisor.[13] Despite the associated physical and psychological suffering, if an employee does not agree to be algorithmically monitored and controlled, the individual will lose his or her job.[14]

   Cashiers, truck drivers, nursing home workers, and many other lower-paying jobs across various sectors have followed suit in adopting Amazon's algorithmization of workers' performance evaluation, aimed at maximizing productivity per capita per second and automating constant micromanagement. Employees who are under such performance evaluation programs can feel pressured to skip interval breaks and bathroom or coffee breaks to avoid adverse consequences.[15] According to a recent in-depth study published in *The New York Times*, eight of the ten largest corporations in the United States have deployed systems to track, often in real time, individual workers' productivity metrics under varied frameworks of data-driven control.[16] The global COVID-19 pandemic has further prompted corporations under profit pressures to keep tighter tabs on employees by means of online and real-time AI evaluation, thus accelerating a paradigm shift of workplace power that was already well underway.[17] Many of the practices adopted during COVID-19 will likely continue and become normalized in the post-pandemic era.

   White-collar jobs are not immune from the growing algorithmization of worker performance evaluation. Architects, financial advisors, lawyers, pharmaceutical assistants, academic administrators, and even doctors and chaplains can be placed under extensive monitoring software that constantly accumulates records, and they are paid 'only for the minutes when the system detected active work', or are subject to a 'productivity points' management system that calibrates pay based on individual scores.[18] For example, some law firms are increasingly subjecting their contract lawyers to smart surveillance systems that constantly monitor their performance during work days in the name of efficiency facilitation and quality control.[19] It appears evident that the growing automation of worker performance evaluation is not limited to specific industry sectors or incomes, and such practices are spreading at such a rapid rate that regulators struggle to catch up and employees suffer from widening power asymmetry.

   As Ifeoma Ajunwa, Kate Crawford, and Jason Schultz observe, due to recent technological innovations, data-driven worker performance evaluation in the United States is on the rise through tools including employee ratings, productivity apps,

[13] Ibid.
[14] Ibid, 1340. *See also* Katie Schoolov, 'Pee Bottles, Constant Monitoring and Blowing through Stop Signs: Amazon DSP Drivers Describe the Job' (21 June 2021) *CNBC*.
[15] Jodi Kantor and Arya Sundaram, 'The Rise of the Worker Productivity Score' (14 August 2022) *The New York Times*.
[16] Ibid.
[17] Ibid.
[18] Ibid.
[19] Drew Harwell, 'Contract Lawyers Face a Growing Invasion of Surveillance Programs that Monitor Their Work' (11 November 2021) *The Washington Post*.

worker wellness programs, activity reports, and color-coded charts.[20] They further argue that such 'limitless worker surveillance' has left millions of employees at the mercy of minute-by-minute monitoring by their employers that undermines fair labour rights, yet the existing legal framework offers few meaningful constraints.[21]

Indeed, algorithmically powered workplace surveillance and worker performance evaluation are often adopted by enterprises to increase efficiency and improve productivity, expand corporate capacity by shaping expectations, and condition the behaviours of employees.[22] However, the adoption of such systems not only intrudes upon the privacy and labour rights of employees,[23] but also harms their physical and mental well-being under a lasting framework of suppression.[24] In a larger context, the dominance of ADM tools for workplace surveillance and worker performance evaluation may distort the nature of the relationship between the employer and the employed and weaken psychological contracts, job engagement, and employee trust.[25] The gap in power asymmetry is institutionally widened by the systematic use of ADM tools that are neither reliable nor transparent and are also prone to bias and discrimination.[26]

Automated worker productivity monitoring and performance evaluation represents a system of mechanical enforcement without empathy or moral responsibility, which potentially dehumanizes the inherently person-to-person process of work management, reward and punishment allocation, and contractual interactions. These tools, cloaked in the promise of technologically supported management and data-driven efficiency, focus not on process but on results, which are observed and calculated based on arbitrary parameters or existing unfair and discriminatory practices. Given the black box nature of these tools, human supervisors, if any, cannot easily detect and address the mistakes and biases that arise in the ADM process. As a result, the use of algorithmic worker productivity monitoring and performance evaluation systems is increasingly contested and criticized for its controversial economic, social, legal, and political ramifications.

---

[20] *See generally* Ifeoma Ajunwa et al, 'Limitless Worker Surveillance' (2017) 105 *California Law Review* 101–42.

[21] Ibid.

[22] Anna M Pluta and A Rudawska, 'Holistic Approach to Human Resources and Organizational Acceleration' (2016) 29(2) *Journal of Organizational Change Management* 293–309.

[23] Alfred Benedikt Brendel et al, 'Ethical Management of Artificial Intelligence' (2021) 13(4) *Sustainability* 1974–92.

[24] Brian Patrick Green, 'Ethical Reflections on Artificial Intelligence' (2018) 6(2) *Scientia et Fiedes* 9–31.

[25] *See* Ashley Braganza et al, 'Productive Employment and Decent Work: The Impact of AI Adoption on Psychological Contracts, Job Engagement and Employee Trust' (2021) 131 *Journal of Business Research* 485–94.

[26] *See generally* Citron and Pasquale, 'The Scored Society: Due Process for Automated Predictions'; Frank Pasquale, *The Black Box Society: The Secret Algorithms That Control Money and Information* (Cambridge: Harvard University Press, 2016).

10.3 SORTING TEACHERS OUT? UNPACKING *HOUSTON FEDERATION OF TEACHERS V HOUSTON INDEPENDENT SCHOOL DISTRICT*

Concerns over algorithmic worker productivity monitoring and performance evaluation systems came to light in the recent lawsuit over the use of VAMs in the United States – *Houston Federation of Teachers v Houston Independent School District*.[27] This case presents yet another controversial dimension of algorithmic worker productivity monitoring and performance evaluation in the education sector. *Houston Federation of Teachers v Houston Independent School District* involves the implementation of VAMs by the Houston Independent School District that algorithmically link a teacher's contributions to students' growth on standardized tests, the results of which inform decisions on teachers' tenure or contract (non)renewal. In 2011, the Houston Independent School District, citing low value-added scores, refused to renew its contract with more than 200 teachers. The VAM is proprietary and is not disclosed to those affected, precluding them from gaining an understanding of the internal logic and decision-making processes at work and causing serious harm to due process rights. Similar practices prevail across the United States following the enactment of the 2002 No Child Left Behind Act and the 2011 Race to the Top Act, in conjunction with other federal policy actions. Before the 2017 summary judgment rendered by the Court in *Houston Federation of Teachers v Houston Independent School District*, which ruled in favour of the affected teachers, federal constitutional challenges against the use of VAMs for termination or nonrenewal of teachers' contracts were generally rejected. Nevertheless, the case was subsequently settled and has interestingly received little attention. This chapter unpacks the case and endeavours to offer a critical analysis of its legal and policy ramifications.

Since 2010, the Houston Independent School District has applied a data-driven approach to monitor and evaluate teachers' performance with the aim to enhance the effectiveness of teaching from an outcome-based perspective. The algorithmically powered evaluation system implemented by the Houston Independent School District has three appraisal criteria – instructional practice, professional expectations, and student performance.[28] To narrow down the parameters for discussion, it should be noted that the primary focus of the case, *Houston Federation of Teachers v Houston Independent School District*, resides in the third component – student performance. Under the algorithmic work performance evaluation system, it is assumed that student growth and improvement in standardized test scores could appropriately reflect a specific teacher's impact on (or added value to) individual

---

[27] *Hous. Fed'n of Teachers v Hous. Indep. Sch. Dist.*, 251 F. Supp. 3d 1168, at 1171 (S.D. Tex. 2017).
[28] Ibid.

student performance, which is known as the VAM for teaching evaluations.[29] By implementing this system, student growth is calculated using the Educational Value-Added Assessment System (EVAAS), a proprietary statistical model developed by a private software company, SAS, and licensed for use by the Houston Independent School District.[30] This automated teacher evaluation system works by comparing the average test score growth of students taught by the teacher being evaluated with the statewide average for students in the same grade or course. The score is then processed by SAS's proprietary algorithmic program and subsequently sorted into an effectiveness rating system.[31]

In essence, under the VAM model, a teacher's algorithmically generated score was based on comparing the average growth of student test scores of the specific teacher compared to the average number state-wide, and the score was then converted to a test statistic called the Teacher Gain Index.[32] This measure was used to classify teachers into five levels of performance, ranging from 'well above' to 'well below' average.[33] It should be noted that the automated teacher evaluation system was initially used to inform and determine teacher bonuses, but as later implemented by the Houston Independent School District, the algorithmic system was used to automate sanctions on employed teachers for low student performance on standardized tests.[34] The Houston Independent School District declared in 2012 its management goal of ensuring that 'no more than 15% of teachers with ratings of ineffective are retained', and around 25 per cent of the 'ineffective teachers' were 'exited'.[35]

The plaintiff in this case, Houston Federation of Teachers, argued that the use of EVAAS violated the following elements of the Fourteenth Amendment.[36] First, the use of EVAAS violates the procedural due process right of the plaintiff because of the lack of sufficient information needed to meaningfully challenge terminations of contracts based on low EVAAS scores. Second, the substantive due process right is also violated, as there is no rational relationship between EVAAS scores and the Houston Independent School District's goal of employing effective teachers. Furthermore, since the EVAAS system is too vague to provide notice to teachers regarding how to achieve higher ratings and avoid adverse employment consequences, the use of EVAAS again violates the plaintiff's substantive due process right. Third, the plaintiff's right to equal protection is harmed by the Houston

[29] Ibid, 1172.
[30] Ibid.
[31] Ibid.
[32] Ibid.
[33] Ibid.
[34] Ibid, 1174.
[35] Ibid, 1174–75.
[36] Ibid, 1172–73.

Independent School District's policy of aligning teachers' instructional performance
ratings with their EVAAS scores.

The court began its analysis with the plaintiff's protected property interests.[37]
Referring to past jurisprudence, the court notes that, regardless of their employment
status under probationary, term, or continuing contract, teachers generally have a
protected property interest under their respective employment contracts (either
during the term of the contract or under continued employment, according to the
type of contract).[38] In this sense, the teachers who were adversely impacted by the
use of EVAAS in the present case have a constitutionally protected property interest
derived from the contractual relationship. The court denied the Houston
Independent School District's argument that 'a due process plaintiff must show
actual deprivation of a constitutional right'.[39] Importantly, the plaintiff in the present
case sought 'a declaratory judgment and permanent injunction' barring the use of
EVAAS in determining the renewal or termination of teacher contracts rather than
monetary compensation and seeking an institutional and systematic outcome.
According to past jurisprudence relevant to this case, '[o]ne does not have to await
the consummation of threatened injury to obtain preventive relief'. Such a statement recommends that a demonstration of 'realistic danger' be sufficient.[40] As the
facts of the case demonstrate a relationship between EVAAS scores and teacher
employment termination, the court found that the VAM evaluation system 'poses a
realistic threat to protected property interests' for those teachers.[41]

The court then turned to the procedural due process issue, which consists of the
core value of 'the opportunity to be heard at a meaningful time and in a meaningful
manner' to ensure that governmental decisions are fair and accurate.[42] The Houston
Federation of Teachers argued that the Houston Independent School District failed
the minimum procedural due process standard to provide 'the cause for [the
teacher's] termination in sufficient detail so as to enable [the teacher] to show any
error that may exist'. The algorithms and data used for the EVAAS evaluation system
were proprietary and remained unavailable and inaccessible to the teachers who
were affected, and the accuracy of scores could not be verified.[43] To address this
issue, the court first acknowledged that, as the Houston Independent School District

---

[37] Ibid, 1173 ('The Fourteenth Amendment prohibits a state from depriving any person of life,
liberty, or property without due process of law … To evaluate such a claim, a court must first
consider whether there is sufficient evidence implicating a protected property right in plaintiff's
employment').

[38] Ibid (Citing *Frazier v Garrison I.S.D.*, 980 F.2d 1514, 1529 (5th Cir. 1993)).

[39] Ibid, 1174 (HISD had cited *Villanueva v McInnis*, 723 F.2d 414, 418–19 (5th Cir. 1984)).

[40] Ibid (Citing *Pennsylvania v West Virginia*, 262 U.S. 553, 593, 43 S.Ct. 658, 67 L.Ed. 1117
(1923); *Pennell v City of San Jose*, 485 U.S. 1, 8, 108 S.Ct. 849, 99 L.Ed.2d 1 (1988)).

[41] Ibid, 1175.

[42] Ibid, 1175–76.

[43] Ibid, 1172, 1176–77 (Citing *Ferguson v Thomas*, 430 F.2d 852 (5th Cir. 1970), the court has
deemed that in the case of public school teacher termination, the minimum standards of
procedural due process include the rights to

had admitted, the algorithms were retained by SAS as a trade secret, prohibiting access by the teachers as well as the Houston Independent School District, and any efforts to replicate the scores would fail. Furthermore, the calculation of EVAAS scores may be erroneous due to mistakes in the data or the algorithm code itself. Such mistakes could not be promptly corrected, and any reanalysis would potentially affect all other teachers' scores.[44]

The court then agreed to the plaintiff's application of the following standard from *Banks v. Federal Aviation Admin.*, 687 F.2d 92 (5th Cir. 1982), that 'due process required an opportunity by the controllers to test on their own behalf to evaluate the accuracy of the government-sponsored tests'.[45] When a potential violation of constitutional rights arises from a policy that concerns trade secrets, 'the proper remedy is to overturn the policy, while leaving the trade secrets intact'.[46] Even if the Houston Independent School District had provided the teachers some basic information (e.g., a general explanation of the EVAAS test methods) under the standard adopted in *Banks v Federal Aviation Admin.*, the measure still falls short of due process, since it does not change the fact that the teachers are unable to verify or replicate the EVAAS scores.[47] Since it is nearly impossible for the teachers to obtain or ensure accurate EVAAS scores and they are therefore 'unfairly subject to mistaken deprivation of constitutionally protected property interests in their jobs', the Houston Independent School District was denied summary judgment on this procedural due process claim.[48]

The issues involved in the substantive due process are twofold. The first issue relates to whether the challenged measure had a rational basis.[49] The Houston Federation of Teachers argued that EVAAS went against the protection of substantive due process, since there was no rational relationship between EVAAS scores and the Houston Independent School District's goal of 'having an effective teacher in every [Houston Independent School District] classroom so that every [Houston

---

(1) be advised of the cause for his termination in sufficient detail so as to enable him to show any error that may exist;
(2) be advised of the names and testimony of the witnesses against him;
(3) a meaningful opportunity to be heard in his own defense within a reasonable time;
(4) a hearing before a tribunal that possesses some academic expertise and an apparent impartiality towards the charges).

[44] Ibid, 1177.
[45] Ibid, 1178 (In *Banks v Federal Aviation Admin.*, 687 F.2d 92 (5th Cir. 1982), two air traffic controllers were dismissed on the grounds of drug usage. However, their urine samples were subsequently destroyed and were unavailable for independent testing. The lab tests that showed traces of cocaine became the only evidence of drug use in the record. The Fifth Circuit found that the controllers had been denied due process).
[46] Ibid, 1179.
[47] Ibid.
[48] Ibid, 1180.
[49] Ibid. (Citing *Finch v Fort Bend Independent School Dist.*, 333 F.3d 555, 563 (5th Cir. 2003), the challenged law or practice should have 'a rational means of advancing a legitimate governmental purpose').

Independent School District] student is set up for success'.[50] However, the court
cited several examples of case law which supported the argument that a rational
relationship existed in the present case and that 'the loose constitutional standard of
rationality allows governments to use blunt tools which may produce only marginal
results'.[51] The second issue surrounding substantive due process concerned vagueness. The general standard for unconstitutional vagueness is whether a measure 'fail
[s] to provide the kind of notice that will enable ordinary people to understand what
conduct it prohibits' or 'authorize[s] and even encourage[s] arbitrary and discriminatory enforcement'.[52] On the other hand, the court also acknowledged that a lesser
degree of specificity is required in civil cases and that 'broad and general regulations
are not necessarily vague'.[53] The court determined that the disputed measure in the
present case was not vague, as the teachers who were impacted had been noticed or
advised of the general information and possible effect of the use of the EVAAS
evaluation system by their institutions.[54]

Finally, the court reviewed the plaintiff's equal protection claim. If a measure
lacks a rational basis for the difference in treatment, that is, if the classification
system used to justify the different treatment fails to rationally relate to a legitimate
governmental objective, it may violate the Equal Protection Clause.[55] However, in
this present case, the court denied the plaintiff's claim that the EVAAS rating scores
represented a classification system. Even if they had, the court deemed that a
rational basis existed, as explored with regard to the substantive due process claims.[56]
In summary, the Houston Independent School District's motion for summary
judgment on the procedural due process claim was denied, but summary judgment
on all other claims was granted.[57]

10.4 JUDICIAL REVIEW AS ALGORITHMIC GOVERNANCE? CONTROVERSIES, RAMIFICATIONS, AND CRITICAL REFLECTIONS

It should be noted that, before the summary judgment ruling was reached in
Houston Federation of Teachers v Houston Independent School District, some
existing literature mentioned the issue of policy failures within the Houston

---

[50] Ibid.
[51] Ibid, 1180–82 (Citing *Cook v Bennett*, 792 F.3d 1294 (11th Cir. 2015); *Wagner v Haslam*, 112 F.Supp.3d 673 (M.D.Tenn. 2015); *Trout v Knox* Cty. Brd. of Educ., 163 F.Supp.3d 492 (E.D. Tenn. 2016)).
[52] Ibid, 1182 (Citing *City of Chicago v Morales*, 527 U.S. 41, 56, 119 S.Ct. 1849, 144 L.Ed.2d 67 (1999)).
[53] Ibid.
[54] Ibid, 1182–83.
[55] Ibid, 1183.
[56] Ibid.
[57] Ibid.

Independent School District's algorithmic work performance evaluation systems and the subsequent measures implemented on the teachers who were adversely affected. Some policies have noted that, while high-quality teachers can greatly benefit students, the 'effectiveness' of teachers may be difficult to assess because it correlates with non-observable characteristics.[58] To address the challenges of teacher evaluation and management, better information on real-world quality contributes to the productiveness of personnel policies and management decisions, but the accuracy of such information and its correlation with student performance cannot be easily observed.[59]

Julie Cullen and others conducted an empirical study that compared the patterns of attrition before and after the implementation of the Houston Independent School District's automated work performance evaluation system as well as the relationship between these patterns and student achievement. These researchers found that, although the algorithmic work performance evaluation system seemingly improves the quality teacher workforce, as it increases the exit rate of low-performing teachers, the statistics that imply this relationship are exclusively more obvious in low-achieving schools, as opposed to middle- and high-achieving schools.[60] More importantly, Cullen et al. also found that the exits resulting from the automated work performance evaluation system were too poorly targeted to induce any meaningful gains in student achievement and net policy effects.[61] They further suggested that the Houston Independent School District's algorithmic work performance measures were ineffective and proposed other substitutive measures via recruitment of new teachers or improvements in existing teaching employees.[62]

Bruce Baker and colleagues discussed legal controversies over unfair treatment and inadequate due process mechanisms since such automated teacher evaluation models are embedded with problematic features and parameters, such as non-negotiable final decisions, inaccessible information, and the use of imprecise data.[63] Algorithmic teacher evaluation models like EVAAS systems are prone to structural problems. First, such systems require that all 'objective measures of student achievement growth' be considered, which may lead to inaccurate outcomes, since the model disregards the fact that the validity and reliability of these measures can vary and that random errors or biases may occur, with no opportunity to question and reassess the validity of any measure.[64] Second, the standards for placing teachers into

---

[58] Cullen et al, 'The Compositional Effect of Rigorous Teacher Evaluation on Workforce Quality' (2021) 16(1) *Education Finance and Policy* 7–41.

[59] Ibid.

[60] Ibid, 21.

[61] Ibid, 21–26.

[62] Ibid, 26.

[63] Bruce D Baker et al, 'The Legal Consequences of Mandating High Stakes Decisions Based on Low Quality Information: Teacher Evaluation in the Race-to-the-Top Era' (2013) 21(5) *Education Policy Analysis Archives* 1–65 at 5.

[64] Ibid, 5–6.

effectiveness score bands and categories are unjustifiable, as the numerical cutoffs are rigid and temporally static. A difference in one point or percentile does not necessarily indicate any actual differences in the performance of the evaluated teachers. However, it can lead to a distinctly different effectiveness category and consequentially endanger a teacher's employment rights.[65] While models that are based on VAMs theoretically attempt to reflect student achievement growth that can be attributed (directly) to a specific instructor's teaching quality and performance, they can hardly succeed in making a fair connection in reality, since it is nearly impossible to discern whether the evaluation estimates have been contaminated by uncontrollable or biased factors, and the variation in ratings is quite broad.[66] By dismissing teachers under such an arbitrary evaluation system, possible violations of due process rights under the Fourteenth Amendment in the form of harm to liberty interests by adversely affecting teachers' employment or harm to property interests in continued employment may likely occur, as shown in *Houston Federation of Teachers v Houston Independent School District*. Likewise, VAMs may be challenged against procedural or substantive due process claims surrounding the technical flaws of value-added testing policies, including the instability of the reliability of those measures along with their questionable interpretations, the doubtful validity of the measure and the extent to which it proves a specific teacher's influence over student achievement, and the accessibility and understandability of the measures to an evaluated teacher as well as the teacher's ability to control relevant factors.[67] VAMs are limited measures in terms of properly assessing teacher 'effectiveness', and 'it would be foolish to impose on these measures, rigid, overly precise high stakes decision frameworks'.[68]

In *Houston Federation of Teachers v Houston Independent School District*, the court found a procedural due process violation mainly because those teachers had no way to replicate and challenge their scores. In addition, the court also indicated concern over the accuracy issue of the algorithmic tool, which has never been verified or audited whatsoever.[69] In a way, the case marks 'an unprecedented development in VAM litigation', and as a result, VAMs used in other states and elsewhere in education management policies should garner greater interest and concern.[70] As per the judge in *Houston Federation of Teachers v Houston Independent School District*, when a government agency adopts a management policy of making highly consequential decisions with regard to employment renewal

---

[65] Ibid, 6.
[66] Ibid, 9.
[67] Ibid, 10–11.
[68] Ibid, 18.
[69] *Hous. Fed'n of Teachers v Hous. Indep. Sch. Dist.*, 251 F. Supp. 3d 1168, at 1177–80 (S.D. Tex. 2017).
[70] Audrey Amrein-Beardsley, 'The Education Value-Added Assessment System (EVAAS) on Trial: A Precedent-Setting Lawsuit with Implications for Policy and Practice' (2019) *eJournal of Education Policy* 1–11 at 7.

and termination based on opaque algorithms incompatible with minimum due process, the court is poised to offer a proper remedy to overturn the use of this algorithmic tool.[71] After *Houston Federation of Teachers v Houston Independent School District*, other states and districts in similar situations have been strongly incentivized to reconsider their use of the EVAAS algorithmic teacher evaluation system or other VAMs by separating consequential personnel decisions from evaluation estimates to avoid potential claims of due process violations.[72] On the other hand, the use of EVAAS (or other VAMs) for low-stakes purposes should also be reconsidered, as the court in *Houston Federation of Teachers v Houston Independent School District* expressed its concern over the actual extent to which 'teachers might understand their EVAAS estimates so as to use them to improve upon their practice'.[73]

As a number of states have adopted automated teacher performance evaluation systems that allow VAM data to be the sole or primary consideration in the decision-making process with regard to review, renewal, or termination of employment contracts, the outcome of *Houston Federation of Teachers v Houston Independent School District* and its legal and policy ramifications might demonstrate a broad reach.[74] Indeed, the lawsuit itself has opened up the possibility for teachers (at least those employed in public schools) to seek remedies for the controversial use of VAMs and other algorithmic teacher performance evaluation systems, especially when the teachers who had challenged such systems had been generally unsuccessful. *Houston Federation of Teachers v Houston Independent School District*, despite being ultimately settled, paves a viable litigation path to challenge the increasingly automated worker performance evaluation in the education sector.

Now it seems possible that due process challenges (at least procedural due process) will persist, as the court drew attention to 'the fact that procedural due process requires a hearing to determine if a district's decision to terminate employment is both fair and accurate'.[75] As noted by Mark Paige and Audrey Amrein-Beardsley, *Houston Federation of Teachers v Houston Independent School District* raised awareness about concerns over government transparency and 'control of private, for-profit corporations engaged in providing a public good',[76] especially with regard to the use of black box algorithmic decision-making tools in the

[71] *Hous. Fed'n of Teachers v Hous. Indep. Sch. Dist.*, 251 F. Supp. 3d 1168, at 1179 (S.D. Tex. 2017).

[72] Amrein-Beardsley, 'The Education Value-Added Assessment System (EVAAS) on Trial: A Precedent-Setting Lawsuit with Implications for Policy and Practice', 8.

[73] Ibid; *Hous. Fed'n of Teachers v Hous. Indep. Sch. Dist.*, 251 F. Supp. 3d 1168, at 1171 (S.D. Tex. 2017).

[74] Mark A Paige and Audrey Amrein-Beardsley, '"Houston, We Have a Lawsuit": A Cautionary Tale for the Implementation of Value-Added Models for High-Stakes Employment Decisions' (2020) 49(5) *Educational Researcher* 350–59.

[75] Ibid, 355.

[76] Ibid.

education sector. The case strongly questions the reliability of the EVAAS system in assessing and improving teacher quality, especially since undetectable errors can lead to significant consequences, including calls for public scrutiny, and seems to offer the potential to compel policymakers and practitioners to both re-examine and reflect on the level of importance (if any) VAM estimations should play in personnel decisions. An independent study on automated decision-making on the basis of personal data in the context of comparison between European Union and United States, which has been submitted to the European Commission's Directorate-General for Justice and Consumers, also underlines that the court's decision in *Houston Federation of Teachers v Houston Independent School District* 'demonstrates that the Due Process Clause can serve as an important safeguard when automated decisions have a legal effect'.[77]

Nevertheless, regrettably, the controversial characteristics of such worker performance evaluation algorithms – the proprietary, black box, inaccessible, and unexplainable decision-making routes[78] – have not occupied a critical spot of concern for legal challenges. The lawsuit in no way means that VAMs and other algorithmic worker evaluation systems should be systematically examined, fixed, or abandoned. As noted, the dominance of automated tools for workplace surveillance and worker performance evaluation may distort the nature of the relationship between the employer and the employed and weaken psychological contracts, job engagement, and employee trust. The gap in power asymmetry has been institutionally widened by the systematic use of algorithmic tools that are neither reliable nor transparent and are also prone to bias and discrimination. All of these issues remain out of the scope of examination in terms of judicial review. In line with this argument, Ryan Calo and Danielle Citron point out the problems of this growingly Automated State, noting a number of controversial cases, including *Houston Federation of Teachers v Houston Independent School District*. The researchers cite the 'looming legitimacy crisis' and call for a reconceptualization and new vision of the modern administrative state in the algorithmic society.[79] They argue that, while scholarly have been asking how we might ensure that these automated tools can align with the existing legal contours such as due process, broader and structural questions on the legitimacy of automating public power remain unanswered.[80] Indeed, without proper gatekeeping or accountability mechanisms, the growing algorithmization of worker performance evaluation can go unharnessed, especially when such practices are

77 Gabriela Bodea et al, *Automated Decision-Making on the Basis of Personal Data that Has Been Transferred from the EU to Companies Certified under the EU-U.S. Privacy Shield Fact-Finding and Assessment of Safeguards Provided by U.S. Law* (Final Report submitted to European Commission Directorate-General for Justice and Consumers Directorate C: Fundamental Rights and Rule of Law Unit C.4 International Data Flows and Protection, 2018) 92.
78 *See* Hannah Bloch-Wehba, 'Access to Algorithms' (2020) 88 *Fordham Law Review* 1265–314.
79 *See generally* Ryan Calo and Danielle Keats Citron, 'The Automated Administrative State: A Crisis of Legitimacy' (2021) 70(4) *Emory Law Journal* 797–845.
80 Ibid.

spreading at such a rapid rate that regulators struggle to catch up and employees face widening power asymmetry.

10.5 CONCLUSION

Automated worker productivity monitoring and performance evaluation indicate a system of mechanical enforcement, if not suppression, which practically dehumanizes the inherent person-to-person process of work management without empathy[81] or moral responsibility. The algorithmic tool, as implemented widely in *Houston Federation of Teachers v Houston Independent School District*, focuses not on process but on results, which are observed and calculated based on arbitrary parameters or the existing unfair and discriminatory practices. Cloaked in technologically supported management and data-driven efficiency, algorithmic worker productivity monitoring and performance evaluation systems create and likely perpetuate a way to rationalize automatic layoffs without meaningful human supervision. Given the black box characteristics of these automated systems, human supervisors cannot easily detect and address mistakes and biases in practice.

The court in *Houston Federation of Teachers v Houston Independent School District* provides a baseline for future challenges in the use of these algorithmic worker productivity monitoring and performance evaluation systems by public authority (not the private sector). Here, judicial review appears necessary and to some extent effective to ensure a basic level of due process protection. However, the ruling arguably only scratches the surface of the growing automation of workplace management and control and the resulting power asymmetry. Indeed, it merely touches on procedural due process and leaves intact critical questions such as algorithmic transparency, explainability, and accountability. In this sense, judicial review, with the conventional understanding of due process and rule of law, cannot readily serve as an adequate form of algorithmic governance that can harness data-driven worker evaluation systems.

Again, salient in *Houston Federation of Teachers v Houston Independent School District*, the affected teachers encountered formidable challenges to examine proprietary algorithms developed by a private company to assess public school teacher performance and make consequential employment decisions. The teachers who were 'exited' had no access to the algorithmic systems and received little explanation or context for their termination. Experts who were offered limited access to the source codes of the EVAAS also concluded that the teachers had no way to meaningfully verify their scores assigned by the system. The algorithmization of worker performance evaluation and surveillance is not and will not be limited to specific industry sectors or incomes. Individuals in other professions may not enjoy comparable social and economic support systems as the teachers in *Houston*

---

[81] See also Chapter 9 in this book.

Federation of Teachers v Houston Independent School District to pursue judicial review and remedies, and the algorithmic injustice they face may never be addressed.

Finally, the increasingly blurred line between public and private authorities and their intertwined collaboration in designing and applying these algorithmic tools pose new threats to the already weak effectiveness of rule of law and due process protection under the existing legal framework.[82] Any due process examination falls short at the interface of public and private collaboration, since the proprietary algorithms held by the private company constitute a black box barrier. The court in *Houston Federation of Teachers v Houston Independent School District* expressed significant concerns over the accuracy of the algorithmic system, noting that the entire algorithmic system was flawed with inaccuracies and was like a house of cards – the 'wrong score of a single teacher could alter the scores of every other teacher in the district' and 'the accuracy of one score hinges upon the accuracy of all'.[83] However, the black box process and automation itself were not considered problematic at all. Due process is needed in the context of the growing algorithmization of worker monitoring and evaluation so that affected employees may be able to partially ascertain the rationale behind data-driven decisions and control programs,[84] but it must be reconceptualized and retooled to protect against the above-mentioned threats to the new power dynamics.

---

[82] The court dismissed the substantive due process claim because the 'loose constitutional standard of rationality allows government to use blunt tools which may produce marginal results'. The court hinted that the algorithmic evaluation system would pass the rationality test even if the system and scores were accurate only a little over half of the time. *Hous. Fed'n of Teachers v Hous. Indep. Sch. Dist.*, 251 F. Supp. 3d 1168, at 1178 (S.D. Tex. 2017).

[83] Ibid.

[84] Sonia K Katyal, 'Democracy & Distrust in an Era of Artificial Intelligence' (2022) 151(2) *Daedalus* 322–34 at 331; *see also* Aziz Z Huq, 'Constitutional Rights in the Machine-Learning State' (2020) 105 *Cornell Law Review* 1875–954.

11

Supervising Automated Decisions

Tatiana Cutts

11.1 INTRODUCTION

AI and ADM tools can help us to make predictions in situations of uncertainty, such as how a patient will respond to treatment, and what will happen if they do not receive it; how an employee or would-be employee will perform; or whether a defendant is likely to commit another crime. These predictions are used to inform a range of significant decisions about who should bear some burden for the sake of some broader social good, such as the relative priority of organ transplant amongst patients; whether to hire a candidate or fire an existing employee; or how a defendant should be sentenced.

Humans play a critical role in setting parameters, designing, and testing these tools. And if the final decision is not purely predictive, a human decision-maker must use the algorithmic output to reach a conclusion. But courts have concluded that humans also play a corrective role[1] – that, even if there are concerns about the predictive assessment, applying human discretion to the predictive task is both a necessary and sufficient safeguard against unjust ADM.[2] Thus, the focus in academic, judicial, and legislative spheres has been on making sure that humans are equipped and willing to wield this ultimate decision-making power.[3]

I argue that this focus is misplaced. Human supervision can help to ensure that AI and ADM tools are fit for purpose, but it cannot make up for the use of AI and ADM tools that are not. Safeguarding requires gatekeeping – using these tools just when we can show that they take the right considerations into account in the right way. In this chapter, I make some concrete recommendations about how to determine

---

[1] See e.g. *State v Loomis* 881 N.W.2d 749 (Wis. 2016) at [71].
[2] Ibid at [92].
[3] See e.g. Reuben Binns, 'Algorithmic Decision-Making: A Guide for Lawyers' (2020) 25 *Judicial Review* 2, 6.

whether AI and ADM tools meet this threshold, and what we should do once we know.

11.2 THE DETERMINATIVE FACTOR

In 2013, Eric Loomis was convicted of two charges relating to a drive-by shooting in La Crosse, Wisconsin: 'attempting to flee a traffic officer and operating a motor vehicle without the owner's consent'.[4] The pre-sentence investigation (PSI) included COMPAS risk and needs assessments.[5] COMPAS (Correctional Offender Management Profiling for Alternative Sanctions) is a suite of ADM/AI tools developed and owned by Equivant.[6] These tools are designed to predict recidivism risk for individual offenders and patterns across wider populations, by relying upon inferences drawn from representative pools of data. The sentencing judge explicitly invoked each COMPAS assessment to justify a sentence of six years in prison and five years of extended supervision.[7]

Though the literature often refers to 'the COMPAS algorithm',[8] COMPAS is not a single algorithm that produces a single risk-score; rather, the COMPAS software includes a range of ADM tools that use algorithms to predict risk, which are described by Equivant as 'configurable for the user'.[9] The tools available include: Pre-Trial Services,[10] which principally concern the risk that the accused will flee the jurisdiction; and three assessments (the General Recidivism Risk scale (GRR), the Violent Recidivism Risk scale (VRR), and the 'full assessment') which involve predictions about recidivism. The GRR, VRR, and full assessment are designed to inform public safety considerations that feed into decisions about resource-allocation across populations,[11] and are used in several jurisdictions to decide how to treat individual offenders.

---

[4] See e.g. Brief of Defendant-Appellant, *State v Loomis*, No 2015AP157-CR (Wis Ct App 2015), 2015 WL 1724741, 1–3; *State v Loomis* at 754.

[5] See e.g. '*State v Loomis*: Wisconsin Supreme Court Requires Warning before Use of Algorithmic Risk Assessments in Sentencing' (2017) 130 *Harvard Law Review* 1530.

[6] Previously Northpointe.

[7] See e.g. Brief of Defendant-Appellant, *State v Loomis*, 9.

[8] See e.g. Ellora Israni, 'Algorithmic due Process: Mistaken Accountability and Attribution in *State v Loomis*' (31 August 2017) *JOLT Digest* <https://jolt.law.harvard.edu/digest/algorithmic-due-process-mistaken-accountability-and-attribution-in-state-v-loomis-1> (accessed 25 August 2022); Leah Wisser, 'Pandora's Algorithmic Black Box: The Challenges of Using Algorithmic Risk Assessments in Sentencing' (2019) 56 *American Criminal Law Review* 1811.

[9] Northpointe Institute for Public Management, *Measurement and Treatment Implications of COMPAS Core Scales* (Report, 30 March 2009) 4.

[10] Ibid.

[11] See generally ibid and Equivant, *Practitioner's Guide to COMPAS Core* (2019). Dr David Thompson testified at the post-conviction hearing, telling the court that COMPAS was originally designed to help corrections allocate resources and to identify individual needs in the community. Brief of Defendant-Appellant, *State v Loomis*, 13.

As the COMPAS software is a trade secret, only the score is revealed to the defendant and court. Nevertheless, Equivant's public materials explain that the GRR includes factors such as: 'criminal associates';[12] 'early indicators of juvenile delinquency problems';[13] 'vocational/educational problems';[14] history of drug use;[15] and age.[16] The enquiry into 'vocational/educational problems' in turn includes data points that are identified by defendants' responses to questions such as: 'how hard is it for you to find a job above minimum wage'; 'what were your usual grades in school'; and 'do you currently have a skill, trade, or profession at which you usually find work'.[17] Equivant notes that these data points are strongly correlated to 'unstable residence and poverty', as part of a pattern of 'social marginalisation'.[18]

The 'full assessment'[19] is designed to assess a much wider set of 'criminogenic need'[20] factors, which are identified by the literature as 'predictors of adult offender recidivism'.[21] These include 'anti-social friends and associates';[22] poor family and/or marital relationships (including whether the defendant was raised by their biological parents, parental divorce or separation, and family involvement in criminal activity, drugs, or alcohol abuse);[23] employment status and prospects;[24] school performance;[25] and 'poor use of leisure and/or recreational time'.[26]

Some of these factors are assessed according to the defendant's own input to a pre-trial questionnaire, some are subjective observations made by the assessing agent, and some are objective data (such as criminal record). Scores are then incorporated by the agent into an overall narrative, which forms the basis of a sentencing recommendation by the district attorney. COMPAS is used by corrections departments, lawyers, and courts across the United States to inform many elements of the criminal process, including decisions about pre-trial plea negotiations; 'jail

---

[12] Northpointe Institute for Public Management, *Measurement and Treatment Implications of COMPAS Core Scales*, 6.

[13] Ibid.

[14] Ibid.

[15] Ibid.

[16] Ibid, 31.

[17] Northpointe Institute for Public Management, *Measurement and Treatment Implications of COMPAS Core Scales*, 21.

[18] Equivant, *Practitioner's Guide to COMPAS Core*, 31, 45, 57.

[19] Northpointe Institute for Public Management, *Measurement and Treatment Implications of COMPAS Core Scales*, 4.

[20] Equivant, *Practitioner's Guide to COMPAS Core*, 36ff.

[21] Paul Gendreau, Tracy Little, and Claire Goggin, 'A Meta-Analysis of the Predictors of Adult Offender Recidivism: What Works!' (1996) 34 *Criminology* 575.

[22] Equivant, *Practitioner's Guide to COMPAS Core*, 36.

[23] Northpointe Institute for Public Management, *Measurement and Treatment Implications of COMPAS Core Scales*, 13.

[24] Ibid, 22.

[25] Ibid, 23.

[26] Northpointe Institute for Public Management, *Measurement and Treatment Implications of COMPAS Core Scales*, 44.

programming' requirements; community referrals; bail applications; sentencing, supervision, and probation recommendations; and the frequency and nature of post-release contact.[27]

Loomis' PSI included both risk scores and a full criminogenic assessment, and each assessment informed the trial court's conclusion that the 'high risk and the high needs of the defendant' warranted a six-year prison sentence with extended supervision.[28] Loomis filed a motion for post-conviction relief, arguing that the court's reliance on COMPAS violated his 'due process' rights in three ways: first, Loomis argues that 'the proprietary nature of COMPAS' prevented him from assessing the accuracy of predictive determinations;[29] second, Loomis argued that use of COMPAS denied him the right to an 'individualized' sentence;[30] finally, he argued that COMPAS 'improperly uses gendered assessments'.[31] The trial court denied the post-conviction motion, and the Wisconsin Court of Appeals certified the appeal to the Supreme Court of Wisconsin (SCW).

Giving the majority judgment, Ann Walsh Bradley J. rejected the claim that Loomis had a right to see the internal workings of the COMPAS algorithms; it was, she said, enough that the statistical accuracy of the COMPAS risk scales had been verified by external studies,[32] and that Loomis had access to his own survey responses and COMPAS output.[33] She noted that 'some studies of COMPAS risk assessment have raised questions about whether they disproportionality classify minority offenders as having a higher risk of recidivism'.[34] Nevertheless, the judge felt that this risk could be mitigated by requiring that the sentencing court be provided with an explanatory statement outlining possible shortcomings in overall risk prediction and the distribution of error.[35]

Addressing Loomis' argument that use of the COMPAS scores infringed his right to an 'individualized' sentence, the judge considered that '[i]f a COMPAS risk assessment were the determinative factor considered at sentencing this would raise due process challenges regarding whether a defendant received an individualized sentence'.[36] By contrast, 'a COMPAS risk assessment may be used to enhance a judge's evaluation, weighing, and application of the other sentencing evidence in

---

[27] See generally State of Wisconsin Department of Corrections, *State of Wisconsin Department of Corrections Electronic Case Reference Manual* (Web Page) <https://doc.helpdocsonline.com/arrest-and-adjudication> (accessed 25 August 2022). For instance, Wisconsin DOC recommends that probation be imposed if one of the 'eight criminogenic needs' identified by COMPAS is present.

[28] See e.g. Brief of Defendant-Appellant, *State v Loomis*, 10.

[29] *State v Loomis* at [6].

[30] Ibid at [34].

[31] Ibid.

[32] Ibid at [58].

[33] Ibid at [55].

[34] Ibid at [61], [100].

[35] Ibid at [100].

[36] Ibid at [104], [120].

the formulation of an individualized sentencing program appropriate for each defendant',[37] as 'one tool available to a court at the time of sentencing'.[38] The judge emphasised that the court, like probation officers, should feel empowered to disagree with algorithmic predictions as and where necessary.[39]

Finally, the judge rejected Loomis' arguments about the 'inappropriate' use of gendered assessments, noting that 'both parties appear to agree that there is statistical evidence that men, on average, have higher recidivism and violent crime rates compared to women'.[40] Indeed, the judge concluded that 'any risk assessment which fails to differentiate between men and women will misclassify both genders'.[41]

Applying these considerations to the instant case, the judge concluded that there had been no failure of due process, because the COMPAS score had been 'used properly'.[42] Specifically, 'the circuit court explained that its consideration of the COMPAS risk scores was supported by other independent factors, its use was not determinative in deciding whether Loomis could be supervised safely and effectively in the community'.[43]

Human reasoning clearly feeds into processes of AI design and development, and humans are often needed to use the predictive outputs of algorithmic processes to make decisions. The question is whether the SCW was correct to conclude that, even if there are doubts about the quality of the algorithmic assessment (overall accuracy, distribution of the risk of error, or some other concern), human supervision at the time of decision-making is a sufficient safeguard against unjust decisions.

11.3 INDIVIDUALISM AND RELEVANCE

Justice is sometimes described as an 'individualistic' exercise, concerned with the 'assessment of individual outcomes by individualized criteria'.[44] Prima facie, this seems to be a poor fit use of statistics to make decisions about how to treat others. As a science, 'statistics' is the practice of amassing numerical data about a subset of some wider population or group, for the purpose of inferring conclusions from the former about the latter. And in Scanlon's words, 'statistical facts about the group to which a person belongs do not always have the relevant justificatory force'.[45]

---

[37] Ibid at [92]; *Malenchik v State* (2010) Ind 928 NE 2d 564, 573, emphasis added.
[38] Ibid; *State v Samsa* 359 (2015) Wis 2d 580 at [13], emphasis added.
[39] Ibid at [71]. Wisconsin Department of Corrections guidance states that 'staff should be encouraged to use their professional judgment and override the computed risk as appropriate' (n 27).
[40] Ibid at [78].
[41] Ibid at [83].
[42] Ibid at [104].
[43] Ibid at [9].
[44] J Waldron, 'The Primacy of Justice' (2003) 9 *Legal Theory* 269, 284.
[45] See e.g. TM Scanlon, *Why Does Inequality Matter?* (Oxford University Press, 2017) 27.

But we often make just decisions by reference to the characteristics of a group to which the decision-subject belongs. During the COVID-19 pandemic, decisions about how to prioritise vaccination and treatment were made by governments and doctors across the world on the basis of facts about individuals that were shared with a representative sample of the wider population. There being statistical evidence to demonstrate that those with respiratory or auto-immune conditions were at an aggravated risk of serious harm, patients with these conditions were often prioritised for vaccination, whilst mechanical ventilation was reserved for seriously ill patients who were likely to survive treatment.[46] Making 'individualised' decisions does not require us to ignore relevant information about other people; it simply requires us *not* to ignore relevant information about the decision-subject.

In this context, 'relevant' means rationally related to the social goal of improving health outcomes. A doctor ought to consider features of particular patients' circumstances that shape their needs and likely treatment outcomes. She might, for instance, decide to ventilate an older but healthy patient – taking into account the patient's age and an assessment of their overall well-being to conclude that treatment survival is highly likely. This is an 'individualised' assessment, in that it takes into account relevant facts, which are characteristics that this patient shares with others. By contrast, her decision should be unaffected by facts that do not bear on treatment success, such as whether the patient is a family member.

So, to justify a policy that imposes a burden on some people for the sake of a social goal, the policy must aim at some justified social goal, to which our selection criteria must be rationally related. The next question is whether ADM and AI tools can help us to make decisions on the basis of (all and only) relevant criteria.

11.4 STATISTICAL RULES AND RELEVANCE

In 1943, Sarbin published the results of a study comparing the success of 'actuarial' (statistical) and 'clinical' (discretionary) methods of making predictions.[47] The goal of the exercise was to determine which method would predict academic achievement more accurately. To conduct the experiment, Sarbin chose a sample of 162 college freshman, and recorded honor-point ratios at the end of the first quarter of their freshman year.[48]

Actuarial assessments were limited and basic: they were made by entering two variables (high school percentile rank and score on college aptitude test) into a two-variable regression equation. Individual assessments were made by the university's

---

[46] See e.g. British Medical Association, *COVID-19 Ethical Issues: A Guidance Note* (Report, 2020) <www.bma.org.uk/media/2226/bma-covid-19-ethics-guidance.pdf> (accessed 25 August 2022).

[47] Theodore R Sarbin, 'A Contribution to the Study of Actuarial and Individual Methods of Prediction' (1943) 48 *American Journal of Sociology* 593.

[48] The ratio of credits to grades that have been converted into honour points.

clinical counsellors and included a far broader range of variables: an interviewer's form and impressions; test scores for aptitude, achievement, vocation, and personality; and the counsellor's own impressions.

Sarbin found that the actuarial method was more successful by a small margin than the individual method at predicting academic achievement, concluding that 'any jury sitting in judgment on the case of the clinical versus the actuarial methods must on the basis of efficiency and economy declare overwhelmingly in favour of the statistical method for predicting academic achievement'.[49]

Many other studies have produced similar results across a range of different areas of decision-making, including healthcare, employee performance, and recidivism.[50] Conrad and Satter compared statistical and discretionary predictions about the success of naval trainees in an electrician's mate school.[51] They pitted the output of a two-factor regression equation (electrical knowledge and arithmetic reasoning test scores) against the predictions of interviewers on the basis of test scores, personal history data, and interview impressions. Their conclusions favoured the statistical method.

In principle, human reasoning that is unconstrained by (statistical or other) rules can be sensitive to a limitless range of relevant facts. But there are several caveats to this promising start. First, humans are easily influenced by irrelevant factors, or over-influenced by relevant factors, and extremely poor at recognising when we have been influenced in this way. There is now a great deal of literature detailing the many 'cognitive biases' that affect our decision-making, such as: 'illusory correlation' (hallucinating patterns from a paucity of available data) and 'causal thinking' (attributing causal explanations to those events).[52]

Second, the availability of more information does not necessarily translate into a broad decision process. Indeed, Sarbin found that the high-school rank and college aptitude test accounted for 31 per cent of the variance in honour-point ratio and for 49 per cent in the clinical predictions in his experiment[53] – which is to say, the counsellors *overweighted* these two factors, and did not take into account any other measures available to them in a systematic way.

Thus, this theoretical advantage often fails to translate into better decision-making. Yet, AI and ADM tools are no panacea for decision-making under conditions of uncertainty. Predictive success depends on many factors, one of which is the relationship between the chosen proxy and the social goal in question. Sarbin himself noted the limitations of using honour-point ratio as a proxy for academic

---

[49] Sarbin, 'A Contribution to the Study of Actuarial and Individual Methods of Prediction', 600.
[50] See e.g. Daniel Kahneman, *Thinking Fast and Slow* (Penguin, 2011) 222.
[51] HS Conrad and GA Satter, *Use of Test Scores and Quality Classification Ratings in Predicting Success in Electrician's Mates School* (Office of Social Research and Development Report No 5667, September 1945).
[52] See e.g. Kahneman, *Thinking Fast and Slow*, 77, 115.
[53] Sarbin, 'A Contribution to the Study of Actuarial and Individual Methods of Prediction', 596.

achievement,[54] and the same concerns arise in many other areas of decision-making. For instance, predictions about recidivism are hampered by the fact that crime reports, arrest, and conviction data poorly mirror the actual incidence of crime.

Predictive success also depends upon the quality of the data, including whether that data is representative of the wider target population. The anti-coagulant medication warfarin is regularly prescribed to patients on the basis of dosing algorithms, which incorporate race as a predictor along with clinical and genetic factors.[55] Yet, most of the studies used to develop these algorithms were conducted in cohorts with >95 per cent white European ancestry, and there is now robust evidence that these algorithms assign a 'lower-than-needed dose' to black patients, putting them at serious risk of heart attack, stroke, and pulmonary embolism.[56]

The Model for End-Stage Liver Disease (MELD) is used to calculate pre-treatment survival rates in liver transplant patients, on the basis of factors such as levels of bilirubin and creatinine in the blood. MELD scores are used to make decisions about which patients to prioritise for transplant. Yet, the MELD was developed on the basis of several studies that either did not report sex data, or which reported a statistical makeup of 70 per cent men (without disaggregating data in either case),[57] and a recent study has found that women have a 19 per cent increased risk of wait-list mortality compared to men with the same MELD scores.[58]

So, AI and ADM tools can sometimes help us to make decisions on the basis of criteria that are rationally related to our social goal. Whether they do have this effect depends (inter alia) upon the quality of the data and the relationship between the chosen proxy and social goal in question. Yet, there may be countervailing reasons to *exclude* certain relevant factors from the decision-making process. I turn to these considerations now.

11.5 CHOICE

Overdose deaths from opioids across the United States increased to 75,673 in the twelve-month period ending in April 2021, up from 56,064 the year

[54] Ibid, 594.

[55] 'Race-Specific Dosing Guidelines Urged for Warfarin' (February 2017) *Ash Clinical News* <https://ashpublications.org/ashclinicalnews/news/2145/Race-Specific-Dosing-Guidelines-Urged-for-Warfarin> (accessed 25 August 2022).

[56] Nita A Limdi et al, Race Influences Warfarin Dose Changes Associated with Genetic Factors (2015) 126 *Blood* 539, 544.

[57] See e.g. Russell Wiesner et al, 'Model for End-Stage Liver Disease (MELD) and Allocation of Donor Livers' (2003) 124 *Clinical-Liver, Pancreas, and Biliary Tract*; B Brandsaeter et al, 'Outcome Following Liver Transplantation for Primary Sclerosing Cholangitis in the Nordic Countries' (2003) 38 *Scandinavian Journal of Gastroenterology* 1176.

[58] CA Moylan et al, 'Disparities in Liver Transplantation before and after Introduction of the MELD Score' (2008) 300 *JAMA* 2371.

before.[59] In 2020, more people in San Francisco died of opioid overdoses than of COVID-19.[60] A significant portion of that uptick has been attributed to a pattern of aggressive and successful marketing of the prescription opioid OxyContin between 1996 and 2010. When OxyContin was reformulated in 2010 to make it more difficult to abuse, many of those who were addicted to prescription opioids switched to heroin and, eventually, fentanyl. One study found that 77 per cent of individuals who used both heroin and nonmedical pain relievers between 2011 and 2014 had initiated their drug use with prescription opioids,[61] and there is now a broad consensus that the introduction of OxyContin can 'explain a substantial share of overdose deaths' over twenty years.[62]

Many different measures have been taken to prevent addiction and abuse, and to support those who are suffering from addiction. One preventative measure is the Opioid Risk Tool (ORT), which was published in 2005 on the basis of several studies that identified correlations between certain facts and opioid misuse.[63] This questionnaire, which is used in several jurisdictions across the world, consists of ten scorable components, including family or personal history of substance abuse or psychological disorder; patient age; and (if the patient is female) a history of preadolescent sexual abuse.

According to Webster, author of the ORT, his goal was 'to help doctors identify patients who might require more careful observation during treatment, not to deny the person access to opioids'.[64] Yet, the ORT is in fact used in clinical practice to decide whether to deny or withdraw medical treatment from patients,[65] which has had a severe impact on patients, particularly women, who suffer from severe and chronic pain.[66] High ORT scores have resulted in the termination of doctor–patient

---

[59] See e.g. Centres for Disease Control and Prevention, National Center for Health Statistics, *Drug Overdose Deaths in the US Top 100,000 Annually* (Report, 17 November 2021) <www .cdc.gov/nchs/pressroom/nchs_press_releases/2021/20211117.htm> (accessed 25 August 2022).

[60] See e.g. 'Last Year, More People in San Francisco Died of Overdoses Than of Covid-19' (15 May 2021) *The Economist* <www.economist.com/united-states/2021/05/15/last-year-more-people-in-san-francisco-died-of-overdoses-than-of-covid-19> (accessed 25 August 2022).

[61] Pradip K Muhuri, Joseph C Gfroerer, and M Christine Davies, 'Associations of Nonmedical Pain Reliever Use and Initiation of Heroin Use in the United States' (2013) *CBHSQ Data Review* <www.samhsa.gov/data/sites/default/files/DR006/DR006/nonmedical-pain-reliever-use-2013.htm> (accessed 25 August 2022).

[62] 'Patrick Radden Keefe Traces the Roots of America's Opioid Epidemic' (13 May 2021) *The Economist* <www.economist.com/books-and-arts/2021/05/13/patrick-radden-keefe-traces-the-roots-of-americas-opioid-epidemic> (accessed 25 August 2022).

[63] Lynn R Webster and Rebecca M Webster, 'Predicting Aberrant Behaviors in Opioid-Treated Patients: Preliminary Validation of the Opioid Risk Tool' (2005) 6 *Pain Medicine* 432.

[64] Lynn Webster, 'Another Look at the Opioid Risk Tool' (29 June 2022) *Pain News Network* <www.painnewsnetwork.org/stories/2022/6/29/another-look-at-the-opioid-risk-tool> (accessed 25 August 2022).

[65] See e.g. NR Brott, E Peterson, and M Cascella, *Opioid Risk Tool* (StatPearls Publishing, 2022).

[66] Jennifer D Oliva, 'Dosing Discrimination: Regulating PDMP Risk Scores' (2022) 110 *California Law Review* 47.

relationships, as well as attracting negative interpersonal treatment by members of medical staff, adding emotional distress to physical pain.[67]

Many authors have objected to use of the ORT to make prescribing decisions on the basis that this practice discriminates against women.[68] Yet, 'discrimination' is an umbrella term. The wrongfulness of discrimination lies in the fact that the characteristics upon which we make decisions that disadvantage certain groups do not justify that treatment,[69] and there are different reasons to object to policies that have this effect.

The first reason that we might invoke to object to decision-making policies or practices that rely upon the ORT is that our decisions are based on criteria (such as the preadolescent sexual abuse of women) that are not rationally related to the social goal of preventing and reducing opioid addiction.[70] The second reason concerns the broader significance of this failure to develop and implement sound medical policy. It might, for instance, indicate that policymakers have taken insufficient care to investigate the connection between the sexual abuse of women and opioid abuse. When the consequence is placing the risk of predictive error solely upon women, the result is a failure to show equal concern for the interests of all citizens.[71] Finally, we might object to use of the ORT on the basis that the policy reflects a system in which women are treated as having a lower status than men – a system in which practices of exclusion are stable, so that women are generally denied opportunities for no good reason.[72]

But there is also an objection to policies that rely upon the ORT that has nothing to do with inequality. The argument is that, when we impose burdens on some people for the sake of some benefit to others, we should (wherever possible) give those people the opportunity to avoid those burdens by choosing appropriately. Policies that impose burdens upon individuals on the basis of facts about the actions

[67] Maia Szalavitz, 'The Pain Was Unbearable. So W Did Doctors Turn Her Away?' (11 August 2022) *Wired* <www.wired.com/story/opioid-drug-addiction-algorithm-chronic-pain/> (accessed 25 August 2022).

[68] Oliva, 'Dosing Discrimination: Regulating PDMP Risk Scores'.

[69] See e.g. Scanlon, *Why Does Inequality Matter?*, 26.

[70] See e.g. Constanza Daigre et al, 'History of Sexual, Emotional or Physical Abuse and Psychiatric Comorbidity in Substance-Dependent Patients' (2015) 2293 *Psychiatry Research* 43.

[71] On equal concern generally, see Scanlon, *Why Does Inequality Matter?*, ch. 2.

[72] This is often what we mean when we talk about discrimination, and Webster makes an allegation of this sort when he says: 'the ORT has been weaponized by doctors who are looking for a reason to deny patients – particularly, women – adequate pain medication'; Lynn R Webster and Rebecca M Webster, 'Predicting Aberrant Behaviors in Opioid-Treated Patients: Preliminary Validation of the Opioid Risk Tool'. See also 'The Opioid Risk Tool Has Been Weaponized against Patients' (21 September 2019) *Pain News Network* <www.painnewsnetwork.org/stories/2019/9/21/the-opioid-risk-tool-has-been-weaponized-against-pain-patients> (accessed 25 August 2022).

of others, such as sexual abuse and patterns of family drug abuse, deny those opportunities.

Take the following hypothetical, which I adapt from Scanlon's *What We Owe to Each Other*:[73]

> *Hazardous Waste*: hazardous waste has been identified within a city's most popu-
> lous residential district. Moving the waste will put residents at risk by releasing some
> chemicals into the air. However, leaving the waste in place, where it will seep into
> the water supply, creates a much greater risk of harm. So, city officials decide to take
> the necessary steps to move and dispose of the waste as safely as possible.

City officials have an important social goal, of keeping people safe. That goal involves the creation of a 'zone of danger' – a sphere of activity that residents cannot perform without serious risk of harm. Accordingly, to justify such a policy, officials need to take precautions that put people in a sufficiently good position to take actions to avoid suffering the harm. They should fence the sites and warn people to stay indoors and away from the excavation site – perhaps by using posters, main-stream media, or text message alerts.

Scanlon uses this hypothetical to explore the justification for the substantive burdens imposed by criminal punishment.[74] There is an important social goal – keeping us safe. The strategy for attaining this goal entails imposing a burden – denying that person some privilege, perhaps even their liberty. Thus, there is now a zone into which people cannot go (certain activities that they cannot perform) without risk of danger. To justify a policy of deliberately inflicting harm on some people, we should give those people a meaningful opportunity to avoid incurring that burden, which includes communicating the rules and consequences of trans-gression, and providing opportunities for people to live a meaningful life without transgression.

We can apply this logic to the ORT. The ORT was created with an important social goal in mind: preventing opioid misuse and addiction. A zone of danger is created to further that goal: certain patients are denied opioids, which includes withdrawing treatment from those already receiving pain medication, and may include terminating doctor–patient relationships. Patients may also suffer the burden of negative attitudes by medical staff, which may cause emotional suffering and/or negative self-perception. Yet, this time, the patient has no opportunity to avoid the burden of treatment withdrawal: that decision is made on the basis of facts about the actions of others, such as the decision-subject's experience of sexual abuse and/or a family history of drug abuse.

The question, then, is how human oversight bears on these goals: first, making sure that decisions about how to impose burdens on certain individuals for the sake

---

[73] TM Scanlon, *What We Owe to Each Other* (Harvard University Press, 1998), 256ff.
[74] Ibid, 263ff.

of some social good take into account all and only relevant facts about those individuals; second, making sure that our decisions do not rely upon factors that (even if relevant) we have reason to exclude. In the rest of this chapter, I will look at the knowledge that we need to assess algorithmic predictions, and the threshold against which we make that assessment. I argue that those elements differ markedly according to whether the prediction in question is used to supply information about what a particular decision-subject will do in the future.

11.6 GROUP ONE: PREDICTIONS ABOUT FACTS OTHER THAN WHAT THE DECISION-SUBJECT WILL DO

The first set of cases are those in which the predictive question is about the (current or future) presence of something other than the actions of the decision-subject, such as: the success of a particular course of medical treatment, or the patient's chances of survival without it; social need and the effectiveness of public resourcing; and forensic assessments (e.g., serology or DNA matching). To know whether we are justified in relying upon the predictive outputs of AI and ADM tools in this category, we need to determine whether the algorithmic prediction is more or less accurate that unaided human assessment, and how the risk of error is distributed amongst members of the population.

There are three modes of assessing AI and ADM tools that we might usefully distinguish. The first we can call 'technical', which involves understanding the mechanics of the AI/ADM tool, or 'opening the black box'. The second is a statistical assessment: we apply the algorithm to a predictive task across a range of data, and record overall success and distribution of error. The final mode of assessment is normative: it involves identifying reasons for predictive outputs, by exploring different counterfactuals to determine which facts informed the prediction.

To perform the second and third modes of assessment, we do not need to 'open the black box': the second can be performed by applying the algorithm to data and recording its performance; the third can be performed by applying the algorithm to data and incrementally adjusting the inputs to identify whether and how that change affects the prediction.[75]

To know whether the AI/ADM tool performs better than unaided human discretion, we must perform a statistical assessment. We need not perform either the first or third mode of assessment: we do not need to know the internal workings of the algorithm,[76] and we do not need to know the reasons for the prediction.

---

[75] See Sandra Wachter, Brent Mittelstadt, and Chris Russell, 'Counterfactual Explanations without Opening the Black Box: Automated Decisions and the GDPR' (2018) 31 *Harvard Journal of Law and Technology* 841.

[76] As Raz puts it, 'Sometimes we can tell that we or others are good at judging matters of a certain kind by the results of our judgements. That would suggest that we, or they, should be trusted

TrueAllele, developed by Cybergenetics and launched in 1994, is an ADM tool that can process complex mixtures of DNA (DNA from multiple sources, in unknown proportions). Prior to the development of sophisticated AI/ADM tools, human discretion was required to process mixtures of DNA (unlike single-source samples), with poor predictive accuracy.[77] Probabilistic genotyping is the next step in forensic DNA, replacing human reasoning with algorithmic processing.

Like COMPAS, the TrueAllele software is proprietary.[78] In *Commonwealth v Foley*,[79] which concerned the defendant's appeal against a murder conviction, one question amongst others was whether this obstacle to accessing the code itself rendered TrueAllele evidence inadmissible in court. On appeal, the defendant argued that the trial court had erred in admitting the testimony of one Dr Mark Perlin, an expert witness for the prosecution, who had communicated the results of a TrueAllele assessment to the Court.

In *Foley*, a sample containing DNA from the victim and another unknown person was found underneath the fingernail of the victim. The mixed sample was tested in a lab, and Perlin testified that the probability that this unknown person was someone other than the defendant was 1 in 189 billion.[80] The defendant argued that the testimony should be excluded because 'no outside scientist can replicate or validate Dr Perlin's methodology because his computer software is proprietary'.[81] On appeal, the Court concluded that this argument 'is misleading because scientists can validate the reliability of a computerized process even if the "source code" underlying that process is not available to the public'.[82]

The TrueAllele prediction is not about what the defendant has done; assessments of guilt or innocence are assessments that the Court (official or jury) must make. Rather, it is about the likelihood of a DNA match – specifically, that the unknown contributor to the DNA sample was someone other than the defendant. In this category of case, I have argued that the Court was correct to indicate that a statistical assessment is sufficient – if such an assessment is sufficiently robust.[83]

If the statistical assessment reveals a rate and distribution of predictive success that is equal to or better than unaided human decision-making, we can justify using the

---

even when they cannot explain their judgements'. 'This is especially so', he says, 'when understanding of matters in that area is slight'. Joseph Raz, *Engaging Reason: On the Theory of Value and Action* (Oxford University Press, 2002), 246.

[77] Katherine Kwong, 'The Algorithm Says You Did It: The Use of Black Box Algorithms to Analyse Complex DNA Evidence' (2017) 31 *Harvard Journal of Law & Technology* 275, 278.

[78] Though that may be changing: '*People v H.K*', Justia US Law (Web Page) <https://law.justia.com/cases/new-york/other-courts/2020/2020-ny-slip-op-50709-u.html>.

[79] *Commonwealth v Foley* 38 A 3d 882 (PA Super Ct 2012).

[80] Ibid, 887.

[81] Ibid, 888–89.

[82] Ibid.

[83] This ought to require assessment by independent entities – entities other than the owner/developer of the algorithm. See e.g. Kwong, 'The Algorithm Says You Did It: The Use of Black Box Algorithms to Analyse Complex DNA Evidence'.

prediction to make decisions. And if it is, we should do consistently, resisting the urge to apply our own discretion to predictions. Of course, we will often take into account the margin of error when applying our judgement to the algorithmic output. For instance, the TrueAllele assessment is only 97 per cent accurate, this ought to affect the weight that we assign to that output in drawing a conclusion about guilt or innocence. But that is a very different exercise from using human judgement to determine the probability of a DNA match in the first place.

If, by contrast, the statistical assessment reveals a rate and distribution of predictive success that is worse than unaided human decision-making, we cannot justify using the prediction to make decisions; there is no meaningful sense in which individual decision-makers can compensate for predictive flaws on an ad hoc basis, and no reason to try, given the availability of a better alternative.

In *Loomis*, the SCW concluded that wrinkles in the COMPAS assessment process and output could be remedied by the application of discretion: '[j]ust as corrections staff should disregard risk scores that are inconsistent with other factors, we expect that circuit courts will exercise discretion when assessing a COMPAS risk score with respect to each individual defendant'.[84] This, I have argued, is an unhappy compromise: either the AI/ADM tool has a better rate and distribution of error, in which case we should not be tempted to override the prediction by applying a clinical assessment, or the AI/ADM tool has a worse rate and distribution of error, in which case unaided human decision-making should prevail unless and until a comprehensive and systematic effort can be made to revise the relevant algorithm.

11.7 GROUP TWO: PREDICTIONS ABOUT WHAT THE DECISION-SUBJECT WILL DO

The second type of case involves the use of AI and ADM tools to make predictive assessments about what the decision-subject will do. This includes, for instance, whether they will misuse drugs or commit a crime, how they will perform on an assessment, or whether they will be a good employee or adoptive parent. To assess whether we are justified in using the predictive outputs of this category of AI and ADM tool, we need to know the facts upon which the prediction is based. This requires us to conduct a counterfactual assessment.

If the prediction is based only on facts that relate to the past actions of the decision-subject, and if the decision-subject has been given a meaningful opportunity to avoid incurring the burden, we may be justified in using the outputs to inform decisions. Whether we are will turn also on the same assessment that we made above: statistical accuracy and the distribution of error. But if the algorithmic output is *not* based only upon facts that relate to the past actions of the decision-subject, we

---

[84] Ibid, 71.

cannot justify using it to make decisions. If we do so, we deny the decision-subject the opportunity to avoid the burden by choosing appropriately.

Those who have evaluated COMPAS have challenged both its overall predictive success, and its distribution of the risk of error.[85] But there is an additional problem: each of the COMPAS assessments, most notably the wider 'criminogenic need' assessment, takes into account a range of facts that either have nothing to do with the defendant's actions (such as family background), or which are linked to actions that the defendant could never reasonably have suspected would result in criminal punishment (such as choice of friends or 'associates'). Thus, they deny the defendant a meaningful opportunity to choose to act in a manner that will avoid the risk of criminal punishment. And if the prediction takes into account facts that we have good reason to exclude from the decision, the solution is not to give the predictive output *less* weight (by applying human discretion). It is to give it no weight at all.

11.8 SAFEGUARDS

We cannot safeguard effectively against unjust decisions by applying human discretion to a predictive output at the time of decision-making. Appropriate 'safeguarding' means ensuring that the decision-making tools that we use take into account the right information in the right way, long before they enter our decision-making fora. I have made some concrete recommendations about how to determine whether the ADM/AI tool meets that threshold, which I summarise here.

The first question we should ask is this: is the prediction about what the decision-subject will do? If the answer to that question is no, we can in principle justify using the ADM/AI tool. Whether we can in practice turns on its predictive success – its overall success rate, and how the risk of error is distributed. We can assess these things statistically – without 'opening the black box', and without identifying reasons for any given prediction. If the ADM/AI tool fares just as well or better than humans, we can use it, and we can offer explanations to the decision-subject that are based on how we use it. If it does not fare just as well or better than humans, we cannot.

If the prediction is about what the decision-subject will do, we need to know the reasons for the prediction, which we can determine by using the counterfactual technique. We can only justify using the ADM/AI tool if three conditions are satisfied: (i) as above, the prediction is accurate and the risk of error is distributed evenly; (ii) the prediction is based solely on what the decision-subject has done; and (iii) the defendant has had sufficient opportunity to discover that those actions could result in these consequences.

---

[85] See e.g. Tim Brennan, William Dieterich, and Beate Ehret, 'Evaluating the Predictive Validity of the COMPAS Risk and Needs Assessment System' (2009) 36 *Criminal Justice and Behavior* 21.

It bears emphasis that the concern about policies that deny individuals a meaningful opportunity to avoid incurring certain burdens is not confined to the sphere of ADM. Courts in Wisconsin are permitted to take into account educational background and PSI results in sentencing decisions,[86] and the Wisconsin DOC directs agents completing the PSI to take into account a range of factors that include: intelligence; physical health and appearance; hygiene and nutrition; use of social security benefits or other public financial assistance; the nature of their peer group; and common interests with gang-affiliated members.[87] Thus, safeguarding efforts should not merely be directed towards ADM; they should take into account the broader law and policy landscape, of which ADM forms one part.

When we impose burdens on some people for the sake of some benefit to others, we should (wherever possible) present these people with valuable opportunities to avoid those burdens by choosing appropriately. And when the burdens that we impose are as exceptional as criminal incarceration, this requirement is all the more urgent: we cannot justify sending people to prison because they received poor grades in school, because their parents separated when they were young, or because of choices that their friends or family have made; we must base our decision on the choices that they have made, given a range of meaningful alternatives.

---

[86] *State v Harris*, 119 Wis2d 612, 623, 350 NW 2d 633 (1984).
[87] State of Wisconsin Department of Corrections, *Wisconsin Department of Corrections Electronic Case Reference Manual*.

Against Procedural Fetishism in the Automated State

Monika Zalnieriute[*]

12.1 INTRODUCTION

The infamous Australian Robodebt and application of COMPAS tool in the United States are just a few examples of abuse of power in the Automated State. However, our efforts to tackle these abuses have largely failed: corporations and states have used AI to influence many crucial aspects of our public and private lives, from our elections to our personalities and emotions, to environmental degradation through extraction of global resources to labour exploitation. And we do not know how to tame them. In this chapter I suggest that our efforts have failed because they are grounded in what I call *procedural fetishism* – an overemphasis and focus on procedural safeguards and assumption that transparency and due process can temper power and protect the interests of people in the Automated State.

Procedural safeguards, rules and frameworks play a valuable role in regulating AI decision-making and directing it towards accuracy, consistency, reliability, and fairness. However, procedures alone can be dangerous for legitimizing excessive power, and obfuscating the largest substantive problems we are facing today. In this chapter, I show how *procedural fetishism* acts as an obfuscation and redirection of the public from more substantive and fundamental questions about the concentration and limits of power to procedural micro-issues and safeguards in the Automated State. Such redirection merely reinforces the status quo. Procedural fetishism detracts from the questions of substantial accountability and obligations by diverting the attention to 'fixing' procedural micro-issues that have little chance of changing the political or legal status quo. The regulatory efforts and scholarly

[*] This chapter incorporates and adapts arguments advanced in my other work on procedural fetishism, and in particular M. Zalnieriute, 'Against Procedural Fetishism: A Call for a New Digital Constitution' (2023) *Indiana Journal of Global Legal Studies*, 30(2), 227–64. I thank Angelo Golia, Gunther Teubner, Sofia Ranchordas, and Tatiana Cutts for invaluable feedback.

debate, plagued by procedural fetishism, have been blind to colonial AI extraction practices, labour exploitation, and dominance of the US tech companies, as if they did not exist. Procedural fetishism – whether corporate or state – is dangerous. Not only does it defer social and political change, it also legitimizes corporate and state influence and power under an illusion of control and neutrality.

To rectify the imbalance of power between people, corporations, and states, we must shift the focus from soft law initiatives to substantive accountability and tangible legal obligations by AI companies. Imposing data privacy obligations directly upon AI companies with an international treaty is one (but not the only) option. The viability of such an instrument has been doubted: human rights law and international law, so it goes, are state-centric. Yet, as data protection law illustrates, we already apply (even if poorly) certain human rights obligations to private actors. Similarly, the origins of international law date back to powerful corporations that were the 'Googles' and 'Facebooks' of their time. In parallel to such global instrument on data privacy, we must also redistribute wealth and power by breaking and taxing AI companies, increasing public scrutiny by adopting prohibitive laws, but also by democratizing AI technologies by making them public utilities. Crucially, we must recognize colonial AI practices of extraction and exploitation and paying attention to the voices of Indigenous peoples and communities of the so-called Global South. With all these mutually reinforcing efforts, a new AI regulation will resist *procedural fetishism* and establish a new social contract for the age of AI.

12.2 EXISTING EFFORTS TO TAME AI POWER

Regulatory AI efforts cover a wide range of policies, laws, and voluntary initiatives at national level, including domestic constitutions, laws and judicial decisions; regional and international instruments and jurisprudence; self-regulatory initiatives; and transnational non-binding guidelines developed by private actors and NGOs.

Many recent AI regulatory efforts aim to tackle private tech power with national laws. For example, in the United States, five bipartisan bills collectively referred to as 'A Stronger Online Economy: Opportunity, Innovation and Choice' have been proposed and seek to restrain tech companies' power and monopolies.[1] In China, AI companies once seen as untouchables (particularly Alibaba and Tencent) have faced a tough year in 2021.[2] For example, the State Administration for Market

---

[1] The bills include the American Innovation and Choice Online Act, the Platform Competition and Opportunity Act, the Ending Platform Monopolies Act, the Augmenting Compatibility and Competition by Enabling Service Switching (ACCESS) Act, and the Merger Filing Fee Modernization Act, see House Lawmakers Release Anti-Monopoly Agenda for 'A Stronger Online Economy: Opportunity, Innovation, Choice', U.S. House Judiciary Committee (2021) <https://judiciary.house.gov/news/documentsingle.aspx?DocumentID=4591> (last visited 13 October 2021).
[2] Charlie Campbell, 'How China Is Cracking Down on Its Once Untouchable Tech Titans' *Time* (2021) <https://time.com/6048539/china-tech-giants-regulations/> (last visited 13 October 2021).

Regulation (SAMR) took aggressive steps to rein in monopolistic behaviour, levying a record US$2.8 billion fine on Alibaba.[3] AI companies are also facing regulatory pressure in Australia targeting anti-competitive behaviour.[4]

At a regional level, perhaps the strongest example of AI regulation is in the European Union, where several prominent legislative proposals have been tabled in recent years. The *Artificial Intelligence Act*,[5] and the *Data Act*[6] aim to limit the use of AI and ADM systems. These proposals build on the EU's strong track record in the area: for example, EU *General Data Protection Regulation (GDPR)*[7] has regulated the processing of personal data. The EU has been leading AI regulatory efforts on a global scale, with its binding laws and regulations.

On an international level, many initiatives have attempted to draw the boundaries of appropriate AI use, often resorting to the language of human rights. For example, the Organisation for Economic Co-operation and Development (OECD) has adopted *AI Principles* in 2019,[8] which draw inspiration from international human rights instruments. However, despite the popularity of the human rights discourse in AI regulation, international human rights instruments, such as the *International Covenant on Civil and Political Rights*[9] or the *International Covenant on Economic, Social and Cultural Rights*,[10] are not directly binding on private companies.[11] Instead, various networks and organizations try to promote human rights values among AI companies.

---

[3] Andrew Ross Sorkin et al, 'Alibaba's Big Fine Is a Warning Shot' (12 April 2021) *The New York Times* <www.nytimes.com/2021/04/12/business/dealbook/alibaba-fine-antitrust.html> (last visited 23 September 2022).

[4] John Davidson, 'Big Tech Faces Tough New Laws under ACCC Plan', *Australian Financial Review* (2021) <www.afr.com/technology/big-tech-faces-tough-new-laws-under-accc-plan-20210905-p58por> (last visited 13 October 2021).

[5] Proposal for a Regulation of the European Parliament and of the Council laying down harmonized rules on artificial intelligence (Artificial Intelligence Act) and amending certain Union legislative acts COM (2021) 206 final.

[6] Proposal for a Regulation of the European Parliament and of the Council on European data governance (Data Governance Act) COM (2020) 767 final.

[7] Regulation (EU) 2016/679 of the European Parliament and of the Council of 27 April 2016 on the protection of natural persons with regard to the processing of personal data and on the free movement of such data, and repealing Directive 95/46/EC (General Data Protection Regulation) (2016) OJ L 119/1.

[8] 'OECD Principles on Artificial Intelligence – Organisation for Economic Co-operation and Development' <www.oecd.org>.

[9] International Covenant on Civil and Political Rights, *opened for signature* 19 December 1966, 999 U.N.T.S. 171 (entered into force 23 March 1976); G.A. Res. 2200, U.N. GAOR, 21st Sess., Supp. No 16, at 52, U.N. Doc. A/6316 (1967).

[10] International Covenant on Economic, Social, and Cultural Rights, *opened for signature* 16 December 1966, 993 U.N.T.S. 3 (entered into force 23 March 1976) [hereinafter ICESCR].

[11] Monika Zalnieriute, 'From Human Rights Aspirations to Enforceable Obligations by Non-State Actors in the Digital Age: The Case of Internet Governance and ICANN' (2019) 21 *Yale Journal of Law & Technology* 278.

However, these efforts to date have been of limited success in taming the power of AI, and dealing with global AI inequalities and harms. This weakness stems from the proceduralist focus of AI regulatory discourse: proponents have assumed that procedural safeguards, transparency and due process can temper power and protect the interests of people against the power wielded by AI companies (and the State) in the Automated State. Such assumptions stem from the liberal framework, focused on individual rights, transparency, due process, and procedural constrains, which, to date, AI scholarship and regulation have embraced without questioning their capacity to tackle power in the Automated State.

The assumptions are closely related to the normative foundations of AI and automated decision-making systems (ADMS) governance, which stem, in large part, from a popular analogy between tech companies and states: how AI companies exert quasi-sovereign influence over commerce, speech and expression, elections, and other areas of life.[12] It is also this analogy, and the power of the state as the starting point, that leads to the proceduralist focus and emphasis in AI governance discourse: just as the due process and safeguards constrain the state, they must now also apply to powerful private actors, like AI companies. Danielle Keats Citron's and Frank Pasquale's early groundbreaking calls for technological due process have been influential: it showed how constitutional principles could be applied to technology and automated decision-making – by administrative agencies and private actors.[13] Construction of various procedural safeguards and solutions, such as testing, audits, algorithmic impact assessments, and documentation requirements have dominated AI decision-making and ADMS literature.[14]

Yet, by placing all our energy on these procedural fixes, we miss the larger picture and are blind to our own coloniality: we rarely (if at all) discuss the US dominance

---

[12] For literature making such analogies see Julie E Cohen, *Between Truth and Power: The Legal Constructions of Informational Capitalism* (2019); Julie E Cohen, 'Law for the Platform Economy' (2017) 51 *UCD Law Review* 133, 199; Hannah Bloch-Wehba, 'Global Platform Governance: Private Power in the Shadow of the State' (2019) 72 *SMU Law Review* 27, 29; Rory Loo, 'Rise of the Digital Regulator' (2017) 66 *Duke Law Journal* 1267.

[13] Danielle Keats Citron, 'Technological Due Process' (2007) 85 *Washington University Law Review* 1249. Although Citron's original work did not focus on tech platforms, but argued that administrative agencies' use of technology should be subjected to due process; See also Danielle Keats Citron and Frank Pasquale, 'The Scored Society: Due Process for Automated Predictions Essay' (2014) 89 *Washington Law Review* 1 arguing for due process for automated credit scoring.

[14] See, e.g., Margot Kaminski and Gianclaudio Malgieri, 'Algorithmic Impact Assessments under the GDPR: Producing Multi-Layered Explanations' *International Data Privacy Law* 125–26 <https://scholar.law.colorado.edu/faculty-articles/1510>; Deven R Desai and Joshua A Kroll, 'Trust but Verify: A Guide to Algorithms and the Law' (2017) 31 *Harvard Journal of Law & Technology* 1, 10 (arguing for ex ante testing of AI and ADMS technologies); Andrew D Selbst, 'Disparate Impact in Big Data Policing' (2017) 52 *Georgia Law Review* 109, 169 (arguing for Algorithmic Impact Statements); Andrew D Selbst and Solon Barocas, 'The Intuitive Appeal of Explainable Machines' (2018) 87 *Fordham Law Review* 1085 at 1100–5 (arguing for algorithmic impact assessments and recoding requirements).

in AI economy, we seldom mention environmental exploitation and environmental degradation caused by AI and AMDS technologies. We rarely ask how AI technologies reinforce existing power disparities globally between the so-called Global South and Imperialist West/North, how they contribute to climate disaster and exploitation of people and extraction of resources in the so-called Global South. These substantive issues matter, and arguably matter more than a design of a particular AI auditing tool. Yet, we are too busy designing the procedural fixes.

To be successful, AI regulation must resist what I call *procedural fetishism* – a strategy, employed by AI companies and state actors, to redirect the public from more substantive and fundamental questions about the concentration and limits of power in the age of AI to procedural safeguards and micro-issues. This diversion reinforces the status quo, reinforces Western dominance, accelerates environmental degradation and exploitation of the postcolonial peoples and resources.

12.3 PROCEDURAL FETISHISM

Proceduralism, in its broadest sense, refers to 'a belief in the value of explicit, formalized procedures that need to be followed closely',[15] or 'the tendency to believe that procedure is centrally important'.[16] The term is often used to describe the legitimization of rules, decisions, or institutions through the process used to create them, rather than by their substantive moral value.[17] Such trend towards proceduralism – or what I call *procedural fetishism* – also dominates our thinking about AI: we believe that having certain 'safeguards' for AI systems is inherently valuable, that those safeguards tame power and provide sufficient grounds to trust the Automated State. However, procedural fetishism undermines our efforts for justice for several reasons.

First, procedural fetishism offers an appearance of political and normative neutrality, which is convenient to both AI companies and policymakers, judges, and regulators. Proceduralism allows various actors to 'remain agnostic towards substantive political and moral values' when 'faced with the pluralism of contemporary societies'.[18] At the 'heart' of all proceduralist accounts of justice, therefore, is the idea that, as individual members of a pluralist system, we may agree on what amounts to a just *procedure* (if not a just outcome), and 'if we manage to do so,

---

[15] Jens Steffek, 'The Limits of Proceduralism: Critical Remarks on the Rise of "Throughput Legitimacy"' (2019) 97 *Public Admin* 784 at 784.

[16] Paul MacMahon, 'Proceduralism, Civil Justice, and American Legal Thought' (2013) 34 *University of Pennsylvania Journal of International Law* 545 at 559.

[17] Jordy Rocheleau, 'Proceduralism' in Deen K Chatterjee (ed), *Encyclopedia of Global Justice* (2011) 906 <http://link.springer.com/10.1007/978-1-4020-9160-5_367> (last visited 2 June 2021).

[18] Steffek, 'The Limits of Proceduralism' at 784.

just procedures will yield just outcomes'.[19] However, procedural fetishism enables various actors not only to remain agnostic, but to avoid confrontation with hard political questions. For example, the courts engage in procedural fetishism to appear neutral and avoid tackling the politically difficult questions of necessity, proportionality, legitimacy of corporate and state surveillance practices, and have instead come up with procedural band-aids.[20] The focus on procedural safeguards provides a convenient way to make an appearance of effort to regulate without actually prohibiting any practices or conduct.

A good example of such neutralizing appearance of procedural fetishism is found in the AI governance's blind eye to very important policy issues impacted by AI, such as climate change, environmental degradation, and continued exploitation of the resources from the so-called Third World countries. The EU and US-dominated AI debate has focused on inequalities reinforced through AI in organizational settings in business and public administration, but it has largely been blind to the inequalities of AI on a global scale,[21] including global outsourcing of labour,[22] and the flow of capital through colonial and extractive processes.[23] While it is the industrial nations in North America, Europe, and East Asia who compete in the 'race for AI',[24] AI and ADM systems depend on global resources, most often extracted from the so-called Global South.[25] Critical AI scholars have analyzed how the production of capitalist surplus for a handful of big tech companies draws on large-scale exploitation of the soil, minerals, and other resources.[26] Other critical scholars have described the processes of extraction and exchange of personal data itself as a form of dispossession and data colonialism.[27] Moreover, AI and ADMs systems have also

---

[19] Emanuela Ceva, 'Beyond Legitimacy: Can Proceduralism Say Anything Relevant about Justice?' (2012) 15 *Critical Review of International Social and Political Philosophy* 183 s at 191.

[20] Monika Zalnieriute, 'Big Brother Watch and Others v. the United Kingdom' (2022) 116 *American Journal of International Law* 585; Monika Zalnieriute, 'Procedural Fetishism and Mass Surveillance under the ECHR: Big Brother Watch v. UK' *Verfassungsblog: On Matters Constitutional* (2021) <https://verfassungsblog.de/big-b-v-uk/> (last visited 9 August 2021).

[21] Padmashree Gehl Sampath, 'Governing Artificial Intelligence in an Age of Inequality' (2021) 12 *Global Policy* 21.

[22] Aneesh Aneesh, 'Global Labor: Algocratic Modes of Organization' (2009) 27 *Sociological Theory* 347.

[23] Nick Couldry and Ulises A Mejias, *The Costs of Connection: How Data Is Colonizing Human Life and Appropriating It for Capitalism* (2019) <https://doi.org/10.1093/sf/soz172> (last visited 23 September 2022).

[24] Kathleen Walch, 'Why the Race for AI Dominance Is More Global Than You Think' *Forbes* <www.forbes.com/sites/cognitiveworld/2020/02/09/why-the-race-for-ai-dominance-is-more-global-than-you-think/> (last visited 23 September 2022).

[25] Kate Crawford, *The Atlas of AI: Power, Politics, and the Planetary Costs of Artificial Intelligence* (2021).

[26] Ibid.

[27] Nick Couldry and Ulises Ali Mejias, 'The Decolonial Turn in Data and Technology Research: What Is at Stake and Where Is It Heading?' (2023) 26(4) *Information, Communication & Society* 786–802; Couldry and Mejias, *The Costs of Connection*; Jim Thatcher, David

been promoted as indispensable tools in international development[28] but many have pointed how those efforts often reinforce further colonization and extraction.[29] Procedural fetishism also downplays the human labour involved in AI technologies, which draws on the underpaid, racialized, and not at all 'artificial' human labour primarily from the so-called Global South. The AI economy is one in which highly precarious working conditions for gig economy 'click' workers are necessary for the business models of AI companies.

12.3.1 *Legitimizing Effect of Procedural Fetishism*

Moreover, procedural fetishism is used strategically not only to distract from power disparities but also to legitimize unjust and harmful AI policies and actions by exploiting people's perceptions of legitimacy and justice. As early as in the 1980s, psychological research undermined the traditional view that substantive outcomes drove people's perception of justice by showing that it was more about the procedure for reaching the substantive outcome.[30] Many of the ongoing proceduralist reforms, such as Facebook's Oversight Board, are primarily conceived for this very purpose – to make it look that Facebook is doing the 'right thing' and delivering justice, irrespective of whether substantive policy issues change or not. Importantly, such corporate initiatives divert attention from the problems caused by the global dominance of the AI companies.[31]

The language of 'lawfulness' and constitutional values, prevalent in AI governance debates, is working as a particularly strong legitimizing catalyst both in public and policy debates. As critical scholars have pointed out, using the terminology, which is typically employed in context of elected democratic governments, misleads, for it infuses AI companies with democratic legitimacy, and conflates corporate interests with public objectives.[32]

O'Sullivan, and Dillon Mahmoudi, 'Data Colonialism through Accumulation by Dispossession: New Metaphors for Daily Data' (2016) 34 *Environment and Planning D* 990.

[28] Jolynna Sinanan and Tom McNamara, 'Great AI Divides? Automated Decision-Making Technologies and Dreams of Development' (2021) 35 *Continuum* 747.

[29] Couldry and Mejias, 'The Decolonial Turn in Data and Technology Research'; Michael Kwet, 'Digital Colonialism: US Empire and the New Imperialism in the Global South' (2019) 60 *Race & Class* 3; Shakir Mohamed, Marie-Therese Png, and William Isaac, 'Decolonial AI: Decolonial Theory as Sociotechnical Foresight in Artificial Intelligence' (2020) 33 *Philosophy & Technology* 659.

[30] Tom R Tyler, 'Why People Obey the Law' (2006), 5, 9 s <www.degruyter.com/document/doi/10.1515/9781400828609/html> (last visited 23 September 2022) (summarizing the procedural justice literature suggesting that process heavily influences perception of legitimacy).

[31] Victor Pickard, *Democracy without Journalism?: Confronting the Misinformation Society* (2019), 17.

[32] Salomé Viljoen, 'The Promise and Limits of Lawfulness: Inequality, Law, and the Techlash' (2021) 2 *Journal of Social Computing* 284.

In the following sections, I suggest that this language is prevalent not accidentally, but through sustained corporate efforts to legitimize their power and business models, to avoid regulation, and enhance their reputation for commercial gain. AI companies often come up with private solutions to develop apparent safeguards against their own abuse of power and increase their transparency to the public. Yet, as I have argued earlier, many such corporate initiatives are designed to obfuscate and misdirect policymakers, researchers, and the public in the bid to strengthen their brand and avoid regulation and binding laws.[33] AI companies have also successfully corporatized and attenuated the laws and regulations that bind them. Through many procedures, checklists, and frameworks, corporate compliance with existing binding laws has often been a strategic performance, devoid of substantial change in business practices. Such compliance has worked to legitimize business policy and corporate power to the public, regulators, and the courts. In establishing global dominance, AI companies have also been aided by the governments.

12.3.2 *Procedural Washing through Self-Regulation*

First, corporate self-regulatory AI initiatives are often cynical marketing and social branding strategies to increase public confidence in their operations and create a better public image.[34] AI companies often self-regulate selectively by disclosing and addressing only that which is commercially desirable for them. For example, Google, when creating an Advanced Technology External Advisory Council (Council) in 2019 to implement *Google's AI Principles*,[35] refused to reveal the internal processes that led to the selection of a controversial member, anti-LGBTI advocate and climate change denial sponsor Kay Coles James.[36] While employees' activism forced Google to rescind the Council, ironically, this showed Google's unwillingness to publicly share the selection criteria of their AI governance boards.

---

[33] Monika Zalnieriute, '"Transparency-Washing" in the Digital Age: A Corporate Agenda of Procedural Fetishism' (2021) 8 *Critical Analysis of Law* 39.

[34] Christina Garsten and Monica Lindh De Montoya, 'The Naked Corporation: Visualization, Veiling and the Ethico-politics of Organizational Transparency' in Christina Garsten and Monica Lindh De Montoya (eds), *Transparency in a New Global Order: Unveiling Organizational Visions* 79–96; See also Ivan Manokha, 'Corporate Social Responsibility: A New Signifier? An Analysis of Business Ethics and Good Business Practice' (2004) 24 *Politics* 56.

[35] Kent Walker, 'An External Advisory Council to Help Advance the Responsible Development of AI', *Google* (2019) <https://blog.google/technology/ai/external-advisory-council-help-advance-responsible-development-ai/> (last visited 17 June 2020).

[36] Scott Shane and Daisuke Wakabayashi, '"The Business of War": Google Employees Protest Work for the Pentagon' (30 July 2018) *The New York Times* <www.nytimes.com/2018/04/04/technology/google-letter-ceo-pentagon-project.html> (last visited 24 October 2018).

Second, AI companies self-regulate only if it pays off for them in the long run, so profit is the main concern.[37] For example, in 2012 IBM provided police forces in Philippines with video surveillance technology which was used to perpetuate President Duterte's war on drugs through extrajudicial killings.[38] At the time, IBM defended the deal with Philippines, saying it 'was intended for legitimate public safety activities'.[39] The company's practice of providing authoritarian regimes with technological infrastructure is not new and dates back to the 1930s when IBM supplied the Nazi Party with unique punch-card technology that was used to run the regime's censuses and surveys to identify and target Jewish people.[40]

Third, corporate initiatives also allow AI companies to prevent any regulation of their activities. A good example of pro-active self-regulation is Facebook's Oversight Board, which reviews individual *decisions*, and not overarching policies. Thus, the attention is still diverted away from critiquing the legitimacy or appropriateness of Facebook's AI business practices themselves and is instead focused on Facebook's 'transparency' about them. The appropriateness of the substantial AI policies themselves are obfuscated, or even legitimated, through the micro procedural initiatives, with little power to change *status quo*. In setting up the board, Facebook has attempted not only to stave off regulation, but also to position itself as an industry regulator by inviting competitors to use the Oversight Board as well.[41] AI companies can then depict themselves as their own regulators.

12.3.3 *Procedural Washing through Law and Help of State*

Moreover, AI companies (and public administrations) have also exploited the ambiguity of laws regulating their behaviour through performative compliance with the laws. Often, policymakers have compounded this problem by creating legal provisions to advance the proceduralist agenda of corporations, including via international organizations and international law, and regulators and courts have enabled corporatized compliance in applying these provisions by focusing on the quality of procedural safeguards.

For instance, Ezra Waldman has shown how the regulatory regime of data privacy, even under the GDPR – the piece of legislation which has gained the

---

[37] See Beth Stephens, 'The Amorality of Profit: Transnational Corporations and Human Rights' (2002) 20 *Berkeley Journal International Law* 45.

[38] George Joseph, 'Inside the Video Surveillance Program IBM Built for Philippine Strongman Rodrigo Duterte', *The Intercept* (2019) <https://theintercept.com/2019/03/20/rodrigo-duterte-ibm-surveillance/> (last visited 17 June 2020).

[39] Ibid.

[40] Edwin Black, *IBM and the Holocaust: The Strategic Alliance between Nazi Germany and America's Most Powerful Corporation-Expanded Edition* (2001).

[41] Karissa Bell, 'Facebook Wants "Other Companies" to Use the Oversight Board, Too' *Engadget* (2021) <www.engadget.com/facebook-oversight-board-other-companies-202448589.html> (last visited 6 October 2021).

reputation as the strongest and most ambitious law in the age of AI – has been 'managerialized': interpreted by compliance professionals, human resource experts, marketing officers, outside auditors, and in-house and firm lawyers, as well as systems engineers, technologists, and salespeople to prioritize values of efficiency and innovation in the implementation of data privacy law.[42] As Waldman has argued, many symbolic structures of compliance are created; yet, apart from an exhaustive suite of checklists, toolkits, privacy roles, and professional training, there are hardly substantial actions to enhance consumer protection or minimize online data breaches.[43] These structures comply with the law in name but not in spirit, which is treated in turn by lawmakers and judges as best practice.[44] The law thus fails to achieve its intended goals as the compliance metric developed by corporations becomes dominant,[45] and 'mere presence of compliance structures' is assumed to be 'evidence of substantive adherence with the law'.[46] Twenty-six recent studies analyzed the impact of the GDPR and US data privacy laws and none have found any meaningful influence of these laws on data privacy protection of the people.[47]

Many other laws itself have been designed in the spirit of procedural fetishism, enabling corporations to avoid liability and change their substantive policies by simply establishing proscribed procedures. For example, known as 'safe harbours', such laws enable the companies to avoid liability by simply following a prescribed procedure. For example, under the traditional notice-and-consent regime in the United States, companies avoid liability as long as they post their data use practices in a privacy policy.[48]

Regulators and the courts, by emphasizing procedural safeguards, also engage in performative regulation, grounded in procedural fetishism, that limits pressure for stricter laws by convincing citizens and institutions that their interests are sufficiently protected without inquiring substantive legality of corporate practices. A good example is Federal Trade Commission's (FTC) audits and 'assessment' requirements, which require corporations to demonstrate compliance through checklists.[49] Similar procedural fetishism is also prevalent in jurisprudence, which does not assess specific state practices by reference to their effectiveness in advancing the

---

[42] Ari Ezra Waldman, 'Privacy Law's False Promise' (2019) 97 *Washington University Law Review* 773 at 778.

[43] Ibid at 5.

[44] Lauren B Edelman, *Working Law: Courts, Corporations, and Symbolic Civil Rights* (University of Chicago Press, 2016); Waldman, 'Privacy Law's False Promise'.

[45] Waldman, 'Privacy Law's False Promise'.

[46] Ibid at 792–94.

[47] Filippo Lancieri, 'Narrowing Data Protection's Enforcement Gap' (2022) 74 *Maine Law Review* 15.

[48] Joel R Reidenberg et al, 'Disagreeable Privacy Policies: Mismatches between Meaning and Users' Understanding' (2015) 30 *Berkeley Technology Law Journal* 1 at 41.

[49] Chris Jay Hoofnagle, *Federal Trade Commission Privacy Law and Policy* 166 (2016).

proclaimed goals, but rather purely to the stringency of the procedures governing that practice.[50]

12.3.4 *Procedural Washing through State Rhetoric and International Law*

Procedural washing by AI companies have also been aided by executive governments – both through large amounts of public funding and subsidization to these companies, and through the development of the laws, including international laws, that suit corporate and national agenda. Such support is not one-sided, of course, the state expands its economic and geopolitical power through technology companies. All major powers, including the United States, European Union, and China, have been active in promoting their AI companies. For example, mutually beneficial and interdependent relationship between the US government and information technology giants has been described as the *information-industrial-complex, data industrial complex*, and so on.[51] These insights build on Herbert Schiller's work, who described the continuous subsidization by US companies of private communications companies back in the 1960s and 1970s.[52] For example, grounding their work on classical insights, Powers and Jablonski describe how the dynamics of the *information-industrial-complex* have catalyzed the rapid growth of information and communication technologies within the global economy while firmly embedding US strategic interests and companies at the heart of the current neoliberal regime.[53] Such central strategic position necessitates continuous action and support from the US government.

To maintain the dominance of US AI companies internationally, the US government aggressively promotes the global free trade regime, intellectual property enforcement, and other policies that suit US interests. For example, the dominance of US cultural and AI products and services worldwide is secured via the *free flow of information* doctrine at the World Trade Organization, which the US State Department pushed with the GATT, GATS, and TRIPS.[54] The *free flow of information* doctrine allows the US corporations to collect and monetize personal data of individuals from around the world. This way, data protection and privacy are not part of the 'universal' values of the Internet, whereas strong intellectual property protection is not only viable and doable, but also strictly enforced globally.

---

[50] Zalnieriute, 'Big Brother Watch and Others v. the United Kingdom'; Zalnieriute, 'Procedural Fetishism and Mass Surveillance under the ECHR' at 185–92.

[51] See, e.g., Shawn M Powers and Michael Jablonski, *The Real Cyber War: The Political Economy of Internet Freedom*, 1st ed (2015).

[52] Herbert Schiller, *Mas Communications and American Empire*, 2nd ed (1992) 63–75.

[53] Powers and Jablonski, *The Real Cyber War* at 47.

[54] Herbert I Schiller, *Culture, Inc: The Corporate Takeover of Public Expression* (1991) 118; Schiller, *Mas Communications and American Empire* at 93.

Many other governments have also been complicit in this process. For example, the EU AI Act, despite its declared mission to 'human centred AI' is silent about the environmental degradation and social harms that occur in other parts of the world because of large-scale mineral and resource extraction and energy consumption, necessary to produce and power AI and digital technologies.[55] The EU AI Act is also silent on the conditions under which AI is produced and the coloniality of the AI political economy: it does not address precarious working conditions and global labour flows. Thus, EU AI Act is also plagued by procedural fetishism: it does not seek to *improve* the global conditions for an environmentally sustainable AI production. Thus, at least the United States and EU have prioritized inaction, self-regulation over regulation, no enforcement over enforcement, and judicial acceptance over substantial resistance. While stressing the differences in US and EU regulatory approaches has been popular,[56] the end result has been very similar both in the EU and the United States: the tech companies collect and exploit personal data not only for profit, but for political and social power.

In sum, procedural fetishism in AI discourse is dangerous for creating an illusion that it is normatively neutral. Our efforts at constraining AI companies are replaced with the corporate vision of division of power and wealth between the corporations and the people, masked under the veil of neutrality.

12.4 THE NEW SOCIAL CONTRACT FOR THE AGE OF AI

The new social contract for the age of AI must try something different: it must shift its focus from soft law initiatives and performative corporate compliance to substantive accountability and tangible legal obligations by AI companies. Imposing directly binding data privacy obligations on AI companies with an international treaty is one (but not the only!) option. Other parallel actions include breaking and taxing tech companies, increasing competition and public scrutiny, and democratizing AI companies: involving people in their governance.

12.4.1 *International Legally Binding Instrument Regulating Personal Data*

One of the best ways to tame AI companies is via the 'currency' which people often 'pay' for their services – the personal data. And the new social contract should not

---

[55] Mark Coeckelbergh, 'AI for Climate: Freedom, Justice, and Other Ethical and Political Challenges' (2021) 1 *AI Ethics* 67 at 67–72; Payal Dhar, 'The Carbon Impact of Artificial Intelligence' (2020) 2 *Nature Machine Intelligence* 423 at 423–25; Emma Strubell, Ananya Ganesh, and Andrew McCallum, 'Energy and Policy Considerations for Modern Deep Learning Research' (2020) 34 *Proceedings of the AAAI Conference on Artificial Intelligence* 13693.

[56] James Q Whitman, 'The Two Western Cultures of Privacy: Dignity versus Liberty' (2003) 113 *Yale Law Journal* 1151; See, e.g., Giovanni De Gregorio, 'Digital Constitutionalism across the Atlantic' (2022) 11 *Global Constitutionalism* 297; Oreste Pollicino, *Judicial Protection of Fundamental Rights on the Internet: A Road towards Digital Constitutionalism?* (2021).

only be concerned with the procedures that AI companies should follow in continuing to exploit personal data. Instead, it should impose substantive limits on corporate AI action, for example, data cannot be collected and used in particular circumstances, how and when it can be exchanged, manipulative technologies and biometrics are banned to ensure mental welfare, and social justice.

Surely, domestic legislators should develop such laws (and I discuss that below too). However, given that tech companies exploit our data across the globe, we need a global instrument to lead our regulatory AI efforts. Imposing directly binding obligations on AI companies with an international treaty should be one (but not the only!) option. While exact parameters of such treaty are beyond the scope of this chapter, I would like to rebut one misleading argument, often used by the AI companies, that private companies cannot have direct obligations under international law.

The relationship between private actors and international law has been a subject of intense political and scholarly debate for over four decades,[57] since the first attempts to develop a binding international code of conduct for multinational corporations in the 1970s.[58] Most recent efforts have led to the 'Third Revised Draft' of the UN Treaty on Business and Human Rights released in 2021, since the process started with the so-called Ecuador Resolution in 2014.[59] The attempts to

---

[57] See, e.g., Steven Bittle and Laureen Snider, 'Examining the Ruggie Report: Can Voluntary Guidelines Tame Global Capitalism?' (2013) 2 *Critical Criminology* 177; Olivier de Schutter, 'Towards a New Treaty on Business and Human Rights' (2016) 1 *Business & Human Rights Journal* 41; Frédéric Mégret, 'Would a Treaty Be All It Is Made Up to Be?', *James G Stewart* (2015) <http://jamesgstewart.com/would-a-treaty-be-all-it-is-made-up-to-be/> (last visited 10 September 2020); John G Ruggie, 'Get Real or We'll Get Nothing: Reflections on the First Session of the Intergovernmental Working Group on a Business and Human Rights Treaty', *Business & Human Rights Resource Centre* (2020) <www.business-humanrights.org> (last visited 10 September 2020).

[58] The Commission on Transnational Corporations and the United Nations Centre on Transnational Corporations (UNCTNC) were established in 1974; the UN, Draft Code on Transnational Corporations in UNCTC, TRANSNATIONAL CORPORATIONS, SERVICES AND THE URUGUAY ROUND, Annex IV at 231, was presented in 1990. For history of the controversy of the issue at the UN, see Khalil Hamdani and Lorraine Ruffing, *United Nations Centre on Transnational Corporations: Corporate Conduct and the Public Interest* (2015) <www.taylorfrancis.com/books/9781315723549> (last visited 18 September 2020).

[59] Binding Treaty, *Business & Human Rights Resource Centre* <www.business-humanrights.org/en/big-issues/binding-treaty/> (last visited 25 September 2022) (providing the latest developments and progress on the UN Treaty on Business and Human Rights); U.N. Human Rights Council, 'Open-Ended Intergovernmental Working Group on Transnational Corporations and Other Business Enterprises with Respect to Human Rights', *OHCHR* <www.ohchr.org/en/hr-bodies/hrc/wg-trans-corp/igwg-on-tnc> (last visited 25 September 2022); Elaboration of an International Legally Binding Instrument on Transnational Corporations and other Business Enterprises with Respect to Human Rights, 26th Sess., U.N. Doc. A/HRC/26/L.22/Rev.1 (2014) <https://ap.ohchr.org/documents/dpage_e.aspx?si=A/HRC/RES/26/9> (last visited 25 September 2022) (resolution adopted by twenty votes in favour, thirteen abstentions, and fourteen against).

impose binding obligations on corporations have not yet been successful because of enormous political resistance from private actors, for whom such developments would be costly. Corporate resistance entail many fronts, here I can only focus on debunking a corporate myth that such constitutional reform is not viable, and even legally impossible because of the state-centric nature of human rights law. Yet, as data protection law, discussed above, illustrates, we already apply (even if poorly) certain human rights obligations to private actors. We can and should demand more from corporations in other policy areas.

Importantly, we must understand the role of private actors under international law. Contrary to the popular myth that international law was created by and for nation-states, '[s]ince its very inception, modern international law has regulated the dealings between states, empires and companies'.[60] The origins of international law itself date back to powerful corporations that were the Googles and Facebooks of their time. Hugo Grotius, often regarded as the father of modern international law, was himself counsel to the Dutch East India Company – the largest and most powerful corporation in history. In this role, Grotius' promotion of the principle of the freedom of the high seas and his views on the status of corporations were shaped by the interests of the Dutch East India Company to ensure the security and efficacy of the company's trading routes.[61] As Peter Borschberg explains, Grotius crafted his arguments to legitimize the rights of the Dutch to engage in the East Indies trade and justify the Dutch Company's violence against the Portuguese, who claimed exclusive rights to Eastern Hemisphere.[62] In particular, Grotius aimed to justify the seizure by Dutch of the Portuguese carrack *Santa Catarina* in 1603:

> [E]ven though people grouped as a whole and people as private individuals do not differ in the natural order, a distinction has arisen from a man-made fiction and from the consent of citizens. The law of nations, however, does not recognize

---

[60] José-Manuel Barreto, 'Cerberus: Rethinking Grotius and the Westphalian System', in Martti Koskenniemi, Walter Rech, and Manuel Jiménez Fonseca (eds), *International Law and Empire: Historical Explorations* (2016) 149–76, arguing that 'international law does not only regulate the relations between nation states' but that '[s]ince its very inception, modern international law has regulated the dealings between states, empires and companies'; Erika R George, 'The Enterprise of Empire: Evolving Understandings of Corporate Identity and Responsibility' in JenaMartin and Karen E Bravo (eds), *The Business and Human Rights Landscape: Moving Forward, Looking Back* (2015) 19 <www.cambridge.org/core/books/busi ness-and-human-rights-landscape/enterprise-of-empire/ 100EFD4FBD897AAC4B3A922E1DAB0D3A> (last visited 25 September 2022).

[61] See Antony Anghie, 'International Law in a Time of Change: Should International Law Lead or Follow the Grotius Lecture: ASIL 2010' (2010) 26 *American University International Law Review* 1315; John T Parry, 'What Is the Grotian Tradition in International Law' (2013) 35 *University of Pennsylvania Journal of International Law* at 299, 236–327, 337.

[62] See Peter Borschberg, 'The Seizure of the Sta. Catarina Revisited: The Portuguese Empire in Asia, VOC Politics and the Origins of the Dutch-Johor Alliance (1602–c.1616)' (2002) 33 *Journal of Southeast Asian Studies* 31.

such distinctions; it places public bodies and private companies in the same category.[63]

Grotius argued that moral personality of individuals and collections of individuals do not differ, including, to what was for Grotius, their 'natural right to wage war'. Grotius concluded that 'private trading companies were as entitled to make war as were the traditional sovereigns of Europe'.[64]

Therefore, contrary to the popular myth, convenient to AI companies, the 'law of nations' has always been able to accommodate private actors, whose greed and search for power gave rise to many concepts of modern international law. We must therefore recognize this relationship and impose hard legal obligations related to AI on companies under international law precisely to prevent tech companies' greed and predatory actions which have global consequences.

12.4.2 *Increased Political Scrutiny and Novel Ambitious Laws*

We must also abolish the legislative regimes that have in the past established safe harbours for AI companies, such as the *EU-US Transatlantic Privacy Framework*,[65] previously known as *Safe Harbour* and *Privacy Shield*. Similarly, regimes, based on procedural avoidance of liability, such as the one under Section 230 of the US *Communications Decency Act 1996*, should be reconsidered. This provision provides that websites should not treated as the publisher of third party (i.e., user submitted content); and it is particularly useful for platforms like Facebook.

Some of the more recent AI regulatory efforts might be displaying first seeds of substantive-focused regulation. For example, many moratoriums have been issued on the use of facial recognition technologies across many municipalities and cities in the United States, including the state of Oregon, and NYC.[66] In EU too, some of the latest proposals also display an ambition to ban certain uses and abuses of technology. For example, the *Artificial Intelligence Act* provides a list of 'unacceptable' AI systems and prohibits their use. The *Artificial Intelligence Act* has been subject to criticism about its effectiveness,[67] yet its prohibitive approach can be

---

[63] Hugo Grotius, *Commentary on the Law of Prize and Booty* (2006) 302.

[64] Richard Tuck, *The Rights of War and Peace: Political Thought and the International Order from Grotius to Kant* (2001) 85.

[65] The White House, 'United States and European Commission Announce Trans-Atlantic Data Privacy Framework', *The White House* (2022) <www.whitehouse.gov/briefing-room/state ments-releases/2022/03/25/fact-sheet-united-states-and-european-commission-announce-trans-atlantic-data-privacy-framework/> (last visited 25 September 2022).

[66] Monika Zalnieriute, 'Burning Bridges: The Automated Facial Recognition Technology and Public Space Surveillance in the Modern State' (2021) 22 *Columbia Science and Technology Review* 314.

[67] Michael Veale and Frederik Zuiderveen Borgesius, 'Demystifying the Draft EU Artificial Intelligence Act – Analysing the Good, the Bad, and the Unclear Elements of the Proposed Approach' (2021) 22 *Computer Law Review International* 97; Vera Lúcia Raposo, 'Ex machina:

contrasted with earlier EU regulations, such as GDPR, which did not proclaim that certain areas should not be automated, or some data should not be processed at all/ fall in the hands of tech companies. On an international level, the OECD has recently announced a landmark international tax deal, where 136 countries and jurisdictions representing more than 90 per cent of global GDP agreed to minimum corporate tax rate of 15 per cent on the biggest international corporations which will be effective in 2023.[68] While this is not tackling tech companies business practices, it is aimed at fairer redistribution of wealth, which too must be the focus of the new social contract, if we wish to restrain the power of AI.

12.4.3 *Breaking AI Companies and Public Utilities Approach*

We must also break AI companies many of which have grown so large that they are effectively gatekeepers in their markets. Many scholars have recently proposed ways to employ antitrust and competition law to deal with and break big tech companies,[69] and such efforts are also visible on political level. For example, in December 2020, the EU Commission published a proposal for two new pieces of legislation: the Digital Markets Act (DMA) and the Digital Services Act (DSA).[70] The proposal aims to ensure platform giants, such as Google, Amazon, Apple, and Facebook, operate fairly, and to increase competition in digital markets.

We already have legal instruments for breaking the concentration of power in AI sector: for example, the US *Sherman Act 1890* makes monopolization unlawful.[71] And we must use the tools of competition and antitrust law (but not only them!) to redistribute the wealth and power. While sceptics argue *Sherman Act* case against Amazon, Facebook, or Google would not improve economic welfare in the long

---

Preliminary Critical Assessment of the European Draft Act on Artificial Intelligence' (2022) 30 *International Journal of Law and Information Technology* 88; Lilian Edwards, *Expert Opinion: Regulating AI in Europe. Four Problems and Four Solutions* (2022) <www.adalovelaceinstitute .org/report/regulating-ai-in-europe/> (last visited 25 September 2022).

[68] Organisation for Economic Co-operation and Development, *International Community Strikes a Ground-Breaking Tax Deal for the Digital Age* (2021) <www.oecd.org/tax/international-community-strikes-a-ground-breaking-tax-deal-for-the-digital-age.htm> (last visited 25 September 2022).

[69] See, e.g., Manuel Wörsdörfer, 'Big Tech and Antitrust: An Ordoliberal Analysis' (2022) 35 *Philosophy & Technology* 65; Zephyr Teachout, *Break 'Em Up: Recovering Our Freedom from Big Ag, Big Tech, and Big Money* (2020); Nicolas Petit, *Big Tech and the Digital Economy: The Moligopoly Scenario* (2020) <https://cadmus.eui.eu/handle/1814/68567> (last visited 25 September 2022); Dina Srinivasan, 'The Antitrust Case against Facebook: A Monopolist's Journey towards Pervasive Surveillance in Spite of Consumers' Preference for Privacy' (2019) 16 *Berkeley Business Law Journal* 39.

[70] See Giorgio Monti, *The Digital Markets Act – Institutional Design and Suggestions for Improvement* (2021); Luis Cabral et al, *The EU Digital Markets Act: A Report from a Panel of Economic Experts* (2021).

[71] The Sherman Antitrust Act of 1890 (26 Stat. 209, 15 U.S.C. §§ 1–7).

run,[72] we must start somewhere. For instance, as Kieron O'Hara suggested, we could prevent anticompetitive mergers and require tech giants to divest companies they acquired to stifle competition, such as Facebook's acquisition of WhatsApp and Instagram.[73] We could also ring-fence giants into particular sectors. For example, Amazon's purchase of Whole Foods Market (a supermarket chain) would likely be prevented by that strategy. We could also force tech giants to split its businesses into separate corporations.[74] For instance, Amazon would be split into its E-commerce platform, physical stores, web services, and advertising business.

However, antirust reforms should not obscure more radical solutions, suggested by critical scholars. For example, digital services could be conceived as public utilities: either as closely regulated private companies or as government-run organizations, administered at municipal, state, national, or regional levels.[75] While exact proposals of 'Public utility' approach vary, they aim at placing big AI companies (and other big enterprises) under public control.[76] This provides a strong alternative to market-driven solutions to restore competition in technology sector, and has more potential to address the structural problems of exploitation, manipulation, and surveillance.[77]

12.4.4 *Decolonizing Technology Infrastructure*

We should also pay attention to the asymmetries in economic and political power on global scale: this covers both the US dominance in the digital technologies and AI, US influence in shaping international free trade and intellectual property regimes, rising influence of China, as well as EU's ambitions to set global regulatory standards in many policy areas and both business and public bodies in the so-called Global South on the receiving end of Brussels demands of what 'ethical' AI is, and how 'data protection' must be understood and implemented.[78]

[72] Robert W Crandall, 'The Dubious Antitrust Argument for Breaking Up the Internet Giants' (2019) 54 *Review of Industrial Organization* 627 at 645–49.

[73] Kieron O'Hara, 'Policy Question: How Can Competition against the Tech Giants Be Fostered?' *Four Internets* (2021), 117–19 <https://oxford.universitypressscholarship.com/10 .1093/oso/9780197523681.001.0001/oso-9780197523681-chapter-10> (last visited 7 October 2021).

[74] Teachout, *Break 'Em Up: Recovering Our Freedom from Big Ag, Big Tech, and Big Money.*

[75] Dan Schiller, 'Reconstructing Public Utility Networks: A Program for Action' (2020) 14 *International Journal of Communication* 12; Vincent Mosco, *Becoming Digital: Toward a Post-Internet Society* (2017); James Muldoon, *Platform Socialism: How to Reclaim Our Digital Future from Big Tech* (2022).

[76] Thomas M Hanna and Michael Brennan, 'There's No Solution to Big Tech without Public Ownership of Tech Companies' *Jacobin* (2020) <https://jacobin.com/2020/12/big-tech-public-ownership-surveillance-capitalism-platform-corporations> (last visited 25 September 2022).

[77] James Muldoon, *Do Not Break Up Facebook – Make It a Public Utility* (2020) <https://jacobin .com/2020/12/facebook-big-tech-antitrust-social-network-data> (last visited 25 September 2022).

[78] More on EU's influence in setting regulatory standards, see Anu Bradford, *The Brussels Effect: How the European Union Rules the World* (2020).

We should also incorporate Indigenous epistemologies – they provide strong conceptual alternatives to dominant AI discourse. Decolonial ways to theorize, analyze, and critique AI and ADMS systems must be part of our new social contract for the age of AI,[79] because people in the so-called Global South relate very differently to major AI platforms than those who live and work where these companies are headquartered.[80] A good example in this regard is the 'Technologies for Liberation' project which studies how queer, trans, two-spirit, black, Indigenous, and people of colour communities are disproportionately impacted by surveillance technologies and criminalization.[81] Legal scholars must reach beyond our comfortable Western, often Anglo-Saxon position, and bring forward perspectives of those who have been excluded and marginalized in the development of AI and ADMS tools.

The decolonization however must also happen in laws. For example, the EU's focus on regulating AI and ADMS as a consumer 'product-in-use' requiring individual protection is hypocritical, and undermines the claims to regulate 'ethical' AI, for it completely ignores the exploitative practices and global implications of AI production and use. These power disparities and exploitation must be recognized and officially acknowledged in the new laws.

Finally, we need novel spaces for thinking about, creating and developing the new AI regulation. Spaces that are not dominated by procedural fetishism. A good example of possible resistance, promoted by decolonial data scholars, is a Non-Aligned Technologies Movement (NATM) – a worldwide alliance of civil society organizations which aims to create 'techno-social spaces beyond the profit-motivated model of Silicon Valley and the control-motivated model of the Chinese Communist Party. NATM does not presume to offer a single solution to the problem of *data colonialism*; instead it seeks to promote a collection of models and platforms that allow communities to articulate their own approaches to decolonization'.[82]

---

[79] Abeba Birhane, 'Algorithmic Injustice: A Relational Ethics Approach' (2021) 2 *Patterns* 100205; Jason Edward Lewis et al, *Indigenous Protocol and Artificial Intelligence Position Paper* (2020) <https://spectrum.library.concordia.ca/id/eprint/986506/> (last visited 25 September 2022); Stefania Milan and Emiliano Treré, 'Big Data from the South(s): Beyond Data Universalism' (2019) 20 *Television & New Media* 319.

[80] R Grohmann and WF Araújo, 'Beyond Mechanical Turk: The Work of Brazilians on Global AI Platforms' in Pieter Verdegem (ed), *AI for Everyone?: Critical Perspectives* (2021) 247–66; Mary L Gray and Siddharth Suri, *Ghost Work: How to Stop Silicon Valley from Building a New Global Underclass* (2019).

[81] Brenda Salas Neves and Mihika Srivastava, 'Technologies for Liberation: Toward Abolitionist Futures', *Astraea Foundation* (2020) <www.astraeafoundation.org/FundAbolitionTech/> (last visited 25 September 2022); Important also here is the broader 'design justice' movement see Sasha Costanza-Chock, *Design Justice: Community-Led Practices to Build the Worlds We Need* (2020) <https://library.oapen.org/handle/20.500.12657/43542> (last visited 25 September 2022).

[82] Non Aligned Technologies Movement, <https://nonalignedtech.net/index.php?title=Main_Page> (last visited 25 September 2022).

12.5 CONCLUSION

The new social contract for the age of AI must incorporate all these different strategies – we need a new framework, and not just quick, procedural fixes. These strategies might not achieve substantive policy change alone. However, together, acting in parallel, the proposed changes will enable us to start resisting corporate and state agenda of procedural fetishism. In the digital environment dominated by AI companies, procedural fetishism is an intentional strategy to obfuscate the implications of concentrated corporate power. AI behemoths legitimize their practices through procedural washing and performative compliance to divert the focus onto the procedures they follow, both for commercial gain and to avoid their operations being tempered by regulation. They are also helped and assisted by states, which enable corporate dominance via the laws and legal frameworks.

Countering corporate procedural fetishism, requires, first of all, returning the focus back to the substantive problems in the digital environment. In other words, it requires paying attention to the substance of tech companies' policies and practices, to their power, not only the procedures. This requires a new social contract for the age of AI. Rather than buying into procedural washing as companies intend for us to do, we need new binding, legally enforceable mechanisms to hold the AI companies to account. We have many options, and we need to act on all fronts. Imposing data privacy obligations directly on AI companies with an international treaty is one way. In parallel, we must also redistribute wealth and power by breaking and taxing tech companies, increasing public scrutiny by adopting prohibitive laws, and democratizing and decolonizing big tech by giving people power to determine the way in which these companies should be governed. We must recognize that AI companies exercise global dominance with significant international and environmental implications. This aspect of technology is related to global economic structure, and therefore cannot be solved alone: it requires systemic changes to our economy. The crucial step to such direction is developing and maintaining AI platforms as public utilities, which operate for the public good rather than profit. The new social contract for the age of AI should de-commodify data relations, rethink behaviour advertising as the foundation of the Internet, and reshape social media and internet search as public utilities. With all these mutually reinforcing efforts, we must debunk the corporate and state agenda of *procedural fetishism* and demand basic tangible constraints for the new social contract in the Automated State.